D1596557

Unclear Physics

A VOLUME IN THE SERIES

Cornell Studies in Security Affairs

Edited by Robert J. Art, Robert Jervis, and Stephen M. Walt

A list of titles in this series is available at www.cornellpress.cornell.edu.

Unclear Physics

Why Iraq and Libya Failed to Build Nuclear Weapons

MÅLFRID
BRAUT-HEGGHAMMER

Cornell University Press

Ithaca and London

Cornell University Press gratefully acknowledges receipt of a subvention from the Department of Political Science, University of Oslo, which aided in the publication of this book.

First published 2016 by Cornell University Press

Printed in the United States of America

Library of Congress Cataloging-in-Publication Data

Names: Braut-Hegghammer, Målfrid, author.
Title: Unclear physics : why Iraq and Libya failed to build nuclear
    weapons / Målfrid Braut-Hegghammer.
Description: Ithaca : Cornell University Press, 2016. | Series: Cornell
    studies in security affairs | Includes bibliographical references
    and index.
Identifiers: LCCN 2016010768 | ISBN 9781501702785
    (cloth : alk. paper)
Subjects: LCSH: Nuclear weapons—Political aspects—Iraq. | Nuclear
weapons—Political aspects—Libya. | Hussein, Saddam, 1937–2006. |
    Qaddafi, Muammar.
Classification: LCC UA853.I75 B73 2016 | DDC 623.4/511909567—
    dc23 LC record available at http://lccn.loc.gov/2016010768

Cloth printing   10 9 8 7 6 5 4 3 2 1

Contents

Illustrations

Acknowledgments

This book could not have been written without the assistance, funding, and support of many individuals and organizations. It gives me great joy to acknowledge these debts, and express my deep and heartfelt gratitude.

This project has had several homes, including the Norwegian Institute for Defence Studies, London School of Economics and Political Science (LSE), the Belfer Center at the John F. Kennedy School of Government at Harvard University, the Center for International Security and Cooperation (CISAC) at Stanford University, and the University of Oslo. It has been generously supported by the Stanton Foundation, the MacArthur Foundation, CISAC, the Norwegian Ministry of Defence, and the Department of Political Science at the University of Oslo.

The Norwegian Defence University College was the incubator and first home. Warm thanks are due to Louise K. Dedichen, Torunn L. Haaland, Sven G. Holtsmark, Kristine Offerdal, the late Olav Riste, and Rolf Tamnes. Numerous nuclear fellows gave feedback along the way, including Kristin Ven Bruusgaard, Damon Colletta, Eliza Gheorghe, Henrik Hiim, Gaurav Kampani, Sebastien Miraglia, Maral Mirshahi, and Jayita Sarkar. I completed the book at the Department of Political Science, University of Oslo. I am indebted to my colleagues there, particularly Ida Weseth Bjøru, Dag Harald Claes, Bjørn Høyland, Anne Julie Semb, and Håvard Strand, for support and feedback.

In the early stages of my research I conducted fieldwork and interviews in numerous countries, including Libya, Jordan, Egypt, the United Arab Emirates, Qatar, Italy, Canada, and the United States. My fieldwork in the Middle East was facilitated by the Libyan Institute for Graduate Studies, as well as networks of scientists across the region. Many of the individuals I spoke to later requested anonymity; some retracted their statements. These contributions were, in some cases, made at considerable personal risk. They all helped shape my understanding of how scientists, engineers, academics, doctors, military officers, and regime officials lived and worked under extraordinary conditions in Iraq and Libya. I have accessed numerous archives, including the Arab World Documentation Unit at Exeter University, the British National Archives, the Conflict Records Research Center, the International Atomic Energy Agency (IAEA), as well as the private papers and archives of numerous individuals in several countries. Very special thanks are due to the indefatigable Leopold Kammerhofer, Marta Riess, and their colleagues at the IAEA Archives. In Princeton, the Institute of Advanced Study kindly provided a workspace in their beautiful library in 2009–2010 and the summer of 2015.

I have received generous guidance and support at every stage of this project. I am greatly indebted to the senior scholars at the Belfer Center and CISAC. At the Belfer Center, Graham Allison, Matthew Bunn, Martin Malin, Steven Miller, Richard Rosecrance, and Monica Toft generously offered (much needed) advice and guidance. At the LSE, Christopher Coker was consistently encouraging. At CISAC, I was challenged and inspired by Lynn Eden, David Holloway, and Scott Sagan. I cannot overstate how much I have learned, or how much it has meant for this book.

One of the great pleasures of working on this project was joining the community of fellows at the Belfer Center and CISAC. Many of my colleagues became role models, friends and, in several cases, extended family. Special thanks are due to Emma Belcher, James Cameron, Sarah Daly, Michal Ben-Josef Hirsch, Jonathan Hunt, Shiri Krebs, Nelly Lahoud, Benjamin Lessing, Megan MacKenzie, Jonas Meckling, Vipin Narang, Ragnhild Nordås, Negeen Pegahi, Karthika Sasikumar, Paul Staniland, Maya Tudor, Keren Yarhi-Milo, and Melissa Willard-Foster. At Stanford, I received much encouragement and advice from Lisa Blaydes, Amir Goldberg, Norman Naimark, Gil-li Vardi, and Chick Perrow. I am very grateful to the (past and current) codirectors of CISAC: Mariano-Florentino Cuéllar, Siegfried S. Hecker, David Relman, and Amy Zegart. I am much obliged to the incomparable Anna C. Coll, Elizabeth Gardner, Megan Gorman, Tracy Hill, Natasha Lee, Reid Pauly, and the broader CISAC community. Warm thanks are due to Susan Lynch at the Belfer Center.

It has been my good fortune to benefit from the support and friendship of many as the process of writing this book took me (and, frequently, my family) to different places. During our family's time in Princeton, Jeff Colgan, Jeff Domanski and Kristan Flynn, Rachel Riedl, Noah Salomon, Jake Shapiro, and Keren Yarhi-Milo (with families) excelled at all-round menschiness, making this a home away from home. In Palo Alto, Gil-li Vardi and Amir Goldberg, Shiri Krebs and Amit Hetsron, Karthika Sasikumar and Matija Ćuk (with children) became our Californian extended family.

Warm thanks are also due to Hans Blix, Wyn Bowen, Avner Cohen, Charles Duelfer, Rolk Ekéus, Christina and Ariel Ezrahi, Frank Gavin, Gudrun Harrer, Jacques Hymans, Nick Kitchen and family, Amal Obeidi, Leopoldo Nuti, the organizers and participants of the International Nuclear History boot camp in Allumiere, Or Rabinowitz, Elisabeth Röhrlich, and Alison Pargeter. I am very grateful to Robert Kelley for help and advice in preparing the map of Libyan sites. I apologize to anyone I may have forgotten.

In the late stages of this project, CISAC generously organized a manuscript review workshop (which was aptly renamed a "murder board" by Scott Sagan) on 26–27 May 2014. The murder board did in the first draft, and helped me produce a much better manuscript. I am extremely grateful to CISAC and all the participants: Emma Belcher, Lisa Blaydes, Benjamin Buch, James Cameron, Zachary Davis, Lynn Eden, Tom Fingar, Siegfried Hecker, David Holloway, Jonathan Hunt, Neil Joeck, Jeffrey Lewis, Neil Narang, Vipin Narang, Brad Roberts, and Scott Sagan. Special thanks are due to Anna C. Coll, who organized this session, and Lauren Williams who took meticulous notes.

At Cornell University Press, Roger Haydon and the series editors were a dream team for this first-time author. I am deeply grateful to Roger and the reviewers, whose feedback and advice helped me write a better book. I also express heartfelt thanks to Teresa J. Lawson for terrific editing. Philip Schwartzberg of Meridian Mapping created the maps.

While completing the manuscript I received assistance from several graduate students. In Palo Alto, Caroline Abadeer at the Stanford Department of Political Science prepared tables and figures, while Maral Mirshahi helped recheck the facts for several chapters. At the University of Oslo, Karl Bjurstrøm, Martin G. Søyland, and Malin Østevik had the thankless task of rechecking footnotes one last time before the book went to print. Malin Østevik also assisted with preparing tables. Remaining inaccuracies and errors are solely my responsibility.

I owe my greatest debt of gratitude to my family. The love from my children, Arne and Haldis, nurtured me throughout the years spent researching and writing this book. My husband, Thomas, has been a model of kindness and patience, asking the right questions at the right time. You make everything better. My parents, Jarle and Astrid, have always helped and encouraged me in all my efforts. Tone and Odd, my parents-in-law, share my love of books and were supportive as I wrote this one. Finally, my maternal grandparents, Arne and Hanna Nåvik, delighted in my research adventures even as these took me far away from them. I dedicate this book to their memory, with much love and gratitude.

Introduction

This book is about two dictators who failed to get nuclear weapons. It is an account of secret programs and regimes that are now confined to the dustbins of history. Leaders in Pyongyang, Teheran, and Washington have drawn different lessons from these cases; scholars continue to debate their implications. In fact, much of what we thought we knew about the Iraqi and Libyan nuclear weapons programs turns out to be wrong. This book reveals that neither Saddam Hussein nor Muammar Gaddafi was really determined to acquire nuclear weapons. Neither leader was capable of micromanaging these programs, which they mostly left in the hands of scientists. They lacked the capability even to pay close attention to the performance of these programs because they had weakened their states to strengthen their own hold on power. If I am right, we may have to reconsider what else we think we know about these regimes.

To understand how autocrats fare in their pursuit of nuclear weapons programs, we can learn much from how they treat their states. Saddam solidified his hold on power by proliferating and fragmenting state institutions, Gaddafi by dismantling them. These choices later tied their hands by limiting their ability to monitor their nuclear program and to intervene when necessary. Both leaders had much less direct influence over their nuclear weapons programs than has been realized. But Saddam's approach—of proliferating state institutions—ultimately gave him a larger toolbox than Gaddafi, who sought to dismantle the Libyan state. Saddam was able to fix some of the problems facing his country's nuclear weapons program, once he decided to intervene; Gaddafi's attempts met with much less success. This realization helps us make sense of the outcomes of these programs: Iraq's program was on the brink of a breakthrough when it was interrupted by the 1991 Gulf War, while Libya's program was an abject failure when Gaddafi finally dismantled it in late 2003.

This argument highlights the trade-offs personalist leaders face when enhancing their power at the expense of effective state institutions. These trade-offs solve some problems, from the perspective of these leaders, but create others. Some of the consequences—minor corruption, flawed reporting, and underperformance—were calculated risks. Other consequences were unexpected—notably, the difficulties of accounting for an unregulated and widely dispersed industry of multiple weapons of mass destruction (WMD) projects—and later played an important role in the international community's confrontation with Saddam that began in 1991 and culminated in 2003.

This book is based on extensive primary source material collected over a decade, much of which has not been explored by other scholars, as well as fieldwork and interviews with scientists and decision makers. The chapters present the programs as scientists and officials perceived them at the time, as well as visiting foreign experts. Through their perspectives, and by combining what we might term "top-down" and "bottom-up" lenses, the relationship between science and politics in both states is explored in detail. This is a departure from the "high politics" perspective of studying authoritarian regimes through the eyes of their leaders. More broadly, this analysis sheds light on how much each leader knew about their nuclear weapons program at different times. As I show, many important decisions and initiatives came from the scientists, often without the permission or even the knowledge of the senior leadership. Many small decisions made by scientists and engineers cumulatively shaped the performance of each nuclear weapons program while the attention of its leader—Saddam and Gaddafi—was mostly focused elsewhere.

Seen from this perspective, these two nuclear weapons programs look very different from how they have previously been portrayed. Saddam and Gaddafi did not pay close attention to these programs; rather, their scientists did not always have a clear sense of what their objectives were supposed to be. At one point, Iraqi scientists jokingly characterized their program as one of "unclear physics."[1] Scientists who were disobedient or incompetent often got away with it, although Saddam did not hesitate to imprison his leading scientists when he became concerned about their loyalties in the wake of the 1979 Iranian Revolution. Most striking, perhaps, is the fact that Saddam decided to invade Kuwait—a high-risk move that provoked the 1991 Gulf War—just as the Iraqi nuclear weapons program stood on the verge of a major breakthrough. Libya's program, although in many ways still a closed book, is revealed in the following chapters as consistently dysfunctional as the regime's interest in nuclear weapons ebbed and waned.

Misjudging how much leaders know about their nuclear weapon programs, or the determination and effort with which they pursue these weapons, is dangerous and costly. For policymakers, understanding how domestic factors shape the outcomes of nuclear weapons programs is essential for designing nonproliferation policies and countermeasures. For authoritarian leaders who want nuclear weapons, the two cases in this book offer a cautionary tale of difficult trade-offs and costly mistakes. Foreign leaders, viewing Iraq and Libya or other closed authoritarian regimes, had no clear picture of the domestic-level drivers and obstacles to the acquisition of nuclear weapons in these regimes when weighing their policy options. Saddam was toppled in a disastrous U.S.-led war in 2003, well over a decade after the Iraqi nuclear weapons program had been dismantled; U.S. and British diplomats struck a deal with Gaddafi to dismantle his failing nuclear program the same year. These decisions set in motion events that continue to redraw the political map of the Middle East.

The Literature

Scholars have produced important new insights about the domestic politics of nuclear proliferation and, more broadly, how authoritarian leaders make decisions about nuclear weapons and national security. This work explores the mechanics of decision making and the many obstacles facing autocrats seeking the absolute weapon. I hope to build on this literature by shedding new light on two crucial cases and highlighting a variable that is largely unexamined in this body of work, namely the role of state capacity.

The first strand of this literature focuses on decision making in authoritarian regimes seeking nuclear weapons. Etel Solingen's book *Nuclear Logics: Contrasting Paths in East Asia and the Middle East* explores how ruling coalitions' strategies for political survival inform regime decisions regarding whether to pursue or to abandon nuclear weapons programs.[2] Specifically, she argues that ruling coalitions that seek to integrate their domestic economy in the global economy are less likely to pursue nuclear weapons than those who seek isolation. Solingen's work echoes broader debates in political science about how state leaders choose between spending money on guns or butter, that is, their militaries or economic development benefiting the population. In these debates, personalist regimes in oil states (such as Iraq and Libya) are described as being particularly prone to spending their petrodollars on guns. Scholars point to two sets of factors to explain this tendency: Jeff Colgan highlights the crucial role of the oil economy in enabling authoritarian leaders such as Saddam and Gaddafi to invest vast amounts in their militaries, while a body of literature points to the lack of domestic constraints (in terms of weak institutions and these leaders' lack of concern for domestic audiences) as an important enabling factor.[3] For example, Jessica Weeks and Christopher Way argue that leaders such as Saddam and Gaddafi who lack institutional constraints in their regimes are more likely to initiate nuclear weapons programs.[4] These contributions demonstrate the importance of the domestic political context for understanding how different autocrats make decisions about nuclear weapons programs. The evidence presented in this book underlines the need for a better understanding of how authoritarian regimes and their state institutions affect decisions about pursuing nuclear weapons. Iraq and Libya, as we will see, pursued nuclear weapons while seeking integration into the global economy. More broadly, both regimes deliberated how much they should invest in domestic development versus nuclear and conventional arms, reaching different conclusions at different times.

Still, we need more work that examines how other domestic-level constraints, notably in the form of institutional capabilities and resources, affect the implementation of these decisions inside nuclear establishments. In *Achieving Nuclear Ambitions: Scientists, Politicians, and Proliferation* Jacques Hymans takes important steps in this direction. Observing that many authoritarian states struggle to acquire nuclear weapons, he argues that neopatrimonial rulers undermine the professional culture inside nuclear weapons programs through constant interference. Hymans argues that these leaders do so because their weak state institutions permit, and even encourage, such interventions. For this reason, he posits, Libya and Iraq were doomed to fail.[5] Hymans's rich and influential account is representative of what has become the conventional wisdom: that Saddam and Gaddafi essentially micromanaged their nuclear scientists, that they were determined to get nuclear weapons, and that they failed largely because their scientists were unwilling or unable to deliver these capabilities. The findings presented in this book challenge all three elements of this conventional wisdom.

After the fall of Saddam's regime, scholars began to explore the inner life of key institutions including the Baath Party, the intelligence services, and the military. These studies, drawing on extensive archives brought from Iraq to the United States, offer important insights. Joseph Sassoon's *Saddam Hussein's Ba'th Party: Inside an Authoritarian Regime* describes how Saddam held scientists in special esteem, believing they were essential for building a strong and modern state.[6] Furthermore, Sassoon shows how the intelligence services struggled to assess the performance of such specialized agencies and instead focused on indicators of individual loyalty, for example through vetting marriages. Other work explores how the Iraqi regime's efforts to secure political power affected the performance of the armed forces. In *The Dictator's Army: Battlefield Effectiveness in Authoritarian Regimes* Caitlin Talmadge explores how efforts at "coup-proofing," that is, preventive measures to reduce the likelihood that actors can successfully organize and implement a coup d'état, and how threat assessments shaped the performance of the military in Saddam's Iraq.[7] Kevin M. Woods traces the effect of purges and other regime interventions on the Iraqi military's performance in *The Iran-Iraq War: A Military and Strategic History*.[8]

The literature on Libya remains scant, primarily because of the difficulties associated with carrying out fieldwork during Gaddafi's tenure. That being said, excellent studies detail the emergence of the modern state in Libya and the impact of the influx of oil and Gaddafi's revolution on the evolving state apparatus.[9] In *Libya since Independence: Oil and State-Building* Dirk Vandewalle notes the idiosyncratic ways in which the Libyan state evolved after Gaddafi seized power in 1969, even when compared with other authoritarian oil-exporting regimes in the Middle East. It was characterized by a hybridization of formal and informal administrative practices, the Gaddafi regime's undermining of the formal bureaucracy's information-gathering capabilities, and the consequent erosion of planning and decision-making capabilities.[10] This literature notes that the Gaddafi regime sought to dismantle the Libyan state while simultaneously using the state apparatus to distribute oil wealth. Limited attention has been given to the consequences of the uneven development of the Libyan state for different areas of state activities, again primarily because of the difficulties associated with carrying out fieldwork and archival research. The fate of Libya's archives after the Gaddafi regime's fall is still unknown. Many records appear to have been displaced or destroyed during and after the 2011 uprising.

Scholars of nuclear proliferation are paying increasing attention to different domestic-level factors that define a state's capacity to build nuclear weapons. One important variable is the ability to absorb technology and assistance from abroad. Alexander Montgomery argues that neopatrimonial regimes are less capable of absorbing nuclear technology from foreign suppliers.[11] More broadly, a study by R. Scott Kemp of the diffusion of centrifuge technology (a pathway for uranium enrichment adopted by many states including Pakistan, North Korea, and South Africa) concludes that the recipient state's organizational capabilities matter more than access to foreign technology for the performance of a nuclear weapons program.[12] Sonia Ben Ouagrham-Gormley's study of biological weapons programs delves even deeper, showing that it is necessary to disaggregate factors working at the different levels—the regime, state organizations, and laboratories—that influence a state's technological absorption capacity.[13] This suggests that regime type is not a sufficient explanation and that we have to look inside bureaucracies and even laboratories to untangle why some programs fare better than others. Iraq and Libya are pertinent cases for such an analysis because, as this book shows, Iraq was able to benefit much more than Libya from access to foreign assistance and technology.

Some authoritarian leaders use state institutions as vehicles for domination and pursuit of grandiose schemes.[14] Some succeed in this; others fail. Joel S. Migdal notes that inefficiencies are prevalent in many authoritarian states.[15] More broadly, institutional weakness has been a persistent challenge for many postcolonial states in the developing world. In these states, formal state institutions vary in terms of stability (their durability against environmental shocks) and enforcement (their ability to shape behavior). Scholars are paying more attention to how and why institutional strength varies.[16] For authoritarian states in particular, more needs to be done to explain the causes and consequences of varying levels of institutionalization.

As this book shows, the Iraqi and Libyan state institutions were not capable of realizing many of Saddam's and Gaddafi's transformative ideas. In these states, formal institutions were instruments of power, despite their imperfections, but they were also sites of negotiation and even resistance. The expansive literature on principal-agent theory, which explores problems of oversight and control in state bureaucracies, holds pertinent insights for this analysis. At the same time, this study improves our understanding of how states that have weak institutional resources monitor agents and different ways in which regimes nonetheless attempt to enforce agents' compliance with the rules set down by the principal.[17] The chapters in this book show that drift and underperformance were not uncommon in these nuclear programs and explain how and why scientists got away with it.

The Argument

This book explores how state capacity affected the nuclear weapons programs of Iraq and Libya. Put simply, weak states often lack the institutional resources to set up and operate nuclear weapons programs. This is particularly problematic in so-called personalist regimes, such as Iraq and Libya, whose leaders undermine formal state institutions and seek to govern through informal structures of patronage and control. The ways in which these leaders coup-proof their states can further weaken their ability to monitor and intervene in the management of nuclear weapons programs. Personalist leaders choose different strategies to address the resulting problems, with varying outcomes.

The argument developed in this book cuts against the conventional wisdom in numerous ways, by showing that authoritarian leaders in weak states have limited capacity—and sometimes limited interest—in managing their nuclear scientists. To be clear, I am not making an argument about how these dynamics unfold in strong states or other political systems, where the impact of management strategies is likely to be different. But the findings will hopefully offer insights for analyzing other states and regimes, particularly authoritarian ones, that may suffer from similar pathologies.

In this section, I lay out the bare bones of the arguments that I develop further in the exploratory analysis presented in subsequent chapters. First, I define state capacity and explain how it varies. Second, I describe how, in weak states, coup-proofing affects how personalist leaders manage their nuclear weapons programs. Finally, I examine how these leaders deploy different management strategies to cope with their oversight and control problems in the nuclear field.

1) STATE CAPACITY AND NUCLEAR PROLIFERATION

Broadly conceived, state capacity refers to the ability of bureaucracies to carry out tasks on behalf of the political leadership. This is a slippery concept that must be carefully defined and operationalized. For the purposes of this book, I define state capacity narrowly, in terms of the professionalism of the state bureaucracy, following Francis Fukuyama and others.[18] This has two dimensions: the ability to carry out specialized functions; and independence from state elites and the political leadership. Both are essential for creating the strong institutions that underpin a robust state apparatus.

While we often define state capacity as either strong or weak, scholars point out there is a lot of variation within each category. Furthermore, there can be variation within states, as evidenced by "islands of excellence" in otherwise inefficient states.[19] For these reasons, the estimates of strong versus weak state capacity are better conceived of as points on a spectrum rather than binary categories. To estimate state strength, political scientists look at how institutions perform in ensuring compliance with formal and informal rules and how vulnerable these agencies are to changes in their environment.[20] Conventional output measures of state strength, such as extractive capabilities, are difficult to measure in oil-exporting authoritarian states, quite simply because such regimes do not tend to tax their citizens. It is important to distinguish between "output" indicators of how well institutions perform in implementing rules, on one hand, and "input" indicators showing how capable states are of designing rules and developing enforcement and monitoring mechanisms, on the other hand. This distinction is particularly important in weak states, where institutions can be created without receiving the necessary resources from the state principal to effectively implement rules. This happens for different reasons, Steven Levitsky and María Victoria Murillo argue. In some cases, this is intentional "windowdressing," demonstrating that the state apparatus is a façade while real political power resides outside the formal institutions of the state.[21] In Libya and Iraq, for example, nonstate actors (such as the Libyan Revolutionary Committees and tribal leaders) played important roles in monitoring behavior and distributing resources on behalf of the leadership.

State weakness, then, can be the result of two distinct, but sometimes coinciding, causes: the absence of necessary capabilities in the state itself to carry out monitoring and sanction behavior; and a lack of willingness by the state leadership to ensure that institutions serve this purpose. As we will see, these variables can change over time, with distinct consequences for the governance of nuclear programs.

To estimate state capacity in terms of the robustness and enforcement of formal institutions, we can use several indicators: whether bureaucrats are educated and trained for their specific tasks; whether recruitment is meritocratic; whether the public sector is a vehicle of social mobility; whether state institutions are subject to purges following political transitions; whether institutions are directly influenced by the preferences of state elites (or nonstate elites); and whether there is widespread embezzlement and corruption by state officials.[22] In other words, we look for indicators of whether state institutions can perform their tasks consistently over time, without being altered or disrupted by changes in their environment, and whether they have the necessary resources to carry out their tasks (notably whether they can oversee implementation of formal and informal rules and sanction those who fail to comply). It is important to recognize that these measures can change considerably in personalist authoritarian regimes run by a single individual for an extended period, as was the case in both Iraq and Libya. For example, purges associated with a leader's emergence to power can undermine state capacity, or leaders taking measures in response to external threats to enhance the capacity of his military-industrial organizations. During the Iran-Iraq War, for example, Saddam gave such organizations more freedom to develop weapons for the war effort.

It is also important to clarify what state capacity is not. While the level of economic development in a country can have effects that resemble those of state capacity, and scholars at times conflate these effects, these are distinct variables. In this book, state capacity refers to the professionalism of bureaucracies, while economic development is an output variable referring to resources and growth. It is similarly important to distinguish between state capacity and plain ineptitude: if poor performance is the result of uneducated or inadequate staff, this reflects state weakness. If scientists or others who have adequate knowledge to carry out a given task nevertheless perform poorly, this is incompetence.

The combination of personalist rulers and weak state capacity can have puzzling consequences. In the case of Libya, for example, the Gaddafi regime's attempt at agricultural reforms was unsuccessful because the regime was unable to shift sufficient people to work on the new agricultural sites. It failed to set up infrastructure, such as housing and transport, or the administrative apparatus to make this happen. Similarly, Libyan nuclear scientists often simply failed to turn up for work, or they moonlighted at other academic institutions during working hours to add to their salaries, apparently without any consequences.

2) COUP-PROOFING THE STATE

Paradoxically, personalist leaders weaken their states to accumulate power. Their most threatening security challenges come from within, often in the form of army coups or popular uprisings. Still, these leaders need the state apparatus to strengthen their hold on power through repression or co-option. To cope with this dilemma some create a large state apparatus capable of detecting and preempting potential threats but *fragment* state institutions to prevent alternative power centers from forming. Less frequently, leaders *dismantle* their formal state bureaucracy to keep power centers from forming and to deny potential challengers the institutional resources with which they could mobilize.

Either strategy has detrimental consequences for the ability of the state bureaucracy to perform specialized functions. In other words, coup-proofing is an intervening variable defining the strength of state institutions in weak authoritarian states. Fragmentation creates a chaotic system with limited transparency and coordination, while dismantlement (which may be accompanied by the rise of nonstate actors that effectively usurp state functions) robs bureaucracies of vital resources and instruments. In both cases, it is difficult for leaders to secure adequate oversight because they lack institutional mechanisms to vet and assess the performance of specialized activities such as nuclear weapons programs. I argue that these strategies have significant consequences for the development of an effective nuclear weapons program in a weak state and for the ability of authoritarian leaders to monitor and intervene when necessary.

In a weak state governed by a personalist leader, the underdeveloped state apparatus makes it difficult to plan and coordinate complex projects such as nuclear weapons programs. These states are bewildering even to seasoned civil servants; they are designed to give only the senior leadership a clear view of the state and its institutions (but, as we will see, even the senior leadership cannot keep track of everything that goes on inside their byzantine institutions). As a result, managing clandestine activities that, like a nuclear weapons program, require collaboration from several different agencies is uniquely challenging. Collaboration in such systems is fraught with risk, because no one wants to be blamed if a project falls behind schedule or fails altogether. Such a strategy, meant to make the state apparatus opaque from anyone outside the top leadership, also has detrimental consequences for leader scrutiny. To protect themselves from the eyes of the leadership, scientists may inflate the number of ongoing projects or may constantly change the design of their organization to make it nearly impossible for anyone to keep track of their actual progress. Institutions can blame each other for mistakes.

In states with such a fragmented structure and proliferating state institutions, conditions are ripe for turf fights. To encourage innovation and stimulate performance in the state sector, which often suffers from inefficiencies, managers may launch competing projects. At the same time, fierce internal competition creates distrust inside organizations, as scientists and engineers fear that colleagues will steal or claim credit for their ideas, or will secretly report mistakes and failures to the leadership. Under such conditions, collaboration is difficult, and this, in turn, inhibits innovation.

Dismantlement weakens the state through a very different route. A personalist leader may seek to prevent challenges or alternative power centers from forming by eroding institutions, or by creating nonstate organizations that take over some (or all) their key functions. But by thus eroding specialized agencies, or by failing to set them up despite having the economic capacity to do so, the state fails to create resources essential to plan and oversee specialized activities such as technological projects. The absence of formal oversight mechanisms makes it very difficult to create any meaningful audit mechanisms or self-regulation by the nuclear establishment. Informal oversight mechanisms (those that are nonstate agencies, such as back-channel reporting from party members directly to the senior leadership) typically will not be able to assess technical issues effectively. Furthermore, if the dismantlement strategy goes as far as replacing key state functions (such as the diplomatic service) with nonstate agency representatives (such as family members of the leader or representatives from ideological movements who answer to the leader but are not part of the state structure) this can undermine vital resources such as negotiations with other states for nuclear cooperation or assistance.

At a more prosaic level, if the state lacks adequate structures for recruitment and training this undermines the development of human resources for the nuclear weapons program. Furthermore, if the regime is hesitant to invest in higher education because it is seen as a breeding ground for political opposition, this limits the development of a pool of potential recruits. This can also lead the regime to prefer outsourcing of the nuclear program, either to other states through a nuclear cooperation agreement or to black market actors, if the opportunity arises. Such outsourcing inhibits the development of necessary skills and the development of institutional memory and the tacit knowledge essential to enable scientists and engineers to find solutions to the inevitable challenges that emerge. At the same time, this interaction can lead the recipient state to attempt to model its own institutions on those recommended by the supplier without necessarily having the organizational infrastructure in place (or wanting to create this infrastructure) to make this work.

3) MANAGEMENT STRATEGIES

Nuclear weapons programs present autocrats with a severe principal-agent problem: the preferences of the principal and agents are not aligned; there is high information asymmetry; and it is difficult to audit the scientists' performance. In weak states, these challenges are especially acute. This gives nuclear scientists both motive and opportunity to shirk or drift from their task. How do dictators deal with this problem? The conventional wisdom is that they micromanage. I dispute this view. In fact, autocrats attempt to cope with the principal-agent problem in different ways, with varying results.

Management strategy represents a choice between delegation and subordination of the operations of a program. The crucial difference between the two is who makes decisions—scientists or the state leadership—about how the program is organized, what its objectives are, and how these will be achieved. We can evaluate which strategies states opt for by using the following indicators: the quantity and quality of mandates given to the agents by the principal, who sets the goals and deadlines for the nuclear program (and how precise these are); and whether the political leadership defines clear rules for the program.

Either approach has drawbacks: delegation to scientific managers runs the risk that the scientists will abuse this by shirking, while subordination (e.g., to a trusted representative of the regime who lacks technical expertise) could lead to uninformed choices and an unproductive program.[23] But personalist leaders often want to defer committing to a program until they have a better sense of how well it will perform. This creates strong incentives for the leadership to delegate, at least in the early stages of the nuclear program, to avoid the potential costs associated with getting directly involved in a program with an uncertain outcome.

Political scientists debate how choices between delegation and subordination in different political systems affect the performance of nuclear weapons programs and other large projects in the military-industrial sphere.[24] The conventional wisdom suggests that delegation may lead to drift, where bureaucrats redefine their tasks and objectives according to their own preferences. On the other hand, interventions such as frequent changes of leadership create instability inside bureaucracies; purges rob organizations of scarce expertise; and political vetting undermines meritocracy and recruitment. The historical literature shows that autocrats have used various strategies. Stalin, for example, granted more freedom to nuclear scientists than to those in other branches of science for a while (noting that they could always shoot the scientists later.[25]) But when it comes to authoritarian regimes and nuclear weapons programs, Matthew Evangelista and Hymans suggest that subordination is bad. I argue that the results of either strategy depend on state capacity.

This argument may seem counterintuitive. There is a prevalent view, consistent with the impression Saddam and Gaddafi wanted to give, that these leaders had a clear view of what was going on inside their states. Leaving aside the issue of whether they were capable of doing this for the moment, is it even possible that these leaders did not have clear idea of how their nuclear scientists performed?

Consider the example of the Iraqi military-industrial complex. The process of research and development in the Iraqi military-industrial complex under Saddam's rule differed from that of other highly centralized states (such as the Soviet Union). The investigations by United Nations (UN) inspectors into Iraq's past WMD programs show that this was in many ways a bottom-up process, where scientists and officials could pitch projects to senior officials. Iraqi documents that emerged after the 2003 U.S.-led invasion also show that—contrary to assumptions held by policymakers and academic studies—the regime did not monitor or follow up on many of these projects because they lacked the know-how and institutional resources. In a meeting of senior Iraqi regime officials in the fall of 1995, the following exchange between Saddam and an outspoken senior general is revealing:[26]

General Amir: Sir, there are projects that at best are meaningless. I really would prefer not to use a more cruel word. . . . Sir, when someone comes up with an idea and says: "Let me use this biological toxin, because once I use it, the entire Iranian Army will disappear." No one then would dare to discuss it with him because it is something more difficult to judge than, say, a bomb or a rocket. [Consequently], they give him the green light to start and they support him. . . . There are many secondary biological programs that did not bring any results, produce any weapons, or do anything of value. . . . But you know them; there is a type of exaggeration to the issue. He is taking advantage of this—[*interrupted*]

Saddam [Hussein]: Did not they know of this earlier?

General Amir: Definitely not, Sir, because the [biological activities] did not bring any results or anything of substance. . . .

As this exchange suggests, the Iraqi regime did not systematically vet WMD projects in terms of their scientific or technological merit.[27] There was no meaningful peer review or monitoring of smaller projects, while larger programs (such as the nuclear program) often reported their achievements and objectives to the political leadership in ambiguous terms. Failure in this "cottage industry" was apparently inconsequential, as the responsible individuals were not punished for failing to deliver what they had promised. This pattern, which appears to have intensified after 1991 until the fall of the regime in 2003, stands in sharp contrast to the notion that the regime consistently interfered in the running and management of sensitive projects. As we will see in the following chapters, this pattern also applied to the nuclear program.

It is important to distinguish between management strategy and control mechanisms. Irrespective of the management strategies they select, state leaders can impose various control mechanisms—such as reporting procedures, budget approval, informal rules, and norms—to monitor and respond to the performance of their scientists and managers.[28] In states with weak institutions, leaders face additional hurdles to the imposition of effective control mechanisms. In such cases, leaders can resort to other mechanisms to induce compliance, such as economic incentives, or fear.

The argument that authoritarian leaders of weak states, such as Saddam and Gaddafi, do not necessarily favor micromanagement may seem counterintuitive. But micromanagement is very costly in personalist regimes. Information asymmetries between technical specialists and the political leadership make this especially difficult when it comes to technical and scientific projects. This, in turn, makes it possible for scientists and managers to exaggerate their progress and their achievements. The personalist leader has limited capacity to process technical information, and multiple issues compete for his attention. Saddam and Gaddafi were aware of these challenges. But for them, the nuclear weapons program was not "Problem Number One" as it was for other authoritarian leaders, such as Stalin. Saddam and Gaddafi were very concerned, however, about the trustworthiness of the designated leaders of their nuclear programs. As we will see, this concern overrode other considerations, even at the cost of bringing the Iraqi program to a halt.

Sources

When I began this research in 2005, much information presented in this book was unavailable. Libya was in the process of dismantling its WMD programs, while Iraq was in the throes of war. I began by carrying out fieldwork across the Middle East and North Africa where I met statesmen, scholars, scientists, military officers, and journalists. What I learned suggested that many of the presumed facts and assumptions that had informed Western analyses were inaccurate.[29]

Years later, I was granted access to primary documents from several different sources. This material yielded rich new insights, particularly the contemporary assessments by scientists and visiting consultants. What I found enabled me to develop a much more detailed account of each program than I had earlier thought possible, leading me to set aside the initial version and start again, using these sources as my vantage point. The material included archival documents from Iraq, Italy, the United States, and the International Atomic Energy Agency (IAEA). I was also fortunate to gain access to many private archives of diplomats, scientists, weapons inspectors, and scholars. These sources are, as a whole, more comprehensive than those supporting any other study of these programs.

For the Iraqi case, I have been able to gather a rich set of primary and secondary sources. In the early stages of this research I met most of the senior scientists who planned, organized, and restructured the Iraqi nuclear weapons program. I also met a number of scientists who worked at lower levels of the organizations. Some of these individuals requested anonymity out of concern for their safety, while others asked me not to cite the information they gave me. I have used public reports from the IAEA and the United Nations Special Commission (UNSCOM) that oversaw the dismantlement of Iraq's WMD programs after the 1991 Gulf War. I also consulted the 2004 report by the Iraq Survey Group that summarizes the findings of the U.S., British, and Australian inspectors searching for WMD programs after the 2003 war.

Gradually, I obtained access to private papers from several Iraqi scientists, including unpublished memoirs and reports from the nuclear program. I also received access to key Iraqi documents and transcripts from meetings between UN inspectors, Iraqi officials, and other state leaders. A key source was the Iraqi record of the state's nuclear program submitted to the UN Security Council in late 2002, which has not been released to the public.

I have also explored archival material in several other countries. I accessed records from the British archive on early assistance to the Iraqi program in the 1950s through the Baghdad Pact. At the Conflict Records Research Center at the National Defence University in Washington, DC, I explored captured Iraqi records of Cabinet conversations, transcripts from high-level meetings, correspondence, and intelligence reports. Some of these documents have since become available online in new translations. I have sought to include the link to online versions of these and other documents whenever possible. The National Security Archives, also in Washington, provided several valuable sources. I also examined records from the IAEA detailing correspondence between the agency and the Iraqi nuclear establishment. The Technical Assistance archive included reports from visiting IAEA consultants on the pertinent institutions, individuals, and organizations from the late 1950s until the mid-1980s. It also held correspondence between IAEA consultants and senior officials in Vienna commenting on draft reports; on proposals from the Iraqi Atomic Energy Commission; and on how to respond to requests from the host state. These files include the IAEA experts' confidential assessments of the Iraqi state's ability to absorb assistance in several fields and analyses of its bureaucratic capacity to manage and oversee technological projects.

The case of Libya remains much more difficult to research. Few official Libyan statements or documents about the nuclear program have been released. I have analyzed public statements by Libyan officials about the nuclear program, trial records after the unraveling of the Abdul Qadeer Khan network, and IAEA reports on Libya's efforts to account for their past clandestine program. In 2005 and 2006, I carried out fieldwork in Libya where I interviewed senior regime officials, academics, officials involved in the disarmament process, and journalists.[30] During meetings with lower-level officials there were occasionally intelligence officers in the room. Some of my interviewees were told not to speak to me, or got into heated arguments with their colleagues in my presence about whether they ought to talk to me, while others later retracted their statements. I have honored those requests. While this book mainly builds on archival sources, these interviews were crucial in making me aware of different perceptions within the regime on Libya's nuclear program and the decision to dismantle this project.

While the available evidence suggests a complete absence of oversight mechanisms in Libya, my conclusions are necessarily tentative. The Libyan regime made few public statements about its nuclear program, and those who were in charge had strong incentives not to implicate themselves in its existence. It is unclear what further evidence can be unearthed from the former regime's archives, especially as records have been lost or destroyed in the wake of the fall of Gaddafi.

The IAEA Technical Assistance archives, which I first explored in early 2013, offered a wealth of new information about the organization and management of the Libyan program. For the first time I was able to examine the organization of each nuclear establishment and its formal and informal links with other state actors in detail. These sources also afforded important new insights into the absorption capacity problem. The IAEA experts gave detailed assessments of the capacity of the Libyan scientists to adopt recommendations for the organization and planning of their nuclear programs; the extent to which the Libyan staff benefited from IAEA training courses; and their ability to install and use new technical instruments and equipment acquired with the assistance of the agency. Furthermore, technical requests from the Libyan nuclear experts show their assessments of their existing resources and how they planned to begin and expand their nuclear program. Sudden changes, such as abrupt shifts in each regime and their nuclear establishment's priorities and geographical limitations on where IAEA consultants could travel, are also reported in these files.

For both case studies, I examined contemporary intelligence assessments of their nuclear programs. In particular, U.S. intelligence assessments and the perspectives of various other foreign intelligence services on the Iraqi program after the 1991 Gulf War are useful indicators of what was known about the program at the time. Reviews of U.S. intelligence assessments after the 2003 war point to lessons learned from their earlier analytical errors in estimating the technical capacity of both Iraq and Libya.

Methods

This is an exploratory analysis of what state capacity is and how it works in the context of nuclear weapons programs in weak states run by personalist regimes. I develop my arguments through two iterations. First, I explore the emergence of the Iraqi nuclear program in four consecutive chapters. The following four chapters analyze Libya's nuclear program. The final chapter explores how state capacity and management strategies shaped each program and influenced their outcomes. I also briefly apply the argument to another case, Syria's nuclear program, and indicate some broader lessons for policymakers and scholars in the concluding chapter.

For both states, I begin by tracing the development of state organizations from independence, looking at early state-building efforts through monarchial rule, coups, and revolutions; Saddam and Gaddafi's rise to power; and their reforms of their state apparatus. I also examine attempts at large-scale reforms (including land redistribution, collective agriculture, education, and economic reforms) to see how these were planned and implemented. These observations give a broader basis for assessing these states' resources for planning and project implementation. I describe the available infrastructure and human resources, and each state's administrative capabilities. Against this backdrop I trace the nuclear prehistory of each state in detail, exploring the emergence of nuclear research and development programs, with close attention to how these activities were organized and managed under different rulers and regimes. I also compare the emerging nuclear program in each state with the contemporaneous exploration of chemical and biological weapons. This analysis sheds light on the background of individuals and institutions that would later become involved in the nuclear weapons program.

In chapters analyzing the shift toward nuclear weapons research and the performance of the nuclear weapons programs, I trace changes in the management of these programs, and how this compared with sideprojects and crash programs that emerged along the way, such as the Iraqi crash program to develop a nuclear device after the 1990 invasion of Kuwait. Here, I distinguish between formal and informal mechanisms of oversight, such as formal performance reviews versus secret reporting by colleagues to the domestic intelligence agencies about the political preferences of their senior managers, or secret reporting directly to the state leader. I also note how the nuclear weapons program related to ministries and agencies overseeing these programs; including instances of passive resistance and obfuscatory reporting as well as direct clashes and confrontation.

In focusing on the management and organization of these nuclear programs, this book neglects several other interesting aspects. For example, I do not systematically examine how other states assessed these nuclear programs, except when particular states intervened to end or delay them. I do not focus on grand-strategic deliberations or Cabinet discussions on strategic issues, except when these are directly relevant to the performance of the nuclear weapons program.[31] I do not examine the Iraqi Baath Party or the Libyan Revolutionary Committees as organizations, except to note when and where they played an important role in the management of the nuclear project. Finally, for the sake of scope and clarity, I do not explore the process of dismantlement of these programs, nor do I explore what kind of nuclear weapons states Libya and Iraq might have become.

Case Selection

Iraq and Libya are crucial cases for understanding the process of nuclear proliferation at the unit level in both theory and practice. Given the small number of states that have pursued nuclear weapons in a serious manner, these cases are inherently important for those interested in understanding why some states pursue but do not acquire these weapons. The outcomes of these programs have also had an outsized effect on international relations. These factors make it all the more important to establish what we got right and what we got wrong.

I was initially drawn to these cases because of their apparent similarities, at a time when little was known about the inner lives of either program. But what I learned suggested that their differences have not been fully realized or adequately explained. Iraq and Libya were both oil-rich Middle Eastern states. Fueled by a booming oil economy, both countries began a series of aggressive foreign policy adventures in the 1970s. After launching dedicated programs to develop nuclear weapons in the early 1980s, they experienced defeats in protracted wars with their neighbors. Ultimately, neither acquired nuclear weapons. This has led many political scientists to treat them as equal cases and outcomes. But this runs the risk of obscuring important differences. For example, even though Libya had more access to foreign technology and had more time than Iraq to develop nuclear weapons, its program performed much worse. Furthermore, the Libyan state under Gaddafi's rule evolved in a highly idiosyncratic manner, which was quite distinct from where the Iraqi state was headed after Saddam seized power.

When it became clear to me that there was significant variation in terms of the governance and performance of both programs, I reframed this project and started again. While I was still seeking to explain why neither state acquired nuclear weapons, I also wanted to explain the differences of the performance of each program, and why Saddam and Gaddafi tried to apply similar treatments to their programs with varying results.

Organization of the Book

In this book I first examine Iraq, and then Libya, in two main sections. Chapters 1–4 examine the emergence of a nuclear program in Iraq between the late 1950s and the 1991 Gulf War. These chapters step inside the Iraqi nuclear establishment, whose emergence was shaken by frequent political turmoil, revealing the controversial origins of the nuclear weapons program. The conventional wisdom argues this program was launched in the early 1970s, at Saddam's behest.[32] But, as I demonstrate, it began as a bottom-up initiative by Baath Party members inside the nuclear establishment. I trace how pro-bomb coalitions and scientists interested in developing nuclear energy each sought to shape the direction of this program in the 1970s, while the senior political leadership sent ambiguous signals about its preferences and intentions.

My analysis of the nuclear weapons program of the 1980s, after an Israeli air raid on an Iraqi nuclear reactor, shows that the scientists organized and ran the program with little interference. This led to drift and inefficiencies, which in turn sparked a series of internal conflicts and reorganization. The scale of the delays in the program was not, however, communicated to Saddam. After the leaders of the program picked a fight with Saddam's son-in-law, the powerful minister of the military-industrial establishment, over whose fault these delays were, Saddam intervened. The program made progress toward the weapons threshold during the second half of the 1980s, despite facing many difficult obstacles, but the leaders continued to report selectively (and even broke Saddam's rules with impunity, in some cases). The program was disrupted after Saddam blundered into the 1990 invasion of Kuwait. This led to the decision to launch a nuclear crash program, which the scientists knew was a mission impossible from the outset.

Chapters 5–8 detail, for the first time, how the Libyan nuclear program was organized and how it actually operated. I show that the nuclear program began earlier than other studies have suggested; explore the ambitious plans the Libyan scientists made at this early stage; and identify how changes in the state after Gaddafi's takeover affected the program's management and performance. The first two chapters explore the Libyan regime's plans for a nuclear program and how research and development were carried out. A striking finding is the growing gap between the regime's ambitions and the actual activities on the ground.

Chapter 8 details how, after the collapse of the nuclear energy program, the Libyans focused their energies on the weapons route. After a decade of failing to build centrifuges at home, the regime made a strategic decision to try another approach: outsourcing. The program was taken over by a regime insider, not a scientist, who spent a fortune buying centrifuges from the nuclear black market. This program, however, suffered a fate similar to the nuclear energy program: while the regime focused on procurement, the scientists were preoccupied with other issues. The program struggled, but senior regime figures were led to believe that a nuclear weapons option could soon be within reach. Gaddafi maintained an ambivalent position on the nuclear question until, at the recommendation of his advisers, he dismantled the program in late 2003.

In the concluding chapter I compare the findings from Iraq and Libya and explore their implications for scholars and decision makers. Finally, I suggest questions for further research and implications for policy.

PART I. IRAQ

Iraq Explores the Atom, 1956–1973

This chapter explores the origins of the Iraqi nuclear weapons program and traces its fate between the 1958 coup d'état, the decisive ascent of the Baath regime in 1968, and Saddam Hussein's restructuring of the Iraqi Atomic Energy Commission (IAEC) in 1973. Little is known about Iraq's nuclear "prehistory," namely what happened before the launching of the weapons program. This chapter fills several gaps in our knowledge by describing how Iraq first came to explore nuclear science and when its earliest interest in a nuclear weapons option emerged.

Scholars dispute basic facts about the Iraqi nuclear weapons program such as when the order to develop a weapons capability was first given; with what level of determination it was implemented; and what role civilian infrastructure was intended to play in this clandestine project.[1] Armed with new evidence, this chapter and those that follow in this part provide more comprehensive answers to these questions. The analysis also highlights two issues that have received less attention, namely how Iraq's nascent state capacity and management strategies shaped the nuclear program during its initial formative stages.

Seen from this perspective, a surprising picture emerges: the Iraqi program was characterized by the absence of strong leadership, and the earliest nuclear weapons ambitions were articulated by scientists, not the senior leadership. As Iraq began to explore nuclear science and technology, the state lacked the institutional capacity to plan and oversee these activities. Iraq's political leaders remained aloof and left the planning and management of the nuclear program in the hands of foreign suppliers and Iraqi scientists. The result was a program at drift, without clear objectives or guidelines. As this chapter shows, this ambiguity nurtured different visions for the future inside the nuclear establishment. Still, with few institutional resources and limited support from the political leadership different factions struggled to achieve their preferred alternatives. In contrast to the conventional wisdom, this chapter demonstrates that Baath scientists harboring nuclear weapons ambitions tried but largely failed to redefine the goals and objectives, i.e., "capture" the program in the early 1970s. This was not a program driven toward developing a weapons option; it is far from clear that the program actually had any objectives.

A Fragile Monarchy

When it achieved independence in 1932, the Kingdom of Iraq was a relatively affluent young state with a modest-sized population, estimated at about three million, and proven (but not fully exploited) petroleum resources. The kingdom was a fragile political entity, comprising diverse ethnic groups with few common ties. King Faisal I saw several challenges ahead, as he noted in a confidential memorandum in March 1933: "There is still—and I say this with a heart full of sorrow—no Iraqi people but unimaginable masses of human beings, devoid of any patriotic idea, imbued with religious traditions and absurdities, connected by no common tie, giving ear to evil, prone to anarchy, and perpetually ready to rise against any government whatever. . . . Out of these masses we want to fashion a people which we would train, educate, and refine."[2]

Over the next two decades, Iraq faced a series of shocks and transformations that further complicated the task of creating a modern state more or less from scratch. In a landmark history of Iraqi political movements, Hanna Batatu lists some of these upheavals: "rapid buildup of monarchic state institutions, the world-wide depression of 1929, the land settlement policies of 1932 and 1938, the severe shortages and the spiraling inflation during the Second World War and in the immediate postwar years, the mass exodus of Jews in the late forties and early fifties, the sudden inpouring of oil money after 1952, and the fourfold increase of the population of Baghdad between 1922 and 1957."[3]

But the young king did not want to develop a strong state or a strong civil society for that matter. Faisal based his rule on support from the British and tribal leaders.[4] He repeatedly banned political parties to prevent a strong civil society from emerging. Access to the center of power was restricted. There was little social mobility in Iraq, and the civil service was not considered particularly prestigious. While the number of government officials rose steadily (from only 3,143 in 1920 to 20,031 in 1958), the security forces (including the police and royal guard) grew at a faster pace (from 2,470 in 1920 to 23,383 in 1958).[5] The military was the strongest institution in the state. Universal male conscription made it a formative institution for the young state's male citizens, and the officer corps offered one of the few routes to social mobility. However, the officer corps was divided along several political and ethnic lines. This resulted in intermittent coup attempts but also prevented the armed forces from posing a unified challenge.

Iraq's new leaders had modest ambitions in the field of development, but still struggled to develop and implement reforms given the limited state institutions. The monarchy gave priority to expanding primary education. Primary education was free, but far from universal. In 1958, more than six-sevenths of Iraqis were illiterate.[6] Nonetheless, Iraq was, along with Syria and Lebanon, one of the Arab states with the highest number of university students, although it was considerably behind Egypt.[7] Ambitious students could also pursue postgraduate degrees abroad, some funded privately and others by government scholarships. In 1959, 2,000 Iraqi students went to the United Kingdom, 1,500 to the Soviet Union, and 1,050 to the United States; an additional 1,685 studied in other countries.[8]

During the 1950s, oil money enabled the monarchy to reshape the Iraqi state. Between 1950 and 1958, the state income from oil exports rose from £5.2 million to £79.8 million.[9] While foreign companies, especially British ones, had a heavy-handed role in shaping the Iraqi oil industry and exports, this oil boom enabled a series of transformations in the Iraqi state. It also made the state more independent from society. From this point on, the Iraqi government set out to develop more systematic economic planning and a more prominent role for the state.[10]

But neither history nor infrastructure had prepared Iraq for rapid technological or industrial development. Iraq was an agrarian society, with roughly three-quarters of the population working in the agriculture sector. Nearly all manufactured goods were imported, and the existing Iraqi industries could not meet local demand. The oil industry was managed by foreign companies at this time, with little spillover to Iraqi society, and was the most important economic and industrial activity in the country. The government's industrialization policy was incremental: developing large-scale industrial resources outside of the oil sector was not a matter of urgency.

With few exceptions, industry and trade remained small-scale and local. In the mid-1940s, only 0.5 percent of the population worked in industry. According to a contemporary British study, "The few undertakings worthy of the name 'industrial' owe their existence partly to state support which, by the way, is given in a less active and systematic form than in other Middle East countries such as Turkey and Iran."[11] In 1953, a survey identified only 269 industrial units that employed more than twenty people across the entire country.[12] One of the oldest modern industries in Iraq was production of weapons and munitions. The British had established local factories for the production of machine guns and rifles during the 1930s.[13] These factories continued to produce British-designed weapons, but Iraqis did not develop new weapons systems. The Iraqi military-industrial complex remained small and did not spur technological innovation.

Given the relatively small population (estimated at 6.5 million in 1957) and underdeveloped economy, it is not surprising that electricity was not widespread. By the late 1950s construction of three large electric power stations was under way to supply the three main regions (Kirkuk, Basra, and Baghdad).[14] In 1959 Dhiya Jafar, the minister of development, inaugurated the

Dukan and Darbandikhan hydropower dams in Kurdistan. Despite the expansion of the national power grid, there were no indications of an interest in exploring nuclear energy or acquiring nuclear weapons at this stage.

THE BAGHDAD PACT BRINGS NUCLEAR ASSISTANCE

Nuclear science first came to Iraq as a result of the Baghdad Pact, an uneasy alliance established in 1955 to counter Soviet influence in the Middle East. As a stronghold of British influence Iraq was a key member of this new union, which included Turkey, Pakistan, and Iran. From the outset, this alliance had a nuclear dimension, as the British lacked the capacity or the willingness to provide a conventional defense for their Baghdad Pact allies against Soviet aggression. Instead, Britain envisioned deploying nuclear weapons to deter the Soviets.[15] A group of Iraqi officers, including Abdul Karim Qasim, resented Iraq's entry into this alliance and started plotting a coup.

Britain was also keen to provide nuclear assistance as part of a broader package of economic assistance to Baghdad Pact member states and proposed establishing a nuclear research center in Iraq.[16] This center, which would be located at Salhiya, near the Tigris River in central Baghdad, was intended to showcase British contributions and spur regional industrial development.

At this time the notion of an Iraqi nuclear weapons program must have seemed an alien prospect to the British. Bolstering the anticommunist alliance in the Middle East, on the other hand, was a pressing matter. Sir John Cockcroft, director of the British nuclear establishment, played a central role in designing British nuclear assistance for the Baghdad Pact allies. His motives were fundamentally political, in the sense that he believed science could play an important role in curbing Soviet influence in the world. In his 1951 Nobel acceptance speech, Cockcroft characterized science as a shield against Communism: "overwhelming evil and danger comes not from science but from political ideas which reject the freedom of the human spirit and the values and rights of individual human beings. In these difficult times science can be one of the strongest shields of our Western Civilisation."[17]

In Baghdad, the ambitions for nuclear science had not yet reached a formative stage. In 1956, the state set up the IAEC as part of a broader initiative to nurture science and technology. The IAEC was attached to the Prime Minister's Office and included representatives from key ministries, including industry, agriculture, health, education, transport, and defense. The first secretary-general of the IAEC was Mohamed Kashif Ghita, who had studied physics at the University of Chicago. One of his main supporters was Khalil al-Zobaie, a chemical corps commander who represented the Ministry of Defense.[18] Iraq did not yet have a scientific or technological community capable of taking the lead in these early efforts. Despite setting up an organization to explore the potential benefits of nuclear technology, the Iraqi government did not develop specific plans or objectives in the nuclear field. As the IAEC began to lay the foundation for an indigenous nuclear program over the next few years, they relied heavily on foreign advisers and consultants.

On 31 March 1957, the Baghdad Pact Nuclear Training Centre was formally inaugurated. The opening ceremony was attended by King Faisal II and distinguished guests, with Cockcroft as the inaugural speaker. As Cockcroft noted in *Nature*, "the Centre is an experiment in introducing the new techniques of radioisotopes to an important group of Middle East countries."[19] Furthermore, Cockcroft suggested that Iraq was not a likely candidate for nuclear power in the near term: "The application of nuclear power will not be worthwhile in Iraq and Turkey in the foreseeable future, owing to the abundant supply of oil and hydro power. Iran and Pakistan are, however, interested in the potentialities of nuclear power . . . and the Centre will help by advice to promote this development."[20]

After the ceremony Dhiya Jafar, Iraq's minister for development, invited Cockcroft for lunch at his home in Baghdad. Here, he introduced his guest to his thirteen-year-old son Jafar, later to play a prominent role in Iraq's nuclear programs. The younger Jafar recalls that when Cockcroft asked what he would like to do in the future, he replied that he wanted to build an atomic bomb. But first, he had to go to boarding school.[21]

The Baghdad Pact Nuclear Training Centre was housed in a pleasant two-story building in Salhiya. While this building was initially intended for agricultural research on dates, it was converted to a center equipped with laboratories, a library, a lecture room, and staff offices.[22] The Iraqi hosts were deferential to the advice of British scientists. At the same time, the Iraqis were reluctant to pay the costs of running the center.[23] The center was supposed to be jointly funded by all Baghdad Pact member countries from August 1957, but Britain provided the lion's share of technical assistance and training. The British estimated that the operations of the center would amount to £23,000 per calendar year. During 1956–1957, the United Kingdom spent £29,500 on the Baghdad Pact Nuclear Training Centre; the following year they subsidized it with £75,500.[24]

The British considered providing a nuclear research reactor to the center, but decided against it because they were concerned that this could be seen as favoring Iraq too much in the eyes of the other Baghdad Pact members. Furthermore, they did not consider a reactor necessary for the purposes of the center before 1958–1959. But when they realized that the Americans were considering providing a research reactor to Iraq the British Foreign Office revisited this issue. In early 1957, Foreign Office officials noted that "to make sure of beating the Americans . . . we (probably) should look at the idea again in consultation with the Atomic Energy Authority."[25]

The British Atomic Energy Authority advised the Foreign Office during the development of the Salhiya center, which was staffed and overseen by

British scientists. Britain anticipated that Iraqis (presumably with the support of other Baghdad Pact members) would take over the running of the center within a few years. At the 1957 inauguration, Cockcroft was appointed chairman of the center's scientific council. Professor W. J. Whitehouse, seconded from the British Atomic Energy Research Establishment at Harwell, was appointed director. Four additional Harwell employees were seconded to Baghdad for an initial period of one year.[26] Furthermore, two lecturers would spend six months at the center. In 1956 the first two Iraqi instructors traveled to Harwell in Oxfordshire to receive training. Over the next couple of years (1957–1958), six Iraqi students received training in isotope research at Harwell.[27]

Britain provided technical equipment and staff to oversee the initial planning and development of the center. The United States, for its part, donated a library of books and reports on nuclear energy. These included declassified reports from the Manhattan Project detailing technical pathways to produce the bomb that had been deemed inefficient or overly complex. A Californian company, General Atomics, would supply a 5-megawatt light-water research reactor for the center.[28]

The Salhiya center was set up to provide courses for up to twenty students three or four times a year. These were modeled on Harwell's Isotope School course.[29] They began to train students in basic techniques and the applications of radioisotopes. These early efforts focused on medical diagnostics and therapy for cancer and thyroid disease. Subsequent studies would focus on uses of radioisotopes for the petroleum industry, agriculture, and water conservation.[30]

The Iraqis did not have specific targets or a plan for how the potential of nuclear power could best be tapped. They were prepared to explore the technology given to them by the British as part of a broader modernization project without predefined objectives or expectations. In a 1959 preliminary assistance report by the International Atomic Energy Agency (IAEA), the objectives of the Iraqi program were described as follows:

> Iraq, conscious of the constructive contribution that radioisotope tracer techniques could make towards the development of medicine, industry and agriculture, has taken steps to initiate a long-term programme to meet the requirements of research into these techniques and their applications. That programme covers specialist training in basic and applied nuclear science, the establishment of a training and research centre, the installation of a research reactor, and expansion of the existing Medical Radioisotope Centre.[31]

To say that there was limited local demand for nuclear technology would not be an understatement. However, the Baghdad Museum expressed interest in carbon dating.[32] In early 1958, a carbon-dating course was held as part of a joint project with the British Museum to establish an Iraqi center for dating archaeological finds.[33] One of the participants, Numan Saadaldin al-Niaimi, went on to study radioisotopes in inorganic chemistry at Oxford University and, upon his return, became a senior figure in the Iraqi nuclear establishment.

A Republic Is Born

On 14 July 1958, a group of officers led by Colonel Abdul Salam Arif and Abdul Karim Qasim seized power in a coup d'état. The officers assassinated the Iraqi royal family and their staff in the courtyard, then turned their attention to the former monarchial regime and its supporters.

Qasim soon sidelined the main architect of the coup, Colonel Arif. Arif favored taking a pan-Arab political direction to bring Iraq more in line with Egypt and Syria. Qasim, on the other hand, wanted a more independent political trajectory.[34] Over the next couple of years he severed several of Iraq's pro-Western alliances, fulfilling his long-standing ambition to exit the Baghdad Pact, and attempted to rebalance the Iraqi domestic political landscape. As a result, Arif found himself increasingly isolated and vulnerable.

On the surface, the new republic appeared to be more inclusive than the monarchy had been. Qasim set up a Revolutionary Council with representatives of the three largest ethnic groups and a Cabinet including representatives from across the political spectrum. The Cabinet was dominated by the Baath [Renaissance] Party, which had a socialist and nationalist orientation. The Baath Party had supporters across Arab republics and monarchies, notably including Syria and Egypt. To counter their influence, Qasim enlisted the support of the Iraqi Communist Party, the oldest political party in the country. He also tried to improve his standing with the officer corps and intelligence services.[35] Despite his attempts to build broader support among elites, the state of Iraq was increasingly threatened by fragmentation in the face of a Kurdish push for autonomy.

Behind the scenes, however, Qasim intensified the concentration of decision-making power. State institutions were weak, and factions became embroiled in power struggles. The republic inherited civil servants who had suffered disproportionately relative to other professions in the upper and middle classes during the economic downturns of the 1940s. Civil servants did not recover their pre-Second World War standard of living until after the 1958 coup.[36] Members of the armed forces fared better, enjoying perks such as servant and housing allowances that were not available to civil servants.

The resulting state weaknesses were apparent in the failure to implement ambitious reform programs. Within months of the July coup a series of large-scale reforms was announced. In October 1958 Qasim announced that land was to be distributed among farmers working in cooperatives. Despite the ambitious tone, these initiatives—intended to strengthen the hand of the state in social planning—failed to materialize. Qasim lacked the necessary elite support and institutional capacity.

Qasim's room for maneuver was therefore constrained. The state's main source of income was at the mercy of foreign companies effectively controlling Iraq's oil extraction and export. Qasim could not risk an outright nationalization, having observed the consequences of the 1951 Iranian nationalization, but tried to improve Iraq's income and influence over the foreign companies. His most significant reform was Public Law 80 of 1961, which placed the vast majority of Iraqi oil fields that had up until then been held by foreign oil companies under state control. This, and the establishment of an Iraqi national oil company, signaled stronger state control over its main economic asset.[37]

STARTING OVER AT SALHIYA

The 1958 coup had a transformative impact on Iraq's foreign relations and, consequently, the fate of the Salhiya center. After Iraq formally withdrew from the Baghdad Pact on 24 March 1959, relations with their nuclear benefactors soured. Britain opted to redirect its assistance efforts to a new nuclear center in Tehran. The American research reactor intended for Iraq, but was similarly redirected to Iran. Abandoned by its patrons, Iraq was unable to continue research and development in the nuclear field. The Baghdad Pact Nuclear Training Center closed in the turmoil of the July coup and did not reopen until November 1960.

After the departure of the British scientists, the Salhiya nuclear research center became the temporary home for the IAEC. Salah Izzat Tahsin took over as the commission's new secretary-general. The Iraqi nuclear establishment continued to depend heavily on foreign staff, assistance, and equipment and had to look abroad for other helpers to build their nascent program.

The 1958 coup opened the door to greater Soviet assistance. The Soviet Union was encouraged by Iraq's departure from the Baghdad Pact. The Qasim government saw the USSR as an important source of economic assistance but was reluctant to grant Moscow too much leverage.[38] Nonetheless, a set of agreements between the two states paved the way for a strong Soviet influence on the Iraqi nuclear program. In February 1959, an Iraqi delegation went to Moscow to sign a broad economic cooperation agreement. Under this agreement, signed on 16 March, the Soviet Union provided a credit loan of 550 million rubles (then equivalent to £49 million) and offered technical assistance with the development of Iraqi industrial capabilities for the next seven years. Then, on 17 August 1959, they signed an agreement to collaborate on atomic energy for peaceful purposes. Iraq purchased a 2-megawatt thermal research reactor (IRT-2000) from the Soviets, which they named "14 Tammuz" (14 July) in honor of the 1958 coup. Iraq paid $5.6 million to acquire this reactor.[39] A new nuclear complex, which would be located at Tuwaitha some 20 kilometers outside Baghdad, would also include a radioisotope laboratory, supporting workshops, and a library.[40] This was a fairly standard Soviet starter package, but it heralded a more ambitious approach to exploring nuclear science and technology in Iraq.

While the Iraqis waited for the construction of the Tuwaitha complex, they sought help with developing the institutional and human resources for their nuclear program. Specifically, they pursued nuclear assistance and training through bilateral ties and the IAEA, which was formed in 1957. The IAEA offered training courses and support for planning and managing nuclear research and development. During the 1960s the IAEA focused on supporting nuclear energy programs in developing states, acting as consultants to assess reactor bids and even supplying technical instruments to member states. In 1961, Baqir Husaini joined the Board of Governors of the IAEA as the Iraqi representative. Several of his fellow board members would play important roles in other developing states' efforts to explore the civilian and military applications of nuclear technology.[41]

The IAEA's technical assistance was, at this early stage, closely coordinated with other assistance programs provided by United Nations (UN) agencies in Iraq. In 1959, Ambassador Jens Henrik Malling was appointed UN Resident Representative in Iraq, where he would oversee the administration of a broad portfolio of assistance programs.[42] These efforts were nominally coordinated with Iraqi ministers and local staff, but due to their limited administrative capacity, foreign experts led the planning and implementation of individual projects. They also fulfilled other roles that could not be served by Iraq's limited administrative resources. Malling's successor, U Hla Maung, reported that the Iraqis used foreign experts to assess bilateral programs of technical assistance from the Soviet Union and Eastern European countries. In 1959, Iraq received $4 million in technical aid from the UN, which was primarily used for agricultural projects and telecommunications. At this time, Iraq declined the offer of further nuclear assistance from the UN, citing limited human resources as an obstacle.

The Salhiya center reopened in November 1960, but remained largely idle. Despite being stocked with ample equipment and materials, only routine measurements were conducted.[43] The local staff did not plan any research and development activities and, in any case, Iraq lacked adequately skilled scientists and technicians to take charge of such activities. Some planning activities could be outsourced to foreign experts provided by the Soviet Union and the IAEA. Through the efforts of the IAEA, Iraq would be able to receive foreign experts who advised on how to develop a technical infrastructure and plan research and development activities. But the implementation of this advice largely hinged on the limited organizational and human resources in Iraq. The agency initially offered more assistance than the IAEC was able to absorb, given the conditions at Salhiya. Still, more support was forthcoming. In 1962, visiting IAEA experts recommended an increase to the assistance budget of 33 percent for the coming year.[44]

To benefit from foreign technical assistance the Iraqis needed to overcome two obstacles: limited manpower (some aid programs lacked adequately qualified local counterparts); and limited administrative capability.[45] There were skilled Iraqi counterparts in some project sectors, such as telecommunications and agriculture, while other projects, such as developing an Iraqi census, lacked adequate local support in many other areas. There was a general shortage of staff capable of providing administrative assistance to English-speaking foreigners.[46] While Qasim's government recognized these problems, it was difficult to find short-term solutions. Maung noted, "It is not always desirable—or fruitful—to press governments too hard in this respect, for the required facilities are just not there."[47] For this reason, the UN experts assisted with tasks such as assessment of bilateral assistance programs and, in the nuclear field, selection of candidates for IAEA fellowships. But it proved difficult to find foreign nuclear experts to help Iraq with these matters. In 1961, for example, the IAEA's approved budget for twelve months of expert assistance for Iraq was not utilized as no foreign experts had been recruited.[48]

As a developing country, Iraq faced problems when adapting foreign equipment to local infrastructure and lacked the technical know-how to tackle these problems. Installing and using instruments that sometimes arrived without training or adequate instructions often proved difficult. An IAEA delegation to Iraq in 1962 noted that there was only one physicist working at the Salhiya center. Finding suitable technicians and medical experts was difficult and would remain so for several years.[49] The technicians working in the college laboratories at this time mostly came from other countries, notably Pakistan.

In the face of these challenges, the early initiatives of the Iraqi nuclear establishment had mixed results. The IAEC initially focused on exploring medical applications of nuclear technology in health and agriculture. For example, Ali Hindawi oversaw the development of a radioisotope department at the Republic Hospital.[50] This unit became operational in 1957. Over the next three years his center pioneered efforts to apply radiation therapy in Iraq. Researchers studied anemia, thyroid treatments, and various therapeutic applications of isotopes (see Figure 1.1).[51] In the early 1960s, this hospital opened Iraq's first cancer treatment center in which Hindawi established the country's first radiation therapy center.[52]

The IAEC also planned to set up a National Radioisotope Center. This center was led by Thabit Hiti, who had trained as a resident doctor in Hindawi's radioisotope department. Hiti wanted to develop more interaction with national and international organizations, including the Loma Linda University Hospital in the United States and the IAEA. Foreign experts were supplied by the IAEA in 1961, but apparently got little backing from the IAEC and the Iraqi government. Over the next decade his center continued to languish in a remote building, which had been intended as a temporary location. The center was isolated from the other activities in the nuclear establishment and, curiously, cut off from the hospital they were intended to serve. When an IAEA inspector revisited the site in 1971, he reported that the same "antiquated" equipment he saw in 1961 was still there.[53]

In the early 1960s, agricultural applications were the most active component of the Iraqi nuclear research program. Agriculture was an important part of the Iraqi economy, and nuclear techniques could address problems with soil (e.g., by increasing fertility) and cultivation.[54] The IAEA's technical assistance programs offered equipment, training, and advice for developing states such as Iraq. Abdul Hadri Islail was the director general of the Ministry of Agriculture's Department of Research and Projects. His junior colleague, Lonay Kadri, a soil chemist, led the Soils Division. In this capacity, Kadri interacted with visiting IAEA delegations. He explained to these officials why the Iraqis struggled to absorb foreign assistance and technology. For example, the IAEA had granted $4,800 for equipment supporting agricultural projects but, as Kadri explained, much of the technical equipment Iraq had received was still in the crates they arrived in. The Iraqis feared that serious fluctuations in voltage could destroy the instruments and had not installed them.[55] Moreover, the shortage of skilled manpower remained a key challenge. Iraq lacked technical workers and administrative resources to tackle more complex problems. There was not much that the IAEA could do to solve these problems. While it could provide additional equipment, developing a pool of human resources was a more pressing—and difficult—matter.[56] Although Iraq had dedicated and enterprising scientists who were keen to benefit from foreign assistance programs and develop international connections, the administrative resources of the state continued to fall short.

The Qasim government set up a coordination committee to oversee the technical assistance programs provided by the UN and states from the Eastern bloc. This was a large committee that consisted of twenty-one representatives from government ministries and other academic and governmental agencies.[57] Despite its impressive size and broad representation, the committee did not have the capacity to review all assistance programs, and individual projects were examined incrementally. Salah Izzat Tahsin, the new director of the Salhiya nuclear research center and the second secretary-general of the IAEC, represented the IAEC, which was made part of the Ministry of Industry. The coordination committee experienced frequent changes in leadership.[58] Nouri al-Kadhim was demoted from his position as director of the committee in July 1961. Just two months later his successor, Fakhri al-Qaisi, was replaced by Usamah Kadry. Given this turbulence, the committee largely failed to fulfill its basic mandate.

Figure 1.1. Dr. M. Menarchi of the Iraqi National Nutrition Institute examines pupils for enlargement of the thyroid gland, one of several applications of nuclear medicine in Iraq (IAEA Archives, Photographic Collection, A005).

Developing Human Resources. Educating more scientists, engineers, and technicians was the main priority of the IAEC during its first decade (1956–1966). Iraqi universities could not meet this sudden demand, but a general expansion of science and engineering faculties helped. In 1956, the University of Baghdad comprised twelve colleges and institutes, including schools of science and engineering.[59] Several of their alumni would later join the Iraqi nuclear establishment, notably including Dhafir Selbi, who received a bachelor's degree in mechanical engineering in 1965 and who would play a central role in the Iraqi nuclear program during the 1970s and 1980s.

Iraqi colleges and universities offered education in pure science but lacked resources for experimental research. The University of Baghdad, for example, taught theoretical nuclear science, chemistry, and physics. But the students did not receive much training in practical applications of nuclear technology. After graduation, there was no industry that could generate useful experience for the pool of recruits for the Iraq nuclear establishment. Most of the science faculty was foreign, and the college leaders were keen to strengthen their Iraqi faculty. The college dean requested IAEA fellowships to train departmental scientists abroad, among whom was Abdul Wahab Derwish, who would later emerge as a leader in the development of the nuclear establishment.[60]

The broad agreements of technical cooperation between Iraq and the Soviet Union opened important avenues for education and training. The Soviets had committed to provide a research reactor (14 Tammuz), and they provided hands-on training for Iraqis to operate the reactor. During the early 1960s Iraqi students traveled to the USSR to study reactor operations, in addition to others studying for degrees in science or technology at Soviet universities.[61]

In 1962, IAEA officials visited the Iraqi nuclear establishment. They highlighted human resources and management as key challenges: "The main problem of the Center continues to be the lack of scientific personnel."[62] Unlike the university, the IAEC appeared wary of taking advantage of IAEA training fellowships. The IAEA consultants noted that their individual Iraqi counterpart was reluctant to send an Iraqi candidate for an IAEA fellowship because he was concerned that the commission had to pay half of the candidate's salary. Once he was told this was not the case, there were no further objections.[63]

While the majority of Iraq's first nuclear scientists and engineers were trained in the Soviet Union, the first generation of leaders of the nuclear establishment was educated in the West during the 1940s and 1950s. Postgraduate degrees from Western universities, particularly British and American universities, were considered more prestigious than degrees offered by Soviet institutions. The first two secretary-generals of the IAEC, Ghita and Tahsin, both studied nuclear physics in America. Wahab and his successor at the nuclear research center, A. K. Wahid, studied in Britain and the United States. (Many Soviet-educated scientists were, as we will see, purged from the program in anticommunist campaigns during the 1960s and 1970s, leaving the nuclear program with significantly diminished human resources.)

The second generation of prominent Iraqi physicists primarily studied in Britain, Canada, and the United States during the early to mid-1960s. Several came from important Iraqi families or the upper middle class, but opportunities were also opening for talented individuals from more humble backgrounds. The aforementioned son of the former Iraqi development minister, Jafar Dhiya Jafar, set out to follow in the footsteps of his father by obtaining a doctorate in high-energy physics at Birmingham University. During the early 1960s, Jafar carried out doctoral research at the Rutherford Laboratory in Oxford. He would become a pivotal figure in the civilian and military Iraqi nuclear programs. At the same time Numan Saadaldin al-Niaimi, who came from a more modest family background in Dohuk, northern Iraq, completed his doctorate in inorganic chemistry at Oxford. Another prominent figure in Iraq's nuclear program, Hussein Shahristani, studied in London for a master of science degree in chemical engineering. After graduating from the Imperial College in 1965, Shahristani received a doctorate in activation analysis from the University of Toronto two years later.

While several talented scientists returned to play important parts in the Iraqi nuclear program, inadequate planning contributed to a loss of scarce human resources at lower levels of the organization. For example, there was an apparent lack of in-house institutional planning and selection of candidates for education and training abroad. Visiting IAEA consultants noted that a former IAEA fellowship recipient trained in Japan had not yet been employed at the center, despite the lack of Iraqi nuclear scientists at Salhiya. Two health physicists who had studied in the Soviet Union and West Germany wanted to change fields of specialization after they returned to Iraq, suggesting that the selection of candidates did not sufficiently factor in what candidates were interested in and how this matched the needs of the organization. Another former IAEA fellow estimated that he had spent 90 percent of his time in England studying other subjects.

THE 1963 RAMADAN REVOLUTION

Qasim survived several assassination attempts—including a 1959 plot involving a young Saddam Hussein—but his domestic position was perilous. Furthermore, his radical foreign policy reorientation alienated potential foreign supporters. In the so-called Ramadan Revolution of February 1963, the Baath Party seized power with the help of the armed forces. Qasim was executed on 9 February. In the months that followed, violence and instability shook Iraq to the core.

The Iraqi Communist Party had been a key supporter of the Qasim regime and thus had been an obstacle to the expansion of the Baath Party's influence. The revolution marked the beginning a purge throughout Iraqi society, ultimately causing the deaths of thousands of civilians. Suspected communists were hunted down and killed. The targets included scores of white-collar workers. Hundreds of doctors, teachers, lawyers, and technicians were killed or imprisoned by the Baathists.

On 10 November 1963, a group of army officers overthrew the new regime. Abdul Salam Arif took over as president. He monopolized power and relied on a few trusted individuals. General Ahmed Hassan al-Bakr, a Baathist, became prime minister. The Baath movement was riddled with divisions, both between the Iraqi and Syrian wings and within the Iraqi chapter, and lacked a sound organizational structure. The Iraqi Baath Party was described as "less a party than a confederation of cliques."[64] The purpose of state institutions increasingly appeared to be to concentrate power in the hands of the ruler. After Arif's death in a dubious helicopter crash in 1966, his brother, Abdul Rahman Arif, seized the presidency. Both brothers had wanted to create a more homogenous society and a more unified state, but neither succeeded.[65]

The Baath Party wing associated with Bakr went underground, where they plotted to oust the incumbent regime and seize power. Bakr appointed his relative, Saddam Hussein, as his deputy.

NUCLEAR FUTURES AT TUWAITHA

In the early 1960s the Soviets began constructing a nuclear complex at Tuwaitha. In 1962, experts from the Soviet State Committee for the Peaceful Utilization of Atomic Energy were based in the Iraqi Ministry of Industry to oversee these efforts. Monachov from the Soviet State Committee for the Utilization of Atomic Energy led the delegation, assisted by the project head Kamenski, Toraskin, chief designer of the Iraqi site, and Tikhonov (electric engineer).[66] They oversaw the development of the site assisted by Iraqi counterparts, offered to train Iraqi technicians, and gave advice for suitable research activities. The Soviet Union anticipated playing such a role for Iraq for the foreseeable future and planned a joint nuclear research program.[67] The Soviets agreed to provide additional reactor fuel upon Iraqi requests, and once the reactor was completed laboratories would be added to facilitate research.

The Soviet research reactor became the hub of research activities at Tuwaitha. The Iraqi scientists developed a research program based on recommendations from the Joint Committee of the IAEC and the Soviet State Committee for the Utilization of Atomic Energy.[68] While the IAEC nominally planned on a five-year horizon, little planning actually took place at the senior level. The Soviets were keen to steer the Iraqi program toward peaceful applications and wanted a strong hand in shaping the direction of Iraqi research and development efforts. Their advisers, including A. M. Demidov (who also served as IAEA expert in Iraq on a separate occasion) and M. G. Zemlyanov, proposed that the initial IRT-2000 research program would focus on neutron activation analysis, neutron-diffraction, neutron capture, radiation chemistry, and radiobiology.[69] By 1969 progress had been made in research on neutron capture by Jafar—"whose efficiency has contributed [greatly] to this particular sphere of works"—with the assistance of IAEA experts Josef Kajfosz and Z. Kosina.[70] This technique, which can detect the chemical composition of matter, has applications for mineral exploration (such as uranium).

The Tuwaitha complex was intended to spur basic research activities, which had thus far been taking place in scattered locations, and lay the foundation for more advanced research and development. The estimated start-up date was October 1963. Ghazi Abdul Wahab Derwish was the first director of the Nuclear Research Center (NRC) at Tuwaitha.[71] Construction ran behind schedule, and the research reactor finally went critical in December 1967. By January 1968 the reactor was fully operational, although it did not produce radioisotopes on a regular basis until the end of 1969.

Neither the NRC leadership nor the IAEC played a central role in the planning of research activities. Individual scientists, in collaboration with IAEA and Soviet experts, planned much of the research activities. In the mid-1960s these activities were loosely structured into the five departments: Nuclear and Radiochemistry (headed by Numan Saadaldin al-Niaimi); Nuclear Physics (headed by Zuhair Mahdi al-Saffar); Health Physics (headed by Subhi al-Hashimi); Radiobiology (headed by Faisal al-Khalisi); and Nuclear Geology (headed by Ibrahim al-Fadhli).[72] Within each department researchers were free to explore basic and applied research in their own fields. The NRC continued to explore basic applications for agriculture and medicine. Figure 1.2, below, illustrates one of the early applications of health physics in Iraq.

During the lengthy construction process, several students returned from abroad with advanced degrees. Jafar joined the NRC in February 1967 and was appointed research scientist in nuclear physics. He was warmly welcomed by the director, Derwish, and Numan, who had joined the chemistry department upon his return from Oxford.[73] Jafar and Shahristani, who returned from Toronto in 1970, brought theoretical insights about reactors back to the Iraqi nuclear establishment.

The NRC offered research opportunities that began to attract postgraduate Iraqi students and experts studying or working abroad. Tuwaitha also facilitated collaboration with foreign experts. To reap this potential, the NRC started planning a series of conferences and seminars to engage Iraqi scientists, engineers, and technicians living abroad.[74]

The late 1960s was also a time of organizational expansion in the nuclear field, which led to some institutional growing pains. As students returned from studies abroad, the IAEC acquired a pool of graduates who could benefit from opportunities such as scholarships and assistance from the IAEA. Students returning from the Soviet Union with advanced graduate degrees included three physicists, two radiobiologists, a geologist, and a health physicist. The influx of graduates spurred initiatives to carry out research in new areas including nuclear and solid-state physics, agriculture, isotope production, reactor physics, and engineering.[75] From late 1969, the NRC produced radioactive isotopes for medical purposes.[76] These activities were directed by individual scientists, while the senior leadership at Tuwaitha was preoccupied with administrative matters. But this growth spurt was not matched in terms of administrative capacity. Despite ample funding, everyday operations were struggling. Even basic items were lacking at the NRC, such as adequate calculators and a copying machine. The following observations, made by a visiting IAEA expert in late 1968, are revealing: [77]

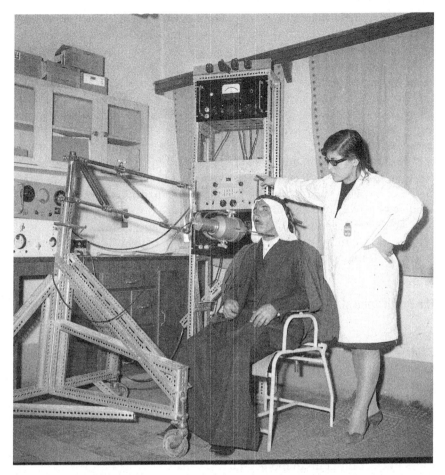

Figure 1.2. An Iraqi technician from the Radioisotope Department of the National Nutrition Institute measures radioiodine uptake in a patient in a village near Baghdad (IAEA Archives, Photographic Collection, A007).

Although I have been informed that very adequate funds are available from the Iraqi Government for support of the Tammuz Reactor Centre, a stringent situation seems obvious, particularly evidenced in securing funds for day-to-day operating supplies. There are two reasons for this. First, the administrative organization has not advanced in capability fast enough to take care of the expanded laboratory staff, i.e. the administrative organization is geared to handle the needs of 60 people instead of 200 to 250 people. Secondly, more industry members are needed on the Iraq Atomic Energy Committee, who will use their influence to provide more funds for operating needs.

With a fully operational research reactor (14 Tammuz), the scene was set for a broader range of experiments. The Iraqis set out to develop a data-processing system with the assistance of foreign experts to process the complex data acquired from experiments. By mid-1969, this system was capable of measuring experiments in areas such as activation analysis and nuclear spectroscopy.[78] Once this infrastructure was set up, experiments could be carried out. Iraqi researchers—notably Jafar, Khalid Ibrahim Said, and Abdullah Khail—carried out a series of experiments in the research reactor. Their efforts were guided and facilitated by Soviet scientists, as the Iraqis had entered into a cooperative agreement with the Soviet Union. As part of this agreement, two scientists went to the Kurchatov Institute in Moscow to study activation analysis techniques (to facilitate more reactor experiments) in 1968. Fifteen Iraqi scientists were trained by Soviet experts in Baghdad in fields such as nuclear physics, neutron activation analysis, and solid-state physics.[79] The Kurchatov Institute also provided material (seven separated stable isotopes), equipment (pneumatic tubes), and visiting staff (A. M. Demidov and L. I. Govor) to the NRC. Their initial experiments were promising and produced valuable new data.

The Baath Coup of 1968

In 1968, Iraq once again was subject to forcible change of government. The Baath Party wing led by Hassan al-Bakr and his deputy, Saddam Hussein, seized power on 17 July with the support of the armed forces. Bakr became president and Saddam his deputy. Saddam took charge of the intelligence services and became deeply involved in overseeing Iraqi economic institutions. Over the next few years, Saddam worked to increase his personal influence. In this section, we will survey some of the broader changes and reforms that followed the 1968 coup before exploring the consequences for Iraq's nuclear program in more detail.

The Baath coup led to a transformation of the size and scope of the Iraqi state. This enabled the new regime to design and implement reforms, notably in the field of education, where other leaders had failed. At the same time, Iraq's new rulers continued their predecessors' efforts to concentrate power in their own hands. The regime wanted to use state institutions as instruments of power and also to detect and deter dissent through a series of purges and infiltration of the state bureaucracy. Baath Party members set up organizations in their workplace from which they sought to influence local planning and management. Behind the scenes, Saddam built a network of influential regime officials at the senior leadership level. This network was motivated primarily by a desire for power and material interest, not a unified ideological vision.[80] The net result was an expansion of the state and at the same time a fragmentation of state power, as party and elite networks sought to assert their power at the expense of formal institutions.

The initial Baath program appeared to be ambitious: a broad socialist vision, including collectivization of agriculture and building a strong state.[81] The armed forces were a key priority. To this end, the regime set out to provide state-sponsored training of scientists and engineers to develop a pool of human resources that could create a modern and well-equipped military. The new regime also set out to revitalize the languishing military-industrial sector. Between 1968 and 1972, for example, Iraq built industrial complexes at Musayyab, Yarmuk, and Abu Ghraib for production of conventional small arms of Soviet design.[82]

From 1970, primary education was free, universal, and mandatory. The expansion of the education system was fueled by oil wealth; an ideological emphasis on education was also seen as a means to fulfill the Baath Party's socialist objectives. Within a decade this campaign had placed the Iraqi primary education system among the best in the Middle East. The Ministries of Education and Research developed a national curriculum, provided teacher training and increased salaries, and required universal attendance during the first six years of primary school. Education's share of the national budget increased from 11.5 percent in 1976 to 13.9 percent in 1978.[83] The government further demonstrated its commitment to higher education by exempting enrolled students from military service.

In the mid-1970s the Baath government launched a series of campaigns to reduce illiteracy and teach basic mathematics. These efforts yielded impressive results. Between 1978 and 1987 illiteracy was reduced from 48.4 percent to 19.9 percent, an effort that was recognized by several United Nations Educational, Scientific and Cultural Organization (UNESCO) awards.[84] In 1975 the ruling Revolutionary Command Council (RCC) passed a law to develop vocational education to meet Iraq's development challenges. By 1978 the percentage of students enrolled in vocational courses had doubled from 9.8 percent in 1972 to 17.8 percent.[85] Over the next decade student recruitment for technical subjects increased threefold, reaching over 120,000 in 1986.[86]

The government also expanded higher education facilities in other major cities and regions. At that time, the majority of university colleges and technical institutes were concentrated in the Baghdad area. These provided education in basic science and various technical fields (notably the Foundation of Technical Institutes and the University of Technology in Baghdad). By the late 1970s, fourteen technical institutes provided two-year training courses for mid-level technicians.[87]

In the mid-1970s, the government greatly expanded efforts to send military officers and university graduates abroad for postgraduate degrees. Gifted individuals from rural backwaters could rise through the ranks in the Baath Party or the state through state schools and scholarships in selected fields. The Ministry of Higher Education and Scientific Research and the

Mukhabarat (the main intelligence organization) organized these efforts. They prioritized scientists, engineers, and military officers who could acquire skills that were relevant for Iraqi military industries.[88] However, Iraqi postgraduates could pursue degrees in various technical and scientific fields, including medicine and pure sciences. The majority of these students did not work in the Iraqi weapons programs after returning home from their studies.[89]

The new regime's leaders sought to purge state institutions of potential dissent, particularly in sensitive areas such as defense and the military. In the first months after the 1968 coup, the regime rounded up suspected political opponents, including communists, Baathists who favored the pan-Arab ideology of the Syrian wing of the party, Nasserists, and pro-Western businessmen; it also purged the civil service and officer corps.[90] The new ruling clique persecuted its perceived enemies and, in a series of executions and public trials, demonstrated the costs of suspected opposition to the wider public.

At Tuwaitha, the nuclear establishment braced itself for change. The center was renamed the Tammuz Center, in honor of the July revolutions of 1958 and 1968, but was referred to as the Nuclear Research Center (NRC) by the staff. Within six months of the 1968 coup, new leaders (with Baath credentials) were installed. In 1969 Moyassar al-Mallah replaced Awadh as secretary-general of the IAEC, just a few months after returning from studies in nuclear engineering in the United States.[91] The IAEC was made a part of the Ministry for Higher Education and Research, and the minister of this department was also the chairman of the commission. Although this was the formal arrangement, the IAEC emerged as a largely autonomous entity that was monitored by the security and intelligence services (which were under the purview of Saddam Hussein).[92] Then, in the fall of 1969, Ali Atiya Abdulla was appointed as the new head of the NRC. He replaced Jafar, who had served as acting director from mid-1968 until early 1969 while the then director, Derwish, was on technical assignment for the IAEA in Syria.

These changes made it clear to the nuclear establishment that party affiliation could affect their career prospects. In fact, several ambitious scientists (including Jafar and Shahristani) did not join the Baath Party. But at this early stage, the regime sent a clear signal that senior management positions would be reserved for party members. Scientists could get away with not joining the party as long as they were found trustworthy (i.e., not suspected of harboring communist sympathies or other political affiliations). Over the next couple of years, as we will see, the regime carried out purges against non-Baathist scientists suspected of communist sympathies. While many of these scientists were later welcomed back to the nuclear program, it was clear that the perceived loyalty and trustworthiness of scientists was becoming a more central concern in the hiring and management of the nuclear program. In addition, the presence of two factions—party members and nonparty members—created a cleavage inside the nuclear establishment that would become increasingly tense over the next decade.

Visiting IAEA experts observed that the change in leadership had little or no consequence for the research activities, as the senior management mainly focused on administration.[93] Most of the research activities continued to be developed by Iraqi scientists in conjunction with foreign experts. Over the next couple of years, scientists and engineers that did join the party tried to exert a strong influence on the activities at Tuwaitha and lobbied to secure higher-level interest and support for the nuclear program. This created new conflicts and divisions within the nuclear establishment. From 1970, the Baath group's efforts were increasingly disruptive. The Baathists sought to sideline their nonaffiliated colleagues. They targeted graduates from Soviet or East European universities, who formed the majority of the scientists and engineers in the IAEC.[94] These individuals were reassigned to provincial academic positions (such as the Salah Al-Din University in Sulaimaniyah) and mid-level government posts. As a result, the NRC lost qualified scientists, engineers, and technical workers. This also included some senior scientists who had not studied in the Eastern Bloc but were dissatisfied with the intensifying politicization in Tuwaitha.

Between 1969 and 1970, several senior figures opted to leave the NRC, having grown tired of the stifling conditions at Tuwaitha. In 1970, Jafar left to work in the Physics Department at London's Imperial College.[95] Shahristani, a rising star in the Iraqi nuclear establishment, was transferred to a university position in Mosul in 1973. The following year he became an assistant professor at the University of Baghdad, where he assumed a leading role in radioisotope production and nuclear chemistry. Numan opted to work in the academic sector but was transferred back to the NRC some months later.

This reduced the already small pool of scientists and engineers in the nascent nuclear program. Recruitment for the nuclear program was not always easy. Competent candidates were dissuaded by the restrictions of the IAEC. The NRC was more security-minded than universities. For example, employees could not publish their research unless they had official approval. Also, some were deterred by the harsh treatment of those suspected of supporting prohibited political parties. On a more prosaic level, Tuwaitha was a lengthy commute for many, compared with the campus of Baghdad University.[96]

The turbulence of this period did not affect the Bakr regime's commitment to ensure continued access to foreign nuclear assistance. Iraq signed the Nuclear Non-Proliferation Treaty in Moscow on 1 July 1968, less than three weeks before the Bakr coup, and ratified it in late October 1969. Three years later Iraq signed an additional safeguards agreement to facilitate IAEA inspections of declared nuclear facilities. This paved the way for further assistance and development. An IAEA adviser based in Baghdad reported in January 1969 that the country remained "outwardly calm . . . attempts are being made by the present [Bakr] administration to draw together divisive elements."[97]

The IAEA experts traveling to Iraq in the late 1960s were staying for longer stretches, several weeks or months, and provided assistance with several aspects of these programs. They assisted the Iraqis with organizational planning, creating new avenues of research, and delivered lectures as well as hands-on training. The younger scientists in particular welcomed these experts, instruments, and information, as they were keen to explore new avenues of research.

The Iraqi scientists were beginning to form their own preferences with regard to the direction of their research activities and weighed these against the advice from foreign agencies and experts. For example, foreign experts repeatedly recommended that a greater portion of these activities should be dedicated to applied research (to increase the contributions to development), but the Iraqis continued to explore both basic and applied areas. At this time, nuclear energy was not yet on the Iraqi horizon.

Gilbert Smith, the IAEA expert based in Baghdad in early 1969, developed a new research program suitable for staff with undergraduate degrees at the request of the acting NRC director, A. K. Wahid (who would be replaced by Jafar as acting director in the fall of 1969 before Abdulla took over as director). This program focused on practical applications of neutron activation analysis for mineral surveys carried out by the geological department. Despite the Iraqi nuclear establishment's exploration of radioisotopes over the past decade, few industrial applications had been developed. One area highlighted by IAEA experts as particularly promising was the application of nuclear technologies to oil refining.[98] The IAEA consultants developed a program reaching out to such organizations as the Petroleum Research Institute, the UN Food and Agriculture Organization, and the Institute for Applied Research on Natural Resources.[99] Still, the Iraqi scientists appear to have had limited interest in industrial applications of nuclear technology.

"DEPARTMENT OF UNCLEAR PHYSICS"

By the late 1960s, the broader objectives and purpose of the NRC remained largely undefined. Neither political nor scientific elites had yet developed clear preferences for Iraq's nuclear future. Jafar recounted how his secretary erroneously typed the heading "Department of Unclear Physics," and drily told Numan that this was an accurate characterization.[100]

With infrastructure in place, and students returning from abroad with new expertise, a pressing challenge was to organize a research program. According to IAEA consultant Kajfosz, who spent several months advising the Iraqi nuclear establishment, "The crucial service point seems now to be the organisation of the scientific work."[101] He further noted: "This question will most probably determine to what extent all this effort will result in a successful and continuous scientific work and growth of this group in future. This, however, is a complicated problem which is related to the character of the people and general conditions, which can be hardly influenced by technical assistance."[102]

At Tuwaitha, the absence of a strong central leadership gave younger scientists opportunities for bottom-up initiatives. The level of leadership, planning, and interaction varied between the five departments, which by 1970 focused on the following areas: reactors, isotopes production, physics, radiobiology, and geology.[103] Some departments made good progress, due to the leadership of ambitious young scientists, while others made more limited advances.

Several new projects exploring uranium deposits and extraction techniques emerged as bottom-up initiatives. These produced some valuable findings, but their implementation suffered from poor management and coordination. The Geology Department at Tuwaitha started to explore the uranium content in Iraqi soil. This was a bottom-up initiative and was not directed by the senior leaders. Due to outdated equipment, this project, and another effort to map oil fields, made very limited progress. Visiting IAEA consultants noted that if this department had cooperated more closely with other departments, and the NRC had invested in adequate equipment, this project could have made more rapid advances.[104] Nonetheless, surveys identified Iraq's western desert as a source of uranium. The chemists at Tuwaitha studied techniques to extract uranium from phosphate ore, but these efforts did not advance beyond initial experiments.[105]

Jafar's Physics Department was noted for making significant progress in scientific experiments, in addition to acquiring necessary equipment for further experimentation, which was credited to his initiative and leadership.[106] Other research projects within this department, notably neutron activation analysis, lacked a dedicated leader and team. As a result, this research appeared scattered and lacked a clear sense of direction. When Shahristani returned from postgraduate studies in North America in 1970, he became a capable leader of this unit. In other departments, the progress of research and development was determined by whether mid-level managers and individual scientists took any initiatives in this direction. The youngest department, Radiobiology, which was headed by al-Khalisi, was in the early stages of staking out a research program in agricultural applications.[107]

The lack of central direction, combined with institutional growth and competing power centers, encouraged competing visions for Iraq's nuclear future. By the early 1970s, factions were vying for control over the nuclear establishment. This was a tumultuous time in Iraqi politics, following an unsuccessful 1973 coup attempt led by the head of the state security services. The RCC, by now effectively under the control of Saddam Hussein, formally oversaw the nuclear establishment through the IAEC. The Baath group based at Tuwaitha, led by Abdul Razzak al-Hashimi (a scientist from the Geology

Department), sought to increase its own relative standing within the center. This made working life at Tuwaitha unpleasant and, in some cases, intolerable for non-Baathist employees. These bullying tactics were toned down in 1972–1973, as the Baath regime attempted to co-opt the Iraqi Communist Party. In 1972, Numan, not a member of the Baath Party, was appointed director of the Tammuz Center. Others were also asked to return. Jafar returned in 1975 at the invitation of the IAEC.[108] Shahristani was also invited back by Humam Abdul Khaliq, a nuclear physicist and Baathist who became head of the NRC in 1978, to head the Chemistry Department. Both scientists were committed to developing and strengthening the research and development activities at Tuwaitha, and to strengthening the management of these activities at the senior level. Their return introduced different perspectives and preferences with regard to Iraq's nuclear futures into the senior tier of scientists at Tuwaitha.

During this period there were some increasingly creative attempts by factions at Tuwaitha to demonstrate relevance to the senior political leadership. In September 1972, the IAEC chairman instructed a committee to reanalyze a lunar soil sample provided by the Soviet Union and present the results as their own findings. This committee was led by al-Hashimi, a prominent Baathist at the NRC, the center's director, Numan, and the IAEC secretary-general, al-Mallah.[109] This apparently pointless exercise was intended to demonstrate that the nuclear establishment was capable of carrying out advanced tasks.

Within the Baath group at Tuwaitha, nuclear weapons ambitions began to rise to the surface in 1971–1972.[110] They began to openly challenge the leadership concerning the direction of the nuclear program. In December 1972, al-Hashimi walked in during the Scientific Council's annual assessment meeting. He criticized their plans and proposals and recommended what Jafar regarded as "glamorous projects" intended to attract funding and attention.[111] Senior scientists dismissed his suggestions as unrealistic, given the limits of Iraq's knowledge base and infrastructure.

While these overtures may have encouraged higher-level interest, there was no rush to develop a nuclear weapons option. Saddam was well placed to call for the development of a nuclear weapons option if he had wanted to.[112] He appeared to hold a special affection for nuclear science and gave scientists a privileged position.[113] Saddam even told the RCC: "we all love Iraq; one atom of it is equivalent to one atom of enriched uranium."[114] Rhetoric aside, there was no green light for a nuclear weapons program yet. That would not change until after Saddam seized the formal reins of power at the end of the decade.

This chapter challenges persistent ideas about Iraqi decision making and decisions during this early period. First, this updated history challenges the widespread impression that the Iraqi nuclear program was a highly centralized, focused, and hierarchical program geared toward developing nuclear weapons. Second, the chapter demonstrates that prior to 1973, the program was exploratory and, for all practical purposes, aimless.

Despite extensive nuclear assistance, and the emergence of an authoritarian regime, there was a striking absence of pro-bomb drivers during this period. This finding, which stands in striking contrast to earlier analyses and theories of nuclear proliferation, underlines perhaps the greatest puzzle of Iraq's early nuclear history: despite Saddam's apparent interest in the nuclear program and lobbying by pro-bomb coalitions, the program simply continued to drift.

As this chapter has demonstrated, state capacity and management strategy are crucial for explaining this outcome. Successive leaders had undermined Iraqi state institutions, and oil wealth made the state more autonomous from society. As a result, the state apparatus remained weak. The planning and administration of the nuclear program was largely outsourced. This was the result of two different, but mutually enforcing, factors: the absence of human and organizational resources to plan and implement a nuclear program; and several foreign offers of assistance with all aspects of launching nuclear research and development programs. These administrative shortcomings remained constant through several political transitions between 1958 and 1968. This slowed down domestic capacity building (as the state lacked a strong influence on planning and implementation) and absorption of foreign assistance.

The nuclear program was subject to formal oversight mechanisms, including oversight committees and government ministries (and, after 1968, the RCC). But these mechanisms lacked the capacity to effectively monitor and oversee the nuclear program. As most of the research activities were set up in cooperation with foreign advisers, the formal oversight mechanisms did not set rules, targets, or priorities. On the ground, Baathist scientists competed with non-Baathist scientists to control the program and set its future direction. Departments struggled to coordinate, not to mention collaborate, which inhibited their work from going beyond basic studies. When more scientists and engineers joined the nuclear establishment in the late 1960s, the supporting administrative resources at Tuwaitha were clearly outpaced. The result was a program that by default focused on basic research rather than industrial applications, let alone nuclear energy or a weapons option.

Ambiguity and Ambition, 1973–1981

Between 1973 and 1981, the Iraqi nuclear establishment pursued a nuclear energy program. But were they also developing a weapons option? This chapter sheds new light on this contested question. Contemporary sources show that as the program was taking an ambiguous turn it was open to different interpretations among technical and political elites. This led to growing tensions inside the Iraqi nuclear establishment, detailed for the first time in this chapter, while the Iraqi leadership was led to believe a weapons option was coming within reach.

As Saddam Hussein worked behind the scenes to increase his power and influence, he instructed a group of scientists to launch a nuclear power program and explore the nuclear fuel cycle. This was an ambitious, but also ambiguous, project, whose long-term objectives (i.e., nuclear power or nuclear weapons) were largely undefined. The implementation of this project was left in the hands of the nuclear scientists, and much of their work was treated as secret. Saddam placed new managers in charge of administering this program and made sure that the best scientists were hired and placed in leading technical positions. But Saddam and the Revolutionary Command Council (RCC) lacked institutional mechanisms to vet or review their progress, despite making large investments in nuclear technology. Furthermore, the secrecy that Saddam imposed on this project stood in the way of peer review inside the nuclear establishment.

After Saddam finally sidelined the ailing President Bakr in 1979, he began to openly signal his nuclear weapons ambitions to his scientists and the general public. Still, even at this stage there was no plan, budget, or organization dedicated to developing a weapons capability at Tuwaitha. Nor had the scientists assessed what resources they would need for a weapons program, or how the technology they were buying from other countries would fit with a clandestine weapons program.

The administrative leaders of the nuclear program became anxious as they began to realize that the weapons option Saddam apparently wanted was not within immediate reach. As it turned out, they got away with it because

Israel bombed a research reactor complex at Tuwaitha in June 1981. This removed the possibility of carving out a future plutonium route to nuclear weapons and necessitated redesigning the entire Iraqi program. Meanwhile, their colleagues were less fortunate: Saddam imprisoned the two scientists he had put in charge of the sensitive new projects before the Israeli strike because he had doubts about their loyalty. Trust was more important, or urgent, than acting on his weapons ambition because Saddam feared the 1979 Iranian Revolution would spill over into Iraq. Saddam still wanted these scientists to lead the future weapons program, but even after he asked them to take charge of the future weapons program they remained prisoners. This, and much more, changed after Israel bombed Tuwaitha.

Two Five-Year Plans

In June 1972, the Iraqi government nationalized the national petroleum company. The windfall profits, which surged after the 1973 Organization of the Petroleum Exporting Countries (OPEC) crisis, were spent on guns and butter.[1] Iraq undertook the most dramatic and sustained arms buildup of any Arab state in the region and began to explore opportunities for developing nonconventional weapons at home. A sprawling military-industrial complex emerged, which outpaced the state's mechanisms for oversight and monitoring.

While the arms buildup was primarily driven by financial opportunity, the Arab confrontation with Israel and enmity with Iran were important motivating factors. The Iraqis aspired to increase their regional status following Egypt's defeat against Israel in the 1973 Yom Kippur War.[2] In October 1973, Egypt and Syria launched a surprise attack on Israel to reclaim lands that had been occupied by the Israelis since the 1967 Six-Day War. After the joint conventional assault failed, Iraq's government wanted to develop better conventional and nonconventional weapons systems. Furthermore, they were concerned about Iran's larger and more powerful army. Saddam ordered new industrial and technological projects to bolster Iraq's military capabilities. Science and technology programs were, from his perspective, long-term investments in prestige and national security. Iraq's 1979 declaration to the United Nations (UN) Conference on Science and Technology for Development cited the regime's commitment to developing "the armament industry in order to achieve self-reliance and national security for both Iraq and the Arab world."[3]

As part of the military buildup, Saddam initiated reform of the once languishing military-industrial sector. These efforts would proceed in two stages, defined in separate and partly overlapping five-year plans. The first focused on creating industrial capabilities, and the second focused on exploring and developing new weapons options through science and technology programs.

The first five-year plan (starting in 1973–1974) focused on strengthening Iraq's basic industrial capacity to produce conventional weaponry. The Ministry of Industry set up a committee to coordinate these efforts, the so-called Military Industry Follow-Up and Executive Committee, headed by the minister of industry, Yasin Ramadan.[4] Iraq would import technology to jump-start indigenous research and development. This created industrial facilities that would later support conventional and nonconventional weapons projects, including the nuclear weapons program. One such facility was the sprawling Al Qaa Qaa General Establishment, which produced explosives, propellants, and pyrotechnics. The second five-year plan (starting in 1974) emphasized exploring new conventional and nonconventional weapons options. A 1974 government decree ordered research and development efforts to explore possible applications for defense in chemistry, biology, and physics.[5] This led to research on weapons applications in all three fields over the next few years, with mixed results.

The pattern of research and development in the Iraqi military-industrial complex differed from other highly centralized authoritarian regimes such as the Soviet Union. In Iraq, low-level officials or individual academics usually pitched projects to senior officials. If the idea or proposal met with interest, the applicants were asked to submit a more detailed proposal. Saddam would examine the proposal personally, usually after a review by a higher-level official. If he gave the green light to go ahead, scientists would be appointed as managers responsible for the entire project, including personnel, procurement, and scientific content.

The investigations by UN inspectors accounting for Iraq's past weapons of mass destruction programs show that this was actually a bottom-up process, where scientists and officials could pitch projects to senior officials. Iraqi documents that have emerged after the 2003 war also show that—contrary to assumptions held by policymakers and made in recent academic studies—the regime did not monitor or follow up on many of these projects because they lacked the institutional resources to do so.

RESTRUCTURING THE IRAQI ATOMIC ENERGY COMMISSION

In early 1973, Saddam restructured the Iraqi Atomic Energy Commission (IAEC) and ordered the senior leaders of the nuclear program to pursue a nuclear energy program. As vice-chairman of the RCC, Saddam became head of the reformed commission. The other members were recruited based on "personal merit," rather than their institutional affiliation.[6] They were instructed to consider the IAEC's work classified. Information about the program, and certain lines of research, was compartmentalized even within the nuclear establishment.

Saddam requested three IAEC members—Khalid Ibrahim Said, Moyassar al-Mallah, and Humam Abdul Khaliq—to prepare a plan for a nuclear power program and, more ambiguously, explore the nuclear fuel cycle. This was their first explicit instruction from the senior leadership to develop a nuclear energy program. The governance of the Iraqi nuclear program was transformed: senior staff members were replaced, a new cooperation policy was instituted with the International Atomic Energy Agency (IAEA), and information about the objectives and activities of the program was compartmentalized within the organization. These developments were doubly ambiguous: first, because the technology could be useful for weapons-related research; and second, because the regime's long-term objectives were increasingly open to different interpretations.

In April 1973, the program, budget, and leadership of the NRC were restructured according to Saddam's edicts. Several research projects, such as the nuclear materials prospecting project, were cut, and more changes soon followed. This had to be explained to the IAEA, who was providing support to the Iraqi nuclear program, in a manner that was consistent with the IAEC's new policy of keeping information about the program secret. In a letter to the IAEA, al-Mallah, the secretary-general of the IAEC, simply stated: "unforeseen circumstances and current developments have dictated on us the revision of our entire programme, especially the priority of committed projects."[7] Subsequently, the Iraqi nuclear establishment limited the IAEA's assistance to a few select areas.

The new emphasis on secrecy made it more difficult for the Iraqi nuclear establishment to deal with foreign actors and agencies providing assistance. This was a challenging balancing act, as Iraq relied on support from these foreign actors. The nuclear energy program would be based on acquiring technology and facilities from abroad, as well as foreign training of personnel. Iraq reached out to several countries to develop research collaboration and purchase technology, including France, Italy, Poland, and Brazil. The Iraqi program would continue to engage with the IAEA and nuclear establishments in the states offering assistance, which included hosting resident foreign experts (Soviet and, later in the decade, French) at Tuwaitha. The compartmentalization created some tensions in Iraq's relations with its foreign suppliers. For example, changes in the leadership within the NRC and reorganization of the research activities in the mid-1970s were reported to the IAEA, but not explained. Technical assistance programs were suddenly interrupted, leaving the foreign experts with nothing to do.[8]

These changes in the governance of the nuclear program affected hiring decisions in ways that ran counter to what we might expect in an authoritarian regime. Saddam instructed the IAEC to recruit scientists based on merit, selecting the staff whose skills would be most useful.[9] As a result, some of the most senior scientists in the program, including Jafar Dhiya Jafar and Hussein Shahristani, were not members of the Baath Party. Over the next two years the IAEC nominated several individuals to be transferred to Tuwaitha from academic positions. These included some previously suspected of being communist or harboring "divergent" political views. However, the senior managerial positions were mostly reserved for party members.

The senior management of the NRC changed after Saddam's intervention in 1973. On 29 July that year, a new director, Husham Sharif, was appointed. Several staff members were reassigned or demoted, including the former head of the Geology Department, Ibrahim al-Fadhli, who was replaced by his former assistant, Salem al-Dabbagh.[10] In 1974 Khalid Said, a party member, was appointed director of Tuwaitha immediately upon his return after obtaining a doctoral degree in the United Kingdom. Another returning doctoral student, Imad Khadduri, recounts that he was told by al-Mallah that if his party credentials had been in order, he could have been appointed instead.[11]

While the regime attempted to increase its control over the IAEC in this manner, the objectives of the nuclear program were increasingly open to interpretation. Several factors contributed to this ambiguity: compartmentalization; a sense among the technical elites that Saddam saw the nuclear program as a lever to increase Iraq's prestige in the region; the emergence of competing visions of Iraq's nuclear future inside Tuwaitha; and growing secrecy in relation to foreign experts and agencies that were supporting the development of a more advanced nuclear infrastructure in Iraq. This ambiguity encouraged speculation about the direction of the program at Tuwaitha. Senior scientists began to suspect that Saddam's long-term objective was to carve out a nuclear weapons option. Still, Saddam did not make any statements to the IAEC clarifying his position at this stage.

This modus operandi—where organizations and bureaucracies explored options while the political leadership delayed making a strategic decision—was not unusual. In fact, it was quite common in Saddam's Iraq. This approach had the benefit of enabling competing factions to pursue their preferred course of action until the senior political leadership—the RCC with Saddam at the helm—made a decision. By delaying their decision in this manner, the decision makers could obtain more information about their options, stimulate competition between different factions, and avoid committing to a failing policy. Absent effective monitoring, competition could stimulate scientists to perform better. In other words, this approach solved the thorny information problem that Saddam faced with regard to assessing technical projects.

The expansion of the nuclear program enabled different actors in the nuclear establishment to further competing agendas. The scientific leaders of the program wanted to develop a strong foundation for science and technology. They were interested in scientific exploration and, to a lesser degree, industrial applications. As seen in the previous chapter, the opportunity to develop an ambitious new program had encouraged scientists such as Jafar and Shahristani to return to Tuwaitha. Meanwhile, the Baathists at the NRC seemed to take the lead in assembling a dual-use infrastructure, creating a future nuclear weapons option.

Apparent inconsistencies between Baghdad's nuclear acquisition efforts and its stated objectives—to explore nuclear technology and develop energy—were duly noted by outside observers. In particular, the Iraqis' emphasis on exploring plutonium extraction and reprocessing at an experimental level—dual-use technologies that could be useful for both an indigenous nuclear power program and for a nuclear weapons program—raised suspicions about Baghdad's nuclear intentions and capabilities.

Other states began to suspect that Saddam had weapons ambitions but were uncertain how far Iraq was from acting on such ambitions. For example, in September 1980 the British Cabinet Office indicated Iraq might acquire nuclear weapons as early as 1990 (or within an eight-to-ten-year time frame) and pondered the consequences for Israel's closeted nuclear posture.[12] While this assessment appears very optimistic, given what we now know about the state of the Iraqi program, it indicates the level of concern raised by that program.

In the mid-1970s, several states in the Middle East contemplated a nuclear option. Israel became known as an undeclared nuclear weapons state by the 1967 war. Among Arab states, Egypt was widely considered the most likely to seek a nuclear weapons option. While President Gamal Abdel Nasser stated that Egypt saw no choice but to match an Israeli nuclear weapons capability, Egypt's nuclear program suffered from limited backing and bickering among the nuclear establishment and the senior executive, and ultimately fizzled out after the 1973 war with Israel. Syria tentatively explored nuclear technology, but made no serious effort to develop nuclear weapons during the 1970s. Iraq's neighbor Iran was making more progress in the nuclear field. Iran's nuclear program was expanding rapidly in the mid-1970s; the shah's public ambiguity about a military dimension for this program caused concern in the international community.

Baghdad monitored the Iranian program closely. The NRC staff submitted regular reports on the Iranian program to Saddam.[13] The shah's reported 1974 statement—that Iran would "certainly" acquire nuclear weapons "sooner than is believed"—did not go unnoticed in Baghdad.[14] For example, this was cited as evidence that the shah was pursuing a nuclear weapons option during the 1970s in a 1994 study forwarded to Saddam.[15] According to Jafar, Iraq's nascent program sought to emulate the Iranian program on a more modest scale.[16] The Iraqis were not competing with the Iranians—the scope and scale of the Iranian program was far greater than the Iraqi efforts—yet Baghdad did not want to fall too far behind.

EXPLORING THE FUEL CYCLE

Iraq's oil revenue increased eightfold between 1973 and 1975, allowing Baghdad to launch a series of ambitious projects in civilian and military fields. While 40 percent of this income was spent on buying weapons, money was also spent on social reforms focused on health, education and housing.[17]

The influx of cash afforded ample business opportunities to well-connected policy entrepreneurs inside the Iraqi state.[18] For the IAEC, and the broader military-industrial complex, the time was ripe for an ambitious procurement campaign. Their immediate objective was to purchase the technological infrastructure that would allow them to explore dual-use nuclear fuel cycle technologies.

The Iraqi nuclear establishment launched an ambitious shopping spree to assemble the technological building blocks of the entire nuclear fuel cycle, from uranium excavation to reprocessing spent reactor fuel. In other words, the Iraqis sought the ability to extract raw uranium, prepare and process it, and then extract and reprocess the spent reactor fuel, which would give them the range of technology necessary for a nuclear energy or weapons program. These efforts unfolded in three steps. First, Iraq asked the Soviet Union to upgrade the IRT-2000 research reactor. Second, Iraq convinced France to supply a new research reactor complex that included laboratory-scale reprocessing technology. This package, which was called 17 Tammuz (17 July) at Tuwaitha, gave Iraq access to the basic science and technology of the back end of the nuclear fuel cycle. Third, Italy provided a uranium fuel laboratory and a radiochemical laboratory. This project package, called 30 Tammuz at Tuwaitha, gave Iraq access to the technology of the front end of the nuclear fuel cycle. In addition to these three large projects, Iraq explored opportunities with other suppliers to purchase technology and even uranium, despite the fact that there was uranium in Iraqi soil. For example, between 1975 and 1976, the Iraqi Ministry of Industry and Minerals (MIM) signed contracts with a Belgian company to construct a unit to extract phosphate, an important step toward extraction of uranium from Iraqi soil.

First, the Iraqis secured an agreement with the Soviet Union to upgrade the 2-megawatt IRT-2000 research reactor at Tuwaitha (called 14 Tammuz) to 5 megawatts (IRT-5000). In 1976, the reactor was shut down in preparation for the upgrade. As part of this process, the fuel was changed from 10 percent and 36 percent enrichment to 80 percent enrichment.[19] This fuel, as we will see in subsequent chapters, played a key role in the 1990–1991 "crash program" to produce a nuclear explosive. The upgrade was completed in mid-1978. Iraq received financial assistance from the IAEA for this project, which was spent on technical equipment and assistance.[20] Furthermore, the Iraqis asked the IAEA to assess whether they were overcharged by the Soviets, as the price they were asked to pay was "2–3 times inflated," according to their estimates.[21] This reactor, once modified, facilitated experimental research and production of radioisotopes.[22] The Iraqis also asked the IAEA to provide "spare parts, machinery and tools for the Institute's workshop and various materials needed for the operation of the reactor."[23]

The IAEC also set out to buy new and more powerful reactors and laboratory-scale reprocessing technology. This created tension in Iraq's relations with supplier states, as Baghdad requested more sensitive technology than they were willing to provide, and tension within the NRC, where turf fights between different groups of scientists were coming to a head.

The French Reactor. In the fall of 1974 Saddam brought a delegation to France that included Humam (IAEC vice-chairman), Said (NRC director) and Ahmed Bashir al-Naib (head of the Iraqi Electricity General Establishment). They wanted to purchase a gas-cooled graphite-moderated power reactor. Because Iraq's electricity grid was much smaller than that of Iran, nuclear scientists believed that a single nuclear power plant was suitable. This type of reactor was especially well suited for plutonium production, which would be useful for a weapons program, but seemed to make less sense for the purposes of a small nuclear power program in a developing country.[24] Their request raised concerns in other states, notably Israel, the United States, and countries in Western Europe.[25] France turned down the Iraqis' request, ostensibly because graphite-moderated power reactors were being phased out, but informally indicated a willingness to supply other research and power reactors.[26]

In November 1976, Iraq signed an agreement with five French companies to provide two reactors. This included an IRT-5000 materials-testing reactor of 40-megawatt thermal power (Tammuz-1), for research and testing of materials for nuclear power plants, and a 500-kilowatt swimming-pool reactor (Tammuz-2).[27] The package also included a materials-testing hot laboratory (called LAMA) for processing and analyzing irradiated fuel rods, a workshop, and waste treatment station. Iraq paid around $450 million for this complex, which the international press referred to as "Osirak," in reference to the French-designed template reactor, which was named Osiris. The entire complex would be under IAEA safeguards, meaning that the site and materials would be inspected regularly. In addition to this nuclear assistance, the French agreed to sell Mirage fighter airplanes to the Iraqi air force and as well as a series of industrial assistance contracts.[28]

Several governments, including those of Israel and the United States, were concerned about the reactor deal. They feared that Iraq could divert material from the reactor fuel to build a bomb, or produce plutonium for the purposes of a clandestine weapons program by modifying the reactor. This was a large research reactor, which foreign observers feared could be reconfigured to produce substantial amounts of plutonium.[29] But Tammuz-1 was designed to be different from similar reactors based on the French Osiris design—notably the Dimona reactor in Israel, which played a central role in the Israeli nuclear weapons program—in order to reduce the risk that the Iraqis could divert the facility for the purposes of a weapons program. For example, the Iraqi reactor was a 40-megawatt reactor, which was considerably smaller than the 70-megawatt Dimona reactor. In addition, the Iraqi reactor would be under IAEA safeguards, unlike the Israeli reactor. Finally, French experts would be on site for the first decade. Their formal role was to assist the Iraqis in operating the new technology, but their presence provided additional transparency to the activities on site.

The concerns that this reactor complex could move Iraq closer to a nuclear weapons option focused on three scenarios: diversion of the reactor fuel in a crash program to quickly assemble a nuclear weapon; reconfiguration of the core of the reactor to increase its production capability; or experimental handling of fuel and plutonium reprocessing in gram quantities to acquire skills that would be useful if Iraq acquired a more powerful reactor, for the purposes of a weapons program, that was not subject to safeguards.[30] I discuss these scenarios below and indicate what Iraqi scientists made of these options, thereby showing, for the first time, that there may have been different views inside the Iraqi nuclear establishment on this question.

Following Israeli allegations that Tammuz-1 could produce up to 12 kilograms of plutonium per year, which would suffice for a nuclear weapon, the Iraqis assessed the production capacity of all their reactors. They concluded that if Iraq withdrew from the Non-Proliferation Treaty (NPT), which would remove their legal obligation not to pursue nuclear weapons and give Iraq the option of discontinuing the IAEA safeguards, the larger reactor (Tammuz-1) could have produced up to 2 kilograms of plutonium per year by irradiating natural or depleted uranium; the smaller Soviet-supplied research reactor could produce up to 250 grams of plutonium per year. These assessments were consistent with later independent studies by IAEA officials.[31] A more recent analysis suggests that if Iraq had withdrawn from the NPT, the Tammuz-1 reactor could have produced the minimal amount of plutonium for a nuclear weapon (8 kilograms) in just over seven years.[32] This estimate assumes that the reactor would operate at its theoretically feasible maximum production level and does not account for probable delays and interruptions. If the Iraqis had made changes to the reactor to further optimize its operation, this could reduce the time frame to just under five years.[33]

Neither option was particularly appealing. Leaving the IAEA, and being cut off from the assistance Iraq needed for its nuclear program, was not a feasible option. Producing enough fissile material for a nuclear weapon between IAEA inspections would be difficult, because such activities would alert French inspectors—who remained on site for the first decade of the reactor's operations—or the IAEA, as the reactor was a declared site subject to inspection every few months. These conclusions were shared by contemporary U.S. assessments.[34] Furthermore, Iraq did not have the ability to reprocess plutonium in large quantities, as reprocessing in the small hot cell facility on site would take a long time; nor did it have the capacity to construct a nuclear weapons device.

Even with these constraints in place, Tammuz-1 could contribute to developing a weapons option in the longer term. It could help to develop skills that would be necessary if and when Iraq opted to develop a nuclear weapons capability. This was an ambition shared by some in the IAEC but, at this stage, there was no plan spelling out how these skills would be developed or sufficiently skilled staff obtained.

Within the Iraqi nuclear establishment, there were different perspectives on whether, and how, the 40-megawatt reactor could contribute to a weapons program. In theory, the reactor could have been diverted for a weapons program, a fact that may have led some Iraqis to believe this was a possibility. In practice, however, this was not feasible given the constraints of the reactor design and the IAEA inspection regime. Jafar did not believe that the reactor could play a direct role in a weapons program. The pro-bomb Baath coalition at Tuwaitha apparently held a different view. A prominent member of this group, Abdul Razzak al-Hashimi, had become director of the NRC and vice-chairman of the IAEC. Mahdi Obeidi, a promising young scientist, was summoned to a meeting with senior IAEC directors including al-Hashimi, Dhafir Selbi, Humam, and Said in late 1979 or 1980, around the time when the IAEC assessed the plutonium production capacity of the reactors. In this meeting, an agitated al-Hashimi asked Obeidi whether Tammuz-1 could serve what he described as strategic purposes. Obeidi got the impression that al-Hashimi was asking whether the reactor could produce enough plutonium for a weapons program, but knew he could not ask for clarification on such a sensitive question. Obeidi did not want to say no to his temperamental boss, and prudently answered that the reactor would fulfill its requirements. Al-Hashimi, who was not reassured by this diplomatic response, turned to the other IAEC members and told them that his head would be the last to be chopped off.[35]

There is an apparent mismatch between the nuclear weapons ambitions held by senior Baathists and the lack of planning and preparation for such a program during the late 1970s.[36] There was apparently no attempt to assess what a nuclear weapons program would require, and the senior IAEC directors' meeting on whether the French reactor complex could play a role in such a project appears to have been an afterthought. Even at this stage, weak management and state capacity slowed Iraq's drift toward a bomb option.

Three years after the Osirak contract was signed, France, following protests from Western and Middle Eastern countries including Syria and Saudi Arabia, proposed a number of changes. It suggested changing the reactor fuel from highly enriched uranium to a new so-called caramel fuel (enriched to just 9 percent). The Iraqi scientists had different opinions about these changes, and how to respond to them. Jafar and Shahristani, who had participated in the technical discussions prior to the signing of the contract along with al-Hashimi and Humam, did not mind: the reactor would still be suitable for a variety of experiments, regardless of the proposed changes in the reactor fuel. Yet the IAEC was adamant that the fuel should not be changed. Al-Hashimi angrily refused to make this amendment to the original contract, protesting that the caramel fuel had not been proven on an industrial scale.

These contracts were part of a set of agreements between France and Iraq that included, along with the reactor sale, training and assistance. In early 1980, some sixty Iraqi technicians, scientists, and engineers were trained in reactor operations for one year at the Saclay Nuclear Research Center.[37] Within the Iraqi delegation, there were disagreements as to whether all members were sufficiently technically qualified. A discussion regarding the selection criteria led to one vocal critic, who had argued that some Baath delegates were not sufficiently qualified, being sent back to Baghdad.[38] During their training abroad, the Iraqis were approached by what they believed were foreign intelligence officers asking questions about the direction of the Iraqi nuclear program.

As these examples suggest, tensions were rising between Baath members and nonmembers in the nuclear establishment. The senior IAEC management held different views about the technical limitations of the technology they had purchased. It is plausible that the pro-bomb lobby gave a misleading impression to the political leadership that the newly acquired technology could help Iraq develop nuclear weapons. Indeed, al-Hashimi's comments to Obeidi strongly suggest that the senior regime level may have believed that Tammuz-1 could play a part in such a program.

Iraq continued to pursue a more powerful reactor that would be able to produce plutonium in greater quantities. In 1976 and 1977, the Iraqi nuclear establishment searched for a supplier who could provide a nuclear power generating plant. Iraqi scientists and technicians visited potential suppliers in Japan, Sweden, and West Germany. In Tokyo, the Iraqis began negotiations with Mitsubishi for a suitable reactor. These talks were interrupted following U.S. pressure. The Iraqis concluded that the United States would resist their efforts to purchase a power reactor.[39] Due to this pressure, the Soviet Union appeared to be their most probable option. Iraq continued discussions for purchasing a power reactor with French, Italian, and Soviet suppliers.[40]

The Italian Contracts. As France emerged as a key supplier of nuclear technology and training, Baghdad nurtured an equally close relationship with Italy. Italy and Iraq had signed a cooperation agreement in 1974 that provided a framework for extensive assistance in industry and development. In January 1976, Iraq also signed a nuclear cooperation agreement with the Italian National Commission on Nuclear Energy. The Italians reached out directly to Saddam in late December 1976, inviting him to Italy to discuss cooperation in several fields of economic development. Prime Minister Giulio Andreotti, who penned the letter to Saddam, noted his country's interest in purchasing Iraqi crude oil.[41] During tense negotiations in 1976–1979, Italy agreed to sell a uranium fuel laboratory and a radiochemical laboratory to Iraq. This package, described as the 30 Tammuz project by the IAEC, marked another important step toward an independent nuclear fuel cycle.

After signing the nuclear cooperation agreement, the Italian National Commission on Nuclear Energy approved a contract for a laboratory-scale radiochemistry laboratory, which could process plutonium in gram qualities, to be purchased by Iraq from the SNIA Viscosa company in 1978.[42] This laboratory was operational by 1979, and this line of research was treated as secret within the IAEC.

Newly discovered sources show how Iraq tried to bargain for technology that would be useful for a weapons program during the talks that led to the 30 Tammuz contract. What the Iraqis asked for—including fuel fabrication, a nuclear power reactor, and a reprocessing plant—involved technology that was be equally applicable to an energy program or a weapons program. For example, during the negotiation of the contract for the so-called Technology Hall in 1976, a facility to recover natural uranium from reactor fuel rods, which contained sensitive chemical separation technology, the Italians seemed to be getting cold feet. The Italian government was aware that this was sensitive technology, and the Foreign Ministry noted in an internal memorandum that "the construction of a 'technology hall' remains a first though small step towards the acquisition of technological knowledge that could be potentially dangerous later on."[43] Italy asked for two postponements of the signing of this contract. Meanwhile, the Iraqis began to make several additional demands. They wanted more and bargained hard. They asked the Italians to commit to provide a nuclear reprocessing plant (i.e., on an industrial scale) and a laboratory for fabricating nuclear fuel.[44] In late October 1977, the Iraqis demanded that Italy grant the authorization by the end of the month or they would pull out of the entire order, which was worth $45 million. The Italians agreed to provide a nuclear fuel laboratory to Iraq, despite the fact that aspects of this were placed on a list defined as "sensitive" by the London Club (of nuclear suppliers).[45] Iraq was politely requested to not use this laboratory for producing nuclear weapons and to subject the facility to IAEA safeguards or bilateral verification with Italy.

The IAEC became more aggressive in their dealings with the Italians in the summer of 1979. As the two parties discussed the contract for the nuclear fuel fabrication laboratory, including supplies of uranium, al-Hashimi criticized the proposed contract as violating Iraqi sovereignty because it stipulated safeguard measures that went beyond Baghdad's basic safeguards associated with the IAEA and the NPT. Al-Hashimi made it clear that Iraq did not want to submit to additional verification measures beyond those of the IAEA and NPT.[46] As in the case of France, attempts to impose additional conditions or safeguard measures that went beyond Iraq's existing agreements were furiously resisted.

Baghdad's rash behavior caused alarm in the Italian company, the SIGEN-GIE consortium, that wanted to sell a 600-megawatt nuclear power station to Iraq. The United States, who held the license for the design of this reactor, strongly objected to the prospective reactor deal. The Italian Foreign

Ministry was less concerned about these protests, apparently believing that this sale would not pose a proliferation risk as the Iraqis would subject the facility to the safeguards of the IAEA and those specified by the London Club.[47]

While the talks eventually stranded, the Iraqi nuclear establishment continued to seek a more powerful reactor. According to U.S. intelligence the Iraqis approached the Italians in the spring of 1981 asking them to provide a plutonium-producing 300-megawatt CIRENE reactor that used natural uranium, which was available in Iraq. This was still a prototype and not commercially available.[48] They also asked the Italians to begin initial feasibility studies in Iraq with the expectation that the reactor would be constructed in nine to ten years. If the Italians had agreed, the Iraqis could have had a reactor that was technically suitable for a weapons program in the country by 1991–1992.[49]

Although Iraq had indigenous uranium sources, the IAEC also went on a uranium shopping spree. The Iraqis wanted to develop basic skills at the front end of the nuclear fuel cycle (i.e., uranium refinement and fuel production) but struggled to do so. In 1979, Iraq purchased 4,000 kilograms of natural uranium (in the form of uranium oxide powder) and 508 kilograms of uranium fuel pellets from Italy. This material was intended to be used for research and development in an Experimental Research Laboratory for Fuel Fabrication. In the same year Iraq also imported over 6 metric tons of depleted uranium from Italy. Between 1979 and 1982, Iraq purchased yellowcake (a uranium concentrate used for production of nuclear fuel or enrichment) from Portugal and Niger and uranium dioxide from Brazil.[50] The yellowcake and uranium dioxide shipments were only partially declared to the IAEA, as neither Niger nor Brazil had joined the NPT at this time.[51] The IAEC submitted design information for the experimental fuel fabrication laboratory to the IAEA in June 1980. In November 1980, a "highly secret" IAEC mission visited China to request the supply of 5 metric tons of uranium hexafluoride (5 percent enriched uranium). This was intended to be the initial feed material for isotope separation experiments, which were necessary for nuclear fuel production, but could also be applied to uranium enrichment. The Chinese ultimately did not follow through on this agreement, citing the outbreak of the Iran-Iraq War.[52]

A new group of leaders was appointed to oversee the negotiation and implementation of the French and Italian contracts. In 1978, Humam was appointed director of the NRC. Humam was a nuclear physicist with solid Baath Party credentials.[53] After obtaining a master's degree in reactor physics from Westfield College in London, Humam became the liaison officer between Saddam's Vice-Presidential Office and the IAEC's Secretariat-General.[54] Jafar and Shahristani were appointed directors general to oversee the scientific planning and infrastructure development associated with the 17 Tammuz (plutonium handling and reprocessing) and 30 Tammuz (fuel production) projects. They were assisted by Khalid Ibrahim Said, head of the IAEC Projects Department. These two projects were large investments, as Iraq spent approximately $600 million on them between 1976 and 1982.[55]

Notwithstanding their efforts, as the procurement campaign forged ahead, advances at home were hobbled by the nuclear establishment's limited organizational and human resources.[56] Consistent with their mandate from Saddam, the IAEC explored a wide range of technologies but did not focus on consolidation in specific areas. For example, Said asked the Chemistry Department to develop research activities in chemical reprocessing, heavy-water production, isotope separation, and helium chemistry.[57] But they lacked sufficient experts to explore these technologies. To address this shortcoming, some graduates started literature surveys and carried out small experiments in conjunction with the Nuclear Research Center in Warsaw.

At Tuwaitha the Iraqi scientists continued to explore the back end of the nuclear fuel cycle, and paid particular attention to plutonium reprocessing. Where possible, the IAEC tried to purchase technology and know-how to compensate for Iraq's limited capacities. Several of these efforts were slowed or halted due to export controls or limited domestic know-how. For example, in 1976 Abdul Qader Ahmed was asked to develop a subcritical assembly to carry out theoretical calculations for a team of reactor physicists.[58] The following year Ahmed approached a West German company, Nukem, to purchase 10 metric tons of depleted uranium pins. This overture failed, as the West German government denied export licenses, yet it raised concerns about the increasingly ambiguous direction of the Iraqi nuclear program.

As these observations suggest, the ambitious procurement efforts were not matched by the activities on the ground. An IAEA expert described Tuwaitha as having "ideal" working conditions, with well-designed laboratories and facilities.[59] But there was a shortage of skilled scientists, and technical and engineering staff were "nearly completely missing."[60] Installing and servicing the new technology was often difficult. More ambitious projects, such as the attempt in 1981 to explore indigenous production of heavy water, which was an essential component for building reactors at this time, was deemed infeasible due to insufficient industrial capacities.[61]

Between 1979 and 1981, Iraqi scientists explored isotope separation techniques. Salman Lami, an electrical engineer working in the Tuwaitha reactor department, led efforts to familiarize Iraqi technicians with isotope separation. They attempted to produce simple ion sources—which could produce ions for research, including separation of uranium—at the Badr Establishment, a mechanical manufacturing site that was part of the military-industrial complex.[62] As part of this effort, Lami traveled frequently to CERN in Geneva.

Even with access to training and technology through bilateral agreements and technical cooperation agreements, the Iraqis struggled to install and use their purchased equipment. For example, in 1976 the Chemistry Department at Tuwaitha received a Varian mass spectrometer, which they intended to use for precision isotope analysis. According to an IAEA technical consultant, the center had not "sufficiently considered" how this instrument would be appropriately used before purchasing it.[63] It took more than a year to install the spectrometer, partly due to delay on the part of the firm but also because the Iraqi scientists were uncertain about appropriate applications.

The activities at Tuwaitha were becoming increasingly diversified and opaque. According to a visiting IAEA expert, it was clear that the leaders of this center were planning on a "big scale," and that they were not "afraid of great expenses." At this stage, he noted, their main challenge was to find enough staff capable of operating and servicing the purchased equipment, as there were hardly any trained engineers or technical staff capable of these tasks. The best foreign-trained Iraqi scientists held senior positions and were not capable of supervising the operation of technological instruments.[64]

On their own initiative, the Iraqi scientists at Tuwaitha explored a series of calculations examining chain reactions and plutonium production. Mastering these calculations, Imad Khadduri and Yehya Meshad analyzed various implosion scenarios that could generate a self-sustaining chain reaction.[65] Their results could be checked against similar studies from the Manhattan Project, which were available in the library. Khadduri and Jafar then began a series of calculations, which were not disclosed to their Egyptian colleague Meshad, on the production of weapons-grade uranium-239 (U-239) from the regular operations of the IRT-2000 research reactor acquired from the Soviet Union. As expected, their calculations showed that it would take decades to accumulate enough U-239 to build nuclear weapons.

There was no plan to divert the Soviet reactor for the purposes of a weapons program. Rather, as Khadduri saw it, the point of the exercise was to develop the appropriate analytic tools for calculating production of weapons-grade plutonium.[66] The Iraqis further calculated the possible production of weapons-grade plutonium from the Osirak reactors, and concluded that the larger reactor could, if natural uranium was introduced, produce about 2 kilograms per year while the smaller reactor could produce 250 grams.[67] To build a reactor suitable for producing significant quantities of plutonium for the purposes of a weapons program would require an extensive research and development effort. It would also require a large site that could not be easily concealed.

By the end of the decade, Iraq had acquired infrastructure to carry out basic experiments in the front and back ends of the nuclear fuel cycle. This raised concerns, particularly in Israel. A series of covert attacks targeted scientists and engineers associated with the Iraqi nuclear program. The first casualty was Meshad, who had played a central role in the acquisition of the Tammuz reactors from France. He was found murdered in a hotel room in Paris in June 1980. Only days later, the last person to see Meshad alive (other than his murderer) was killed. Then, on 13 December 1980, Abdul Rahman Rasoul, a consultant engineer, died in Paris.[68] In the summer of 1981 Lami was found dead in Geneva.

A series of attacks also targeted items that had been purchased by Iraq as well as the companies that were providing technology for Iraq's nuclear program. In early April 1979, the French reactor cores were prepared for transport in the Constructions Navales et Industrielles de la Méditerranée warehouse, in a port near Toulon. On 7 April, two days before shipment, the reactor cores were damaged in an explosion. When the cores arrived in Iraq, it appeared that they were significantly affected.[69] On 7 August 1980, another round of attacks targeted French and Italian companies supplying technology to the Iraqi nuclear program. Two bombs exploded in the Rome offices of SNIA Techint, the company that provided equipment for experimental fuel fabrication, chemical engineering, and materials testing, while a third targeted the home of the director, Mario Fiorelli. Another bomb exploded in the Paris home of a French reactor consultant.[70]

At the same time, export controls and U.S. pressure on states supplying the Iraqi program posed significant obstacles. These covert actions generated unwanted publicity. On 16 September 1980, in a meeting with the RCC, Saddam stated: "The Zionists know us very well and they know the Ba'ath party very well. . . . But everyone else will know us better and better."[71] His adviser responded: "The Arabs, the Zionists, and the Americans are going to work hard against us because they are afraid, which is a problem." Only two weeks later, on 30 September, Iranian jets attempted to bomb the Osirak reactor site in a surprise raid.

SADDAM'S NUCLEAR AMBITION

As Saddam's position in the Iraqi regime grew stronger, his nuclear ambitions began to surface in internal regime discussions as well as public statements. In a June 1978 speech at Al Bakr University, Saddam spoke openly of his desire for nuclear weapons: "From here, we will recognize our true scientific underdevelopment. . . . We should generate the unusual capabilities of the Arab nation, including the capability to have a bomb, and that is no longer a monopolized science. The atom is a widespread and thorough science, and any country can produce the atomic bomb."[72]

Behind the scenes Saddam, still vice president under the now ailing Bakr, prepared his decisive ascent to power. In late 1978 and early 1979, Saddam monitored senior Baathists to ascertain which ones were loyal to his preferred "Iraq first" policy and which leaned toward the Syrian Baath Party's more pan-Arab nationalist orientation.[73] Saddam's statements during this period, even with regard to the nuclear weapons option, were carefully tailored to test his audience, and should be seen in this light rather than taken at face value.

After forcing Bakr to resign on 16 July 1979, Saddam became president. He immediately purged the Baath Party of those he suspected were sympathetic to the Syrian wing and adopted an increasingly nationalist stance. Saddam stated that Baath ideology would be whatever he said it would be.[74]

Saddam's regional ambition underpinned his focus on matching the technological and military achievements of his non-Arab rivals, Iran (then in the throes of revolution), and Israel. He characterized the developmental gap between Iraq and Israel as an instrument of oppression. At a July 1980 press conference, Saddam stated: "The Zionist entity has, with all its sympathizers and supporters, been basing its calculations on the scientific gap between the Zionist entity and the Arab nation."[75] Saddam drew a strong link between modern technology and the regional power balance: "The nation which is lagging behind in knowledge is more easily defeated than a scientifically advanced nation."[76] He considered Iraq's lack of development as increasing its vulnerability to external challenges.[77] Israel's clandestine attempts to deny Iraq nuclear technology were interpreted as evidence for the linkage between superior technological capabilities and regional domination.

While Saddam's nuclear ambitions were growing, his rationale for pursuing a nuclear weapons option was conceived in broad and rather general terms. As Saddam began to discuss the relevance of nuclear weapons for Iraq with other officials, he increasingly referred to how a nuclear weapons capability would bolster Iraq's regional standing in relation to Iran and Israel.

In a meeting on 3 June 1978, Saddam argued that Israel's nuclear monopoly undermined Arab states. He expressed concern that this monopoly enabled Jerusalem to independently define "red lines" and, accordingly, coerce Arab states into compliance. He also noted that once an Arab state acquired nuclear weapons, this would weaken Israel's strategic position, as most Arab states would be able to survive a first nuclear strike while Israel most probably would not.[78] While Iran's nuclear program had not yet produced a weapons option, Israel's nuclear monopoly was an obvious constraint for any Arab state aspiring for a leading regional role, such as Iraq. Furthermore, Saddam believed that Iraq or Egypt was a more likely target of an Israeli strike than Syria or Jordan. A nuclear strike on those states could have damaging consequences for Israel, the Iraqis believed, due to their geographical proximity.[79]

The series of attacks on the Iraqi program convinced Saddam that Israel was committed to preventing Iraq from acquiring an advanced nuclear capacity, let alone a nuclear weapons option. In discussions with senior military officers in 1980, Saddam argued that Iraq was a primary target for an Israeli strike:

> Saddam: And they are waiting for the Iraqi Army to strike them, so they will respond by striking Baghdad, this is if they have an atomic bomb and we don't have it. We have already came to this judgment and figured it out about

4–5 years ago. If we didn't have one or more of these bombs, in the next Arab-Israeli war they will . . .

Air Force and Air Defense Commander: Destroy us.

Saddam: And the first striking target will be Baghdad, not Damascus or Amman.[80]

In the spring of 1979, Saddam told the RCC that Iraq would put pressure on the Soviet Union to acquire a weapon to match Israel's capabilities.[81] Saddam also referred to having made a request to an allied country in early 1979 for a weapon capable of deterring Israel from striking Iraq in a different meeting.[82] Whether such requests were made remains unclear, but Saddam's nuclear appetite was growing.

At a July 1980 press conference, Saddam responded to the series of attacks on the Iraqi program. Criticizing Israel, he did not disguise his ambitions for Iraq's nuclear program: "The Zionist entity and all its supporters and sympathizers should realize that the Arab nation is beginning to rise, and that there is no power to check it, and that the Arabs will know how to deal with atomic energy for peaceful purposes, will know how to use arms and industry, will have millions of Arab graduates every year in various technical fields. Then they should have another view of the Arab nation, their future, their rights."[83] Then Saddam elaborated on his long-term ambitions for the nuclear program: "They [Arab peoples] may lack the practical means of expression, but this is a question of time. So, the people have realized that honour and independence cannot be protected without reaching a stage in scientific development comparable to that achieved by others, including the enemy, and especially the Zionist entity."

Saddam also issued a thinly veiled warning about the consequences of attacking Iraq's nuclear program:

You ask how far Israel has gone to handicap our programme. We have no programme to make a bomb for Israel to handicap. Our programme is known to France, to Italy, to international public opinion and to all who seek the truth. It is using atomic energy for peaceful purposes. The Zionist Mossad and all the Zionist supporters in Europe try to chase all the Arabs with open eyes and minds in their dealing with science, even to the extent of physical liquidation, which is what happened to an Egyptian citizen lately.

He concluded by warning that "whoever wants to antagonize us will find this nation in one state today but in a differently advanced state a few years hence."

Around this time, Saddam discussed how a nuclear option might affect Iraq's regional standing with senior regime figures. He noted that matching Israel's nuclear weapons capability could make Israel more vulnerable to conventional onslaughts, and described a scenario where Iraq could join a coalition assault with Syria and Jordan to recapture the Golan Heights, which were occupied by Israel in the 1967 war.[84] However, as Saddam was also concerned that the Syrian Assad regime would invade Iraq—he had requested Jordanian air support in the event of such an attack—this war alliance was not an entirely realistic one, even in Saddam's eyes.[85] In any case, Saddam knew that Israel had many more nuclear weapons than Iraq would have for the foreseeable future, and that the United States would step in to guarantee their survival in the event of a coalition attack from Arab states.

Underneath his pan-Arab rhetoric, Saddam's ambition for an Iraqi nuclear weapons option was beginning to manifest itself. As Saddam strengthened his hold on power in the late 1970s, he began to articulate his desire for a nuclear ambition to his inner circle and the scientists he wanted to develop this option. During an IAEC meeting in late 1979, Shahristani recalls, NRC director Humam instructed those present that Saddam wanted the nuclear program to take a more "strategic" direction, both in terms of the acquisition process and capacity building.[86] The term "nuclear weapon" was not used, but several scientists assumed that this was what Saddam had in mind.[87] But, by the turn of the decade, Saddam's concerns about internal security effectively ground the program to a halt. This fact, curiously overlooked in the literature, tells us something important about how Saddam wanted to govern his nuclear program as it edged toward carving out a weapons option. Meritocracy trumped nepotism when it came to selecting the scientific leaders of his nuclear program. However, as Saddam was getting in a position to act on his ambitions, in a context where the Iranian Revolution threatened to spill over into Iraq, his security concerns trumped all other considerations.

PURGE

In July and August 1979 Saddam purged political and administrative elites.[88] In a recorded July meeting, Saddam accused senior figures of plotting against him. Some individuals were merely sidelined, including Bakr, but many were imprisoned or executed. Deputy Prime Minister Adnan Hamdani, former minister of planning, was one of twenty-one senior officials sentenced to death. Hamdani had been a popular and powerful figure supported by leading officials from key ministries including Planning, Industry, and Education. It was rumored that Hamdani had objected to Saddam's decision to invest more in defense than in education and industry. He was also said to be at the center of one of several alleged cliques or factions formed by individuals from the RCC or ministries. The executions were carried out in early August, allegedly by party members in the presence of the RCC. The message to those present, which subsequently echoed throughout the regime and state, was that no one was above suspicion. At the same time, Saddam raised salaries for officials and military personnel.[89]

Saddam then appointed his trusted men to key leadership positions. Saddam increasingly governed through patronage networks that were independent of formal state structures. The Baath Party, despite having a central role at the apex of the formal state apparatus, was often bypassed in strategic or sensitive decision-making processes. At the same time, the state bureaucracy was populated by mushrooming institutions whose purpose and actual workings were increasingly ambiguous. Complex routines, even for supposedly simple matters, made it more difficult for officials to understand policymaking and implementation processes. Saddam's tendency to commit to a policy option late in the process, and his preference for verbal communication rather than formal written orders, made it more difficult for state officials to know for certain what he really wanted. This could create paralysis during moments of crisis. On the other hand, it encouraged policy entrepreneurship among senior officials with close ties to Saddam.

Over the next few years, Saddam continued to consolidate his power and increase his personal influence over the Iraqi state apparatus and society. By the early 1980s Saddam was redrawing the Iraqi state according to his own preferences. He had already seized personal control over the oil income in 1977, which he spent as he wished. Once in power, Saddam began to transform the state apparatus, getting rid of suspected opponents or potential rivals, and nurtured new elites.

War, Arrests, and Interruptions

At first, the leadership of the nuclear program was unaffected by Saddam's purge, with one exception. The IAEC's legal adviser, Hamid Younis, was arrested. He was released after several weeks, but his injuries from torture made him unable to return to Tuwaitha.[90] As Saddam was now president, he could no longer serve as chairman of the IAEC. Vice President Izzat Ibrahim took over this role, and received regular briefings about the nuclear program and its progress. Just as Saddam strengthened his hold on power, and set the scene to begin developing a nuclear weapons program in earnest, a series of crises and upheavals disrupted the nuclear program.

The first challenge came in the wake of the Iranian Revolution, which posed an ideological challenge to secular Arab rulers; nowhere was this challenge more keenly felt than in Iraq. Several incidents of political violence, including terrorist attacks apparently targeting senior regime members such as Tariq Aziz, former foreign minister and now deputy prime minister, created growing concern about spillover effects among the majority Shiite population. Shiites were widely arrested in Iraq at this time because the regime feared that they might seek to emulate the Iranian Revolution and rise up against the more secular, Sunni-dominated, Baath regime. A series of terrorist attacks led to further persecution of Shiites and additional scrutiny of non-Baathists in senior positions. On 4 December 1979, Shahristani was arrested by the Tuwaitha security officer on suspicion of being a member of the illegal Da'wa Party. Rumors started circulating at Tuwaitha. Some of his colleagues alleged that Shahristani had criticized mass arrests of Shiites and that he had smuggled Da'wa propaganda back from Paris in toothpaste containers.[91]

Jafar protested Shahristani's arrest, citing the negative impact it had on the nuclear program.[92] Without the leader of the reprocessing project, he argued, the progress of the nuclear energy program would be held back. Jafar wrote to Saddam on 8 December, and again in early January, arguing that Shahristani should be released. Then, Jafar himself was arrested on 16 January 1980. Unlike Shahristani, however, Jafar was not tortured.[93]

In June 1980, still a prisoner, Jafar was taken to meet Saddam's brother Barzan Al-Tikriti, the director of Intelligence Services, and IAEC vice-chairman al-Hashimi. Barzan told Jafar that Saddam wanted him to develop nuclear weapons. This was reportedly the first explicit green light for a weapons program. While Jafar believed he did not have the necessary knowledge or experience to lead a nuclear weapons program, he agreed to try.[94] He was rewarded with a more comfortable house arrest, with a garden, a television, and a telephone. Furthermore, he gained access to books from the IAEC.[95] He found Karl Cohen's *The Theory of Isotope Separation as Applied to the Large Scale Production of U235,* and Manson Benedict and Thomas Pickford's *Nuclear Chemical Engineering* most useful. Over the next few months, Jafar made it clear to Barzan that he would refuse to return to Tuwaitha as long as al-Hashimi remained IAEC vice-chairman.[96]

Shahristani also received a visit from Barzan. On a stretcher, temporarily paralyzed by torture, he received the same proposition: to rejoin the IAEC and develop a nuclear weapons program. This was the first time Shahristani heard the term "nuclear weapon" stated explicitly.[97] He blankly refused, saying that he was both mentally and physically unfit and, in any case, did not have the skills to produce a nuclear weapon.[98] Barzan responded that he ought to do this as a service to his country, but Shahristani remained firm. He would remain in prison for another decade, until he was able to escape during the 1991 Gulf War.

After the 2003 U.S.-led invasion, both Jafar and Shahristani reflected on their respective choices. Looking back more than two decades later, Jafar indicated that he did not have a sense that Saddam was in any rush to develop a bomb or to use it. The lack of urgency was indicated by the absence of any deadline. Moreover, Jafar was not convinced that Iraq could manage to set up a successful nuclear weapons program. But Jafar's future appeared to hinge on his answer to the demand relayed by Barzan. And the scientific and technological challenge—or set of nested challenges—appealed to him professionally.[99]

Iran was still in turmoil after the 1979 revolution, and the armed forces were weakened. This seemed to be an opportune moment for Saddam to put a check on Iranian power. On 22 September 1980, Iraq attacked Iran, apparently hoping to strike their neighbor a powerful blow and thereby prevent the Islamic Revolution from spilling over into their own territory. Saddam's attention switched to the war effort, which turned out to be far more difficult and demanding than the Iraqis had anticipated. On the eve of war, in a meeting between Saddam and his senior advisers on 16 September 1980, one adviser warned that Iran could raise concerns about Iraq's nuclear program: "They want to instill fear [of Iraq] in the Zionists and the Americans and how it is going to affect our efforts regarding the other issue of the nuclear power in Iraq. Iraq does not own a bomb yet and they [the United States and Zionists] are already afraid, so what if Iraq actually owned a bomb! [Laughter]."[100]

After the outbreak of the Iran-Iraq War, the Iraqis immediately began to fear for the safety of the Tuwaitha site. In a conversation among senior regime officials about possible Iranian targets, this question surfaced. As the transcripts reveal, the Iraqi regime was concerned about the vulnerability of the nuclear program. Military personnel told Saddam: "If we were to build [a] nuclear reactor for peaceful purposes in the Baghdad region, we should think differently and not place it in Baghdad, we should place it in a location completely unknown to everyone, including our people, except for a limited number of people; and those locations are in abundance in our country."[101] The Iraqis were well aware that the Tuwaitha site was vulnerable, and noted enemy aircraft, which they suspected were Israeli, near the site.[102] The commander of the Iraqi air force noted that the Iranians were targeting the nuclear reactor and stated plainly that their air defense system on site was inadequate. He recommended approaching the Jordanians and asking for additional antiaircraft machine guns.[103] Saddam disagreed, stating that he would not make this request of the Jordanians, who he believed were a bulwark against a Syrian invasion into Iraqi territory. At Tuwaitha, some precautions were taken. NRC director Humam requested studies of the likely consequences of an air strike against the reactors once they were operational.[104] As the reactor site was only about 20 kilometers from Baghdad, he was concerned about the radioactive fallout that could result from such an attack. Drawing on Soviet ideas, their initial measure was to erect an earth mound around the site rising to 25 meters and two tunnels to protect against floods.[105]

Only a few days into the war, on 27 September 1980, two Iranian F-4 jets broke out from a larger group attacking an electric power plant outside of Baghdad, and struck the Osirak reactors. The strike caused damage to ancillary buildings, but not the reactors. In the aftermath of the attack, the Iraqis once again considered the need for additional protection of the reactor complex. Saddam was concerned about this, describing the Iranian regime as a "tool for Israel to hit the Iraqi nuclear reactor."[106] At this time, Saddam appeared sanguine about this possibility, stating: "In case they destroy the reactor, those who brought its technical equipment can bring again technical equipment."[107]

In the aftermath, few additional protection measures were taken to protect the reactor against future strikes. The options were, at any rate, fairly limited. In a meeting on 1 October, Saddam's military adviser proposed that covering the reactor with sand bags could protect against exploding missiles, but not a direct hit. They also discussed options such as trenches and dirt dams to protect against a more direct hit. During this discussion, Saddam and his advisers expressed anger at the reluctance of the nuclear establishment to build the reactor on a less vulnerable site. The planning director complained that there had been "many efforts" to implement security measures, while Saddam said that scientists had come up "too many troublesome difficulties" and ought to have been punished.[108] The technical establishment's views had prevailed with regard to the location. There had been an earlier proposal to set up a new underground site at Hamrin, presumably for the more powerful reactor Iraq was hoping to acquire, but the scientists had refused (or, in the words of the general secretary of the Ministry of Defense, didn't "want to bother themselves") to move to this location.[109]

The Iranian attack interrupted development of the Osirak complex by a few months, but construction continued after this hiatus. The two reactors were scheduled to receive their initial load of nuclear fuel from France in the summer of 1981. The fuel had arrived in early 1981, and the shipment had been formally registered by the Iraqi representative on the IAEA, Abdul Qader Ahmed.[110] The reactors were expected to become operational some months later. In early June, the smaller reactor was fully loaded with nuclear fuel.[111]

The Iraqis were not alone in expressing concern about possible attacks. In a U.S. intelligence assessment of April 1981, the possibility of a preventive strike on Iraq was raised:

> During the highly asymmetrical and unstable period of transitional vulnerability, those states which wish to retain regional superiority or fear a neighboring state's nuclear intentions would have an incentive to remove nascent threats. Preventive "surgical" strikes against the nuclear facilities of proliferating states are possible. Similarly, countries may be tempted to engage in covert operations against the nuclear programs of suspected proliferator states; this is already happening to Iraq. . . . Long before Iraq is actually capable of a nuclear explosion we may have an Israeli counter action that poses grave regional problems.[112]

And indeed, at dusk on 7 June 1981, the Israelis bombed the reactor complex in a surprise raid. Jafar could hear the bombardment from his house in

Baghdad, where he was under house arrest. Dhafir Selbi arrived on site within fifteen minutes of the attack.

Three facets of this revised history contradict the established narrative of the Iraqi nuclear program between 1973 and 1981 as a centrally directed, transparent, and hierarchical effort. First, the program was characterized by ambiguous objectives and limited oversight. Second, the regime did not always receive reliable information about how far they were from a weapons option even after Saddam began to signal his desire for such weapons in public and in private. Third, the nuclear scientists did not implement Saddam's apparent order to develop a nuclear weapons option. One senior scientist refused to help Saddam build nuclear weapons, while Jafar would only agree to do so on his own terms. When Saddam got Jafar to agree, he remained under house arrest because he refused to return to Tuwaitha as long as al-Hashimi remained on site.

How can we reconcile these surprising observations with the broader argument that Saddam's tactics to strengthen his hold on power eroded the Iraqi state and undermined the nuclear weapons program? First, the expansion of the Iraqi state during this period helps to explain the observed challenges of oversight and monitoring. As the state apparatus proliferated, especially in the military-industrial sector, principals lacked the capacity to keep track of the myriad projects that emerged during the 1970s. Underlying this proliferation, which was intended to make oversight difficult for anyone except the senior political leadership, was a power struggle at the top between the Baath Party and Saddam's efforts to strengthen his personal hold on power. Before Saddam's decisive ascent to power in 1979, this power struggle was also reflected in the management of the nuclear program. Specifically, the Baath Party members at Tuwaitha attempted to increase their influence over the management of the program through direct interventions as well as purges. While they were able to push out several of their colleagues during the early 1970s, after Saddam took a stronger interest in the nuclear program in 1973 he ensured a more meritocratic approach to hiring of the scientific staff, and many of those pushed out were brought back in. Still, the opaque goals of the program fed the emergence of two competing camps at Tuwaitha—a Baath group and another group with apparently opposing preferences for the direction of the nuclear program as it took an increasingly ambiguous direction. As a result of these three factors—lack of oversight, delegated management, and turf fights—the senior Iraqi leadership may have been led to believe a nuclear weapons option was coming within reach when this was, in fact, a fairly distant prospect.

One of the most striking findings is the program's apparent failure to respond to Saddam's requests to begin preparing a weapons option during 1979–1980. The arrest of Shahristani and then Jafar does not explain why the program as a whole appears to have made no tangible advances toward a weapons option in their absence. The scientists at Tuwaitha do not appear to have started preparing for or planning a nuclear weapons program in earnest during this period, even with pro-bomb advocates at the helm. This challenges the influential argument that the Iraqi nuclear program was shaped by Saddam's orders and preferences. Furthermore, it shows that, in absence of action, a clear green light to develop a nuclear weapons option from the senior leadership—which Saddam gave his two top scientists in 1980—is not necessarily a trigger for action in a weak authoritarian state. Even after Jafar agreed to lead a nuclear weapons program, Saddam kept his intended bomb maker under house arrest until the Israeli strike on Osirak forced his attention back to the nuclear program.

As this chapter has shown, Saddam's interest in a nuclear weapons option was inconsistent. His orders to his scientists were ambiguous prior to 1980, and he was apparently not too concerned with whether they were implementing his orders at this time. The nuclear program, including the French reactors, took a back seat to other geopolitical and domestic considerations related to national and regime security. While it is plausible that Saddam was led to believe a nuclear weapons option was coming within reach, before the Israeli strike on Osirak he was in no hurry.

CHAPTER 3

Saddam's Nuclear Weapons Program, 1981–1987

This chapter examines the Iraqi nuclear weapons program that emerged after the strike on Osirak on 7 June 1981 until early 1987. In the wake of the strike, Saddam Hussein asked Jafar Dhiya Jafar to create the capacity for clandestine, large-scale production of fissile material. This project was planned and executed under Jafar's leadership, with minimal involvement from Saddam. The Baath Party's influence was reduced, while a group of scientists, with Jafar at the helm, was given unprecedented autonomy in managing the program. Over the next few years, they encountered difficulties and mounting delays, leading to a crisis in 1987 when Jafar and his colleagues realized that the program was failing to meet its objectives.

This phase of the Iraqi nuclear weapons program has been subject to speculation. Why did the scientists select uneconomic technologies, and why did they make such slow progress? Some have argued that the program was quite simply poorly managed. Others point to their numerous constraints—the Iran-Iraq War, international concerns about the Iraqi nuclear program, and having to adopt a new technological route under international scrutiny.[1] This chapter traces the emergence of this program, analyzing both domestic and international constraints. It also demonstrates that the program was captured by scientists i.e., that they effectively redefined the activities of the program according to their own interests and preferences rather than those defined by the regime principals, and operated with unlimited budgets and weak oversight mechanisms. The program stalled as the technical leadership stuck with their technological preferences and discarded more efficient alternatives.

To make sense of the path the Iraqis followed, we must not only delve deep into the weapons program, but also place it in the context of the Iraqi state at war. This brings several surprising facts to light. During the Iran-Iraq War Saddam's military-industrial complex became an inflated organization in which scientists got away with not delivering results, despite ample funding. Scientists set their own priorities and targets, and Saddam did not intervene in the management of the program. Even in the face of war, the nuclear weapons program was not subject to pressure during the first six years. When finally pressed by the Iraqi leadership to set a deadline in 1985, the nuclear scientists were deliberately opaque about the target they intended to meet. When they realized they would not make this deadline in early 1987, they did not tell Saddam. Instead, they asked for his permission to start working on the design and explosive packaging for a nuclear weapon.

Osirak Bombing: A Watershed Event

After the Israeli attack, Saddam's attention returned to his nuclear program. The destruction of Osirak was a public humiliation that could not be ignored. This view was shared by some of the senior nuclear scientists, who had previously been lukewarm about developing a weapons option. At the same time, Saddam had to calibrate his response to avoid alienating the United States and other moderate Arab states, whose support he needed for the war effort against Iran. The Iraqi Atomic Energy Commission (IAEC) summarized the situation they faced after the attack: "Following the Israeli aggression of June 1981 on the Tuwaitha site, Iraq was forced to resort to self-reliance. . . . There was not a gesture, let alone a guarantee, from anyone ensuring that the aggression . . . would not be repeated."[2]

During the war with Iran, the Iraqi state apparatus was transformed to support the war effort. The military-industrial complex was expanded while the domestic economy suffered. The nuclear weapons program was an exception; shielded from the demands on the conventional arms industries to contribute to the war effort it operated without any budgetary restrictions.

When Saddam responded to the Israeli attack, he was mindful of how his reaction might affect his standing in the regime and abroad. This was a blow to his prestige, at a time when Saddam was aligning himself with the more moderate Arab countries and the United States. Saddam managed to keep their support and was careful not to provoke the United States in his response to the strike. But, as U.S. intelligence documents point out, Saddam's moderate response to the strike, including avoiding criticism of the United States in his official statements, and accepting a compromise resolution at the United Nations (UN) in response to the attack, was unpopular among other senior regime officials. It also intensified the dissatisfaction among senior Iraqi officials about the costs of the war with Iran.[3]

After the bombing raid on 7 June 1981, Saddam ordered his defense minister, General Adnan Khairallah, to examine the damage.[4] Ten Iraqi soldiers and a French engineer had been killed in the attack; the main reactor was destroyed, and unexploded Israeli munitions were still scattered on the site.[5]

A team of soldiers was sent to secure the area. The deputy chairman of the IAEC, Abdul Razak al-Hashimi, and Dhafir Selbi, an engineer at the Nuclear Research Center (NRC), took a closer look at the destruction.

After the military completed its assessment, Saddam requested a meeting with the IAEC.[6] The challenge before them was momentous. Israel's action suggested that any attempt to develop a nuclear energy program (let alone a nuclear weapons program) would be strangled in the cradle. With international suspicion cast upon Iraq's nuclear program, foreign states would be reluctant to supply Baghdad with another, more powerful, reactor. While French companies agreed to replace the destroyed research reactor, this never came to fruition due to reluctance on the part of the French government. To develop a nuclear weapons capability, Iraqi scientists would have to take a completely different technical route.

In the immediate aftermath, Baghdad did not comment on the attack. But over the next couple of weeks Saddam made a series of statements to domestic and foreign media. These were reasonably measured and avoided directly antagonizing the United States. Saddam told the Iraqi public that the strike "will not stop the course of scientific and technical progress in Iraq. Rather, it is an additional strong stimulus to develop this course . . . with even greater resources and with more effective protection."[7] Despite these statements, however, foreign governments believed that the prospect of an Iraqi nuclear weapons capability was more distant than ever.

Two days after the strike, the Israeli prime minister, Menachem Begin, held a press conference where he stated that Israel would not under any circumstances permit its enemies to develop weapons of mass destruction (WMD). The Israelis had to act, Begin claimed, because the IAEA did not know the true purpose of the Osirak complex and would not be able to detect clandestine activities.

On 12 June, the Iraqi foreign minister Sa'adoun Hammadi spoke to the UN. His remarks mainly focused on the Israeli nuclear weapons program. Hammadi emphasized the point that Israel, a nonmember of the Non-Proliferation Treaty (NPT) and an undeclared nuclear weapons state, had destroyed a declared civilian facility in an NPT member state. Israel's objective, he argued, was to deny Arab states advanced science and technology which could threaten Israel's forcible domination of Arab peoples. He pointed out that Iraq's Western allies had helped Israel develop its nuclear arsenal. Hammadi characterized the Iraqi nuclear program as a "vast and ambitious programme of development."[8] He added: "My Government recognized at an early stage the importance of science and technology, including the peaceful application of nuclear energy, for the achievement of social and economic development. Working towards that goal, we have made efforts to expand our nuclear-research facilities and to widen the scope of the peaceful uses of atomic energy."[9] The Israeli attack, he concluded, was an illegal act intended to "undermine the new Iraq and all that it stands for."[10]

Behind the scenes in Baghdad, the Osirak raid challenged both Saddam's pro-Western shift—at a time when he was embroiled in an unpopular war—and his own position in the regime. As contemporary intelligence assessments indicate, both the Soviet Union and Baath hardliners attempted to use the attack to "reverse Iraq's shift toward the West."[11] But, as a U.S. document indicates, Saddam remained firm, not least because of the need for international support for the war with Iran.[12] Saddam's reaction, and pro-Western inclination, did not go unchallenged at home: "Israel's raid, however, plus deep suspicion that the United States was an accomplice, have bolstered the hand of hardline [Baathists] who oppose Saddam's recent tilt toward the West."[13]

The Board of Governors of the International Atomic Energy Agency (IAEA) met two days after the attack. The credibility of their safeguards and inspections system was dented by the Israeli strike. The deputy director for safeguards said that even "fantasy did not move us to expect an event like the Israeli attack."[14] On 12 June the board adopted a resolution criticizing the Israeli attack, which was subsequently presented to the UN Security Council. Baghdad requested that Sigvard Eklund, director general of the IAEA, participate in the upcoming Security Council discussion of a draft resolution criticizing the Israeli attack.

Eklund refuted the Israeli allegations that Iraq could have used the reactor to produce significant quantities of plutonium or extract highly enriched uranium from the fuel rods, arguing that material balance accounting and visual inspections would have revealed such activities. He also denied the Israeli claim that there was a secret laboratory 40 meters below the reactor (later amended to 4 meters), that inspectors had missed. In fact there was no such laboratory, only a small room for the control rod drives that the IAEA was well aware of.[15]

Eklund pointed out that the attack had grave implications for the credibility of the safeguards regime and the IAEA itself: "A non-NPT country has evidently not felt assured by our findings and by our ability to continue to discharge our safeguarding responsibilities effectively. . . . One can only conclude that it is the Agency's safeguards system which has also been attacked."[16] On 19 June, the Security Council approved a resolution condemning the attack, saying that it was "in clear violation of the Charter of the United Nations and the norms of international conduct."[17]

In the United States, the attack was described as "a watershed event" that could create new military and political realities in the Middle East and intensify the regional arms race.[18] As Israeli officials rejoiced, Iraq's response remained muted, and Baghdad abstained from retaliation (e.g., sabotage or terrorist sponsorship). While U.S. intelligence reported that Saddam had publicly called for other states to give Iraq a nuclear deterrent against Israel, it assessed that such statements would only make it harder for Iraq to persuade others to assist.[19] This, we will see, was largely but not entirely correct, as Iraq's European suppliers (Italy and France) turned their back on the country while other suppliers entered the Iraqi market. In any case, it would take years to recover what had been lost, as Iraq had to look elsewhere for help with creating a nuclear weapons option.

GOING UNDERGROUND

Immediately after the strike, Humam Abdul Khaliq assembled a team at Tuwaitha to explore technical options for setting up a weapons program.[20] They scoured the NRC library for information on possible technical routes for producing fissile material for a nuclear weapons program.[21] This was their first effort to assess technical, practical, and logistical aspects of different technical pathways to produce fissile material on a large scale. They found that sensitive design information was hard to come by, while the methods detailed in the American Atoms for Peace library had several drawbacks.

In choosing a way forward, a key consideration was the need to make their program less visible to the outside world. Several scientists, including Jafar and Hussein Shahristani, believed that the French had provided information to the Israelis about the design of the reactor complex. In their opinion, it was highly suspicious that the Israelis targeted the particular chimney leading to the reactor core. Shahristani received a visit from Barzan al-Tikriti after the attack, and they agreed it was highly probable that the French had advised the Israelis. Although there was no clear evidence of such collusion, the Iraqis were determined to deny other states information about their nuclear program in the future.

Still under house arrest, Jafar prepared his own memorandum for Saddam recommending technical pathways to creating an indigenous nuclear weapons capability. Jafar had few illusions about the challenges of taking this route. Looking back, he wrote: "Uranium enrichment isn't like baking a cake. It is an incredibly complex process, which requires not only know-how but also hundreds of thousands of components as well as hard work to obtain raw materials, procurement of which was made doubly difficult due to the programme's covert nature. . . . No one in Iraq had prior experience of uranium enrichment or bomb making and, therefore, there was no guarantee our efforts would eventually be successful."[22]

One of the fundamental questions was whether Iraq would remain within the NPT or exit the global nonproliferation regime. Having suffered an attack from a nonmember on a declared facility, Jafar advocated leaving the NPT over the next two years. In his view, it did not make sense to adhere to the constraints of the treaty if the nuclear program could still be attacked with impunity by a nuclear weapons state who had not signed the NPT.[23] The other commissioners disagreed. Withdrawing from the NPT would raise additional concerns about the Iraqi program and could cut off potential avenues of assistance. Furthermore, remaining within the NPT gave Iraq an important alibi that could help protect the new program from detection. It also gave Baghdad the moral high ground in criticizing Israel, in their view. Ultimately, Iraq remained a member of both the NPT and the IAEA.

During the weeks and months that followed the Israeli strike, Saddam made a number of public and private statements suggesting that he wanted a nuclear deterrent. In speeches and interviews with foreign journalists, as well as in closed meetings with advisers and the Revolutionary Command Council (RCC), he invoked the need to defend Iraq from similar attacks. In an interview with American journalist Barbara Walters, Saddam argued: "Whenever 'Israel' has the technical requirements of aggression it will commit it against any Arab country. . . . This, in fact, is the main lesson whose implications and details will no doubt preoccupy us."[24] His conclusion was that Iraq had to match Israel's technical capabilities in the military realm to deter or deny future attacks. In a press conference, Saddam declared that "we will let the Iraqis' minds operate to the maximum, and try by every possible means to protect ourselves."[25]

In a meeting with the Iraqi Cabinet Saddam made clear his determination to get the bomb: "If we stopped work on our atom bomb, they would subsequently say that they caused the failure of the so-called Arab atom bomb. . . . Let everyone realise that those who can bring over a laboratory or a nuclear reactor are also capable of bringing over ten other such laboratories and reactors."[26]

Behind closed doors, Saddam remained hopeful that France would rebuild the destroyed reactors. But Iraq did not receive compensation or assistance with rebuilding the reactors from France or the IAEA. This meant going it alone. Saddam told his Cabinet members to prepare for great obstacles:

Work hard. Work hard. Work hard. Work hard! You know, it is like the neck of a bottle and they do not want us to get out of it. . . . The Israeli strategic planners know better than anyone the meaning that Iraq is building and Iraq is winning militarily. Technically, they are right in all of their attempts to harm Iraq. I do not rule out that they might even hit Iraq with the atomic bomb someday when they reach a certain stage and we are prepared for it, and God willing, we will be ready to face it.[27]

Faced with these constraints, Saddam wanted the most capable minds to oversee the efforts to chart a new course toward a weapons capability. Jafar had already agreed in principle to lead this program, but refused to return to Tuwaitha as long as al-Hashimi remained head of the IAEC. In mid-August, al-Hashimi was promoted to the Ministry of Education.[28] On 1 September 1981, Jafar was summoned to meet Saddam. He was taken to a Presidential Palace in Karradat Maryam where Barzan—Saddam's trusted half-brother—waited for him. As they walked to Saddam's office, Barzan whispered conspiratorially that al-Hashimi was not his favorite person either.[29]

Dressed in military uniform, Saddam lamented that Israel was permitted to have nuclear weapons while Iraq was to be denied nuclear technology. The president stressed the need to rebuild what had been lost and, from this day, to work toward a nuclear deterrent. Without such a deterrent, he noted, Iraq would not be able to ward off future Israeli attacks.[30] This statement, made in the presence of Jafar, Barzan, and Saddam's personal secretary Sabah Mirza Mahmoud, was Saddam's green light. There was no written or formal decree issued, and no specific order detailing what Jafar would do next. In Jafar's eyes, his order was to create the ability to enrich uranium on a large scale. Saddam gave Jafar a piece of paper with the presidential letterhead, and asked him to list his demands. Jafar thought it best to leave the page blank. Saddam then told his half-brother to grant any future requests from Jafar. In effect, this was a blank check. As they were leaving, Barzan told Jafar to give Saddam what he wanted for the sake of their country.[31]

WAR AND NONCONVENTIONAL WEAPONS

Saddam initially believed the war he launched opportunistically in September 1980 would be a short-lived affair. By 1982, the Iranian counteroffensive had made it clear that this war would not be so easily won. Although the Iraqi military machinery had gone through a massive buildup in the years prior to the war, and Iraq received support from several Western states, including French jets and American intelligence support, Iran's new leaders mobilized armies that far outnumbered Iraqi forces. Their sheer numerical superiority quickly became a key concern for the Iraqi leaders. The first three years of the war depleted Iraq's foreign reserves from $30 billion to $3 billion.[32]

The Iran-Iraq War triggered new efforts to explore nonconventional weapons. To meet the Iranian challenge, Iraq's military-industrial complex would develop nonconventional weapons, including chemical and biological weapons. The RCC gave these research and development programs extraordinary autonomy and resources.[33] The majority of decisions regarding technical priorities and resource utilization were effectively delegated to the program managers.[34] Saddam was apprised of the progress of the nonconventional weapons programs by confidential reports from staff, managers, and the Mukhabarat. Chemical weapons were made a top priority for the State Organization for Technical Industries (SOTI).

There are several similarities between the Iraqi chemical, biological, and nuclear weapons programs during the 1980s. These include the timing of key decisions, disruptions at the managerial level, the inclusion of several additional projects of questionable value, competing parallel projects, and limited oversight and auditing by the senior regime. On the other hand, there were important differences. As we will see, during the Iran-Iraq War the chemical and biological programs were requested to contribute to the war effort, while the nuclear program was shielded from such demands.

The chemical and biological programs began in 1973–1974 at the Al-Hazen Ibn Al Haitham Institute (Al-Hazen Institute). Both projects moved from basic research and development to weaponization during the mid-1970s and mid-1980s. In 1974, a government decree ordered state organizations to explore scientific and applied research in chemistry, biology, and physics.[35] During the late 1970s Iraqi scientists synthesized several agents, including nerve gas, on an experimental scale and purchased equipment for pilot-scale production.[36] At the end of the decade, turbulence hit the Al-Hazen Institute. Senior leaders, including the director, were accused of mismanagement and financial fraud. They were imprisoned and the institute was closed in 1978. As a result, research and development activities stalled.

During the war with Iran, however, Iraq's chemical weapons complex became a sprawling enterprise. According to an Iraqi official interviewed by UN inspectors, "anyone who came to us with an idea of a weapon, we would study and try to develop. The fact is that during the [Iran-Iraq] war, it was masses of people attacking Iraq. . . . Any idea that was presented to us to find a solution to this problem on [our] border [with Iran] of 1200 km was welcomed."[37] Over the next few years, Iraq used chemical weapons on a large scale.

The biological weapons program, the most secretive of Iraq's nonconventional programs, began as a research and development effort in the early or mid-1970s. According to Iraqi scientists, little was achieved in the biological program before the 1978 closure of the Al-Hazen Institute.[38] In 1983 a biologist proposed to Baath officials that biological weapons could aid Iraq's struggle against Iranian forces. Then, in late 1985 Iraqi biologists resumed their efforts to explore and develop biological weapons. This project was carried out in more than one location, and different agencies, including the Ministry of Defense and the state security apparatus, ran parallel programs. In this atmosphere, entrepreneurship was relatively low-risk while the rewards were considerable. In late 1986 the director of the Muthanna State Establishment (MSE) requested production of large quantities of botulinum toxin for use in the war.[39]

In early 1987, officials were concerned that the research and development was not advancing fast enough. To accelerate the program, the research activities were reorganized, more staff were hired, and additional equipment purchased. In 1987–1988 weaponization trials began. In 1988, after breakthroughs in research, Hakam was selected as a production site. In parallel with continuing research and development, the program started purchasing technical equipment and growth media. When the Iran-Iraq War ended in 1988, the scientists were instructed to continue the biological weapons production program, but it was made less of a priority.[40] In the fall of 1990 the program was disassembled due to concerns about an imminent bombing attack by the United States.

Exploring Enrichment, 1982–1987

Exploring and preparing for large-scale production of enriched uranium required changes at every level of the nuclear establishment, from the senior levels of the leadership to recruitment. Over the next few years it was expected that several other transformations would follow as the true scope and requirements of the new program were still largely undefined. Saddam had only instructed Jafar to create the ability to enrich uranium on a large scale; no words had been said about how or what the following steps would be. Securing a greater pool of skilled staff was an immediate priority. The IAEC began a recruitment campaign headhunting recent graduates from other sectors in the Iraqi state. Several scientists returned to Tuwaitha, some were motivated by the Israeli destruction of Osirak. The number of technical employees increased every year. From an initial group of 150–200 skilled technical staff, the staff totaled 7,500 by late 1990.[41]

To scale up the pool of Iraqi scientists and engineers, new tactics were necessary. Some, such as Jafar, were told that Saddam personally requested their service. Others, including senior engineers, were simply transferred from other programs despite their own preferences. Material incentives—including attractive plots of land and expensive cars—were also used to recruit and reward scientists. The nuclear scientists enjoyed high salaries—some were paid the equivalent of a government minister's salary—and social status. For particular achievements Saddam would provide scientists with medals and commendations or a new car. Failure was rarely penalized, though it could lead to demotion or being sidelined in extreme cases.

By 1982–1983, the war with Iran was taking a toll on the economy, but strategic sectors were shielded to support the war effort. Indeed, "Army officers and technicians employed in military industries were arguably better off than during the prewar period."[42] The war economy reflected Saddam's increasing dominance in the Iraqi state. According to Tariq Aziz, deputy prime minister at the time, only Saddam could scrutinize the military budget. Individuals could pitch proposals for weapons programs directly to Saddam, who would direct them to Military Industrial Commission (MIC). Even when MIC officials realized these projects were of questionable technical merit, and they failed to produce results, it was difficult to discontinue them.[43] This was wasteful and made planning more difficult. Not even high-ranking officials knew whether there was a budget for the powerful MIC. Looking back, Aziz lamented the lack of transparency and accountability in the military-industrial complex: "God knew how they worked."[44]

There were no financial restrictions on the nuclear weapons program either. Within three years the expenditure for the program increased tenfold. According to the official Iraqi declaration submitted to the UN in 2002, the nuclear program's budgets grew enormously between 1982 and 1985. Starting in 1982, the estimated budget allocation was 918,658 Iraqi dinars (ID), while the final allocation (plus capital investment and spent foreign currency) was 948,134 ID. The following year 1,063,019 ID were allocated and 1,222,959 ID were spent. In 1984 1,919,552 ID were estimated while 3,199,278 ID were allocated. In 1985 2,566,470 ID were estimated while a staggering 9,784,558 ID were spent.[45] The large discrepancies between the estimates and actual expenditure did not lead to any questions, nor did they create any problems, for the leaders of the nuclear weapons program.

REVIEWING TECHNICAL OPTIONS

In the second half of 1981, scientists and engineers at Tuwaitha researched and compared different routes to producing large quantities of fissile material. At this stage, researching and producing large-scale uranium enrichment was their objective. There was no attempt to explore weaponization or develop a weapons design during these first years of the program.

Saddam had one clear order for his nuclear scientists: avoid sensitive foreign assistance that could alert the outside world to the nuclear weapons program.[46] The Iraqis were thus confined to a primarily indigenous route, unlike other developing states seeking nuclear weapons, despite lacking industrial resources similar to those in other states that had produced nuclear weapons previously. Their restrictions were the following: they could not purchase items on export control lists, but items that were not on those lists could be purchased, ideally as a package complete with training. At the same time, they had to select a route that would be practically feasible. These two factors were more important than other issues such as how economical or efficient the method was and how much effort was required in terms of research and development.

When Jafar returned to Tuwaitha in September 1981, he asked a team of scientists and engineers to study the available literature on enrichment technologies. The teams began to scour the literature for options, and then reviewed these in view of Iraq's capabilities and constraints. They faced more constraints than most states have when setting out to develop a nuclear weapons capability: a severe shortage of skilled manpower; underdeveloped industrial capabilities; having to avoid foreign assistance that could alert other states to the true nature of their program; and fear of another Israeli strike.

As a plutonium route was now out of the question, given the threat of future Israeli attacks and the absence of suitable reactors in the country, the Iraqis focused on uranium enrichment technologies. Their initial assessment focused on four options: laser isotope separation; gaseous centrifuges; gaseous diffusion; and electromagnetic isotope separation (EMIS). Some of these were methods that had been discarded by other states better equipped to pursue more advanced alternatives. But the Iraqis' prime concern was not whether a particular method was economical or efficient; they were looking for methods that were feasible given their constraints and would emit few obvious signals to the outside world.

As a frequent observation of the Iraqi program is that technical choices were inefficient and suboptimal, it is useful to examine how Iraqi scientists weighed these options in some detail. Laser isotope separation was not a proven method for producing sufficiently large quantities of enriched uranium, and the Iraqis lacked the basic know-how and the technological capacity to pursue this method. Gaseous centrifuges were deemed too difficult; this method required special materials that could not be indigenously produced, and the engineering challenges associated with the high-speed rotation of the centrifuges were considered too demanding given Iraq's limited know-how. In other words, because centrifuges could not be pursued without foreign assistance they were ruled out at this stage.

Gaseous diffusion, where uranium hexafluoride is separated through a porous membrane, was an old and proven methodology. But this approach presented considerable challenges. First, the NRC lacked the basic technical know-how and industrial capacity to produce the barrier material. Furthermore, the machines required were under export controls and could not be built locally. The IAEC also judged this to be an uneconomical method, requiring thousands of cascades of porous membranes to separate the enriched uranium from the other compounds. Finally, the uranium feed material would be difficult to produce.[47] Notwithstanding these challenges, this approach was found promising.

Finally, EMIS had been used to produce uranium feed material for the Manhattan Project. This method was described in reports from the project gifted to the NRC library in the 1950s. The technology was simple; the magnets could be manufactured in Iraq and the American reports described the method in detail.[48] The Iraqi scientists noted that this was an uneconomic method and that it would necessitate considerable research and development. But the scientists had some basic experience from working with ion sources in Germany and Switzerland. Prior to his death (a suspected assassination), Salman Lami had explored basic isotope separation at CERN. The assessment teams concluded that they could produce a prototype and manufacture the equipment domestically. Furthermore, key pieces of equipment were not subject to export control restrictions. Another advantage lay in the simplicity of this process. EMIS had only two stages of enrichment, while gaseous diffusion and enrichment would require thousands of rounds. EMIS also appeared to be a more robust technology than centrifuges. Whereas the malfunction or power outage of individual centrifuges could disrupt an entire batch of material, and possibly damage other centrifuges, the malfunction of individual EMIS separators would not have compounding effects.[49]

In late 1981 Jafar and his colleagues completed their review. They decided to move forward with EMIS as their primary uranium enrichment technology and explore two alternatives: laser isotope separation and gaseous diffusion. While both seemed to be beyond the industrial and scientific resources of Iraq, the senior leadership insisted they look into alternatives in case they failed with EMIS. Specifically, in the fall of 1981 Humam requested that the Physics Department at Tuwaitha looked into laser isotope separation as a potential enrichment option. This was a relatively new method, developed in the United States during the 1970s. For Iraq, this was a long shot. While the scientists continued to examine this method on a small scale, they were unable to set up an experimental trial.[50]

The research and development efforts would proceed in three steps. First, the scientists would study the available literature. Then, they would carry out research and development to familiarize themselves with the basic process and engineering challenges. The final step would be a pilot-scale trial. Once successful, or even before, the pilot-scale lineup would be scaled up to the production stage. This approach involved considerable uncertainty and—particularly with technologies that required more development and advanced industrial capabilities—risks of delay and failure.[51]

The scientists explored several enrichment technologies with varying levels of effort, and this approach has been criticized for its apparent lack of focus.[52] But in Saddam's Iraq this was the norm. Indeed the Manhattan Project had also set out to explore several technologies, mainly focusing on two main tracks, admittedly with much greater resources. Exploring other technological options, however unrealistic, had the added benefit of creating more activities to report. Accordingly, as instructed by the IAEC, Jafar and his team adopted parallel projects to distribute the risks of failure and delays in the short term, as failure in one area could be compensated by progress in another.

But this policy had several unintended consequences. It spread limited resources thinly and created destructive rivalries in technical communities working toward the same goal. It also created turf fights among officials seeking to increase their portfolio and influence. Some went so far as to plagiarize the work of their colleagues. Others took care to not share the results of their research until an occasion came along, such as an internal seminar, where they could publically claim credit for their achievements, lest others claim credit in the interim. The emphasis on progress led to a tendency among senior managers, and in some cases ministers, to deliver vague reports cluttered with calculations and technical assessments and overly optimistic prognoses for achieving objectives. In this atmosphere, where colleagues had to be wary of each other, the scant expertise available was isolated within the organization.

REORGANIZATION

In January 1982, the IAEC was reorganized in preparation for its new task. This was the first of several organizational changes that shaped information sharing, decision making, and management of the nuclear program. Figure 3.1 below offers a snapshot overview of the organizational changes and adaptations during the 1980s. As with many other organizations in Saddam's war state, the nuclear program became an opaque organization with a bewildering number of offshoots. The scientists, led by Jafar, were given essentially free rein with minimal oversight. They faced the overwhelming task of developing an indigenous nuclear weapons program in secret, at a time of war, but were given no specific targets or deadlines from the political leadership. The program was a priority, as evidenced by Saddam's blank check, but it was not an urgent effort.

The IAEC was restructured into six units: International Relations, the Office of Studies and Development (the OSD), Administration, Management of Building Projects, the NRC, and Manpower Training. The IAEC chairman at this time was Izzat Ibrahim al-Doori, who served in his capacity as RCC vice-chairman. His role was formal, as the IAEC would brief Saddam's office directly about the weapons program (through Saddam's personal secretary) and only briefed Izzat Ibrahim occasionally.[53] The new vice-chairman was Humam. The other commissioners were Rahim Abdul al-Kittal as head of International Relations, Jafar as head of the OSD, Dhafir Selbi as head of Administration, Khalid Said as head of Management of Building Projects, and Moyassar al-Mallah as head of Manpower Training.[54]

The IAEC charged the OSD, led by Jafar, with the uranium enrichment program.[55] The initial staff of the IAEC was around 150 in 1983.[56] Over the next five years, the staff increased and additional departments (as well as subunits) were added to cope with specific tasks. As a result, the program became increasingly byzantine and difficult to monitor.

The commissioners had mixed feelings about their responsibilities. Their task was intimidating in the face of their limited human and industrial resources, especially compared with the Manhattan Project, which had been able to draw upon the expertise of leading scientists from several countries and massive industrial resources. While the Iraqi program, like the Manhattan Project, explored several technical options and scientists would reorganize the program in light of the findings, the restrictions facing the Iraqis made it more difficult to cope with risks and uncertainties. Moreover, they could not pursue the optimal technological pathways for fear of detection. Their limited domestic expertise, experience, and infrastructure made the pursuit of alternative technologies a towering challenge, and diverted manpower from the main priorities of the program. Furthermore, they had no experience with research and development for any project on this scale. It

83

REORGANIZATIONS, 1982–88

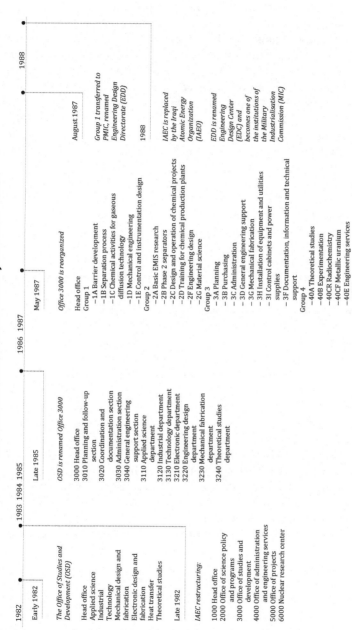

1982   1983 1984 1985   1986 1987

Early 1982

The Office of Studies and Development (OSD)

Head office
Applied science
Industrial
  Technology
Mechanical design and
  fabrication
Electronic design and
  fabrication
Heat transfer
Theoretical studies

Late 1982

IAEC restructuring:

1000 Head office
2000 Office of science policy
  and programs
3000 Office of studies and
  development
4000 Office of administration
  and engineering services
5000 Office of projects
6000 Nuclear research center

Late 1985

OSD is renamed Office 3000

3000 Head office
3010 Planning and follow-up
  section
3020 Coordination and
  documentation section
3030 Administration section
3040 General engineering
  support section
3110 Applied science
  department
3120 Industrial department
3130 Technology department
3210 Electronic department
3220 Engineering design
  department
3230 Mechanical fabrication
  department
3240 Theoretical studies
  department

May 1987

Office 3000 is reorganized

Head office
Group 1
 −1A Barrier development
 −1B Separation process
 −1C Chemical activities for gaseous
   diffusion technology
 −1D Mechanical engineering
 −1E Control and instrumentation design
Group 2
 −2A Basic EMIS research
 −2B Phase 2 separators
 −2C Design and operation of chemical projects
 −2D Training for chemical production plants
 −2F Engineering design
 −2G Material science
Group 3
 −3A Planning
 −3B Purchasing
 −3C Administration
 −3D General engineering support
 −3G Mechanical fabrication
 −3H Installation of equipment and utilities
 −3I Control cabinets and power
   supplies
 −3F Documentation, information and technical
   support
Group 4
 −40A Theoretical studies
 −40B Experimentation
 −40CR Radiochemistry
 −40CF Metallic uranium
 −40E Engineering services
 −40F Design
 −40G Material experiments
 −40N Material characterization
 −40S Metallurgical technology
 −40M Powder technology

August 1987

*Group 1 transferred to
PMIC, renamed
Engineering Design
Directorate (EDD)*

1988

*IAEC is replaced
by the Iraqi
Atomic Energy
Organization
(IAEO)*

*EDD is renamed
Engineering
Design Center
(EDC) and
becomes one of
the institutions of
the Military
Industrialisation
Commission (MIC)*

1988

Figure 3.1. Iraqi nuclear weapons program reorganizations, 1982–88.

was impossible to estimate a timeline. This made planning more difficult and incremental adaptation essential.

The upward chain of command for the IAEC led straight to the Presidential Office, as the formal chain of command, through the RCC, was largely ignored from the beginning. This distinguished the nuclear program from other weapons programs. The chemical and biological weapons programs were formally part of the Ministry of Industry and Military Industrialization (MIMI) and reported to the minister, who was formally junior to the RCC. Since the mid-1970s, by contrast, the nuclear program had acquired a special status within the state apparatus, with the standing of a ministry and enjoying direct access to the center of political power, namely the Presidential Office. Reporting directly to Saddam's office was beneficial for the IAEC, as this streamlined access to resources. Saddam appeared to be genuinely interested when he was briefed about the nuclear program. In contrast, Jafar recounts that when he briefed Izzat Ibrahim, he seemed bored and often changed the subject.[57]

The nuclear weapons program was compartmentalized within the NRC. The senior tier of the IAEC, and those in charge of organizing the enrichment projects, knew that their objective was to produce weapons-grade uranium on a large scale. The second tier (mid-level managers) and regular employees were not informed about this. They were aware that their colleagues explored enrichment technologies but made their own judgments as to whether this was meant to serve peaceful or military purposes in the end. As the program moved forward, the amount of resources poured into the project at a time of war led some to assume that the final objective was to produce weapons. Over time, the internal compartmentalization was undermined by rumors and conversations among colleagues. For example, a radiation physicist at Tuwaitha first heard about the weapons project from a colleague in 1989.[58]

As the IAEC was put in charge of one of the most clandestine and sensitive weapons programs in the Iraqi state, surveillance intensified. Intelligence officers were based at the NRC and watched the offices of senior IAEC members, but most Mukhabarat officers focused on monitoring contacts between the Iraqi nuclear establishment and supplier companies, both domestic and foreign. They would also accompany IAEC staff on any foreign trips. The Iraqi intelligence apparatus gathered personal information about IAEC employees, including their political sympathies. The Baath Party encouraged members working at the NRC to monitor their colleagues.[59] This made scientists cautious but did not affect the technical decisions or priorities as the intelligence lacked the necessary knowledge to effectively monitor the advances of the program.

To move the program from initial research and development toward the production stage, Iraq also had to develop new indigenous production capabilities. During 1980–1981 the MIC finalized a series of contracts to import large quantities of machines, equipment, and raw materials. In late 1981, Humam enquired whether the military production complex could fabricate equipment needed for the new program. This had the added benefit of disguising imports actually intended for the weapons program at Tuwaitha that, if detected, could have attracted unwanted attention. Subsequently, a joint committee was set up between the IAEC and SOTI to facilitate this assistance.[60] This collaboration was similar to that set up between SOTI and the chemical and biological weapons programs.

While the program focused on enrichment technologies, the Iraqis did not yet completely abandon the hope of a plutonium route to a weapons capability. While the planning team had concluded that indigenous uranium enrichment would be the most preferable option for the weapons program, the IAEC tried to persuade France to rebuild the Tammuz reactors. A French consortium agreed to rebuild the reactor on 19 March 1983.[61] But the French government was not willing to assist Iraq with rebuilding their nuclear program. By 1985 it was clear that this was not going to happen. In late 1984 the IAEC launched Project 182 to study the design of a 40 megawatt heavy-water reactor. The project focused on basic reactor design, fuel fabrication, and heavy-water production. Realizing the scope of the challenges associated with building a nuclear reactor suitable for a weapons program in secret and without foreign assistance, the Iraqis began to consider making this an "open" project in order to seek assistance from other countries or the IAEA. Project 182 was scaled down in 1988, when the program was streamlined to focus on enrichment facilities. The project led the scientists to the conclusion that building a reactor indigenously would be too demanding in terms of resources and too vulnerable to air attacks.[62] As this exercise suggests, the IAEC directed scientists to explore an unrealistic option rather than focus scarce resources on creating a large-scale enrichment capacity.

Jafar and his colleagues looked for ways to reduce their infrastructure's vulnerability to future attacks. The NRC at Tuwaitha would remain the hub of all research and development activities. The buildings on site would not receive additional physical protection and were simply painted with camouflage. Manufacturing and production plants would be built elsewhere, either in military-industrial facilities or in new secret locations. The new sites would be designed to be able to withstand air strikes or physical sabotage. These sites were to be scattered around Iraq, so that an attack on all of them would require an extensive air campaign.[63] Documentation from the program was sent to four different sites: two sites at Tuwaitha; a third in the Karradat Maryam district; and a fourth center in a Baghdad guesthouse belonging to the IAEC.[64]

The distribution of sites came into conflict with the need for scientists and engineers to be physically proximate during the research and development process, particularly as these ran in tandem. Also, spreading workshops added costs (as this required duplicating manpower and machines) and de-

lays. Nonetheless, creating a more robust infrastructure was seen as imperative. Eventually, all the sites directly involved in the research and development of uranium enrichment technologies were scattered around Baghdad,
while duplicate sites and facilities focusing on extraction and refinement of
uranium feedstock were located in northwestern Iraq.

As a small group, with Jafar at the helm, was charged with planning,
administering, and implementing the new program, they had limited resources to devote to all of these areas. An element of improvisation also
shaped how the scientific managers decided to organize the weapons program. While this institutional "commotion" could be disruptive for research
and development efforts, it appeared to signal rapid development, and made
it difficult for others to closely track the aggregate progress.

As the nuclear weapons program grew in size and complexity, Saddam
held Jafar and Humam responsible for the progress of the overall program.
The scientific leaders did the planning and much of the management and
the project was overseen by the IAEC commissioners (led by Humam) and
Abdul Kader Abdul Raman Ahmed, the director of the NRC. The program
came to resemble that of other state agencies: frequent reorganization, rapid
institutional growth, and intra-agency competition.

Within a few months the OSD was reorganized into a new administrative
structure comprised of six sections, each distinguished by number: the Head
Office (Office 1000); the Office of Science Policy and Programs (Office 2000);
the OSD (Office 3000); the Office of Administration and Engineering Services
(Office 4000); the Office of Projects (Office 5000); and the NRC (Office 6000).[65]
Over the next three years, these six departments would morph into twelve
sections. (For an overview, please consult Figure 3.1)

Office 3000 (led by Jafar) oversaw several—perhaps too many—crucial areas of scientific and technical development. First, Jafar and colleagues explored technical options for uranium enrichment. Second, this unit was in
charge of finding and developing suitable research, development, and manufacturing resources. This included the construction of laboratories, finding
industrial buildings that could fabricate equipment, and selecting suitable
locations for project sites. This required working with the domestic military-
industrial complex and foreign companies. Figure 3.2, below, illustrates the
sites and facilities associated with the nuclear weapons program. The Al Fao
General Establishment Company built facilities for the chemical and nuclear
weapons programs.[66] Third, Office 3000 was charged with setting up procurement units in other state organizations to avoid foreign detection.[67]

The NRC continued other plausible research activities and international
publishing to reduce foreign suspicions. These activities were completely
separate from those of the clandestine program. The NRC continued to carry
out basic research consistent with previous projects in chemistry, physics,
biology, agriculture, medical diagnostics, and radioisotopes. Their findings
were communicated in scholarly publications and at academic conferences.[68]

Figure 3.2. Map of nuclear and military-industrial sites, Iraq.

In this way, Iraq hoped to distract the outside world from the emergence of its secret program.

RESEARCH AND DEVELOPMENT

Between 1982 and 1985, the scientists studied several enrichment technologies. Their purpose was to develop a clearer understanding of the basic processes of each technique, in theoretical and technical terms and assess whether Iraq could produce or acquire the machines and raw material required for each route.[69] At this stage, no thought was put into bomb design or how a nuclear arsenal would be integrated with Iraq's military capabilities.

Given their limited experience with enrichment, Office 3000 spent more time analyzing technical processes than working on engineering challenges. The usual way in which each stage—laboratory-scale research, pilot-scale test, and large-scale production—would inform the next was compromised by the IAEC's preference to run these processes in parallel. In many cases, production units were constructed simultaneously with initial experimental efforts despite the established principle of following a sequential approach.[70] This entailed risks and a greater need for adaptation and improvisation (i.e., downstream problems). Their guiding principle was to proceed wherever possible, even in pursuing technologies with great uncertainty.[71] Being seen as making tangible progress toward a nuclear weapons capability was imperative. Problems would simply have to be worked around as they arose.

The scientific leaders of the program had more autonomy than during the more ambiguous period of the late 1970s. Jafar had received carte blanche from Saddam, and his position as the scientific head of the clandestine program could not be easily questioned within the organization. The vice-chairman of the IAEC, Humam, had Baath credentials and a good working relationship with Saddam. Over the next few years, Humam helped create a more stable and supportive working environment at Tuwaitha. This was not just the case for the weapons program: other lines of research, such as radiation protection, also had considerable independence. According to one scientist working on radiation issues, for example, Humam made no attempt to steer his research activities.[72]

The absence of clear benchmarks and deadlines did not, however, create a carefree atmosphere. The active role of Baath members in facilitating the arrest of their colleagues over the recent years—and their ongoing monitoring—necessitated caution. Efforts by Jafar and his colleagues had to be seen, both by their Baath colleagues and the Presidential Office, as moving forward. This would come to influence their approach to research and development, and their reporting, over the coming years. Given the highly technical nature of their research and development efforts, few others were capable of vetting or questioning their choices. As a result, Office 3000 enjoyed considerable autonomy. Jafar and his colleagues were able to pursue what they perceived to be the most feasible, if not necessarily the most efficient or economic, enrichment technologies.

The organization of research and development underscored the necessity of incremental adaptation. Individual projects would rapidly move from basic research to development to production or, in many cases, run these processes in parallel. The IAEC's guiding principle was, in their own words, to forge ahead with upstream activities (i.e., creating industrial-scale enrichment facilities) wherever possible, even if downstream efforts (research and development, refinement of uranium feed material) were moving slowly.[73] There may have been several reasons behind this, including a perceived need to make observable progress to ward off accusations of delay or, worse, failure.

As the planning of the enrichment research program was done in haste, implementation was expected to change over the next few years. As it turned out, there would be technical adaptations (such as the choice of open magnets for the production stage of EMIS), and major changes in the choice of enrichment technology (as with the decision to discard gaseous diffusion and adopt centrifuges as a secondary technology) as well as the overall organization of the program. This required flexibility at all levels of the organization, which was difficult to pull off given the highly centralized nature of the program. Furthermore, given the challenges of coordination in Saddam's state, this was a tall order. While there were cases of incremental adaptation, in other areas the leadership remained committed to the basic approach—adaptation through experimentation—and preferred existing technological paths over adapting incrementally.

While the nuclear weapons program was not subject to direct pressure from Saddam or other senior regime officials, tensions grew inside the organization. Despite making real progress in some areas, such as developing an industrial base more or less from scratch with the help of the military-industrial complex, failure to make equally rapid progress in other areas led to mounting frustration within the program sections. Several senior and mid-level managers were frustrated that their proposals for alternative ion sources and enrichment technologies were brushed aside or received scant resources. Their dissatisfaction was aggravated by the management of the program, which followed the classic pattern of military innovation in Iraq: administration, planning, management, and performance reviews were typically carried out by a small number of individuals with little transparency or input from other levels of the organization. Jafar's role as scientific leader of the program was curtailed by the administrative influence and purview of the IAEC. He would at times receive direct orders to start additional tracks or prioritize certain areas of the project, and he was not in a position to object. Nonetheless, these changes led to mounting criticism of Jafar by mid-level project managers in the nuclear weapons program.

Tensions among the project managers and IAEC commissioners mounted toward the mid-1980s. The pressures of the enormous task also began to wear on the scientists and engineers at Tuwaitha. The senior management was stretched to the limit. The experimental approach meant that most teams had to return to the drawing board repeatedly, and the engineering teams became demotivated and exhausted.[74] Under such conditions, and given the stakes of failure, the scene was set for clashes.

Gaseous Diffusion. The Iraqi scientists were interested in gaseous diffusion, despite its challenges, because it could make the EMIS process more efficient. Gaseous diffusion is a process where uranium isotopes are separated through a physical barrier; uranium-235 (U-235) is aggregated through repeated cycles. This low-enriched uranium (LEU) would be used as feed material for EMIS.[75]

In early 1982 a team began to explore the basic science and engineering challenges of this approach. They started research and development to ascertain the technical specifications of key items such as compressors and making the basic configurations work on a miniature scale. This group faced three key challenges: producing suitable porous barriers; understanding how molecules flow through such barriers; and setting up cascades.[76] Their objective was to build several hundred cascades to produce 4–5 tons of LEU (3–4 percent) as feed material for EMIS.[77] Over the next six years, they were unable to develop an appropriate porous barrier, as they lacked the advanced industrial capacity to produce suitable materials.

While gaseous diffusion was a proven technology, it required an advanced industrial infrastructure. Producing the porous barrier and large compressors were well beyond the industrial capabilities of Iraq. Engineers attempted to reverse-engineer compressors procured from the United States. A suitable barrier had 10 trillion holes per square centimeter; producing such material was well beyond the capabilities of the Iraqi industrial establishment.[78] Experimental facilities for testing different barrier designs and diffuser models were built at the NRC and Rashidiya, northwest of Baghdad. Along with research and development efforts focusing on porous barriers, Office 3000 also tried to develop compressors and, when these efforts failed, attempted to purchase compressors from abroad. In late 1988, a barrier material was successfully developed. The next challenge was to design and produce a porous tube. The department developed a suitable design and started laboratory-scale production, but was unable to take this to large-scale production due to their limited industrial capabilities.[79] By late 1989, the gaseous diffusion project was shelved.

EMIS. In early 1982, Office 3000 began a five-year program exploring the basic science and technology of EMIS, considered the most feasible option under the constraints of secrecy and primarily indigenous production. Most of the personnel and resources at the Applied Science Department (subdivision 3110; please see Figure 3.1 for further details) were devoted to this line of research and development. Key personnel included Khaloow Raof Hamdi, Thamer Numan Mawlood, and engineers Razzak Obais Marzook and Lath Jamil Bunni.[80] They planned to proceed in three overlapping stages: initial research and development (focusing on all aspects of EMIS, but primarily magnetic fields and ion sources); setting up a pilot-scale experimental trial; and building a production unit capable of producing 15 kilograms of 93 percent enriched uranium per year (a bomb required at least 8 kilograms and more likely 15–25 kilograms). This output could be increased further by using LEU (rather than natural uranium) as feed material. LEU could be produced through gaseous diffusion, the supporting enrichment method that was being developed (ultimately unsuccessfully) in a separate department (initially this track was pursued by the Technology department 3130, then Group 1 after 1987).

The EMIS method of uranium separation did not require high-speed movement machinery, which led Office 3000 managers to conclude that this was a more realistic option for the limited pool of scientists and engineers who would be responsible for the design and manufacture of these items. As they set out to explore this technology they decided to focus on understanding the scientific principles of magnet separators and to experiment with different types of magnets. Once they had successfully achieved separation of U-235, design and fabrication efforts of the larger equipment was halted while the teams focused on improving ion sources and collectors.[81]

In designing, producing, and operationalizing magnet separators the first challenge was to familiarize Iraqi scientists and engineers with the separation process using magnets in theoretical and practical terms. To do so, Office 3000 set up an initial series of research and development projects (Projects 101, 102 and 103). In Project 101 the Applied Science Department constructed a small-scale model to develop some basic insights into magnet separation. Over the next five years they designed, manufactured, and operated three types of magnets (R40, R50, and R100). In Projects 102 and 103, two identical magnets were fed different ion sources for isotope extraction. In January 1982 they decided to set up a laboratory-scale program for developing uranium tetrachloride, which was the feed material for EMIS.[82] The MSE provided precursor chemicals for these experiments and trials.[83] Once these systems were operational, Office 3000 began to compare the observed magnetic field configuration with their theoretical calculations. Matching results were confirmed in September 1984.[84] Some sixteen months later, in January 1986, they successfully separated uranium isotopes from uranium tetrachloride vapor.[85]

The construction of these magnets was supported by the military industry. The joint committee between SOTI and the IAEC facilitated the import and assembly of the machinery to produce magnets in the Badr General Establishment.[86] The design, production and assembly of the magnets took place at the Office 3000 departments at Tuwaitha. Components were produced at the Badr General Establishment and the General Establishment for Electrical Industries.[87] The separators were assembled with components from the Badr General Establishment, the NRC, and the Oqba Bin Nafi Establishment, while some items (vacuum pumps, gauges, and valves) were procured from abroad.[88]

One of the many important decisions made at this early stage was choosing an ion source for EMIS. While making this decision, the scientists were influenced by the level of experience and familiarity they had with the different options. They decided to focus on PIG because some staff members had been trained in working with similar technology in connection with their earlier efforts to develop linear accelerators. In early 1980 three NRC employees had traveled to Darmstadt in Germany as part of their effort to develop heavy-ion sources. While the methods they learned there were relevant for EMIS, there were important differences (e.g., EMIS required singly charged uranium ions). The benefits of their experience were limited by a lack of detailed information in the literature about PIG. Still, Jafar and colleagues opted for PIG instead of calutron mass spectrometers, an alternative technology used in the Manhattan Project.

The second stage of this research and development ensued in 1983 with a series of projects (104, 105, 106) focusing on fabricating and operationalizing pre-production scale separators. These projects were geared toward setting up a pilot-scale trial of the basic components of EMIS. In Project 105, the Iraqis fabricated a model separator with an open magnetic field. In Project 106 they explored different configurations of ion sources, specifically how double or quadruple ion sources would perform compared with single sources in the separator. In tandem with these projects, a series of research projects explored how to collect the desired uranium from the separators more efficiently.

As the program moved forward, a pressing concern was to produce the feed material in larger quantities. The chemists in Office 3000 developed the capacity to produce 1 kilogram of uranium tetrachloride (the feed material used to test the separators) per day.[89] But collecting the uranium from the separator pockets was a considerable challenge. Finally, in October 1987, Numan and his colleague Abdul Razzak al-Qaraghouli collected a sample tube of uranium dioxide (2–3 percent enriched).[90] To move from such laboratory-scale samples to kilograms would require, as Jafar put it, a quantum leap: it could not be achieved by scientific ingenuity alone but required manufacturing capabilities of a daunting scale and precision.

These challenges had to be addressed in tandem with several other demanding tasks, including the organization and supervision of the development of manufacturing sites at Tuwaitha, the Rabie mechanical workshop, and the Dijla electronics and control workshop.[91]

Jafar and his colleagues began preparations for the production stage in tandem with the first and second series of projects. The production plant (Project 8119) was envisaged as two identical facilities with seventy separators, each producing (at design capacity, which assumed optimum performance) 15 kilograms of highly enriched uranium per year. If their colleagues were able to produce LEU feed (less than 20 percent U-235), or if this could be procured from another country, they could expect increased output and possibly shorten the time required to produce enough highly enriched uranium for one nuclear weapon by two years.[92] In late 1987 the IAEC decided to have two EMIS sites, in case one was attacked or otherwise became nonoperative, and to bolster production when necessary.[93] These two sites were Tarmiya (to be constructed by a Yugoslav company) and Sharqat (a replica of the Tarmiya site built by the Iraqi military-industrial complex). The Fao General Establishment and the nuclear establishment constructed these sites, under the direction of a joint committee.

The collaboration between the IAEC and the General Establishment companies (i.e., the military-industrial production sites) also included several related projects such as development and production of munitions and bombs. One such project was the production of radiological bombs, a project that has received little attention from scholars. In the second half of the 1980s, the IAEC requested that the MSE produce casings for radiological weapons. These designs were based on aerial bombs developed at the Nasr factory since 1984 for dispersal of chemical and biological weapons. In 1988 MSE began feasibility studies of casings for a bomb filled with radiological material. The initial design weighed more than 1,400 kilograms, which meant that only two Iraqi aircraft (TU-16 or TU-22) would be able to deliver them.[94] The teams at MSE, on their own initiative, developed two additional designs that were smaller: a 400-kilogram design called the Muthanna-4 carrying between 500 grams and 1 kilogram of irradiated material; and a 1,000-kilogram bomb.[95]

Preparing Uranium for Centrifuges. To produce feed material for the uranium enrichment program, the so-called front end of the nuclear fuel cycle, geologists and chemists revived earlier efforts to search for and exploit indigenous uranium. During the 1970s teams from Tuwaitha had located uranium deposits in northern Iraq. At that time, indigenous uranium exploration (not to mention mining and refinement) was set aside as the French agreement included provision of reactor fuel. Interest in producing yellowcake (a uranium concentrate powder that can be further refined into nuclear fuel or undergo enrichment) from natural uranium surfaced again in 1979, but it was only after September 1981 that the front end of the fuel cycle (i.e., refining uranium) became a priority.

In May 1982, the Iraqi Ministry of Industry and Minerals (MIM) commissioned a Belgian company to build a unit to extract yellowcake from phosphoric acid. In January 1985 this unit, located at the Al-Qaim Establishment (a phosphate fertilizer production complex established by MIM in 1979), became operational. At design capacity, assuming optimal conditions, this unit could have produced 103 metric tons of yellowcake per calendar year. As it turned out, the plant at Al-Qaim would produce only around 168 tons before it was shut down in mid-1990.[96] This was due to several factors: the low concentration of uranium in the feed material; an extraction rate that was half of the design rate; and fewer days of operation (only 214 days per year).[97] In addition, much of the phosphoric acid at Al-Qaim went directly into fertilizer production rather than uranium extraction.[98]

The next step in the process was to convert the yellowcake to a form that was suitable feed material for EMIS. Specifically, the yellowcake had to be converted into suitable uranium oxide and pure uranium tetrachloride. These products would then be sent to Tarmiya, one of the two EMIS production sites. This was a very challenging step for the chemists at Tuwaitha. In 1983, the Iraqis attempted to build a small plant themselves, but found this too difficult given their lack of experience in this area.[99] A Brazilian plant to convert yellowcake to uranium oxide was commissioned. This design would be modified by the Iraqis and additional equipment purchased to suit their specifications. These design modifications were completed in the late summer of 1987.[100] A site north of Mosul for the conversion plant, named Al-Jazira, was selected in the spring of 1989.

A Deadline, 1985

During the first three years of the nuclear weapons program (1982–1985), there had been no explicit pressure from Saddam to produce weapons. There is no evidence suggesting that anyone had started to think about what kind of weapons these ought to be and how they would be delivered. The roadmap of the program was based on Jafar's memorandum from 1981, which focused on technological options and assessments rather than deadlines or benchmarks. In the spring of 1985, however, this would change.

In April 1985, Saddam summoned the leaders and five senior members of the IAEC—Chairman Izzat Ibrahim, Vice-Chairman Humam, and Commissioners al-Kittal, Said, al-Mallah, Jafar, and Selbi—to review the progress of the weapons program. They were taken to the Radwanya district of Baghdad where he was waiting in a caravan. As the meeting began, Humam reviewed the ongoing projects. His remarks were based on a report he had prepared with Jafar that had not been precirculated to the other commissioners. As they listened to Humam's presentation, the other commissioners were surprised that they had not been consulted or briefed prior to the meeting.

They were even more surprised when Humam completed his presentation by announcing that the program would fulfill its objective within five years, by 1990. Humam did not specify what this objective was, or what exactly would be achieved by 1990. Some of the other commissioners assumed that this was a promise to reach a new milestone in the enrichment programs.[101] But it was not clear what exactly would be delivered. Saddam reacted with visible emotion, according to the recollection of Selbi.[102] When Saddam invited the other commissioners to comment on Humam's presentation they remained silent.

Humam's promise was remarkable for two reasons. It was the first commitment by the IAEC to Saddam with an explicit deadline attached, although it was not clear what exactly would be delivered. Further, the announcement was made while enrichment technologies were being explored at a theoretical or experimental stage, and no significant breakthroughs had yet been achieved. The IAEC had imposed a deadline before the scientists had found an experimentally proven enrichment technology.

After the meeting the commissioners were presented with new cars and mobile caravans. They drove to Tuwaitha, where al-Kittal confronted Humam and demanded an explanation as to why a promise had been made without internal consultation. All of the commissioners would be held responsible for meeting this deadline. The conversation rapidly escalated into a furious argument. Staff were cleared from the corridors so they would not overhear.[103]

Where did the initiative behind this commitment come from? Was it self-imposed by Humam and Jafar, orchestrated behind the scenes by Saddam, or someone else? It seemed out of character, as no one in the nuclear establishment had previously set a timeline or deadline. But a similar promise had been made in early 1985, when the director of the MSE promised the minister of defense he would deliver biological weapons within five years.[104] This ambitious, and quite possibly arbitrary, promise seemed unfounded, given that the program had only just started recruiting scientists. Two years later, the BW program was still focusing on basic experiments. In short, an apparently premature promise was made in both programs by senior managers to senior officials with a seemingly arbitrary deadline. It is possible that Humam's commitment was made on his and Jafar's initiative, to buy some time to make substantial advances toward the production stage. Many of Jafar's colleagues in the IAEC and Office 3000 blamed him and Humam for making what they believed was an unrealistic promise.[105] It is perhaps more likely that senior managers of both the nuclear and biological weapons programs had been asked by senior officials to review their achievements and indicate a deadline.

Most of the reporting of the program was carried out informally through personal briefings and back-channels to the most senior members of the regime. Had Saddam wanted more detailed assessments he would surely have requested them, but, Jafar noted, he seemed content to let the scientists work at their own pace.

The leaders of the nuclear program updated Saddam in a series of occasional meetings. During these Humam and Jafar would describe their progress to Saddam, who typically listened without interruption. According to Jafar's recollection, Saddam never asked about weaponization or hinted at a deadline (or even a time frame) during these meetings. Neither Humam nor Jafar brought up such questions but focused on the developments in the enrichment program in their comments. These sessions were intimate and informal; at times Saddam would come out from a nap and other times he would play with his daughter Hala.[106] The men would at times sit and enjoy a meal together after the update. The intimate setting of these meetings indicated that the two scientists were considered part of Saddam's close circle of advisers.

Saddam and his subordinates in the security services and RCC had few other sources of information about the project. Such information was heavily compartmentalized within the organization. Even the IAEC commissioners felt that Jafar and Humam rarely consulted them about the priorities and challenges facing the program. Nor did they specify exactly what had been achieved and where they were falling behind. This led to frustration and speculation, particularly by those who disagreed with the priorities laid down by Humam and Jafar. From their perspective, their reporting tended to exaggerate the progress of the program. According to some commissioners, quarterly progress reports were "general outlines that were not coupled to target values or measured outcomes nor to scheduled dates."[107] This curtailed the possibility of rigorous internal review, as the commissioners were only able to make general comments rather than focus on the performance of particular projects. Foreign experts later concurred that these reports blurred the lines between what had already been achieved and the anticipated next steps.[108]

The complexity of the program, where downstream and upstream activities were carried out simultaneously, added to the difficulties of monitoring the overall progress toward large-scale uranium enrichment. As the leaders of the nuclear weapons program reported that they were moving forward with the exploration of enrichment technologies, details about the rate of progress, and the challenges they faced, were absent.

GROWING TENSIONS

While the political leadership remained aloof, frustration began to mount within the departments at Tuwaitha. The decision to pursue EMIS as the primary enrichment technology was particularly controversial. Senior scientists and engineers complained that Jafar continued to set the technical priorities of the program while others continued small-scale "pet projects." The mounting delays led to disputes and divisions within the senior tiers of the program.

There were two focal points for these criticisms, both related to the design of the electromagnetic separators. First, there was inadequate theoretical analysis of the behavior of low-charge ions under magnetic conditions to guide the design of the ionization gauze. Second, the PIG models were unstable and basically unpredictable. As some of the engineers bitterly complained, continuing down this track was essentially flogging a dead PIG.[109] Yet their proposal to pursue a less complicated ion source, the calutrons adopted in the Manhattan Project, was brushed aside.

In early 1987, a group of engineers (Selbi, Basil al-Qaisi, and Numan) appealed to Humam to end the stalemate. They argued that their experiments with the PIG failed consistently and that it was necessary to adopt calutrons as an alternative ion source. The decision to do so was made in a larger meeting involving all leaders of related Office 3000 projects (Humam, Jafar, the head of the Electronics and Electrical Engineering Department, the head of the Mechanical Engineering Department, the ion source mechanical designer, and the head of the Mechanical fabrication Workshops).[110] Nonetheless, this decision was not implemented in a serious manner. Months later, it emerged that the prototype calutron—designed by Yahya Nussaief, who was head of manufacturing—was still stored at the mechanical workshops. After yet another meeting, the shift from PIG to calutrons was effected.[111]

The management of research and development activities was also criticized for its emphasis on experimental adaptation to guide both upstream and downstream activities. The research and development process began with basic analysis and then moved to design and pilot-scale development (often in parallel). The lion's share of problem solving was thereby shifted to the second stage of the program, where it was far more costly and complicated, not to mention time-consuming, to make adjustments. The centralized management of the program, whereby Jafar was the key decision maker, also contributed to stifle crucial feedback between the research and development processes. Proposals that could have made the research and development stage more efficient, such as relying more on computer modeling than experimental trials, were ignored.

The slow progress of the enrichment projects led some Tuwaitha scientists and engineers who were not involved with the weapons program to believe that those who were were not keen to produce nuclear weapons. One scientist noted that several of his colleagues did not like nuclear weapons and speculated that some may have wanted to delay the program.[112] But there is no evidence that scientists willingly sabotaged or slowed down the weapons program. The problem was more prosaic: the more the senior leaders invested in their chosen technologies, the more difficult it was to revisit this decision.

When Jafar presented a quarterly progress report to the IAEC in April 1987, however, he seemed nervous.[113] This report went into far more detail than previous quarterly reports, and the conclusion was bleak: it would be impossible to make the major leap forward within the deadline promised to Saddam two years earlier. Having put massive resources into the EMIS research program, they were still not seeing reliable results during pilot trials. Because other approaches had been marginalized in order to pour resources into the EMIS project, little progress was forthcoming elsewhere.

The reactions were strong and immediate. The first commissioner commenting was al-Kittal, who asked whether this finding would be reported to Saddam—it was not. Others asked for a more specific description of the problems in the EMIS project, in the hope that some solution could be found. Even at this stage, the commissioners did not have a full picture of the technical challenges or the status of ongoing programs.[114] Senior participants later described the discussion, which lasted for hours, as the most stressful meeting of the weapons program.[115] While no immediate solution to the technical problems was found, the commissioners agreed to restructure the management of the program to give Jafar more time to focus on the bottlenecks in the EMIS project. More broadly, it was apparent that the management of the program had to be reformed to focus on key challenges and give the commissioners a clearer view of the problems that were accumulating.

The IAEC decided to create a more streamlined organization. The first round of reorganization followed the program leaders' begrudging realization that the program had outgrown the management structure. The weapons program had grown in size and complexity, while the centralized management of all of these projects suffered from over-stretch. The result was a bloated program that did not focus resources on the most promising technological development tracks. Furthermore, the centralized management approach adopted thus far had prevented the other senior figures from helping to solve the outstanding problems facing the program.

In response to the April 1987 report, Selbi volunteered to assume some of Jafar's administrative obligations, while Jafar remained scientific leader of the enrichment-related project portfolio in Office 3000. These changes were reported to IAEC chairman Izzat Ibrahim, but the findings of the internal report of April 1987 were not communicated to him, or to Saddam.[116]

Later that spring, the senior management initiated another round of reorganization of the main research and development units in the program. In May, senior figures in Office 3000 traveled to the Habaniya resort outside Fallujah to discuss the organization of the weapons program. This meeting was set in pleasant surroundings, and the scientists were joined by their families. This set the scene for a constructive discussion. Jafar and Selbi led the deliberations on how to optimize the organization and management of the weapons program.

They decided to reorganize Office 3000 into a simpler structure of three groups, each focusing on distinct clusters of activities. Group 1, led by Mahdi Obeidi, was dedicated to gaseous diffusion; Group 2, led by Jafar, focused on EMIS; and Group 3, led by Selbi, housed various related activities (planning, administration, documentation, procurement, manufacturing, and installation).[117] This revised structure, the scientists hoped, would pool human resources more efficiently. These groups were overseen by a steering committee, Committee 3000, whose members included Jafar (head), Selbi, Numan (director general), Ahmed (director general), and Obeidi (deputy director general). As signs of this turbulence registered at the senior level of the regime, at a time when Saddam was trying to regain control over the proliferating military-industrial complex, the autonomy of the project would be called into question.

A FIRST STEP TOWARD WEAPONIZATION

In early 1987, Humam and Jafar discussed the issue of weaponization.[118] This was a complex challenge in terms of design and engineering. They agreed that it would be unwise to dedicate human resources to another demanding line of research and development at that stage, as Groups 1 and 2 were still facing many challenges with enrichment technologies. Nonetheless, they decided to commission a preliminary report for Saddam's perusal. They asked Kidhir Hamza, who had written one of the earliest proposals for a weapons program in 1971–1972, to prepare this report. Hamza commanded little respect from the senior figures of the IAEC or even his colleagues. The fact that he was chosen to lead the first study of weaponization could be taken to suggest that this line of research was not seen as urgent.

Humam and Jafar agreed that Saddam had to sanction research and development on weaponization. Jafar recommended that this line of research, which they proposed to name the al-Hussein project, should be carried out in a separate location. In Humam's view, weaponization introduced a host of new challenges, including physical risks to buildings, staff, and surroundings, and heightened risks of detection. Thus far, Saddam had only sanctioned the development of a large-scale production of fissile material. Moving forward with weaponization required his explicit approval. Preparing the technical infrastructure would also require collaboration from other institutions in the MIC. For example, the Al-Qaa-Qaa General Establishment would provide the explosive package for the nuclear weapon. The likelihood that word would spread about the highly secretive weapons program further underlined the need to get Saddam's explicit approval.[119]

In April 1987, Humam indicated in a memorandum to Saddam that the program was approaching a new stage. Around this time, the IAEC commissioners suspected that Saddam was receiving unflattering reports about the nuclear program.[120] General Amir al-Saadi, who was the deputy of Saddam's son-in-law, Hussein Kamil, noted that Saddam inserted "eyes" in weapons projects, just as the IAEC suspected. For example, during 1987–1988, Saddam sent a team to record missile tests to provide him with a video independent of the MIC's reporting channels. He also received reports outside of MIC's formal channels. As these measures suggest, the Iraqi leader was aware of the problems of drift and overly optimistic reporting in the military-industrial complex, and was looking for ways to avoid being misled by his officials.[121]

When Saddam received Humam's memorandum he consulted Kamil, who was head of the MIMI. Kamil was a rising star, having merged the General Institute for Industries and the special security agency (Amn Al Khas), and then becoming a minister in rapid succession.[122] His new portfolio included all arms production, including WMD (chemical, biological, and nuclear weapons programs). Kamil recommended lifting the weaponization project from the IAEC and making it his personal responsibility.

Saddam accordingly ordered that Kamil would take direct charge of the weaponization project. This weakened the IAEC's influence over a particularly sensitive dimension of the program, which was a blow to the commission, particularly Jafar and Humam. As the program moved closer to the threshold of a nuclear weapons capability, the exclusive reign of the IAEC was about to end. Kamil transferred a dozen scientists and engineers from Tuwaitha to Amn Al Khas. Kamil told Hamza, the team leader who had lobbied for a weapons program since the early 1970s, to use the name Mohammed Hazem, presumably due to the sensitivity of the project.[123] (Incidentally, when Kamil talked to UN inspectors after his 1995 defection to Jordan, he confirmed that Hazem was Hamza's pseudonym, and characterized him as a "professional liar.")[124]

Hamza and his team would to study the literature to define the challenges of weaponization, assess what resources would be required, and consider what available resources could be mobilized for the weaponization program. They had not received any specifications for the size or basic design preferences of the weapon. The group assumed that their objective was to develop a minimum 10-kiloton weapon.[125] This assumption, along with several others in the study, revealed the lack of direction from the military and political leadership, as well as the group's lack of relevant expertise.[126]

In September 1987, Saddam's secretary Hammadi called a meeting to discuss Hamza's findings. General al-Saadi listed the key conclusions, which specified that a weaponization program would take a decade and require some three hundred specialists and a billion-dollar budget.[127] The initial estimates of the reports cited a need for $600 million worth of equipment and infrastructure, a figure that did not include the establishment of a new power station and several new facilities for explosive tests and laboratories. The other attendees ridiculed these assessments. Said, the director of the NRC, said that this project could be done in five years with the available resources at Tuwaitha. He was promptly put in charge of weaponization. Al-Saadi transferred a group of scientists from the weaponization program back to the IAEC and Tuwaitha in November. They formed a new unit, Group 4, at Tuwaitha dedicated to weaponization.[128]

After the Osirak strike, the Iraqi nuclear program was transformed. It received much greater resources and benefited from a plan and a dedicated organization. The immediate objective was to produce enriched uranium on a large scale. To this end Saddam gave Jafar carte blanche, made him responsible for the planning and implementation of the program, and removed influential Baathists from the senior leadership. Saddam set the basic rules for the program but remained a remote figure between 1981 and 1987.

During this period we can see several indications of capture, as scientists explored technologies that were unlikely to yield results for several years. These choices have previously been attributed to Jafar, but the evidence presented in this chapter shows that the IAEC ordered Jafar and his colleagues to open additional research tracks, which diverted resources from the main priorities of the program. To be clear, this was not the result of Saddam's personal interference or scientists acting "as if" Saddam interfered. As a result, Jafar and Humam designed the program to maximize the number of activities, while constant reorganization made auditing and peer review difficult for the regime, and even for the IAEC. This seems to have been one way of coping with the many uncertainties associated with their momentous task and the potential risks of failure.

Despite increased motivation and resources, the program continued to falter. Undoubtedly, being cut off from foreign support was a contributing cause. Another was the delegatory management of the program that, in the absence of adequate monitoring and auditing mechanisms, facilitated drift. Despite committing to a deadline, the managers of the program did not revise their priorities when their preferred technologies were not working. The absence of effective monitoring mechanisms in the Iraqi state also failed to alert the senior political leadership of the problem. It is telling that the first reorganization of the program came at the initiative of senior engineers, following months of intense in-fighting, and not as the result of external intervention. Meanwhile, the scientists withheld the information that they would not meet the 1990 deadline from Saddam. Instead, they asked for permission to launch a weapons program.

Crises and a Crash Program, 1988–1991

In 1988, tensions came to a head when the leaders of the nuclear weapons program accused the military-industrial complex of delaying their progress. After Jafar Dhiya Jafar and Humam Abdul Khaliq clashed with Hussein Kamil, Saddam's powerful son-in-law (and minister of military industries), Kamil took charge of the program. The program was split into two tracks, focusing on different enrichment technologies. Each was subject to more scrutiny and pressure to deliver. As the war with Iran came to an end in the fall of 1988, both tracks were making progress toward large-scale production of fissile material. Meanwhile, a dedicated group was developing a weapons design.

These two groups played by different rules. Specifically, Jafar's group followed the rules while Kamil's group largely ignored them. Both groups made progress, but Kamil's unit withheld information from Saddam to present their results in a more flattering light. In addition, Kamil exaggerated the prospects of an imminent breakthrough to Saddam by late 1990. Saddam attempted to open his own lines of information, apparently without much success. At any rate, Saddam's attention turned to the economic crisis after the war with Iran ended, which posed a potential threat to his survival. The nuclear program was less important.

After Saddam invaded Kuwait in August 1990, Kamil ordered a crash program to develop a crude nuclear explosive. The scientists knew this was a "mission impossible," due to remaining challenges in basic design and difficulties in scaling up models from experiments to production. Saddam and Kamil, on the other hand, were oblivious of this fact. As the allied forces started a bombing campaign in February 1991, the crash program was interrupted, and subsequently dismantled. Bombing destroyed many of the sites, and within a few months the program was reorganized. The scientists were tasked with rebuilding the destroyed infrastructure.

Reorganization and New Directions

In 1987–1988 the weapons program was reorganized from within and without to create a more efficient and transparent organization. The internal restructuring that followed the April 1987 report described in the previous chapter redefined the project's administrative structure. A second series of changes in 1988 placed the program under Kamil's purview. These changes are summarized in Figure 4.1 below, which illustrates the administrative restructuring of the program, as well as the emergence of competing technical projects within the nuclear weapons program. Under Kamil's direction, Saddam seems to have hoped, the leadership could regain control and bring the program back on track.

In 1988, two additional rounds of reorganization transformed the governance and oversight of the project. First, in early 1988 Saddam replaced the Iraqi Atomic Energy Commission (IAEC) with a new body, the Iraqi Atomic Energy Organization (IAEO), led by Humam as chairman and Jafar as vice-chairman. Some of the former IAEC commissioners became directors general of the IAEO (Dhafir Selbi and Khalid Said); al-Kittal left the commission and took a position at the Iraqi Embassy in Austria.

Second, in late 1988 the program was lifted from the IAEO and placed under Kamil's Ministry of Industry and Military Industrialization (MIMI). In the fall of 1988 Humam sent a report to Saddam describing the status of the program, pointing out (some) problems and suggested solutions.[1] The majority of the bottlenecks Humam identified were blamed on delays caused by the Military Industrial Commission (MIC) in the construction of workshops at the Oqba bin Nafi General Establishment and the Tarmiya site, which was the main electromagnetic isotope separation (EMIS) production site.

Saddam submitted these criticisms to Kamil, as the responsible minister. He then called a meeting of the senior leaders of MIC in October 1988, including Kamil; Directors General Amir al-Saadi, Mahdi Obeidi, Nazar Juma Kaseer, Ahmed Murtadha Ahmed; the director general of the Al Fao General Establishment, Abdul Fattah; as well as directors general from the military-industrial complex.[2] The contingent from the IAEO—Humam, Jafar, and Selbi—was outnumbered. Assuming the role of chair of the meeting, Kamil began by accusing Humam of falling behind with the weapons program. He cited information passed from insiders and deflected any MIC responsibility for delays, blaming poor management of the nuclear weapons program. He also claimed that if the MIMI, under his leadership, were in charge of the program, the situation would improve.[3] The following day, Kamil transferred the nuclear weapons program from the IAEO to the MIMI.

Kamil maintained Group 1, focusing on gaseous diffusion, as a separate entity, to stimulate competition. The remaining projects would be led by

Iraq Nuclear Weapons Program Timeline, 1982–1991

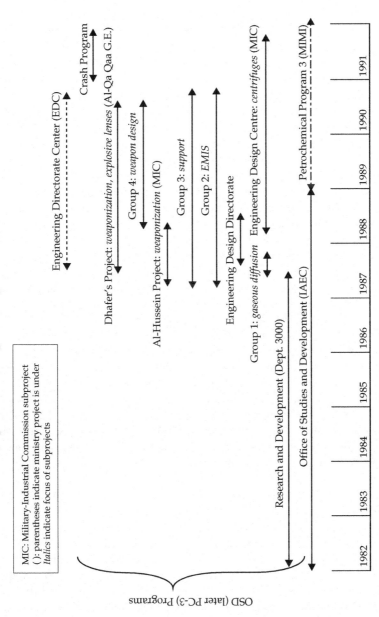

Figure 4.1. Iraq nuclear weapons program timeline, 1982–1991.

Jafar, who was appointed deputy head of the MIMI. He would be supported by Said, Zafir Rashid Salman, and Thamer Numan Mawlood, who were appointed as managers of the new program by Presidential Decree on 1 April 1988.[4] In January 1989, the entire weapons program (Office 3000) was officially transferred to Kamil's ministry and renamed Petrochemical Project No. 3 (PC-3 for short).

Kamil had a reputation for applying ruthless pressure and was known for his success rate in high-level turf fights. Related to Saddam through blood and marriage, he had good access to financial resources. He had already appropriated several large and prestigious projects since taking charge of the MIMI in 1988.[5] Kamil put pressure on PC-3 to make rapid progress, but lacked a realistic understanding of timelines or of the technical requirements to succeed. When staff told him that developing a prototype of an advanced machine would take two years, but could perhaps be done in one, Kamil gave them a deadline of six months.[6] Any delays could mean not being able to leave the site until the work was done. While such deadlines led to acceleration in some areas, other problems could not be easily resolved through rushed intensive campaigns.

These campaigns were grueling, intensive efforts that rarely succeeded in finding breakthroughs, despite Kamil's pressure and scare tactics. In Selbi's recollection, "The meeting would usually last for five or six hours, and until backs ached, to end up with discussing only one or two points of the set agenda. The rest of the time was spent discussing issues outside the stipulated agenda. . . . Discussions would get so diverse and fruitless to the point that many who attended began to label them as meetings that ended in negative results."[7] Selbi also recollects that, under Kamil, "any proven deliberate delay would expose the responsible to be taken to a court of law."[8] This threat was never carried out. But it does suggest that, even during the Iran-Iraq War, the nuclear weapons program's managers struggled with implementation, while the regime lacked the tools to improve the situation. As frustrations grew, Selbi and Jafar proposed that Selbi chair the review sessions to ensure a more focused and problem-oriented approach.

TWO TRACKS: CENTRIFUGES AND EMIS

After Group 1 (initially focusing on gaseous diffusion, then adopting centrifuges as their main technology) was transferred to Kamil in August 1987, most of the staff left Tuwaitha for the new location in Rashidiya, situated northwest of Baghdad. Upon arrival, Group 1 was renamed the Engineering Design Directorate (EDD) and placed under Obeidi's leadership. Under Kamil's direction, the basic strategies of the EDD and the other departments (Groups 2–4) began to diverge. While the EMIS program remained consistent with Saddam's diktat to adopt an indigenous route, the EDD increasingly relied on foreign assistance despite the increased risks of detection. Kamil also encouraged dropping long-standing investments—he decided to abandon gaseous diffusion, for example—and adopted new avenues if these seemed more promising. In this respect, the pace of this group's work seemed faster than their competitors as new activities were constantly added to the overall portfolio. In other respects, Kamil's management style was not that different from other state elites in the military-industrial complex. Kamil compartmentalized information, preferring to report to Saddam only once major progress had taken place. As Kamil came under increasing criticism from other senior regime figures, including for a series of arguments with Saddam's son Uday, he took care to cast his managerial performance in the most positive light possible.

The transition of Group 1 to Rashidiya was not altogether smooth. The scientists experienced challenges and delays in moving from research and development toward developing industrial-scale production, similar to those experienced previously by their colleagues at Tuwaitha. In the face of such problems, Kamil simply postponed reporting to Saddam. Meanwhile, EDD subgroups discreetly started pursuing alternative technologies, such as centrifuges, with the hope of being able to report some much needed success in the near future.[9]

Shortly after their relocation, the EDD teams at Rashidiya were subsumed into a new ministry. In 1988, the MIMI was formally created (having existed since 1987), and absorbed several agencies, including the MIC. The EDD was then given the status of a MIC directorate and renamed the Engineering Design Centre (EDC). The EDC retained its existing five technical departments and gained additional nontechnical departments supporting them. All departments ultimately answered to Kamil.

This organization, now a ministerial department, was not subject to budgetary restrictions or financial planning. There was not even an annual budget during their first two years. Expenditures, including salaries, were funded by loans from the MIMI. From the spring of 1989, annual financial allocations were made by the Ministry of Finance based on the needs and requirements of the program.[10] Its expenditure increased tenfold during the first year (excluding foreign expenditure and costs of construction shouldered by the MIC). Kamil's group at the EDC did not even have a budget until 1989.[11]

The guiding principle for Kamil's group at Rashidiya was to adopt small projects, purchase equipment and raw materials at the design stage (so they could launch quickly into production if the technology proved feasible), and focus resources on design challenges while outsourcing production and manufacturing to other organizations in the military-industrial complex. This led to a proliferation of projects, reaching a total of more than seventy different working teams in 1989. This was ultimately deemed detrimental to the organization, as it diverted resources from the key challenges.[12] Subsequently, resources were focused more sharply on what was then seen as the main task at hand: to produce centrifuges.

While research and development on EMIS was moving forward at Tuwaitha, the EDC's research on gaseous diffusion languished. The Rashidiya building (originally designed to be a water research centre) was not prepared for research and development activities. The Al Fao General Establishment provided designs for laboratories and workshops. While the main building was redesigned, work on gaseous diffusion slowed down. In other words, Jafar's program was performing better than Kamil's group, which became a problem for Kamil, who also had enemies in Saddam's closest circle, including his most volatile son. Despite having dedicated a portion of the weapons program's resources to this line of research (15 percent of labor and funding since 1982), the group working on gaseous diffusion was not making significant progress toward large-scale production. This led Kamil to rethink his options. The difficulties of producing suitable barriers had been apparent to the leaders of this project for a while. Kamil and his scientists began to explore alternative technologies to produce feed material for EMIS, and began to explore centrifuges as an alternative enrichment technology in competition with EMIS.

Gaseous diffusion had been intended to be a complementary approach for EMIS, producing low-enriched uranium to use as feed material for the separation process instead of natural uranium (a much less efficient and more time-consuming option). If this option was going nowhere, an alternative had to be found. In the spring of 1988 the scientists organized a meeting to assess three alternative options: laser isotope separation, mass diffusion, and chemical enrichment. Laser isotope separation had previously been discarded by the IAEC. Mass diffusion was a relatively new method, and the Iraqis had no available information or strong indications suggesting this could be a workable technology. This option was also discarded, as it seemed at least as challenging as gaseous diffusion. They therefore decided to explore chemical enrichment as a potential alternative.

In 1989 and 1990, teams intensively explored ion exchange chromatography (Redox) and solvent extraction (Chemex), two technologies that separate enriched uranium ions from other compounds.[13] While the chemists were optimistic about taking this research to the production stage, this posed numerous challenges. Many of these would—as per usual—have to be tackled later in the process. In late 1990, the Rashidiya group placed orders for a pilot plant producing equipment for chemical extraction.[14] Those efforts did not progress beyond initial design assessments before the 1991 Gulf War broke out.

As the EDC discreetly turned their attention to the centrifuge option, they realized that Saddam's rule about avoiding sensitive nuclear assistance was becoming an important obstacle to making progress. To perform better than their colleagues had done thus far—Kamil had promised Saddam that the scientists would under his leadership—they ignored Saddam's rule and began to seek help from abroad.

First, teams set out to build and assemble an oil-bearing Beams gas centrifuge, an old design that was described in the literature. In December 1987, the first Beams centrifuge was constructed. But the model did not work.[15] It was clear to the scientists that their immediate challenge was to develop better design analysis, to identify what caused the vibration and rotation causing the breakdown of the centrifuges. But even after attempts to improve the design analysis through tools such as computer simulations, which frustrated engineers at Tuwaitha had advocated for years, troubleshooting often failed to identify and target the underlying problems. Two years later, many of the problems had been solved with the help of two German scientists and the Beams centrifuge eventually reached a speed of 50,000 revolutions per minute. Meanwhile, the EDC explored alternative centrifuge designs based on the advice and designs provided by the two foreign scientists. Some of these proposed designs were constructed and tested. By August 1988 the bulk of resources were dedicated to another design, the magnetic-bearing centrifuge.[16]

Cooperating with the military-industrial complex proved problematic. This was particularly troubling for Kamil, who was in charge of this sector. During the construction of the Beams centrifuge model, for example, Iraqi industry was not capable of producing the components with their existing know-how and machinery. This caused delays and high levels of waste. Similarly, the buildings constructed for development and production of centrifuges had insufficient ventilation, making the environment less clean than it ought to be for such sensitive processes. Faced with these challenges, which did not have any obvious short-term solutions, the centrifuge program sought help from foreign companies.

The EDC's main target was to develop enough centrifuges to produce 10 kilograms of highly enriched uranium (HEU) annually by 1994.[17] To get results, the leaders of the centrifuge program pursued design information and the necessary machinery from abroad.[18] This meant searching for highly sensitive design information and purchasing centrifuge components from foreign suppliers, which entailed considerable risk of detection. A significant portion of the most difficult design and manufacturing work was outsourced to profit-driven Western European suppliers. With their assistance—which included training and advice by German engineers traveling to Iraq—the centrifuge program made progress.

In the second half of 1988 they decided to also explore a magnetic-bearing centrifuge, the so-called Zippe model developed in 1960. Over the summer, Obeidi and colleagues tracked down early designs and detailed blueprints from European and American sources. In July or August 1988, a former employee of the MAN company (a Munich-based subcontractor to the Dutch nuclear fuel company URENCO) provided the Iraqis with several early design drawing for magnetic-bearing centrifuges. This triggered the decision to switch from gas centrifuges to the Zippe model.[19] With this information in hand, they decided to immediately begin purchasing manufacturing equipment and raw material to build thousands of centrifuges, even though the design had not been fully assessed or tested. They were not yet certain that they could make the centrifuge model work.

The decision to move forward with large-scale sensitive procurement at this early stage led to considerable internal discussion. Some warned that this was a high-risk strategy, given that there was not yet even a prototype that could prove the actual performance of this centrifuge model. Nonetheless, the EDC ordered the construction of a development and manufacturing site at Yousifya called Al Furat.[20] Here, a pilot cascade of one thousand centrifuges would be built after the prototype design had been tested experimentally.[21] This site had to be constructed according to very specific criteria, beyond Iraq's existing industrial capabilities, to be suitable for the production of highly sensitive components.

In 1989 another former MAN employee gave the Iraqis further design drawings, technical reports, and specifications for producing and operating centrifuges sourced from URENCO from the 1970s and 1980s.[22] In 1989–1990 the Iraqis also purchased twenty specialized centrifuge rotors from Germany.[23] Some sensitive items, including maraging steel and computer numerically controlled (CNC) machines (necessary to produce key components for centrifuges), were seized at Frankfurt Airport by the authorities.[24] Despite some difficulties, much of the ordered equipment began to arrive in the fall of 1989. Still, construction of the Al Furat plant was delayed. An alternative building at Rashidiya was used as a temporary site, where a small cascade of 120 centrifuges would be set up.

In 1989–90, other states were beginning to suspect that the Iraqi nuclear program had a military dimension, but agencies remained unaware of the actual scope and progress of the Iraqi program.[25] In February 1989 the Central Intelligence Agency (CIA) prepared a report concluding that Iraq had a strong interest in nuclear weapons, citing their procurement activities and suggesting that Iraq could have a nuclear weapon by "the mid-to-late 1990's," perhaps within two years.[26]

At home, the program was also subject to increasing scrutiny. Obeidi, who was the head of the centrifuge program, recalled: "Saddam's security men at Rashidiya began asking technical questions well beyond their understanding. Some of my engineers told me they seemed to be probing for flaws in our program that they could report to their superiors."[27] In other words, Saddam was not prepared to fully trust Kamil or his scientists to provide a realistic appraisal. However, security service officers lacked the technical ability to confirm what the scientists told them.

In early 1990 Obeidi and his colleagues began to work on a prototype magnetic centrifuge. Obeidi was now under so much pressure that he developed a heart condition. Having failed with the initial Beams centrifuge, it was now imperative for him to deliver results. After intensive efforts, a successful test was carried out of a single magnetic centrifuge in the spring of 1990.[28] Looking forward to the production stage, initial projections suggested producing a pilot-scale cascade of one thousand oil centrifuges during the first year and then scaling up to four thousand centrifuges.[29] After the switch to the magnetic Zippe centrifuge model, the centrifuge team focused on setting up an initial pilot cascade of one thousand centrifuges.

As these cascades were being planned and prepared, the EDC began to prepare sites that would produce feed material for the centrifuges (uranium hexafluoride [UF6]) in addition to other preparations for scaling up centrifuge enrichment. As locations were selected to house these new facilities, the EDC was keen to avoid distant locations because this ran the risk of spreading scarce resources too thin. While this made sense from an organizational perspective, it violated the principle of geographical dispersal to make the program less vulnerable.

SCALING UP EMIS

At Tuwaitha, Jafar prepared to scale up EMIS. Despite the inevitable delays in building highly sophisticated infrastructure and machinery, long-standing technical challenges were being resolved. Jafar's group had remained faithful to the principles Saddam had established for the program by relying on indigenous resources and taking secrecy seriously.

Their next step was to build production sites for feed material, EMIS, and weapon development. Beyond Tuwaitha, the sites for production of feed material were given a higher status, and Jazira was made a directorate. Group 4, focusing on weaponization, moved to a new site called Atheer, 50 kilometers west of Baghdad. Several new directorates were established to oversee the development of the industrial-scale buildings required for the next phase of the program.[30]

In late 1987 and early 1988, Group 2 began developing the EMIS production sites. The construction of the Tarmiya plant started in late 1987. The plant would have seventy R120 separators (1,200 millimeters wide) and twenty R60 separators (600 millimeters wide).[31] The uranium feedstock would first enter the R120 separators, where up to 18 percent enriched uranium would be collected. This uranium would then be passed on to the R60 separators, where the enrichment would increase to 93 percent. The Iraqis assessed that, at design value, the R120 separators could collect 55 kilograms of 18 percent enriched uranium per year, while the R60 separators could collect 11 kilograms of 93 percent highly enriched uranium per year.[32]

Between February and September 1990, the first eight R120 separators were installed at Tarmiya. By 1991, another seventeen separators had been manufactured but not yet installed.[33] The process of installing the separators turned out to be riddled with difficulties. The performance of the separators was far below the design capacity (none reached above 20 percent).

As a result, only 685 grams of uranium (4 percent enriched) was produced at Tarmiya.[34] This did not come as a surprise, given that the pilot separators at Tuwaitha had an average performance of 7.2 percent enrichment and only produced 640 grams of enriched material.[35] Between July 1990 and January 1991, three of the seventeen separators of the second R120 series were installed. In total, five R60 separators were constructed. In November preparations started for the installation of the R60 separators, although these efforts were ultimately interrupted the following year.[36] During initial runs the performance was only 16 percent.[37]

As the installation of separators at the production sites was delayed, the production of the feed material was halted. But large-scale production of feed material was not an immediate concern, given the delays in the installation of separators. Production of uranium oxide began at the Jazira plant in 1989, while the production of uranium tetrachloride was halted in 1990, due to the delayed installation at the two EMIS production sites.[38] Meanwhile, a series of research projects explored how to recover uranium more efficiently from EMIS separators and how to purify uranium tetrachloride.[39] In addition, chemists were developing various supporting systems to prepare the sensitive feed material to be fed into the EMIS separators. Despite inevitable delays in scaling up both the production of feed material and separators from the pilot programs, the scientists and engineers were overcoming long-standing challenges.

WEAPONIZATION MOVES FORWARD

Group 4 at Tuwaitha had to juggle several different tasks, including the preparation of HEU into a metal sphere and designing and producing the explosive package and weapons components. Weaponization work required theoretical analyses, chemical work, design, and manufacturing of high explosives and trigger mechanisms. The scientists and engineers at Tuwaitha had to prepare for these tasks using what they could find in the available literature.[40] The program was divided into two subcomponents. Group 4 remained responsible for the overall design, production, and testing of the bomb. A separate unit, the Dhafir Project, focused on detonators and explosive lenses.[41] The theoretical and chemical work was carried out at Tuwaitha, while the components for the bomb and the high explosives were to be developed and tested at Atheer.[42]

Group 4 began by specifying the requirements for weaponization and setting up the organization of this project. This group was led by Said, who had extensive administrative experience from serving as the director of the Nuclear Research Center (NRC). He had committed to completing this project, with no additional resources, within five years.

Initially, Said and his staff did not have any specifications in terms of the size and weight of the bomb. In April 1988, Group 4 started developing the explosive casing for the weapons core. During an initial planning meeting, MIC staff cited the American "Fat Man" design—the bomb used against Nagasaki on 9 August 1945—as a possible template.[43] This was accepted as a working model, at least for the time being, and some even referred to the device as "Fat Man." Prior to the formation of Group 4, the earliest theoretical studies of weaponization (in the al-Hussein project) focused on a gun-type device. By 1988, the Iraqis had selected an alternative design: an implosion fission device with an expected yield of 20 kiloton.[44] This was a more complicated design than the gun-type weapon but would require a smaller quantity of HEU.[45]

Less thought was given to how this weapon would be delivered at this stage. Quite simply, the Iraqis assumed that the weight of the bomb would determine whether it could be delivered by missile or airplane.[46] It was only in December 1990, much later in the process, that Group 4 started serious discussions about coordination with Iraq's missile program.[47] When the scientists engaged with the missile project, they learned that the initial weapons design was too heavy and too large to fit on even the largest missile design. Specifically, the estimated weight of the device (1,200 kilograms) had to be reduced to about 700 kilograms to fit in the missile load. Group 4 modified their design to reduce the total weight to about one ton or less.[48] In addition, engineers were working on the placement of the nuclear warhead inside the missile warhead. Working with an empty warhead, delivered on site in September 1990, they developed several different proposals for how to mount the warhead inside the missile.[49]

Group 4 prepared a very detailed plan with specified deadlines for 962 individual tasks. This plan also gave estimates for how long it would take to achieve these tasks, taking into consideration the limits of their experience and manpower, but for some tasks they did not have the information to be able to estimate the date of completion. The report, finished by August 1988, concluded that it would take three years to design and construct a nuclear weapon. One month later, Group 4 reported to the IAEC president in September 1988 citing late 1992 as their target date.[50] Initially, staff submitted monthly reports for individual projects, which were fed into a rigorous system. Within a few months, this system was found too cumbersome and was replaced by verbal reporting.[51]

The weaponization project was run in a different manner to the hierarchical managerial style of the IAEC. The activities were subject to three sets of internal reviews: periodic group meetings, periodic activities meetings, and open lecture seminars. This produced a more interactive atmosphere and fostered a more concerted approach to overcoming challenges. Between 1988 and 1990 the project was reorganized five times, due to changes in the "understanding of the work and the technical requirements."[52] This entailed moving technical teams, which may have had some disruptive effects.

The Atheer site was developed for the weaponization project at the cost of 1 million Iraqi dinars. This site was designed to "develop, fabricate and cold-test a nuclear weapon and its individual components."[53] Most of the Group 4 departments relocated to Atheer; three departments remained at Tuwaitha. This site was designed to facilitate various tests and construction activities, including experiments with explosive material of up to 1 metric ton. The layout of the site was carefully designed to avoid raising suspicion.[54] There were many delays in the construction of this new site, which took at least a year. These were caused by several factors: late arrival of equipment, poor management, and some design errors. Even in May 1990 the site was not ready, as basic utilities were still not in place, including electricity, water, and suitable air systems.[55]

To make up for lost time, a series of measures were taken in the late spring of 1990. Each task that was lagging behind was now subject to an intensive review. In addition to this internal review process, Kamil frequently inspected Atheer, putting further pressure on those responsible for constructing the laboratories and the assembly hall where the nuclear bomb would be constructed.[56] The design teams started producing items such as metal spheres of various dimensions and experimented with detonator systems. In late 1990 the teams at the Al-Qa-Qaa General Establishment (QGE) carried out CNC machining—a highly precise manufacturing tool—to produce high explosives.[57]

In early 1990 preparations began for developing a test site. Group 4 intended to carry out an underground test, which required finding a suitable location. Several sites in Western Iraq near Najaf and Muthanna were considered from mid-1990 until January 1991.[58] The group envisioned a 300-metre-long vertical tunnel, with a diameter of 90–100 centimeters to accommodate the nuclear bomb.[59] This posed yet another engineering challenge, as Iraq's largest drills were no larger than 30 centimeters in diameter.

First, the QGE assisted with the development of an explosive package for the weapons design. The Dhafir Project carried out tests and development during 1990. Specifically, the scientists and engineers made progress with explosives research through a series of tests, and with the manufacturing of components for the explosive package of the weapon (notably lenses).

Still, their collaboration with Group 4 was not free of tension. The nuclear scientists criticized the Dhafir Project members for their experimental approach, arguing that they had to adopt the more systematic analytic methods of Group 4 in assessing the results of explosive tests. By the second half of 1990, the Dhafir Project and Group 4 improved their cooperation, realizing that this would be necessary to move forward in the program.[60]

The weaponization program attracted international attention to the Iraqi nuclear program, as Humam had anticipated. Two incidents in particular alerted the international community to the possibility of a nuclear weapons program in Iraq, which involved Iraqis getting caught buying sensitive equipment abroad and a loud bang at home.

Since November 1987, the QGE had worked on sophisticated triggering mechanisms for an implosion bomb. By late 1989, the staff placed an order for such mechanisms, so-called krytrons, with a U.S. company. This led to a sting operation at Heathrow in March 1990, where five Iraqis were arrested. The QGE also placed an order for high-speed detonators in 1989, which was intercepted by U.S. authorities, drawing attention to the Iraqi program in the international media. This especially annoyed Jafar and his colleagues, as Group 4 had not requested the QGE staff to place these orders.[61]

In mid-August 1989 a huge explosion rocked the QGE. This was heard in Baghdad and Tuwaitha and led to foreign press speculation, including allegations that the blast could have been a nuclear accident.[62] In fact, the blast was not the first accident at QGE, and an investigation determined it was caused by human error and inadequate safety procedures. The incident damaged several buildings on site, including a nitric acid production building. A British journalist, Farzad Bazoft, who traveled to Iraq to investigate this accident, was apprehended and subsequently executed. The regime was concerned about espionage, particularly because they feared it would enable Israel to launch targeted strikes against the nuclear program. When Saddam discussed the execution of Bazoft with other senior officials, he expressed concern that Bazoft was gathering information that would help Israel and Iran attack the Iraqi nuclear facilities. Saddam elaborated:

> We are dealing with a country that considers the war between us not to be over, with aggressive purposes, and this country applied this concept by attacking the Iraqi nuclear reactor. . . . Therefore, the issue of dealing with a spy for this country or any other foreign country becomes more significant when he is a spy for Israel—a country with which we are still in a state of war. . . . Moreover, we do not have a truce with Israel, so what does this mean? It means that it is going to ease the mission for Israel to hit Iraq, as it was hit in 1981. So, isn't it the right of every citizen in this [weapons] factory, being a target of Israel, to hit him [the spy] and kill him inside the factory? Isn't this his right, as well as the right of neighboring villages or factories, to defend their selves from this [attack] according to the code of human rights?[63]

As these comments suggest, the Iraqis were concerned that Israel would strike again because the Iraqi nuclear weapons program was making progress and the war with Iran had ended. After the 1981 Osirak strike, the main purpose of developing nuclear weapons became to deter another conventional or nuclear attack from Israel, a possibility taken very seriously by the Iraqi regime. The regime feared Israel might launch another conventional attack and even considered a nuclear strike by Israel. In other words, the Iraqi regime feared that Israel would not allow an Arab state to acquire nuclear weapons and believed Tel Aviv was prepared to use force to prevent this from happening. In late 1990, for example, civilian defense plans were prepared in case of a strike by a 20-kiloton nuclear weapon on Baghdad.[64]

Project 22: Plutonium Extraction. While the secret reactor development program, Program 182, did not go beyond initial design studies, the Iraqis did not completely abandon research and development in this vein. Between 1988 and 1990 a group of scientists studied the basic techniques of the plutonium route to a nuclear weapons capability. They fabricated reactor fuel and carried out experiments where they extracted plutonium from irradiated fuel pins.

Between April 1988 and April 1990 scientists carried out three series of experiments in the hot cell laboratory at Tuwaitha using PUREX technology to extract plutonium.[65] The first two series of experiments used fuel pins from the Soviet-supplied IRT-5000 research reactor, while the third used three fuel cassettes produced by the Iraqis. The Iraqis had requested, and received, permission from the International Atomic Energy Agency (IAEA) to exempt the fuel pins from the IRT-5000 reactor from safeguards. As a result, they carried out experiments that helped create know-how and relevant experience. The Iraqis separated a total of 5 grams of plutonium and extracted 11 kilograms of uranium.

Why did the Iraqis launch another line of research with little prospect of contributing to the ongoing nuclear weapons development? This can seen as another new offshoot from the program that was pleasing to industrious scientists but bore little direct relation to the main challenge at hand. While this experiment had little applicability to the enrichment work, these experiences would turn out to be directly applicable to the crash program that emerged after the invasion of Kuwait in the fall of 1990.

Invasion and War, 1990–1991

After the end of the drawn-out war with Iran in August 1988, Iraq was left with a large war machine and a decimated economy. While Iran had suffered greatly during the war, Iraq's Arab neighbors (notably the United Arab Emirates and Kuwait) had produced more oil than their quota stipulated by the Organization of the Petroleum Exporting Countries. This reduced Iraq's oil income and undercut its economic recovery, which was of concern to Saddam for several reasons, including his own political survival. These concerns trumped other considerations, including the progress in the nuclear weapons program.

On 2 August 1990, Iraq's Republican Guard invaded Kuwait. While Saddam had repeatedly expressed dissatisfaction with the Kuwaitis, particularly their refusal to raise the oil price despite Iraq's struggling economy, this act surprised Iraqis and the international community alike. This was a fairly impulsive move; according to Saddam, the decision came only one month before the invasion.[66] Tariq Aziz recalls the Revolutionary Command Council (RCC) discussing the invasion in mid-July 1990, suggesting that most senior officials supported the idea to placate Saddam.[67] But there were exceptions. Aziz warned Saddam that this could lead to war with the United States, while Vice President Izzat Ibrahim al-Doori remained silent.[68] Kamil was in charge of the Republican Guard forces that carried out the invasion, and he joined his forces in Kuwait.[69] The invasion was not particularly well planned. The military intelligence did not have detailed maps of Kuwait, and the generals had to use tourist maps during the invasion.[70]

This was perhaps Saddam's most consequential strategic blunder, because he underestimated how the United States would react to his attempt to annex a neighboring state. Saddam's high-risk move came at a sensitive time in the nuclear weapons program, as the scientists were scaling up toward industrial-scale enrichment. Surprisingly, perhaps, this does not appear to have influenced his decision to invade Kuwait.

The fact that Saddam made a high-risk move at such a sensitive time in the nuclear weapons program underscores a bigger point: for Saddam, the nuclear weapons program was not the main priority. In other words, he never made it "problem number one." His economic concerns did not lead him to pursue nuclear weapons with greater determination; they led him to take a risk that ultimately jeopardized the program.

After the invasion, a series of United Nations (UN) Security Council resolutions imposed sanctions on Iraq and demanded that Iraqi forces withdraw from Kuwait. Having gotten away with numerous transgressions over the past few years, including massive use of chemical weapons against Iranian soldiers and Iraqi civilians, Saddam had emerged as an ally of the West. Iraq had secured support from many important states in the international community—notably the United States—by challenging Iran as a regional power. Now these former supporters were preparing for a militarized confrontation unless Saddam withdrew from Kuwait, while the sanctions imposed on Iraq by the Security Council had broad impact, including halting the arrival of equipment ordered for Group 4 and the PC-3 program.

Faced with these reactions, a new sense of purpose emerged for the nuclear weapons program. Shortly after Kamil's return from Kuwait, on 18 August he traveled to the NRC where he met with al-Saadi, Said, Numan, and Jafar.[71] Kamil told them to initiate a "crash program" to develop a nuclear bomb. This would involve taking irradiated fuel from the safeguarded research reactor and using it as feed material for HEU for a nuclear weapon. This program, they estimated, could produce 26 kilograms of HEU.[72]

Numan countered that this would violate the Nuclear Non-Proliferation Treaty, but Kamil ignored this objection. Jafar offered a technical response that appeared to defuse the tension in the meeting room. According to Numan and Jafar's recollection:[73]

[Kamil] now turned his attention to Jafar and once again laid out his vision of the new programme. Rather than point out obstacles, Jafar initiated a discussion concerning the technical aspects of such a plan, which [Kamil] took to be an implicit acceptance of his order. He immediately demanded the new programme be put into effect without delay and afforded the highest priority. Jafar had little choice other than to acquiesce and with that the meeting was brought to a close.

Jafar and colleagues found this plan dangerous and misguided. First, removing safeguarded material would alert the IAEA that clandestine activities were taking place. The IAEA inspections were scheduled to take place at regular intervals of two to three months, and refusing to admit the inspectors would immediately alert the international community to Iraq's efforts. The scientists realized that this was a mission impossible. They did not believe the crash program could succeed in such a short time frame, given the scope of the challenge.

Refusing Kamil what he wanted was not an option, even though what he asked for could not be done. Similarly, telling him something could not be done was an equally unattractive option from the scientists' point of view. Still, Jafar requested confirmation of the order to be on the safe side, given the high-risk nature of this move.[74] Kamil remained unaware of the numerous obstacles facing the crash program, such as the fact that the centrifuges were still facing challenges, and the weaponization group could not easily accelerate its advances. Neither Kamil nor Saddam realized that the nuclear crash program was doomed to fail up against an unrealistic deadline and a mounting international crisis over the invasion of Kuwait.

THE CRASH PROGRAM

To plan and manage the crash program, a new committee was established under Numan's leadership. This committee prepared a detailed plan for a breakout project from the clandestine nuclear weapons program. The program consisted of four components: extract reactor fuel (Project 601); conversion of HEU into uranium metal (Project 602); further enrichment of the extracted uranium in centrifuges (Project 521C); and weaponization. All subprojects included designing, producing, and operating new capabilities. To support these activities, resources would have to be reallocated from the regular program.[75]

True to form, Kamil set a deadline of six months for the crash program.[76] He allocated more resources to some of the existing projects and additional projects would be established. Constructing new process equipment was a steep challenge, especially in such a short time.

The first challenge was to extract uranium from fuel rods. Project 601 focused on the design, construction, and operation of a small-scale reprocessing plant. During the meeting with Kamil in August, Jafar had committed to completing the extraction within two to three months.[77] Uranium would be extracted from French and Russian fuel cassettes (sixty-eight fresh rods and thirty-eight lightly irradiated fuel pins).[78] The design portion of the uranium extraction project could draw on earlier research and development in the LAMA radiochemical laboratories (Project 22). But new equipment had to be constructed. A new lab in the hot cells at Tuwaitha to extract the uranium from the fuel rods was completed in December 1990. This lab was intended to process between one and two fuel rods per day.[79] When the lab was ready, however, Kamil did not grant permission to begin processing the fuel rods. Three fuel elements were opened a few days before the beginning of the Gulf War in January 1991, but none were processed.[80]

The extracted HEU from Project 601 would be handed over to Project 602, for conversion into metal suitable for the nuclear weapon core.[81] The conversion process would consist of several stages and required developing several fabrication units. The design phase was completed rapidly and construction began at Tuwaitha in late 1990.[82] Installation was scheduled from early 1991 but was delayed, as components were still being constructed in January. At this time the uranium tetrafluoride (UF4) plant was near completion, and a first round of 10 kilograms of uranium oxide was processed. During the Gulf War air campaign, Building 64, which housed these activities, was hit, and the conversion process was halted.[83]

In September 1990, the EDC was asked to set up a centrifuge cascade to convert the UF4 (produced in Project 602) to UF6 through centrifuge enrichment. No decision was made as to what chemical form the UF6 would take.[84] The cascade of forty-nine or fifty centrifuges was to be designed, built, and constructed at Rashidiya using some foreign-supplied components and others that were indigenously constructed.[85] This cascade was expected to include different types of centrifuges, distinguished by their rotors. The installation of the cascade was delayed by two months, pushing back the planned first run to July 1991. While preparations to set up the intended production hall began, no efforts were made to assemble the centrifuges before the cease-fire agreement. One reason is that some of the equipment to manufacture centrifuge components had not been shipped, and transport was halted by the trade embargo put in place after the invasion of Kuwait.[86]

In parallel with these efforts, Group 4 teams began to prepare a new production unit and to design a small explosive device. After the crash program was launched, the weaponization teams focused on developing an initial design to enhance the skills and expertise of their engineers. One of their main technical bottlenecks was the production of explosive lenses for the weapon package. Initially, the Dhafir Project was given two months to produce such lenses. By late October it was clear that this would not be achieved before late December at the earliest. The overall deadline for the program was then adjusted to four months after the production of spherical lenses.[87] During the second week of January 1991, several pressed lenses were tested, and the project could move forward to the production stage.

The scientists also had to find suitable delivery vehicles. They assessed two options: an adaptation of the al-Hussein missile already explored in the weapons program, which could deliver a 1-ton nuclear warhead within a range of 650 kilometers; if this was unsuccessful, they could use an unmodified al-Hussein missile with a range of 300 kilometers.[88]

In the fall of 1990, Iraq received an offer of assistance with its nuclear weapons program from Abdul Qadeer Khan, a prominent figure in the Pakistani centrifuge program who was running a for-profit proliferation network on the side. In early October 1990, he offered Iraq a project design for a nuclear warhead and assistance with purchasing enrichment technology from Western European countries.[89] Khan could provide technology and materials from his extensive network. His stated objective was personal financial gain. This was not the first offer of this nature made to the Iraqi intelligence service. The offer was considered, and scientists were keen to request more information to be able to better assess the offer, but officials were wary.

The centrifuge program had pursued foreign assistance over the past couple of years, and had found that any such proposal required extreme caution. The Khan offer could be a setup by a foreign intelligence service, a ploy by investigative journalists (as the Iraqis had experienced previously), or simply a hoax. Nonetheless, some senior figures believed that it would be sensible to ask to see some of this material in case it could help the program move forward more quickly.[90] The scientists suggested asking for more information to assess the quality of what the Khan network could provide, but the Iraqi intelligence services did not follow up. The internal correspondence on this matter cited the current circumstances—presumably the highly charged international atmosphere—as a reason not to meet with Khan.[91] While we cannot know if the Iraqis would have taken up Khan's offer if their circumstances had been different, it is clear that the centrifuge program had benefited greatly from similarly sensitive assistance from German scientists.

In November 1990 Kamil brought Jafar to the Radhwaniyah Palace to brief Saddam on the progress of the crash program. Kamil told Saddam that the project was making good progress and that a nuclear weapon could be produced within months. However, Jafar left the meeting with the impression that the president was preoccupied and not particularly impressed by Kamil's message.[92]

On 16 January 1991, the U.S.-led alliance began the Gulf War campaign to drive Iraqi forces from Kuwait. Bombing raids targeted several sites associated with Iraq's nonconventional weapons programs, including the nuclear weapons program. After Iraq accepted UN Security Council Resolution 687 (the so-called cease-fire resolution) on 6 April 1991, all crash program efforts were halted.[93] The nuclear weapons program was dissolved, but the IAEO remained intact. After the bombing campaigns of 1991, Jafar and his colleagues focused on other tasks, such as rebuilding the Iraqi power grid. Between 1991 and 1998, UN inspectors unraveled the story of Iraq's past weapons of mass destruction programs and destroyed any remaining components and infrastructure.

DISTANCE FROM THE NUCLEAR WEAPONS THRESHOLD

How far were the Iraqis from the nuclear weapons threshold when they were attacked in January 1991? The consensus view, supported by the 1997 assessment of the IAEA, is that Iraq was at, or close to, the nuclear weapons threshold.[94] Furthermore, the IAEA assessed that the crash program could have reduced Iraq's distance from the weapons threshold by two years.[95] For the IAEA, this assessment was deeply troubling, as the weapons program had been carried out clandestinely in a declared facility subject to routine inspections within a member state.

To assess how far Iraq was from a nuclear weapons capability in 1991 we must distinguish between producing a single crude device (the aim of the crash program) and producing an arsenal of several weapons (the aim of the regular nuclear weapons program). Let us begin by comparing estimates by Iraqis, scientists and managers, and foreign governments before and after the 1991 Gulf War. While these actors may have different views on the definition of "threshold" and how far the Iraqis were from it, they concur that the program could have produced a nuclear weapons option during the 1990s.

When Saddam invaded Kuwait, the regular weapons program was in the process of scaling up production of fissile material. The installation of EMIS separators at Tarmiya had been delayed. Undoubtedly, this process would have encountered several engineering challenges over the next few months. Meanwhile, the centrifuge program at Rashidiya was making progress. Their initial target was to produce 10 kilograms of HEU per annum by 1994.[96] This target proved overly optimistic; Iraqi scientists later estimated that Iraq would have been able to set up the pilot-scale one thousand-centrifuge cascade around 1997 or 1998.[97]

The weaponization project was behind schedule due to the delayed construction of the main facilities but was moving forward. The infrastructure, including the construction of sites for hot and cold tests, was under way. Jafar later estimated that production and cold testing of a nuclear weapon could have started in 1993.[98] Kamil, as per usual, had a different deadline in mind. In late 1995, a senior Iraqi official wrote to Saddam that Kamil had said that he believed a nuclear weapons option was between eight and twelve months away in 1991.[99]

The crash program was lagging behind the unrealistic six-month deadline imposed by Kamil. This is not surprising, given Kamil's poor understanding of the technical challenges facing this effort, and the fact that this program added new and time-consuming demands, such as preparation of process equipment and weapon components, on top of long-standing challenges. In late 1990, Obeidi's team calculated that a fifty-centrifuge cascade, once operational, could process enough HEU (70 percent enriched) for a weapon within a few months.[100] In light of delays in individual projects, the crash program's deadline was adjusted to July 1991. Looking back later, Jafar indicated that the crash program could have succeeded within one to two years, in other words by about mid-1992.[101] Of course, further delays would have incurred, notably if the Iraqis wanted to deliver the weapon on their missiles.

Several Iraqi scientists concur that a realistic completion date for the regular nuclear weapons program could have been the mid-to-late 1990s. But it is not at all clear that the timelines imagined by the leadership were consistent with the scientists' timelines. While we know little about Saddam's perspectives on this, these are likely to have been informed by Kamil. Kamil's assessment was far more optimistic than those of the scientists and may have shaped the expectations of the senior tier of the Iraqi leadership as to the nuclear weapons threshold.

What were the assessments of other states before the 1991 Gulf War? In early 1991, the international community was largely oblivious to the size and scope of Iraq's nuclear weapons program. Before the Gulf War, British intelligence assessed that Iraq was at least a decade away from the nuclear weapons threshold.[102] In 1989, the CIA assessed that Iraqi the program could succeed in the mid-1990s, possibly even before.

When other states learned about the scope and achievements of the Iraqi weapons program after the 1991 Gulf War, they revised their earlier assessments. In late 1992, the British Ministry of Defence acknowledged to UN officials that Iraq had been much closer to being able to produce a nuclear warhead than they had expected.[103] At the same time, French experts assessed that the Iraq program had been about two years away from this threshold.[104] While there were varying estimates of the exact timelines, in light of this new information there was a broad consensus that Iraq was not far away from a major breakthrough in 1990–1991. New evidence presented in this chapter suggesting that added delays were likely to incur does not undermine the long-standing judgment that the Iraqi program was well on its way toward a nuclear weapons capability.

In retrospect, Saddam's invasion of Kuwait prevented Iraq's acquisition of a nuclear weapons capability. That was Kamil's conclusion in 1995, and this view was shared by other senior figures of the program, including Jafar, many years later. While this statement was undoubtedly self-serving from Kamil's point of view, his basic assessment appears to have been essentially correct.

More recently, however, Jacques Hymans has argued that the Iraqis would never have succeeded: "Even if the Gulf War had not intervened the Iraqi nuclear weapons project would probably have been no more successful in the 1990s than it had been in the 1980s. Indeed, it would likely have run definitively into the ditch."[105] As this and the foregoing chapters in this book have suggested, the weight of the evidence does not support this interpretation.

The reorganization and changing management of the Iraqi nuclear weapons program in the late 1980s brought the program back on track, but the leadership still lacked a clear picture of the program's progress and likely timelines. These changes were initiated by scientists who persuaded the leaders of the program that a different organization was necessary. They were proven right, as the EMIS program made important breakthroughs after the 1987 reorganization. When the senior level of the regime intervened after the leaders of the nuclear program quarreled with the powerful MIC, the program made increasingly rapid progress.

Ultimately, however, their efforts were in vain. Despite a series of long-awaited breakthroughs toward the end of the decade, Saddam was distracted or simply lost interest. He remained distant from the program, and his high-risk move against Kuwait in August 1990 resulted in its interruption and dismantlement.

But while the Iraqi regime was able to regain control over the program, Saddam still struggled to get a clear sense of how well the scientists were performing, and he appears to have been unaware that Kamil broke his rules for the program. The results of the intervention were mixed, but overall the program made important advances with regard to both EMIS and centrifuges between 1988 and August 1990. Kamil's annexation raised the risks of detection and encouraged scientists to drop approaches that were not yielding results. He was also able to mobilize the resources of the vast MIMI, which assisted the nuclear weapons program with its implementation as it approached the production stage. Furthermore, the infusion of foreign assistance into a more efficient organization gave the centrifuge program a welcome boost.

On the other hand, Kamil did not always understand the consequences of his decisions. He lacked technical know-how, which the scientists occasionally exploited by obscuring their reports and recommendations in overly technical language. When they received the order to begin the crash program, the scientists did not tell him that it would be impossible to succeed within the given deadline. As Iraq stood on the precipice of the 1991 Gulf War, Kamil and Saddam may have believed that a nuclear weapon was within reach.

PART II. LIBYA

CHAPTER 5

Searching for Uranium in Libya, 1951–1973

While the outcome of Libya's nuclear weapons program is well known, the origins and operational details of this program remain murky. Libya disclosed very little about the program after it was dismantled in late 2003, and less has emerged since. So little has been known that scholars have concluded that little can be said about Libya's nuclear program except that those responsible did not seem to know what they were doing.[1]

This chapter, which draws extensively on International Atomic Energy Agency (IAEA) archival sources that have not previously been available to scholars, presents the emergence of nuclear research and development in Libya against the backdrop of an unusually underdeveloped state. The chapter sheds new light on the drivers and constraints facing the Libyan nuclear project and reveals that the few facts and assumptions that have shaped our understanding of this program are misleading. For example, the Libyan nuclear program began as early as 1970, not in 1973 as Libya later declared. Furthermore, contrary to the conventional wisdom, the Gaddafi regime had very little control over the program, particularly after the 1973 Cultural Revolution eroded Libya's weak state institutions. Foreign scientists and advisers led this program with minimal input from the Libyan state, which lacked the capacity to plan and implement technical projects. Gaddafi remained distant and noncommittal.

To make sense of the Libyan program, which seemed to stumble from one costly blunder to another, we must first understand its highly unusual environment. The Libyan state during this period was a case of extremes: a move from poverty and underdevelopment to rapid economic growth, followed by a revolution that sought to dismantle the state. After Gaddafi seized power in 1969, state institutions were dismantled and rendered powerless. When bureaucracies and academics became targets of the Cultural Revolution, even a privileged project such as the nuclear program struggled to develop basic institutional capacities. While scientists made sound plans, they lacked the institutional resources to fulfill them.

Libya's nuclear program was characterized by ample funding and virtually no planning. The Libyans not only sought technology from other states, they also outsourced much of the planning and operations to foreigners. But Libya's nuclear establishment, modeled on Western nuclear organizations, failed to assume these tasks even after the emergence of a nuclear energy program in 1970. As a result, Libya struggled to establish a viable research program. This pattern persisted over the next three decades, even as the project attempted to launch a nuclear energy program and pursued nuclear weapons. The mismatch between the regime's plans and the program's performance deepened as the program drifted toward exploring a weapons option.

This chapter begins by tracking the emergence of the Libyan state during the 1950s and 1960s and tracing early Libyan interest in uranium exploration during the final days of the monarchy. Here, I explore Libya's extreme underdevelopment and how this shaped the state's state institutions prior to Gaddafi's coup, as well as the virtual absence of educated elites and industrial resources. Then, I investigate the impact of Gaddafi's 1969 coup on the state's capacity to plan and implement a nuclear program. Against this background, subsequent chapters trace the curious trajectory of the Libyan nuclear program over the next three decades to its end in 2003.

State of Sand

When the United Libyan Kingdom became an independent country on 24 December 1951, it was perhaps the poorest state in the world. The desert country had been ravaged by the brutal colonial rule of Italy and the battles of the Second World War. Libya's population of less than one million, scattered over the fifth-largest country in Africa, shared few formative experiences other than displacement and poverty. Unlike many other postcolonial states, Libya did not inherit an educated elite or class of bureaucrats.[2] With no industry, an illiterate population, and a meager 2 percent of its land suitable for agriculture, Libya was unlikely to be able to maintain its gross domestic product, already one of the lowest in the Middle East.

Given its lack of natural resources, development experts looked to Libya's population as the country's main asset.[3] Libya was an attractive target for foreign aid because, with a small population, smaller interventions could have a bigger impact.[4] At the same time, Libya's most fundamental challenges revolved around its limited human resources. A 1948 study had noted some of the development challenges facing the future Libyan state: a 94 percent illiteracy rate; fewer than twenty Libyan college graduates; an annual income of just £15 per capita; a 40 percent infant mortality rate; and a population suffering from a host of preventable diseases.[5] More than 80 percent of the labor force worked in agriculture.[6]

Adrian Pelt, a Dutch diplomat appointed United Nations (UN) high commissioner for Libya in 1949, oversaw the preparation of Libya's constitution. He described Libya as being in "the greatest need of help."[7] Libya did not have the resources to solve its challenges alone. In his first official report, Pelt wrote that the new state would need "as much financial and technical assistance as the United Nations can supply. . . . It is obvious that the country requires very substantial outside assistance in order to maintain even its present standards, and yet more for development in the economic and social fields." If these needs were not met, he warned, this could "jeopardise the very existence of the new State."[8]

Notwithstanding these challenges, Pelt handed over power to Libya's new monarch on 24 December 1951. King Idris al-Senussi had limited ambitions for the new state. His rule was supported by alliances with key tribal leaders and with foreign powers, notably Great Britain and the United States.[9] His foreign policy, seen as moderate by Western powers, was not favored by the Libyan public. There was widespread popular support for the Free Officers Movement led by Gamal Abdel Nasser, which had overthrown the British-friendly Egyptian monarch in 1952, and for the growing Baath movement that espoused Arab unity and socialism.[10] Idris did not favor a strong state or military. He required, for example, that Libya's small military seek his approval before carrying out any field exercises.[11] His reservations may have arisen after the Free Officers Movement seized power in Egypt, and to prevent the military from emerging as an independent political force he split the armed forces, while mobilizing tribal ties to secure loyalty.[12]

Idris was reluctant to support the development of a central state apparatus with strong institutions. Libya was a federation of three provinces—Cyrenaica, Fezzan, and Tripolitania—each of which comprised a number of municipalities. The provincial governments were, generally speaking, better equipped, in terms of civil servants and administration, than the central state apparatus.[13] The central government in Tripoli, headed at independence by Prime Minister Mohammed Montasser, provided grants to the provinces, which also received financial and military aid directly from foreign countries. Building central state institutions was a heavy economic burden. For example, setting up an army of just one thousand, in a country of about one million people, was beyond the new state's financial means.[14] The minimal state apparatus lacked the resources to extract taxes or to build a centralized system of government.

Underdeveloped institutionally, the young state also lacked a healthy civil society. After the first election in February 1952, the opposition coalition was banned.[15] Power increasingly rested with powerful families in eastern Libya. Observers decried the absence of political order at the national level, pointing out that Libya was a "non-party state."[16] The business of running the new state was largely in the hands of a handful of oligarchical families while the average person remained disenfranchised.[17] While the population at large harbored support for Arab nationalist movements—and for Egyptian leader Nasser, in particular—this was manifested in single-issue protests, and street demonstrations were met with repression. In 1968, for example, more than one hundred citizens were detained preventively. In the southwestern province of Fezzan, a young Muammar Gaddafi was expelled from school for organizing a demonstration to protest Syria's withdrawal from the United Arab Republic.[18] He nevertheless was later able to join Libya's military, and it was there in the mid-1960s that Gaddafi and a group of his military academy friends began to plot a coup.[19]

SCIENCE, INDUSTRY, AND EDUCATION

Libya was an unlikely candidate for nuclear technology. The scale of its underdevelopment was extreme, even by comparison with other developing states. There was no indigenous industry to speak of, and the main exports—prior to the discovery of oil fields—were esparto grass (used for making goods such as paper and cords) and scrap metal from the battlefields of the Second World War. Development experts characterized Libya as "a prototype of poor country . . . where there are no sources of power and no mineral resources, where agricultural expansion is severely limited by climatic conditions . . . where there is no skilled labour supply and no indigenous entrepreneurship. . . . Libya is at the bottom of the range in income and resources and so provides a reference point for comparison with all other countries."[20]

Against this backdrop, Libya's first development plan (1963–1968) focused on education. There was little to build on. During the Italian colonial era, education and training for Libyans had largely been neglected. There were only three secondary schools for Libyans in 1939, focused on religious studies or crafts; seven secondary schools were reserved for Italian children.[21] Modern subjects such as mathematics were taught in Italian, a language that the majority of the Libyan population did not speak.[22] During the Second World War, the education system had largely shut down. After the Allied defeat of Italy in 1943, the situation did not improve, and a local petition criticizing the lack of primary education and the continued exclusion of Libyans from public institutions was delivered to the British chief administrator of Tripoli and Cyrenaica.[23]

Libya continued to lag behind in higher education too, as well as in the fields of science and technology. In late 1955, Libya's first university was founded in Benghazi, in eastern Cyrenaica, with thirty-one students. The faculty was largely foreign, mostly from Egypt.[24] Nasser had agreed to provide four lecturers for the new Libyan University for its first four years.[25] About a decade later, two colleges were established in 1966 and 1967 in

Tripoli; they later merged as the new University of Tripoli and were renamed the Colleges of Engineering and Education.[26] Notwithstanding these initiatives, the state did not make technical education a priority. Science and technology were not seen as important for Libya's economy or development; instead, the main purpose of the colleges was to train civil servants and administrators. Between 1957 and 1967–1968, the number of enrollments fell, possibly reflecting an effort to curtail or prevent political protest movements.[27] Contemporary observers believed that "the two sources of upheaval and revolution in the political life of the Middle East, the students and the army, have remained calm in Libya."[28] This would soon change.

With a largely unskilled labor force and without energy resources—no hydropower, no coal and, at that point, no known oil fields—Libya's industrial potential was almost nonexistent.[29] Postwar migration to the newly created state of Israel, which left only seven thousand Libyan Jews in the country, decimated the small-scale entrepreneurial sector of the economy.[30] Italians owned the larger enterprises and banks. Most foreign observers assumed, like Pelt, that the way to stimulate economic development would be through foreign aid and technical assistance. But the shortage of natural and human resources made it impossible to launch larger development projects.[31] There were diverging views among Libyan leaders as to how they could spur economic development, but it clearly would require extensive foreign assistance with training, financial aid, and basic state-building. Libya lacked the ability to collect information, make plans, or see that they were implemented.

Energy—both its production and transmission—was an early priority. An immediate challenge was to improve the power supply to the capital as a first step toward creation of a national grid. The cost of electricity was very high. The Italian-built electrical power plant in Tripoli was defective and required subsidies; between 1956 and 1958, the new government spent over $4 million on repairs.[32] The United States gave the government a loan for a new electrical power station, which became operational on 24 December 1961.[33]

The issue of nuclear weapons first emerged in Libyan public debate in the early 1960s, in connection with the lease of the Wheelus Air Base outside Tripoli to the United States.[34] This arrangement was controversial domestically, with the population roused by Nasser's pan-Arab rhetoric and by Baath socialism.[35] Fears that the United States could use this air base to support Israel against hostile Arab neighbors, perhaps even with nuclear weapons, caused stormy discussions and threats by Idris of abdication. To calm critics in the press and in the parliament, the Libyan prime minister asked the U.S. ambassador in June 1960 for assurances that nuclear weapons would not be stored at Wheelus.[36] In response, the United States said that such weapons were not stored on the base.[37] Still, rumors circulated in Tripoli that the U.S. bases were preparing to store nuclear and hydrogen bombs and were constructing rocket-launching pads.[38] After the 1967 Six-Day War, suspicions that Wheelus had been used to support the Israeli war effort once again made the base a sensitive issue between Libya and the United States.

OIL AND URANIUM

The discovery of large oil deposits in Libya in the mid-1950s transformed the economy and the state. After extensive surveys for petroleum and mineral resources, the first oil fields were being commercially exploited in late 1961. As an array of foreign companies arrived, it became necessary to develop institutional resources at the national level to facilitate these projects and, following the large influx of petrodollars, to build an oil economy.

Whereas newly independent Libya had been described as an extreme example of an impoverished country, its economic growth during the 1960s was extraordinary.[39] The gross national product per capita increased by 42 percent from 1966 to 1967, and income per capita grew from $40 at independence to $1,018 in 1967.[40] These newfound riches suggested that Libya's poverty and underdevelopment could soon be history. This extraordinary and unpredictable growth also made large-scale planning a challenge, notably with regard to building up industry.[41] Libya's lack of skilled manpower, an obstacle to development prior to the discovery of oil, continued to hinder development even as Libya experienced rapid economic growth. While skilled labor could be imported from other countries, development also required sound planning and implementation at the national level. Libya's institutions could not keep up. In 1963, therefore, Idris abolished the federal system and sought to streamline the central state apparatus.[42]

The scope of these challenges was apparent in the 1963–1968 development plan and its implementation.[43] The plan had emphasized infrastructure projects to develop the road network, energy supplies, and communication. But industry received only 4 percent of the allocations. In 1961 a Ministry of Industry had been set up to oversee state-owned production and to "plan the development of private and nationalised industries."[44] This was a top-down effort on a modest scale and was not seen as a significant priority at the time. By 1969, there were only 189 industrial enterprises in the country, of which only a small minority were Libyan-owned.[45]

Given this context, nuclear science and technology were not obvious priorities for the monarchial government. No measures were taken to explore nuclear science; physics was not taught at the university. Nonetheless, the kingdom joined the IAEA in 1963, and it signed the Nuclear Non-Proliferation Treaty in 1968 as one of several states that had neither ongoing research and development in the nuclear field nor plans to carry out such activities.

In January 1969, the Ministry of Industry received a request from the Oceanic Exploration Company of Denver, Colorado, for exclusive prospecting rights for uranium, thorium, and other radioactive materials.[46] This alerted the Libyan government to the possibility of becoming an exporter in the lucrative uranium market. The company wrote to the ministry again on 14 April, narrowing down their preferred exploration to two areas: Jabal Ben Ghenemeh near the border with Chad; and Jabal al Awaynat near the border with Sudan.[47] In June 1969, Abdul Alim Shaari, the Libyan minister of industry—who would play a central role in the development of Libyan industry over the next decades—traveled to the IAEA in Vienna asking for assistance with either setting up a Libyan uranium-prospecting project or assessing the offer from the U.S. company. He followed up with a formal request for IAEA assistance on 16 June.[48] The assistant undersecretary of state, Ahmed al-Attrash, then requested IAEA assistance with developing a uranium-prospecting program on 19 August 1969.[49] The agency was prepared to provide consultants to help with prospecting carried out either indigenously or by the Oceanic Exploration Company.

The kingdom's first interest in nuclear material was driven by a desire to exploit the commercial potential of uranium, a raw material for nuclear energy and nuclear weapons. Refining this raw material to suitable feed material for enrichment requires the development of sophisticated infrastructure, but there were no indications that the Libyan government intended to set up such capabilities at this stage. Natural uranium could be exported to states that were able to refine this material indigenously. The global uranium market was lucrative, with relatively few suppliers. Uranium was one of several raw materials whose commercial potential appealed to the Ministry of Industry. It does not appear that the option of a nuclear weapons program was considered at this stage, although it is possible that this was part of the discussion behind closed doors.

DEVELOPMENT AND DEFENSE

Libya's first development plan allocated only 5 percent of the country's budget to defense, roughly half the rate typical for most Arab states at the time.[50] The army was small and Libya's borders were difficult to defend—in 1968, there was one Libyan soldier per 100 square miles.[51] The police force outnumbered the armed forces because Idris was more concerned about domestic challenges to his rule than foreign threats. Nonetheless, Libya had to develop national defenses. In 1966–1967, the government established a navy and an air force, and considered purchasing missiles. In 1967 a new prime minister, Abdul Hamid Bakkush, increased the armed forces.[52] Bakkush, a thirty-two-year-old technocrat from the petroleum sector, developed a more ambitious national program based on socialist and nationalist ideas and brought a new young cadre of skilled professionals into the state administration and planning departments. He was also a driving force behind negotiations with Britain to obtain missiles for Libya's armed forces.[53] Within a year, however, conservative forces around the king deemed Bakkush too progressive and replaced him with Wannis Gaddafi (no relation to Muammar Gaddafi).[54]

133

To the Libyan government, a missile system appealed for several reasons. First, the armed forces were kept small to prevent the military from becoming an independent political actor. Political considerations aside, the severe shortages of skilled manpower and the need to find candidates for the civil service also contributed to government reluctance to prioritize expansion of the armed forces.[55] Given the combination of Libya's geography and its small population, a missile system seemed to be an ideal solution: it could be purchased from abroad, complete with the training of technicians, and it required few operators. A mobile system was particularly useful for a country with such vast borders. This idea had taken hold by late 1966, and the Six-Day War enhanced the desire for a highly mobile defense system.[56] While it was not really apparent who Libya's enemies were—relations with neighboring states were good—Tripoli's defense plans were based on technical fixes that would, they hoped, compensate for their limited human and infrastructural capabilities.

Conveniently, a package comprising radar, communications, missiles, and aircraft could be purchased from Great Britain.[57] One of Prime Minister Bakkush's achievements during his short tenure was to finalize the contract for purchasing a missile system from Great Britain. This deal, announced in May 1968, included the purchase of a complete missile air defense system, making it more expensive than any previous British contract in this area.[58] The package included Rapier and Thunderbird missiles, radar systems, and training courses for the Libyan army. The large missile system contract was the first in a series of acquisitions: Libya needed aircraft for its new air force, and possibly also tanks, as it remodeled its military along more modern lines.[59]

By the late 1960s, a number of plots against the monarchy were under way. Dissident groups believed that a coup was inevitable; the only real question was when it would happen. One such group included Muammar Gaddafi and the seventh graduating class from the Military Academy.[60] Gaddafi and his officer comrades began to prepare a coup d'état in August 1968 when they were assembled at the Garrison Command Camp in Tripoli. They opted to make their move in early September 1969 when, they believed, they were about to be apprehended by the internal security forces.[61]

1 September 1969: Gaddafi Seizes Power

On 1 September 1969, at 6:30 a.m., a representative of the self-proclaimed Revolutionary Command Council (RCC) announced a coup from a radio station in Benghazi. His brief statement declared that Libya would now be known as the Libyan Arab Republic and that the "hour of work has come."[62] The monarch's strategy for retaining power—relying on tribal loyalties and a weak army divided into rival factions—had failed. The Libyan state was seized by a small group that did not even have to resort to violence.

Gaddafi and his officer colleagues did not have a plan or clear sense of what would come next. For more than a week after the coup, the RCC members refused to reveal their identities. They did not initially announce any kind of political program, beyond reassuring foreign oil companies that their contracts would be respected. Egypt's Nasser soon intervened, arguing that unless the individuals leading the coup stepped forward they risked losing power. Gaddafi emerged as the face of the new government, and chairman of the RCC, but it took four months after the September coup before the membership of his Council of Ministers was made public.[63] The first Council of Ministers of the Libyan Arab Republic did not include any of the Free Officers who had brought Gaddafi to power.[64] This was the first indication that the organs of the state would be kept remote from the center of real power.

To create a "new society," the RCC set out to dismantle the administrative structures of the state.[65] A series of trials were held by new People's Courts and military tribunals to purge the state of remnants of the former regime, such as former Prime Ministers Bakkush and al-Muntasir (the latter died in prison within a year), leading to the detention of key figures of the small tier of Libyan technocrats. Those who escaped this purge, such as the former minister of industry Shaari, and others who replaced the purged officials, had to be extremely cautious to avoid accusations of working against the revolution. To fill senior government posts, the new regime proceeded in an apparently haphazard manner. Astonishingly, Gaddafi asked a group of students for recommendations—an indication of how little importance he placed on the formal structures of the state.[66] He would rely instead on his closest co-conspirators, most notably his deputy, Abdessalam Jalloud. With Gaddafi at the helm, the twelve men of the RCC, whose numbers would soon decline following internal tensions, would be the supreme decision-making body, accountable to no one.

If the RCC's initial reticence suggested a lack of preparation for power, its attempts to shore up support demonstrated how unprepared its members were to govern. The military had emerged as the most important source of political power in Libya, which also made it a crucial arena for securing support and removing potential opposition. Initially only sixty to eighty officers formed the core of the RCC's support in the army. The majority of the officers were more inclined toward pan-Arab nationalism and Baathist ideology, and many had been trained in Baghdad. To placate them, Gaddafi bankrolled a conventional military buildup during the 1970s. However, he also wanted to prevent the army from becoming a powerful actor inside the state and closed the Ministry of Defense shortly after the coup.

The RCC isolated itself from the formal structures of government.[67] The council governed from seclusion at the Aziziya base in central Tripoli, where Gaddafi also took up residence. This seclusion, combined with purges and a general atmosphere of fear, brought the operation of public institutions to a halt during this period. During the 1970s the distance between weak state institutions and the real center of decision making—at first the RCC but increasingly Gaddafi himself and a small circle of individuals around him—would increase further.

At this stage, Libya appeared to adopt the state-centered model of governance seen in other Arab republics, notably Egypt. However, real decision-making power lay with the RCC. To secure their fragile hold on power, they sought to remove alternative structures of authority and influence, including, at this early stage, tribal and religious leaders, whose authority they saw as a potential challenge. Coupled with their initial purge of former officials, the RCC put students and intellectuals on trial in the People's Courts. During the 1970s, the persecution of individuals suspected of opposing the regime would intensify. Over the next decades, the Gaddafi regime prevented the formation of alternative power centers inside the bureaucracy "through an intricate mix of ideology, the constant reshuffling of personnel, the dissolving of ministries, the threat of further decentralizing the country's bureaucratic system, and the creation of new bureaucratic structures when the old developed a potential to be politicized."[68]

It was unclear what the new Libyan republic would become. The RCC did not issue edicts specifying its program. Gaddafi gave many speeches suggesting that he intended to recast the Libyan state and society, but did not set out a program for such a transformation. His deputy Jalloud said that the RCC had to develop a program for radical change "to convince the people and the world at large that it was not a movement aiming only at seizure of power. This was the way army leaders could prove that they had led not a military coup d'état but a revolution."[69] Their premise was the malleable concept of "people power," which would take precedence in Libya over state or other organizations such as unions or political parties. The RCC would tap people power directly, without any intermediate state structures, as such structures were said to "corrupt" the revolution. Gaddafi declared that bureaucracy was incompatible with revolution: "The age of dealing with the problems which disturb the classes of the toiling masses by means of counterfeit promises from air-conditioned offices has now irrevocably ended."[70]

The remaining state institutions did not, however, join the revolution voluntarily. For example, civilian judges would on occasion acquit students and intellectuals accused of working against the revolution.[71] Widespread popular reluctance to embrace the revolution led to the RCC experiencing increasing frustration with the model of government seen in Egypt.[72] Gaddafi, frustrated with the lack of progress of the revolution, blamed the "pecuniary lust . . . rooted in the hearts of officials."[73] To remove this obstacle, he argued, people power had to be mobilized against those "who have formed a barrier between the revolution and the masses . . . [against] this bourgeois class, the bureaucrats. . . . The masses must destroy bureaucracy and destroy barriers."[74]

The new regime's foreign policy ambitions were vague but radical. Gaddafi wanted to reduce the influence of former colonial states such as Italy,

France, and Britain in the Middle East and North Africa. Israel was denounced as the main example of European postcolonial influences at work in the Middle East. The Libyan regime adopted a confrontational set of policies, including support for various terrorist organizations, which it would pursue primarily by oil wealth, through funding proxy actors pursuing goals that the Libyans deemed consistent with their own radical principles, rather than engaging in direct military confrontations with other states.

Despite its fiery rhetoric, Libya was not in a position to pose a military challenge to her neighbors, let alone the Israeli armed forces. Even developing a military that would be capable of defending the long Libyan borders posed a great challenge. According to Mohamed Ennami, who would emerge as a senior figure in the Libyan nuclear establishment during the 1980s, national security was "the number one priority [after the 1969 revolution]. . . . Libya started rebuilding its armed forces, buying military equipment from all over the world, [as well as] establishing new educational and industrial institutions (schools, universities, training centers, research and development units, hospitals, farming and construction industries, etc)."[75]

But Gaddafi's initial defense policy was strongly influenced by his concern to secure a loyal military. Expenditure on military hardware surged to 30 percent of the budget after the 1969 coup.[76] The new regime's approach mirrored that of the monarchy as it purchased sophisticated military equipment and technology from abroad. A strong air force seemed to address Gaddafi's basic dilemma, so purchasing airplanes was also a priority for the regime. In January 1970, Libya purchased Mirage jets from France with the tacit acceptance of the United States. In 1974 the Libyan regime signed an agreement with the Soviet Union to supply MIG-23 and TU-22 aircraft, SCUD-B missiles, and surface-to-air missiles.[77]

After seizing power, the RCC prepared to "launch a frontal attack" on the oil industry, which was dominated by foreign companies, to ensure greater revenues for the state and increase decision-making power for the Libyan oil organization.[78] The regime renegotiated the oil price and terms of operation directly with the companies operating in the country and managed to raise the price—and thus their own income—by 35 percent. Then, in 1971–1973, Libya nationalized the Sarir oil field that had belonged to British Petroleum and the U.S. Bunker Hunt Oil Company and secured a 51 percent participation share in the management and property of the foreign oil companies, while other Organization of the Petroleum Exporting Countries (OPEC) members only asked for 20 percent. Equipped with much stronger influence over prices and sales than several Gulf oil exporters, Libya reaped great benefits from the OPEC crisis after the Yom Kippur War in October 1973.

From 1973, Libya's oil-fueled economic boom enabled a tremendous conventional buildup. By the late 1980s, Libya would become one of the main importers of military equipment in the Arab world.[79] The Gaddafi regime purchased much advanced equipment without ensuring that it suited the needs or capabilities of the armed forces and often without provision for training the armed forces to use what had been purchased.[80] As a result, the Libyan military's performance, as later chapters will show, was often abysmal even against far less equipped adversaries.

Supplying the military with more advanced equipment did not resolve concerns about political challenges from the armed forces. For example, regime officials were concerned that airplanes could be hijacked.[81] Gaddafi's solution was to weaken the armed forces as an organization; he introduced "revolutionary" actors into their ranks and undermined formal lines of authority. Gaddafi in this way deprived the armed forces "of the authority they require to operate effectively. Strong institutions were "anathema to [Gaddafi's] demand for total dominance. . . . His dominance and security values . . . create[d] much . . . ambivalence and apparent unpredictability in [his] behaviour toward Libya's political institutions."[82]

SEEKING NUCLEAR OPTIONS

Despite the general slowdown of the Libyan state apparatus after the coup, the new regime immediately started exploring several options for acquiring nuclear weapons. Some of these efforts are well known: Gaddafi's henchmen contacted other nuclear weapons states for help in acquiring nuclear weapons and also requested nuclear assistance from non-nuclear weapons states. At the same time, new sources show, the Ministry of Industry began to explore options for a nuclear energy program with the assistance of the IAEA in December 1970.

Why did the Libyan regime begin to explore these options when they were barely capable of running the country? Looking back at these efforts, a senior figure in Libya's nuclear program described how "falling behind in areas of education, health, technology and services, in addition to the increasing gap . . . especially in industrial-technological productivity and services . . . [contributed] to feelings of insecurity."[83] Thus Libya's early interest in nuclear technology was shaped by its comparative underdevelopment. The desire for regional status was another important motive behind the regime's nuclear weapons ambitions. Looking back on this in 2005, a senior Libyan official indicated to the author that Israel's nuclear advances became another key motivating factor for the Libyan regime's early nuclear aspirations.[84]

Gaddafi's nuclear weapons ambition was informed more by his political ambitions than by strategic assessments. In the early 1970s, the nuclear weapons project was cast in terms of a "pan-Arab project" that Libya would undertake on behalf of the Arab world.[85] Acquiring nuclear weapons would provide Tripoli a leading regional role in the confrontation with Israel and, at the same time, position Libya as a candidate to supplement or—after

Nasser's death—replace Egypt as the leading confrontational Arab state. Looking back on these issues in 2004, Gaddafi stated that "in 1969 and early 1970s we did not reflect on where or against whom we could use the nuclear bomb. Such issues were not considered. All that was important was to build the bomb."[86]

In 1970, the Gaddafi regime started to examine options for setting up a nuclear program exploring research and energy applications, and sought assistance to begin these efforts from the IAEA.[87] In March 1972, the regime set up the National Committee for Atomic Energy (NCAE), as an autonomous agency of the Ministry of Industry to plan and oversee the establishment of an indigenous nuclear program. There was no research and development program at this early stage and the Libyans focused on developing basic resources for teaching nuclear physics at the graduate and postgraduate levels. No budget was set aside, nor had the Ministry of Industry—in charge of the plans for uranium exploration and technical assistance in the nuclear field—prepared a plan.[88]

After Libya's nationalization of oil and the 1973 rise in oil prices due to OPEC action in 1972–1973, the Gaddafi regime did not have significant financial constraints: Libya could easily afford to explore several routes to nuclear weapons simultaneously. Even so, the regime's initial plans were remarkable in their ambition and scope. By early 1973, the regime contemplated investing in research reactors and possibly power reactors. The Ministry of Planning included a nuclear-powered desalination facility in its plans for power reactors, even though this did not make sense from an economic perspective, as seven other gas and turbine desalination plants were already planned.[89] In the nuclear field, as elsewhere, the guiding principle of Libyan development planning at this time was to ask for more rather than to prioritize.

A nuclear energy program made sense both as a route to a weapons option and from a development perspective. Although Libya was an oil-exporting state, energy was a pressing concern. The country's entire power supply at this time came from thermal (petroleum) sources. The national power grid was still a work in progress. Nuclear energy appeared to be a good option for diversifying the national power supply. In 1973, total Libyan power production amounted to 300 megawatts out of a total capacity of 600 megawatts.[90] The Libyan Electricity Corporation aimed to integrate the existing networks by 1976 and to create a unified national power network by 1980–1984 with a total capacity of 2,000 megawatts. A nuclear power station was initially envisaged to contribute 300 megawatts. In 1973, only one nuclear power station was being considered, and the Libyans hoped to acquire such a station around 1980–1984.[91] Over the next few years, there was a steep rise in electricity demand, with an estimated 25 percent growth rate per annum between 1974 and 1978, which subsequently moderated to about 10 percent per year.[92] The decision to include nuclear energy in the national grid came from the senior level of the regime.[93] This target was based on the assumption that electricity consumption would continue to grow; estimates indicated, however, that Libya's total consumption would still be at the "lower end of the present OECD range."[94]

The Libyan regime decided to pursue nuclear weapons at a time when Egypt had made the opposition decision.[95] The Arab-Israeli Wars strengthened the appeal of nuclear weapons as a means of enhancing Libya's status in the context of the regional conflict. Israel's resounding military victory over the Arab coalition in the 1967 war had demonstrated a growing gap in military capabilities. As suspicions over Israel's nuclear intentions mounted over the next few years, nuclear weapons became increasingly salient as a lever for adjusting the regional power balance. On the other hand, Libya did not have any obvious enemies or rivals except for those defined by the Gaddafi regime's ideological precept of anti-imperialism, and, by extension, anticolonialism. Closer to home, Libya was not yet involved in conflicts with its neighbors (Egypt, Sudan, Chad, Niger, Algeria, and Tunisia).

Earlier studies of the Libyan nuclear program have argued that the pursuit of nuclear weapons was security-driven.[96] Nuclear weapons appealed to the regime because they could provide a deterrent that did not require a large standing army. Seen from this perspective, nuclear weapons could deter external enemies and help prevent the emergence of threats to the Gaddafi regime at home. But the argument that the Arab-Israeli conflict motivated the Libyan interest in nuclear weapons is not really persuasive: Libya was neither involved in nor directly affected by the conflict. Israel's nuclear weapons arsenal may have motivated the Libyan nuclear ambition, but arguably more as a political and symbolic issue than as a threat. As Ennami's statement above indicates, the Libyans were concerned about the implications of the widening technological gap between Israel and Arab states for the regional power balance. This likely outweighed any potential concern that the Israeli nuclear arsenal represented a direct threat to Libya.

The ideological lenses through which the Gaddafi regime viewed regional issues, along with its preference for advanced technological solutions, further enhanced the appeal of nuclear weapons. First, the regime's ideological opposition to colonialism and imperialism was reflected in its grand strategy and its emphasis on deterrence. Libyan territory had been subject to successive colonial projects, which had a powerful influence on Libya's national legacy and foreign policy outlook. In May 1973 Gaddafi stated: "If [other countries] have the power they will enslave others; and if they know that others are unable to retaliate, they will attack them. This is the crux of imperialism. The big powers make war against other countries without any constraints because they do not fear reciprocal action."[97] Thus it was the legacy of colonialism, rather than imminent threats, which informed Gaddafi's emphasis on deterrence strategies, including nuclear deterrence.

FOUNDATIONS FOR A NUCLEAR PROGRAM

In March 1970, Gaddafi's deputy Jalloud traveled to China to nurture bilateral ties and request cooperation in the areas of science and technology. He reportedly asked for nuclear assistance but was apparently advised to develop an indigenous technological base first. It has been widely reported that Jalloud asked to purchase nuclear weapons, but there is no clear evidence of an explicit request at this early stage.[98]

Gaddafi discussed the possibility of Libya funding Egyptian nuclear research with Nasser, perhaps with the hope of acquiring know-how for Libya's program.[99] After Nasser's sudden death in September 1970, the relationship between Libya's and Egypt's leaders began to cool. Nonetheless, Gaddafi continued to explore the option of cooperation in the nuclear field with Nasser's successor, Anwar Sadat, including Libyan funding for nuclear research in Egypt.[100] In early 1972, Gaddafi appears to have given the green light to develop a nuclear-powered desalination plant to be jointly operated with Egypt.[101] In 1973, the two states discussed entering a political union with Sudan, and Gaddafi and Sadat also envisaged cooperation between their nuclear establishments.[102] After the union failed to materialize, these tentative plans were shelved. The Egyptian nuclear program was scaled down over the next few years as the country's leadership abandoned ambitions to try to match Israel's nuclear capabilities. While formalized cooperation between Libya and Egypt did not come to fruition, Egyptian scientists who left the country as the nuclear program was being downsized would come to play a crucial role in the nascent Libyan program. As we will see, Egyptians formed the majority of scientists in Libya's nuclear establishment initially and many played key leadership roles in the early stages.

Creating an indigenous foundation for a nuclear weapons option was a tall order for a state that was effectively preindustrial and lacked graduates with relevant degrees and experience. However, Libya's unexploited uranium deposits offered another route to a nuclear future, and the IAEA offered resources that the Libyans lacked. By 30 September 1969, the new regime had already contacted the UN resident representative to ask for assistance with planning of prospecting for uranium.[103] The IAEA interpreted the request as having a high priority for the Libyans.[104] Although the Oceanic Exploration Company that had made initial inquiries apparently lost interest after the September coup, the new Ministry of Planning was keen to follow up. Over the next two years, the Ministry requested assistance from the IAEA with setting up a uranium exploration survey, acquiring the technical infrastructure for basic and applied research, and exploring other options for a nuclear energy program.[105]

These plans were taking shape as the new regime prepared its first budget and sought to carve out a development policy. As we will see, there are several similarities between the regime's planning for its industrial development efforts and its planning for a nuclear program. It is useful, therefore, to briefly outline how the regime prepared development efforts in other areas, and the role of state organizations and foreign experts in this process.

The overall approach was characterized by ample funds, a virtual absence of planning, and significant incentives to scale up developments projects. The organizations and departments that were charged with overseeing industrial development did not develop any basic concepts or plans to guide their efforts. They received advice from foreign consultants in a range of areas but tended to ignore their reports. When in 1972 a new three-year development budget was announced, a plan to guide these efforts was suggested but did not materialize.[106] Development planning was not based on any explicit plan but rather on unpublished "guidelines." Development budgets were prepared on a rolling basis on a three-year horizon, with budget updates each subsequent year.[107] In April 1973, for example, the development budget increased by nearly 50 percent compared with the annual budget announced just four months earlier. Simultaneously, the allocations for industry and mineral developments, which included nuclear prospecting and steel production, increased from 174 million to more than 238 million Libyan dinars.[108]

The government had plenty of money, but lacked the vision and capacity to transform an underdeveloped state to an advanced industrialized economy. Although the new regime invested 50 percent more in the development of industry than the monarchy had done, it had few results to show for it. The regime's large investment offered few incentives for entrepreneurship: for example, only smaller enterprises could be private; all medium-to-large industries were state-owned. There was little industry in either state or private hands to begin with. The industrial enterprises on record at the time of the 1969 coup consisted only of "a tobacco factory in Tripoli employing 500 workers; two textile factories in Benghazi; a gypsum factory in Tripoli, with barely more than fifty workers; small plants for the processing of macaroni, olive oil and fizzy drinks, detergents (based on foreign patents) and tomato canning. There was one cement factory."[109] The cement factory was built by the Ministry of Planning under the monarchy to stimulate private enterprise, but "officials complain[ed] that it took four years for private capital to establish a cement factory, although government had provided 80 per cent of the finance."[110] This lack of initiative only worsened under Gaddafi, which was perhaps not surprising in light of the regime's restrictions on how much businesses in private hands could grow, and its growing zeal for redistributing private wealth and property.

In the public sector, too, there was an abundance of funding and a shortage of projects. The funding allocation process—whereby proposals would be forwarded to the Ministry of Planning and then approved by the RCC—encouraged ministries to adopt large projects with inflated budgets.[111] These projects were typically based on foreign assistance and imported technology, following the example of the petroleum industry.[112] For example, agriculture was a key priority for the Gaddafi regime and central to its ideological project of redistributing land and wealth. Between 1970 and 1980, 2,349.9 million Libyan dinars were spent on agricultural projects across the country.[113] By comparison, only 70 percent as much (1,629.1 million Libyan dinars) was spent on industry during the same time period.[114] These projects were nominally run by the state, but in practice oversight was difficult.

At first, the nuclear program adopted a similar approach. The National Committee of Atomic Energy (NCAE) was an agency of the Prime Minister's office (Jalloud was then the Prime Minister) with links to the Ministry of Foreign Affairs, but lacked institutional resources to actually plan and oversee the nuclear project. The first chairman of this committee was chemist Yusuf Elmehrik, who was also the Dean of the Faculty of Science at the University. The Committee had six other members representing the ministries of agriculture, health, education, industry, planning and petroleum. The committee's only employee was its secretary, Mustafa Ghiriyani, who was Secretary at the Prime Ministerial Office.

The program was overseen by the NCAE but in practice Jalloud, who was the most influential figure in the RCC after Gaddafi, took charge of the program. The main purpose of the NCAE was to coordinate technical assistance from the IAEA. Its seven members were from the University of Libya and from the Ministries of Agriculture, Health, Education, Industry, Planning, and Petroleum. The committee had no budget, only one employee—Mustafa Ghiriyani, a secretary from the Prime Minister's Office—and did not carry out any activities or research. The NCAE forwarded information from the IAEA to relevant organizations, provided the agency with information, coordinated national policy on agency matters, submitted requests for assistance to the agency, and secured resources for implementation of any such projects.[115] In other words, the committee had neither a mandate nor resources to prepare proposals or plans for nuclear research and development independently. In fact, no one did.

On 26 April 1970, Mohamed Mughrabi, the deputy director general of the UN Office of Technical Cooperation, approved the proposal of the resident UN representative in Libya to seek IAEA assistance. The IAEA's technical assistance programs could give Libya access to several resources that could, at least initially, substitute for what Libya lacked. The agency offered consultants who could help plan a nuclear research (or power) program, provide detailed expertise in planning procurement, install the equipment upon arrival, give advice on how to set up organizations to run and audit nuclear research and development, and offer peer review of large contracts.

Libya's institutions for planning and technical development were not equipped for carrying out fairly straightforward tasks, let alone planning a project of this nature. Libya at this point apparently had no nuclear scientists or engineers with relevant experience, and its state institutions would remain understaffed until graduate students began to return after completing their degrees abroad later in the 1970s. While Libya was keen to get assistance from the IAEA, along with other UN resources, it did not necessarily follow the advice they gave. Although Libya's bureaucrats may have appreciated sound advice, they often lacked the resources or influence necessary to implement the recommended measures.

In late September 1969 the Ministry of Economy and Industry requested assistance from the IAEA to advise them on how to begin prospecting for nuclear raw materials. This request was framed as part of a program of mineral resources exploration. The IAEA nominated James Cameron, an expert provided by the agency, and Cameron visited Libya for week in early December 1970. The IAEA offered a wide range of advice and technology to support developing states who were interested in nuclear technology but who lacked the institutional resources to plan these programs. Cameron recommended that Libya request an IAEA "Atomic Energy Planner" who, as a later consultant described, could "advise the government on the potential role of nuclear techniques in their economic and social development plans."[116]

The Libyan counterpart organization for the prospecting project was the Industrial Research Center. This center, located some kilometers east of Tripoli, was an autonomous agency of the Ministry of Industry.[117] The center's main responsibility was to assist in industrialization programs.[118] The Libyan point of contact for any nuclear issues was the center's director, Abdul Alim Shaari who, as Minister of Industry, had first contacted the IAEA for prospecting assistance in 1969. Under his capable leadership, the center had overall responsibility for the nuclear portfolio.[119] As early as 1970, Shaari began to explore options for regional nuclear collaboration, including the Middle Eastern Regional Radioisotope Center in Cairo, in addition to assistance from the IAEA and other nuclear supplier states, notably the Soviet Union.[120] He expressed to visiting IAEA consultants a broad interest in nuclear technology.

One of the center's three departments was the General Department of Geological Research and Mining. Directed by Jadallah Azzouz Ettalhi, who would play a pivotal role in developing Libyan industry for decades to come, this unit was responsible for all geological and mineral exploration, including petroleum. With only seven employees, including three foreigners, it had ambitious plans for expansion and generous funding to support institutional growth.[121] However, its staff lacked relevant scientific and technological expertise and the center also lacked the necessary equipment, due not to a lack of financial resources but to insufficient planning and experience. There were still too few Libyan nationals with the education and experience essential for planning and launching an industrial-scale program in the field of mineral resources.

In 1973 IAEA expert J. A. K. Quartey also visited the University of Tripoli to assess the potential recruitment of graduates. Although staffed by foreign faculty and well equipped, the university lacked the expertise to teach physics, chemistry, or other modern applied sciences. The dean of the Faculty of Sciences, Yusuf Elmehrik, who was also the first chairman of the NCAE, asked for help from the IAEA to develop courses in nuclear physics and chemistry. Elmehrik would later emerge as a central figure in the Libyan nuclear establishment.[122] Most of the university's geology graduates (on average fifteen per year) were recruited in the oil sector, but some might also be recruited in the nuclear program.[123] In 1974, the University of Benghazi also set up engineering and science faculties.[124] Despite these additions, there was much competition for the small pool of students from which the nuclear program could recruit.

By 1973, the University of Tripoli was developing resources for postgraduate research in physics. A visiting IAEA consultant found these beginnings to be positive: "There are very-well qualified members of staff to handle this line of research; construction of the required laboratory is well advanced; financial allocation has been made for the years 1972–75, and an order has now been placed for the necessary equipment."[125] The Physics Department seemed to be well on its way to launching postgraduate courses in classical physics.

Given the continuing shortage of skilled personnel, the IAEA's technical assistance was a very useful resource. Ettalhi, the director of the General Department of Geological Research and Mining who would, in the 1980s, serve twice as Libya's prime minister, asked for help in developing a plan for utilizing uranium deposits and establishing training fellowships and other educational opportunities.[126] Ettalhi indicated further that the center was interested in receiving an Atomic Energy Planner from the IAEA.[127] The Agriculture Research Center, set up in March 1972 and staffed primarily by foreign experts, also expressed interest in radioisotopes research. The director, Mohamed Zehni, became a member of the NCAE.[128]

REQUESTING A RESEARCH REACTOR

In December 1970, the Ministry of Industry was contemplating not only a program for uranium exploration but also a nuclear energy program. In late 1971 and the spring of 1972, several requests for further IAEA assistance were made by the Department of International Organizations and Technical Cooperation at the Ministry of Unity and Foreign Affairs. The University of Tripoli also wanted to expand its resources in the nuclear field and, in 1971, its Physics Department requested assistance from the IAEA to acquire a 2-megawatt research reactor with supporting facilities. IAEA experts saw this request, and especially the additional facilities requested by the Libyans, as an indication that the state was "beginning to embark upon studies in atomic energy."[129]

The University of Tripoli's Physics Department wanted the research reactor to be located in the Tripoli area, as part of a broader effort to develop research and training resources in the field of nuclear energy, including "facilities for material testing and isotope production."[130] The request was framed as part of a broad expansion of Libya's technical and scientific education. As the IAEA report noted: "Many other small projects requested by the Libyan University for Benghazi Campus and Tripoli are under study and are of major importance. The execution of these projects requires several tens of millions of dinars which will constitute a heavy burden on the Libyan budget."[131]

The university explained to IAEA representatives that they wanted such a reactor for training and research in the field of nuclear energy.[132] The Libyan nuclear establishment saw the next logical step as acquiring a power reactor, which they expected to obtain during the early 1980s. The IAEA challenged this assumption, and an agency expert noted in a 1973 report to the Libyan government:

> It is recognized that a nuclear research centre, including a research reactor, can contribute greatly to the development of a nuclear power programme [but] it is not a strictly necessary prerequisite to the introduction of nuclear power. Concern was expressed regarding the high drain which would be caused on already scarce scientific manpower. A research reactor did not, therefore, appear to be of a high order of priority. The general view was that while a research reactor may well be incorporated into long-term plans, it was realized and agreed that a programme which would be of more immediate importance and would make a far greater contribution to the country's general development would be one in radioisotope applications in agriculture, medicine, industry, etc.[133]

It is unclear why the Libyan nuclear establishment believed that a research reactor was necessary, but it is also unclear how committed they were to this project in the first place. The Libyans seemed receptive to the points made by the IAEA, but still placed a request for a research reactor (for experiments) with the Ministry of Planning for the 1973–1976 development plan.[134] This may be explained by Libya's laissez-faire approach to planning at this time. Tripoli could afford to pursue both options—a radioisotope laboratory and a research reactor—despite IAEA advice that a research reactor was not a necessary step toward developing a power program.

In light of these remarkable ambitions, it is not surprising that the Libyans created a dedicated organization to oversee the nuclear program already in March 1972, nor that they were soon frustrated with the organization's performance.[135] The members of the NCAE met infrequently to discuss IAEA projects and to serve as liaison with the agency.[136] The mandate of the committee was to lay the foundation for the development of nuclear science and technology in Libya. A year after its inception, the government was apparently not too pleased with its progress. IAEA expert Quartey reported after his 1973 visit that "the Committee faces problems resulting from lack of funds and, within its structure, the Government is preparing a new structure."[137] In 1973, the Libyan government passed the Nuclear Energy Act, placing the responsibility for the nuclear energy portfolio with the NCAE.[138] The same year, however, the committee was merged into a new entity, the National Atomic Energy Authority (NAEA).[139] The NAEA then took charge of carving out a new path for the Libyan nuclear program.

The nuclear scientists at the University of Tripoli were deferential to the NCAE and later the NAEA, and quite frank about the modesty of their activities in communications with the IAEA. Quartey wrote in 1973:

> In view of the links between the Centre and various scientific departments, ministries, and industry generally, and also considering the relatively high concentration of analytical facilities and instruments at the Centre, the adviser discussed the possibility of incorporating radioisotope applications and some nuclear instruments into the Centre. However, the advisor was informed that because of the lack of graduates, interest in nuclear matters so far has been limited to attending conferences, receiving publications, etc. The general feeling was therefore that radioisotope applications equipment should be the responsibility of the National Committee for Atomic Energy.[140]

As Libya's nuclear program was scaling up in its ambition, focusing on the prospect of nuclear energy, Libya's economic boom transformed the state's financial resources. Shukri Ghanem, a Libyan economist who worked at OPEC and would later became prime minister, said that at this time "there was so much money that it was not difficult to follow a policy of 'all things to all people.'"[141] He noted further that the planning of industrial activity was "indiscriminate" with regard to the economic feasibility of individual projects.[142]

The economic boom was also reflected in the nuclear project. The Industrial Research Center had taken a conservative approach to planning the new program, preferring to delay purchasing more nuclear equipment until they had recruited and trained more skilled staff. The new nuclear authorities took a different view: training could be a by-product of larger acquisitions from nuclear supplier states.

As the government chose which projects to fund, they selected several heavy-industry projects such as a steel plant, an aluminum smelter, and several petrochemical projects rather than investing in light-industry or knowledge-based projects.[143] These choices were originally motivated by the rich mineral resources of Libya, but it proved difficult to link these projects with extraction of raw materials. The plants were essentially transplants from abroad, notably Japan, purchased as turnkey projects, and offered few opportunities for building Libyan know-how. Even after their completion, Libya remained unable to extract minerals for these plants from its proven deposits. In a study of the Libyan development economy written in the mid-1980s, Ghanem noted that these industrial projects were based on imported raw materials, imported labor, and imported technical know-how.[144] While this gave cause for concern to economists such as Ghanem, not to mention development experts, the senior tier of the Libyan regime was apparently not worried. As Libya's oil income continued to rise, it was possible to afford both guns *and* butter.[145]

This chapter has presented, for the first time, a history of the emergence of Libya's nuclear program prior to the previously accepted "official" start-up date of 1973. This prehistory shows how the Libyan state's underdevelopment, and the legacy of the monarchy's weak central state apparatus, shaped the nuclear program that emerged after Muammar Gaddafi seized power in September 1969. Most importantly, the acute lack of technical expertise and resources for development planning at the national level led to an inflated set of nuclear ambitions, whose realization required extensive foreign assistance across the board, from staffing research institutes to designing a research and development program, to advising the government on the infrastructure for the nuclear program. On the ground, the embryonic scientific community made sound plans and recommendations but lacked the institutional resources to fulfill their ambitions.

Libya faced many obstacles in its postindependence state-building process. Initially, the state lacked both human and financial resources. After the discovery of oil, unbalanced growth created new opportunities but also introduced additional challenges as the Libyan state apparatus struggled to develop capabilities for development planning and implementation. These challenges, which were key factors limiting the scope and scale of development assistance to the country, only intensified after Gaddafi's coup created greater distance between weak state institutions and the real center of decision making—at first the RCC, but increasingly Gaddafi himself and a small circle of individuals around him. As both Gaddafi's circle and Libya's state institutions lacked the capacity to assess technical recommendations in the nuclear field, the nascent nuclear program mirrored the unbalanced growth that characterized broader trends in Libyan development during the late 1960s and early 1970s.

From the outset, the nuclear program was affected by the division of decision-making authority, which rested with Gaddafi's inner circle, from formal institutional arrangements. The main consequence for the nuclear program prior to 1973 was the shift from a gradual approach to building infrastructure and know-how toward a laissez-faire approach that outsourced most aspects of this process to foreign experts and agencies. But, at a more structural level, the combination of informal lines of authority and oversight, especially by Gaddafi's most important deputy, Jalloud, undermined the tenuous link between the nuclear program and the state. After 1973, when Gaddafi launched a Cultural Revolution to undo the state, the institutional foundation for the nuclear program would erode further.

Cultural Revolution and Nuclear Power, 1973–1981

As Libya's Atomic Energy Authority (NAEA) prepared for a nuclear power program, Muammar Gaddafi set out to eradicate the state. His April 1973 announcement of a "Cultural Revolution," and the radical program it heralded, apparently came as a surprise even to the Revolutionary Command Council (RCC).[1] The Cultural Revolution gave Gaddafi increasingly unrestrained power, created a shadow apparatus challenging the formal institutions of the state, and caused turbulence throughout the country. As Gaddafi pursued increasingly radical policies at home and abroad, fueled by oil wealth and the growing influence of vigilante Revolutionary Committees, the state dwindled.

The ambitious expansion of the nuclear program throughout the 1970s strained Libya's faltering state institutions. This was manifest in increasingly ambitious plans for nuclear power and, by the end of the decade, prospecting for uranium. As International Atomic Energy Agency (IAEA) reports show, foreign experts deemed the initial plans prepared by Libyan scientists sound and appropriate but, by the late 1970s, the Libyan technical community had been outpaced by the regime's ambitions. The main problem was not ineptitude; it was a lack of state capacity. Over the next few years, the Libyan regime struggled with planning and coordination at all levels of the nuclear organization. The scientists seemed demotivated, foreign experts noted, and their new and well-equipped laboratories were often idle.

Because so little is known about the early history of the Libyan nuclear program, scholars have overlooked how the Cultural Revolution affected its early stages. As we will see in this chapter, the Cultural Revolution, which undermined the administrative capabilities of the state to an extreme degree, eroded the Gaddafi regime's resources for monitoring and controlling the nuclear program. At the same time, the Cultural Revolution marked intensifying efforts by the regime to target potential sources of opposition in the state and the student body. These coup-proofing efforts contributed to undermine the nuclear program. Like many of Libya's other technical development projects, the nuclear program was largely planned and operated by foreign scientists and the regime remained disengaged. This combination—a weak state and a delegated nuclear program—explains the striking mismatch between the Gaddafi regime's ambitions and actual developments between 1973 and 1981.

The Cultural Revolution Hits the Nuclear Establishment

In early 1973, having grown disillusioned with trying to emulate Gamal Abdel Nasser, Gaddafi set out to create a new state called "Jamihiriyah," a neologism meaning "state of the masses." This was a radical reformation: there was no longer a Libyan constitution; all laws were abolished; and Gaddafi himself would rule in an informal capacity, as "Brother Leader" and "Guide of the Revolution."

Libya was to become "stateless." The institutions of the state—ministries and official agencies—were to be replaced by "popular committees," and all citizens would participate in grassroots-level committee structures. After this project failed to mobilize the citizenry, Revolutionary Committees were set up to eradicate opposition and further the transformation envisaged by Gaddafi. The members of the Revolutionary Committees were answerable only to Gaddafi, as the "Leader of the Revolution." They would monitor, and in some cases eventually replace, key state institutions—even the diplomatic corps. The committees led a purge of civil servants, academics, and capitalists such as business owners and landlords who were seen as antithetical to Gaddafi's revolutionary ambitions. This further weakened Libya's already fragile administrative capacity. Private companies struggled as Revolutionary Committees seized land and buildings and replaced the managements of public companies.

Some state institutions were carefully shielded to preserve the regime's ability to provide funds and services to the population. For example, the state bank and petroleum company were exempted from the Revolutionary Committees' appropriations. While they were apparently subject to some limits, on the whole these committees took over control of Libya's "centrally unplanned economy," as some contemporary observers described it.[2] They would also come to play a key role in the layered network of surveillance and security organizations that proliferated in Libya's public and private spheres. Even the nuclear program, exempt from most of the other pressures of the Cultural Revolution, was closely monitored by the intelligence services.

Gaddafi's Cultural Revolution set out to recast civil society. Along with his close advisers Abdessalam Jalloud, Abu Bakr Yunis Jabr, Khaled Humeidi, and Mustafa Kharroubi, Gaddafi recognized that the regime's early ideological initiatives, such as sending volunteers to fight in Palestine or to work in remote agricultural settlements, did not inspire the population.[3] To get Libyans more involved in the revolutionary project, they created what has been described as a hybrid state, with institutions representing the formal traditional state organs and parallel institutions representing the revolutionary authorities that held the real power.[4] In practice, this divested the formal state institutions of decision-making authority, as Revolutionary Committees wielded unrestrained power over society and effectively usurped some branches of the state. Particularly affected were the universities and the diplomatic service, both crucial for the development of a nuclear program through a combination of indigenous human resources and foreign technology.

As the regime continued to weaken the institutions of the state in order to avoid challenges, it nevertheless had to maintain some basic state functions, such as distribution of wealth and basic security. Even so, the regime was willing to experiment with some key institutions, such as the armed forces, which seemed to pose a particularly potent latent challenge to the regime's long-term survival. In late 1977 Gaddafi created a "popular army" comprising of the entire adult population. Universal military training was compulsory—at times women were also drafted—and weapons were distributed to citizens. These steps were intended both to strengthen the population's revolutionary zeal and to protect against foreign invasion. As a consequence, the armed forces were effectively deprofessionalized. This move further reduced the standing of the professional armed forces and thus their potential challenge to the Gaddafi regime.

To get rid of residual resistance to the Cultural Revolution, university students and civil servants—whom Gaddafi described as "perverts and deviationists"—were prime targets.[5] The Revolutionary Committees seized control of educational institutions, replacing staff and curricula that were deemed counterrevolutionary.[6] After hundreds, possibly thousands, of students mobilized to protest, Revolutionary Committee members hunted down leading figures in the student community who were subjected to torture and, in some cases, public executions. The secret police also targeted academics, lawyers, intellectuals, and civil servants to deter potential sources of opposition. This disruption affected recruitment in the dwindling state bureaucracy, as well as for the nuclear program, because senior figures in engineering departments were targeted.

The small nuclear establishment thus had to navigate carefully while the state was being transformed and fragmented. The nuclear community at this time largely comprised foreign scientists and technical staff who were mostly Egyptian, Tunisian, or Pakistani, as Libya was still in the very early stages of educating students in these technical fields. Their relationship with the new political elite had to be built from scratch, as there were virtually no existing ties to build on in a state that had been completely overturned since the 1969 September coup. The small technical community had limited resources in terms of organization, infrastructure, and potential new recruits. Scientists were in a particularly difficult position in the changing Libyan state where technocrats were primary targets of the regime's revolutionary zeal. For the departments that formally oversaw the nascent nuclear program, the erosion of formal state institutions left few opportunities to play a direct or active role in overseeing or directing nuclear research and development. The Libyan state's resources for technical planning, coordination, and follow-up were already weak, and the Cultural Revolution aggravated these problems.

Faced with this reality, the Libyan state apparatus had to adapt. One way in which it did so was to delegate detailed planning and implementation to agencies, both domestic and foreign, rather than to carry out coordinated and centralized state planning. This practice was consistent with how planning had been carried out previously under Gaddafi. In April 1973, as IAEA consultant J. A. K. Quartey observed, the role of the Ministry of Planning was to approve long-range general objectives and allocate funding for individual organizations "which, in turn, are responsible for drawing up their own programmes of activities for approval."[7] Such approval, it appears, was usually granted and rarely subject to substantial review or questioning.

From 1973 onward, the links between the regime's ambitions and the activities in the Libyan nuclear field were increasingly tenuous. Initially, contact between the regime and the nuclear establishment had been facilitated through the Ministry of Industry, but it soon shifted to the Prime Minister's Office, under Jalloud. After the Cultural Revolution began, authority was increasingly personalized rather than organizational or institutional. Within government departments, authority and decision-making power depended upon personal connections rather than formal titles and defined responsibilities. This undermined internal lines of authority, and made it difficult for foreign consultants and organizations to provide meaningful input to planning and decision-making processes. The regime's intelligence organizations monitored the nuclear establishment but appear to have been more concerned with vetting candidates for potential foreign trips and scholarships than the activities (or lack thereof) within the nuclear establishment. Efforts to launch nuclear research, including installing and using laboratory equipment, were largely nonexistent, but the regime apparently did nothing to amend the situation.

PLANNING FOR NUCLEAR POWER

In 1973, the University of Tripoli and the University of Benghazi, which were created after the splitting up of the former University of Libya, were expanding in the fields of nuclear physics, engineering, and chemistry with the aim of offering both undergraduate and graduate education in applied science and technology. This required extensive foreign assistance. The

University of Tripoli submitted a request to the IAEA stating that "purely [for] academic reasons, the Faculty of Science has decided to establish the Atomic and Nuclear Physics Laboratory in the Department of Physics, and it will welcome scientists and technicians from IAEA to share information and conduct research and training. . . . The planned research programme . . . is actually the first project in the field of atomic and nuclear physics."[8] The dean of the faculty, Yusuf Elmehrik, was also then head of the National Committee for Atomic Energy (NCAE). The University's plans were ambitious, but did not seem unrealistic. As a 1973 IAEA report noted, the university drew up sound plans, hired qualified staff, enjoyed sufficient funding from the government, and ordered relevant equipment.[9]

To be able to offer postgraduate education in atomic and nuclear physics, the university needed new facilities and equipment for research and training. The faculty already had qualified foreign staff and a laboratory, but more equipment and space was needed to accommodate the new programs. The university allocated additional space for these facilities, including new buildings, equipped with research facilities, for the Chemistry and Civil Engineering Departments.[10]

In the spring of 1973, the university set up a laboratory for basic experiments in physics, started a nuclear measurement project, and made ambitious plans for further expansion.[11] With the assistance of the IAEA, the Faculty of Science ordered equipment for a new radioisotope laboratory to enable students to carry out research experiments. According to Libyan statements and visiting IAEA consultants, this equipment, which included a 400-kiloelectron-volt Van de Graaff generator and a duoplasmatron ion source, was suitable for carrying out "research on basic problems of atomic and low energy nuclear physics, both for undergraduate and post graduate students, and to start research in these topics as a first step to introduce this branch of physics in the Faculty of Science."[12] The faculty proposed a gradual build-up of its capacities, noting in its initial request to the IAEA that "future work and projects of larger scale will follow as more trained graduates become available."[13]

The faculty continued to pursue a nuclear research reactor after its 1971 bid for IAEA support failed. The Libyans argued that this reactor would facilitate additional training, teaching, and research in materials testing and isotope production, which would stimulate basic research and development in a number of fields.[14] However, the IAEA consultants viewed Libya's request for additional equipment, along with the reactor, as suggesting that the Libyans had greater ambitions and wanted to explore nuclear energy, rather than simply carry out basic research and development. When a visiting IAEA consultant asked the Libyans in the spring of 1973 whether they were contemplating embarking upon a nuclear energy program, and whether the request for a research reactor was intended as a step toward an energy program, the answer was yes.[15]

A couple of years later, in June 1975, the Libyans reportedly attempted to purchase a TRIGA (Training, Research, Isotopes, General Atomics) research reactor from the United States.[16] They were denied the TRIGA—a small reactor suitable for research distinguished by the ease with which it can be operated—for reasons IAEA consultants privately described as "strategic."[17] This reflects the nature of planning in Libya at this time, which encouraged scaling up requests rather than prioritizing, and perhaps also suggests that the scientists were less focused on the pursuit of nuclear energy than the regime was and wanted the opportunity to carry out basic research experiments.

The nuclear measurements project at the University of Tripoli was the country's first step toward designing and carrying out a research program in the nuclear field.[18] The government gave the university a generous budget.[19] The Faculty of Science planned to establish the infrastructure for various experiments and basic research including a laboratory for spectroscopic measurements, another for radioactive materials, a high-vacuum laboratory, and a plasma physics laboratory. This rapid expansion was, according to the faculty, driven by an "urgent need for creating opportunities of research in the important field of atomic and nuclear physics" at the undergraduate and graduate levels.[20]

To move forward with these plans, the Libyans pursued assistance from the IAEA and other states, notably the USSR. Initial projects included plans for low-energy nuclear reactions, activation analysis, radiochemistry, and neutron physics. The faculty sought assistance from the IAEA to install the equipment and obtain the associated items necessary to start experiments and research.[21] They also asked for an IAEA expert to train local staff in the operation of this equipment. Nuclear science was a new discipline in Libya; all of its scientists and technicians were young and relatively inexperienced. IAEA consultants noted that "there is obviously no real scientific research tradition in Libya."[22] Despite these challenges, within a decade the faculty had established four areas of research—nuclear physics, theory, plasma physics, and solid-state studies—and its scientists were publishing regularly in international journals.[23]

Although up to two hundred Libyans were pursuing graduate degrees in physics and nuclear science in the mid-1970s, the Libyans still lacked technical staff who were experienced in the installation, operation, or maintenance of nuclear instruments and equipment. Libyan universities started to run courses in nuclear engineering in 1978 but still had far too few technical workers with the skills necessary for operating specialized nuclear instruments. As a result, the Libyans struggled to install the new equipment for the radioactive materials laboratory. In October 1974, the Van de Graaff generator was nearly operational, but essential computing and analytic equipment was still lacking.[24] A year later, some of this equipment was still in its shipping containers as the staff did not have experience or know-how in this area.[25] During 1976–1977, an IAEA consultant helped to install this equipment so that the generator could be used for physics experiments.[26] Even this proved challenging, however, as importing necessary equipment and manuals took several months, partly due to Libya's inefficient postal service and delays by the exporter.

Therapeutic applications were typically an area that interested developing states who were in the early stages of exploring nuclear technology with IAEA assistance. Libya's initial attempts in the early 1970s to develop cancer treatments soon ran into problems, and a decade later there were still no nuclear diagnostics facilities in the country. Libya's minimal forays into this field illustrate the broader challenges facing the nuclear program, particularly manpower and technology absorption.

Setting up basic radiation therapy for cancer treatments proved difficult, for example, despite access to foreign assistance and equipment. In 1972 British health physicist J. Eric Roberts advised the Libyan Central Government Hospital on setting up a radiotherapy cobalt-60 unit supplied by Canada. However, as the IAEA noted, these efforts faced the continuing shortage of Libyan scientists and especially technicians; operating this unit would require two doctors, two graduate physicists, and technicians trained in radiography.[27] Libya had trained one graduate in Egypt but had to recruit two foreign experts specializing in these techniques as there were none in the country.

At the new Physics Department of the University of Tripoli, the staff was expanding: at least twenty PhDs were hired, but most were foreign scientists, mainly Egyptians, on contracts of two or three years.[28] The head of the department, Izzat Abdelaziz, was an Egyptian; he would come to play an essential role in the development of the Libyan nuclear establishment during the second half of the 1970s. The deputy head, Anwar Zaki, was an Egyptian scientist then completing his doctoral dissertation.

The Libyan program continued to suffer from shortages of skilled physicists, chemists, and engineers despite attempts to educate more students. A key problem was the lack of human resources management and opportunities for training. Once graduates returned home, their opportunities for further learning were few and far between. IAEA fellowships for graduate students to visit nuclear research institutions in other countries were an important training resource, especially as the Libyan nuclear establishment did not have the resources to train scientists and engineers in operating and maintaining specialized technological instruments, let alone nuclear reactors. But the Libyans put little effort into human resources management or recruitment. There was apparently no systematic merit-based recruitment or management of fellowship opportunities offered by the IAEA. The agency attempted to help the Libyans select suitable candidates by suggesting procedures and criteria for selection of qualified individuals. These decisions would instead be influenced by the intelligence agencies, who were less concerned with scientific merit than with suspected political sympathies. The Libyan nuclear establishment, notably the NCAE and its successor, the AEA, lacked procedures to select candidates or to identify what kind of placements would be suitable to further an individual's expertise.[29] Candidates applying for such placements often stated very general areas of interest such as "reactors and generators" or "neutron physics" and usually asked to visit the most prestigious institutions such as the U.S. facility at Oak Ridge, Tennessee, despite having very weak foreign language skills.[30] Scientific merit and skill development apparently played very minor roles in their selection.

While these challenges were not seen as a significant concern by the Libyan regime, senior Egyptian scientists attempted to explain the importance of human resources management to Jalloud. They appear to have persuaded him to send more Libyan graduate students abroad.[31] However, regime leaders remained reluctant to scale up their investment in education, preferring to hire foreign scientists. They were perhaps concerned that universities, and especially the faculties of science and engineering, could once again become fertile breeding grounds for political opposition.

The University of Tripoli started to produce small numbers of graduates in the early 1970s. In 1973, the Faculty of Science had a total of 345 students and sent 61 Libyan students abroad for postgraduate studies (12 in chemistry and 9 in physics).[32] By 1975, more than 200 students were pursuing postgraduate degrees in nuclear sciences abroad, with an emphasis on nuclear energy.[33] Of these, 128 students had entered five-year programs in nuclear energy in the United States.[34] By the mid-1970s, senior Libyan officials estimated, there were about 2,500 Libyan students in the United States.[35] Students were expected to return to Libya after their studies, but some did not. Such "brain drain" occurred on a large scale: during Gaddafi's reign an estimated 100,000 citizens, mostly the better-educated, left the country. In addition, large numbers of skilled foreign workers were deported, peaking at 90,000 in 1985 alone.[36] For a population of just a few million, this was a significant loss. But brain drain posed an even more serious problem for the nuclear program, given the very small pool of people with appropriate skills and knowledge.

In the mid-1970s, research in physics progressed slowly at the University of Tripoli. The department's staff continued to expand, but the level of activity was still low. For example, lectures in the fall semester did not start until November each year. In late 1976, Abdelaziz, the Egyptian head of department, resigned and was replaced by a Libyan scientist, S. A. Swedan.[37] At this time, as IAEA observers noted drily, "The atmosphere at the University . . . [was] certainly anything but stimulating . . . [although] future plans seem to be rather impressive."[38]

GADDAFI'S AMBIVALENT NUCLEAR AMBITIONS

In the mid-1970s, as the Libyan regime intensified its efforts to acquire infrastructure necessary to explore the nuclear fuel cycle, Gaddafi made public statements expressing interest in nuclear technology. In April 1975, for example, he told a Sudanese newspaper that he hoped to make Libya a nuclear power, pointing out that nuclear weapons technology was not a secret.[39] While little evidence is available concerning internal regime discussions about the nuclear program at this time, there were disagreements within the RCC during the early 1970s about whether Libya should become an increasingly radical actor on the international arena or invest in "building the revolution at home" through economic development. According to senior regime figures interviewed by the author in 2005 and 2006, the division between those in the senior tiers who wanted to pursue anticolonial policies and those who wanted to invest in economic development remained a key fissure in the regime over the next several decades.[40] While Gaddafi listened to both sides, he did not commit consistently to either faction. Whereas previously the RCC may have been a restraining influence on Gaddafi, by 1974–1975 he acted in an increasingly unrestrained manner.[41]

Gaddafi often sent mixed messages about his policy preferences and delayed committing to any one position (or faction) until late in the decision-making process. This was as true in the nuclear field as elsewhere. Some of Gaddafi's public statements during the mid-1970s strongly suggested that he wanted to acquire nuclear weapons; some stated the opposite, suggesting principled opposition to the notion of an Islamic bomb or the existence of nuclear weapons. Other states, notably Israel and the United States, interpreted them as indications of a nuclear weapons ambition.

Meanwhile, the Libyan nuclear program advanced in a haphazard manner. Even as regime officials entered talks with foreign companies, the nuclear establishment struggled to develop a viable research and development program. The erosion of state structures during this period further undermined the Libyan regime's capacity to manage and monitor large and complex projects. Power and authority rested with Gaddafi, his advisers, and the Revolutionary Committees, but some ministries remained nominally responsible for implementation and oversight of individual projects. Governance under these conditions was often based on guesses or assumptions about Gaddafi's intentions and preferences, rarely explicit instructions. Gaddafi concentrated political power outside the remaining state institutions, while his personal views dictated strategic policy. This was particularly true in the military realm, Gaddafi having closed the Ministry of Defense shortly after the 1969 coup.

There was a puzzling contrast between the uneven advances on the ground and the Gaddafi regime's stated ambitions for nuclear power. This may have reflected a calculated ambiguity or internal disagreement about the direction of the nuclear program. It certainly reflected a mismatch between the regime's far-reaching ambitions and the limited capabilities of its scientists and administrators. The political elite and the nuclear establishment were only tenuously connected, and there were no institutions attempting to regulate or monitor the nuclear program. Jalloud held regular meetings with the senior Egyptian scientists leading the efforts to develop nuclear infrastructure in Libya. Still, Jalloud's limited technical know-how, the frequent turnover of foreign scientists in leading positions, and the absence of oversight mechanisms in the state made monitoring difficult. Nor is it clear what Jalloud reported to Gaddafi about the actual progress of the nuclear program, or how frequently Gaddafi was briefed on this issue.

Notwithstanding Gaddafi's public ambiguity about the long-term objectives of his nuclear program, the nuclear establishment explored the nuclear fuel cycle without interruption and attempted to develop an ambitious nuclear energy program. There is no evidence to suggest that the orientation of the program changed due to a reorientation of the regime's nuclear policy during the 1970s. Inside the nuclear establishment, however, there was no consistent push to fulfill the regime's ambitions. There was no discernible pressure from the regime on the scientists to speed up their efforts, nor were there any deadlines to deliver a nuclear weapons option.

BUILDING NUCLEAR NETWORKS

From 1973, the Libyan nuclear project took an ambiguous turn, exploring technology suited to both nuclear energy and weapons development.[42] Already by 1974, Gaddafi's statements led U.S. intelligence estimates to see Libya as a state pursuing nuclear weapons capabilities.[43] To U.S. analysts, Libya's "shotgun" approach—buying a wide range of facilities and services from abroad—suggested that the regime wanted to launch a crash program.[44] As it turned out, the explanation was more prosaic: Libya's efforts reflected a lot of money and very little planning.

In parallel with the effort to explore applied nuclear technologies with the aid of the IAEA and bilateral nuclear cooperation agreements with several countries, Libya began to explore clandestine technologies associated with sensitive aspects of the nuclear fuel cycle such as uranium enrichment, plutonium production, and reprocessing. In so doing, the Libyans pursued multiple avenues at once: developing indigenous capabilities with foreign help; outsourcing; and purchasing off the shelf. For example, the Libyan nuclear establishment explored the front end of the nuclear cycle (finding uranium and refining it into uranium ore concentrate, or yellowcake, and processing nuclear fuel) with foreign assistance, as well as importing raw materials and technology. The regime imported 2,263 metric tons of yellowcake from Niger.[45] As contemporary U.S. intelligence assessments noted, these amounts were in excess of any existing or foreseeable needs, but they could provide raw material for the power reactors the Libyans were hoping to acquire—or a clandestine weapons program.[46] In 1973 rumors surfaced that the Libyans tried to purchase twenty electromagnets, suitable for enriching uranium, from a French company.[47] This company, Thomson-CSF, had been operating in Libya for several years in connection with servicing French-supplied Mirage planes, and some of its engineers had also assisted the University of Tripoli's Physics Department with establishing its computer systems.[48] By the mid-1970s, U.S. intelligence viewed the Libyan procurement activities, which seemed to pursue several options at once, as geared to "leapfrog" ahead in the development of key capacities to pursue nuclear weapons.[49]

While the Libyan regime continued to rely on other states to supply equipment and know-how, Gaddafi's radical policies were creating tensions in Libya's foreign relations. By the late 1970s, the regime was supporting what it saw as postcolonial resistance movements that often took the form of violent actions against Israel and former colonial powers in Europe, notably France, Italy, Belgium, and Britain. France, Britain, and the United States, who were key suppliers of nuclear technology, were by now reluctant to support Libya's nuclear program. For example, Libya had attempted to purchase a research reactor from the United States in 1975 and would try to secure larger contracts with French and Belgian companies during the 1980s, but these agreements fell through after initial agreements were signed.

The Libyans turned elsewhere, setting up cooperation agreements, formal and informal, with Brazil, Argentina, Pakistan, and the Soviet Union. They also approached India and China: in 1978, senior Libyan officials allegedly offered to pay India's foreign debt in exchange for a nuclear weapon.[50] Two years later, Libyan scientists traveled to nuclear establishments in Bombay, Delhi, and Calcutta requesting assistance with training, apparently without success.[51] The Chinese government was also reluctant to provide nuclear assistance to Tripoli. Despite these difficulties, the Libyan regime was able to nurture two relationships that held the promise of nuclear assistance, namely those with Pakistan and the Soviet Union.

In the early 1970s, Gaddafi struck up a close relationship with the Pakistani premier Zulfikar Ali Bhutto. Bhutto traveled to Libya in early 1972, shortly after he had given the green light for a Pakistani nuclear weapons program. Although Libya's generosity toward the Pakistani program was presumably motivated by a desire for help with its own, this relationship does not seem to have been based on an explicit series of quid pro quo exchanges. Built on a personal connection between the two leaders, it began to fade after Bhutto was ousted from power in 1977. Still, as late as 1979 Libya funded the Pakistani nuclear weapons program with an estimated $133 million.[52]

Libyan support for the nuclear weapons program of Pakistan also included up to 450 metric tons of yellowcake.[53] There is no available evidence to suggest that this led to transfers of sensitive technology from Pakistan to Libya during the 1970s; the Libyans may not even have requested such assistance then, as their program was still in the preliminary stages. However, eighteen Libyan nuclear scientists did receive training at the Pakistani Institute for Nuclear Technology.[54]

Seen from the outside, the Libyans' behavior gave cause for concern: Jalloud had approached other states asking for weapons-sensitive technology; Libya had aided Pakistan's nuclear weapons program; and the Libyans were planning to launch an energy program that could give them the opportunity to develop a weapons program. But, as we have seen, by the mid-1970s the Libyan nuclear program presented, at best, a mixed picture. On the one hand, returning graduates with degrees in nuclear science developed a small, but growing, domestic knowledge base for the nuclear program, which was bolstered by help and advice from the IAEA as well as foreign states. Generous financial allocations permitted the pursuit of more hardware than the nuclear establishment was capable of utilizing. Both the IAEA and the Soviet Union, which was emerging as Libya's main supplier of nuclear technology at this time, tried to help Libya with planning and managing their program. On the other hand, even with such assistance, there was no systematic approach by Libyan authorities to organize research and development activities, nor was there effective coordination of the technical assistance, as the Libyan organizations with ostensible authority over the nuclear program seemed incapable of performing these tasks. There was little room for enterprising scientists: according to an IAEA consultant visiting in 1977 and 1978, the scientists held "mainly nominal functions within the present establishment."[55]

The IAEA provided technical assistance with several key challenges that the Libyans were not capable of handling with indigenous resources—from planning a nuclear energy program, training manpower, advising on nuclear prospecting, sourcing and installing nuclear technology—which gave the agency a clear picture of some of the pressing challenges the Libyan nuclear establishment faced. This led the IAEA's technical assistance effort to prioritize help with training, planning, and managing a nuclear energy program in the second half of the 1970s. But IAEA consultants found it very difficult to make tangible progress. First, consultants who offered training courses were met with an unmistakable lack of enthusiasm on the part of the Libyan staff, who were often absent—occasionally due to vacation or military training but at times just because the training center was too remote. Even candidates for IAEA fellowships stayed away from the training courses offered by foreign experts, and sometimes shunned contact with them. This reluctance was, in all likelihood, at least partly due to security concerns and monitoring by domestic intelligence agencies. Libyan scientists were frustrated by rigid administrative rules, restrictions on contacts with foreigners, and their own limited influence inside the nuclear establishment. This frustration created broader problems: a lack of motivation and a lack of research and development activities, despite the influx of advice and the regime's grandiose plans for nuclear power. During the summer, for example, the laboratories and offices emptied as all staff went on vacation.[56] The high proportion of foreign technical staff slowed the indigenous development of necessary skills and human resources; it also made the organization's institutional knowledge base very vulnerable, as the most senior individuals were foreign nationals. During the 1977 war between Libya and Egypt, the program came to a halt. Some Egyptian scientists left, while others used the opportunity to go on strike for better pay and conditions.

The Physics Department at the University in Tripoli continued to expand its facilities for education and research—described in 1975 as sophisticated and state-of-the-art by visiting IAEA consultants—but apparently little research actually took place.[57] IAEA experts noted that there was a lack of working discipline among the students. As noted above, another challenge was the fact that most of the staff were foreigners, including more than twenty PhDs on short-term contracts. The faculty were nearly all foreign: mainly Egyptian and some Pakistani nationals.[58]

This state of affairs puzzled the foreign experts who were charged with advising the Libyan government. Despite Libya's petrodollars, the country was underdeveloped, and basic services such as telephone and postal services were unreliable. It could take several days to arrange to make a telephone call "if the telephone operator at the post office [was] not in the proper mood."[59] The IAEA consultants struggled to find ways to spur the development of nuclear science under these conditions. Commenting on a 1976 report from an IAEA expert deployed in Libya, IAEA technical officer Joze Dolnicar responded: "Mr. Spits' first Field Report should be evaluated by a sociologist rather than a physicist. . . . At this time, the technical progress is not evident, and there is nothing that the Agency can do to accelerate the activities."[60]

Shopping for Reactors. In the mid-1970s, the Libyan regime started to look for suppliers for nuclear reactors. During this period they were turned down by the United States (in 1975), France (a preliminary agreement was canceled in 1976), and China (in 1978), which led to Tripoli approaching Moscow for a wide array of technical and military assistance.[61] The Libyans requested that the Soviet nuclear establishment provide infrastructure for the complete nuclear fuel cycle, which would constitute an independent technological foundation for a nuclear energy program and give insights into the dynamics of weapons-related technologies as well. Jalloud led a Libyan delegation to Moscow to ask for a heavy-water reactor, a heavy-water plant, and a spent-fuel reprocessing facility, a package that could have given Libya a weapons option.[62] According to a senior Soviet official, it was obvious to both parties that this was intended to be a military program.[63] The estimated price, at this stage, was $10 billion. In 1977, Libya was successful with part of its request: the Soviet state company Atomenergoexport agreed to construct a nuclear plant for power production in Libya.[64] After this initially fairly positive reception, however, the Soviet Ministry of Foreign Affairs raised concerns about possible proliferation risks and dug their heels in.

Libya's decision to seek a nuclear power reactor from the Soviet Union—a request that would be, by 1982, increased to two reactors—was made at the highest level of the regime. This power reactor was ostensibly meant to supply 440 megawatts to the national power grid. But senior regime figures apparently believed that this reactor could be the source of fissile material in a future weapons program.[65] U.S. intelligence later estimated that the two reactors, if built, could have produced enough fissile material for some thirty nuclear weapons annually.[66] Gaddafi's closest circle selected a location for the power reactor at Sirte, Libya's intended new capital and Gaddafi's hometown, apparently without assessing the suitability of the site.[67]

Very little other planning or preparation took place to prepare Libya for a nuclear power program at this stage. As research and development was still at a rudimentary stage, the prospect of operating a nuclear reactor appeared to cause unease in the Libyan nuclear establishment.[68] The Libyan scientists received some advice on how to set up a nuclear energy authority from the IAEA during 1981, but did little to follow up. The details of the power reactor and its intended role in the Libyan nuclear program were only loosely defined. The nuclear establishment did not become involved in any detailed deliberations until later, when the proposed delivery date was much closer.

Under Soviet pressure, Libya ratified the Nuclear Non-Proliferation Treaty and placed all of its nuclear facilities under safeguards as of 8 July 1980.[69] (Figure 6.1 below shows the head of the Libyan nuclear program signing this agreement at the IAEA in Vienna.) The Libyans were noticeably reluctant to discuss their plans with visiting IAEA consultants.[70] While this may have been interpreted as reluctance on the part of Libyan scientists to discuss a project with potentially sensitive dimensions, it is equally possible that the scientists lacked the information to discuss these plans. In fact, during the mid-to-late 1970s, Libya's nuclear establishment does not appear to have been involved with—or informed in any detail about—the senior level of the regime's plans, which illustrates the lack of interaction between the senior tier of the regime and the scientific establishment, even at this stage of the program.

While negotiating for the nuclear power plant, the Libyan nuclear establishment also agreed to purchase a Soviet research reactor. The research reactor was a secondary objective for the Libyans, but remained on the wish list of the nuclear establishment. In a 1975 visit to Libya, Soviet premier Alexei Kosygin discussed providing technical assistance and a research reactor with Libyan officials. In June 1975, the Soviet Union agreed to provide a research reactor. The understanding was that the center would focus on operating low-power nuclear reactors, suitable for research and development as well as familiarizing Libyans with reactor operations. Soviet technicians would remain on site to help with training and general assistance.[71] The research reactor intended for Libya could produce no more than 1.2 kilograms of plutonium per year, meaning that it would take a decade to produce enough fissile material for a single nuclear bomb.[72]

Gaddafi signed the agreement for the research reactor in Moscow in August 1975. The Soviet Union's Kurchatov Institute oversaw its installation and operation, while Atomenergoexport oversaw its construction. Atomenergoexport also shipped 11.5 kilograms of enriched uranium to fuel the reactor, which arrived in early 1981. The 10-megawatt research reactor—which would remain Libya's only nuclear reactor as it turned out—became operational in November 1983. But the Libyans were still negotiating a power reactor agreement with the Soviets, and in 1981 there were no indications that this agreement would not move forward. In November that year, IAEA consultants traveled to Libya to help with planning and preparing for a nuclear energy program. They expected the contract for the two Soviet power reactors to be signed in the near future. Their report also described the schedule they anticipated for the Libyan power program at that stage: "Present plans including the construction of two 440-MW PWR units of the Soviet type, construction to start in early 1982; construction time for the first unit is expected to be six-and-a-half years and the second unit three years later."[73] But within

Figure 6.1. Dr. Abdel Fattah Eskangy, head of the Libyan nuclear program, signs a safeguards agreement with Professor Ivan S. Zheludev, acting director general of the International Atomic Energy Agency, on 8 July 1980 (IAEA Archives, Photographic Collection, A0057).

five years the Libyan regime had squandered their prospects of making another deal with the Soviets. They never received those two reactors.

THE TAJOURA NUCLEAR RESEARCH CENTER

In tandem with their efforts to purchase nuclear reactors, the Libyans wanted to set up a nuclear research center to nurture more training and research and development for the expected power program. In 1977, two years after the contract was signed by Gaddafi in Moscow, construction of a research center began at Tajoura, 25 kilometers outside Tripoli. While the Libyans were expecting that more facilities would be added elsewhere, such as an institute for training nuclear technicians, the Tajoura Nuclear Research Center (TNRC) would become the hub of the Libyan nuclear program.

The AEA was led at that time by two Libyan scientists, Abdel Fattah Eskangy and his deputy, Hajji M. Kershman, who had been the first Libyan nuclear scientist to obtain a PhD during the early 1970s.[74] Eskangy was a nuclear scientist who specialized in radioisotope techniques for groundwater studies, which were of central interest to the regime's ambitious plans for water extraction from the desert.[75] Under Eskangy's directorship, the nuclear program focused on exploring dual-use technologies that would be relevant to both a nuclear energy program and a weapons program. The TNRC was initially directed by Mustapha Torki, a Tunisian scientist. Jalloud headed the committee overseeing the development of the center. He reportedly expressed interest in enrichment technology and plutonium reprocessing to the Egyptian scientists working at the TNRC.[76] Under the leadership of the AEA and the managers of the TNRC, the loosely defined objective of the nuclear program was to examine the nuclear fuel cycle, but it apparently lacked more specific targets or guidelines. Although the leaders of Libya's nuclear establishment set up a small health physics unit and remained interested in nuclear water desalination, which had obvious applications in a desert country, they did not prioritize other applications of nuclear technology.

The development of a large nuclear research center at Tajoura was a welcome boost to the struggling nuclear program. While construction was ongoing, the Libyans set up different research departments for the new research center. These departments could carry out basic research and training for scientists and technical workers while waiting for the new facilities to become operational. By 1977, the TNRC had several departments, but only one—the Activation Analysis Department—had ongoing research activities. There was a Physics Department without a research program or activities; a Plasma Department; a Radiation Protection Department; a Maintenance, Operation and Construction Department; an Engineering Research Unit; and a Computer and Documentation Department.[77] Some of these departments had no staff. The center had a total staff of six hundred, with one hundred engineers, technicians, and workers. The Engineering Research Unit appeared to be particularly strong in the eyes of visiting IAEA experts.[78] The staff held degrees from universities in Libya and abroad but had virtually no practical or professional experience with nuclear power.[79]

As the development of the TNRC moved forward, its approach for acquiring technical instruments was described as "haphazard." Nowhere were there specifications for training staff in how to use this equipment to develop research programs.[80] The Libyan nuclear establishment was keen to buy more instruments even though they continued to have problems with the equipment they had and lacked scientists with the capacity to make use of advanced research equipment.

Inefficient administration and cumbersome regulations stalled initiative and slowed the pace even during this time of expansion. Teaching at the University of Tripoli was now geared toward training students in all aspects of reactors and preparing them to work with the research reactor expected to arrive from the Soviet Union in five years' time (1982).[81] In effect, the Physics Department became the training ground for the staff of the expanding TNRC. Beyond this role, however, there was limited collaboration or coordination between the Physics Department and the center.[82] At times, the TNRC apparently demanded priority access to visiting IAEA consultants who offered classes or other training opportunities, while the university had to wait. Such exclusionary tactics were particularly unproductive since, as noted above, the TNRC scientists rarely bothered to turn up to these classes anyway.

The senior management at the TNRC during this period, and most of the senior technical staff, were foreign experts recruited by the Libyan authorities. For example, the Geology Department was directed by an Egyptian scientist, Mohamed El Aziz; and the AEA was supported by Haschisch, an Egyptian from the Cairo Nuclear Center.[83] The TNRC was initially staffed mainly by about one hundred Soviet technicians training Libyans to operate the site.[84] Visiting foreign experts were nonetheless struck by how understaffed the center was, and encouraged their Libyan hosts to make more efforts to develop an indigenous base of relevant skills and know-how. Paying the scientists and engineers adequately would, of course, also have helped. In January 1975, Gaddafi announced that Libya would seek to recruit Arab scientists from the West to help Libya's nuclear program. A member of the RCC began to approach individual scientists seeking to recruit them.[85] Recruiting scientists and engineers was still a challenge, as was developing a more efficient administration. As a visiting IAEA expert observed in 1976, "the low level of activities may be retraceable to the inefficiency of related services such as the Administration and the Purchase Department. Besides, because of underpayment, it is difficult to attract technicians matching a high standard."[86] While the university planned to graduate about ten students per year in nuclear engineering beginning in about 1982, this would not be enough to satisfy the growing demands of the nuclear power program.[87]

Senior regime figures provided key support for the expansion of the program. Jalloud was a central driving force in Libya's early pursuit of nuclear technology. The committee charged with overseeing the establishment of the nuclear reactor at the TNRC reportedly met every week. The Egyptian scientist heading up the Physics Department, Abdelaziz, who assisted with the expansion of the center, was assured that Gaddafi would provide whatever resources deemed necessary.[88] Gaddafi did not meet Abdelaziz personally, but Jalloud continued to follow the nuclear project closely, and he reported directly to Gaddafi.[89]

The TNRC was becoming operational, but visiting experts from the IAEA were struck by a sense of apathy among its scientists. A visiting IAEA consultant noted that there was a brief flurry of activity in 1975–1976, when several projects were launched, but that the TNRC had become stagnant by 1977–1978.[90] Explanations ranged from inefficient administration and poorly motivated scientists to military service and a halt of activities in preparation for a further expansion of the research center. The acute shortage of skilled staff and the heavy reliance on foreign staff also contributed to make the management and operations vulnerable to disruption.

The lack of planning at the TNRC made little sense. There did not seem to be any meaningful leadership guiding the efforts at the center. According to an IAEA consultant, "the most conspicuous feature is the notable lack of any clearly discernible general plan envisaging specific objectives for the present utilization and future development of this nuclear research center."[91] However, once the Soviet research reactor arrived in 1981, the situation at the TNRC improved. Fathi Nuh, who had studied nuclear physics in the United States and would remain a significant figure in the Libyan nuclear establishment for years to come, and Eskangy, director of the AEA, oversaw the initial operation of the reactor. The IRT research reactor section in the TNRC's Reactor Department carried out a series of experiments.[92]

In tandem with these efforts, the AEA returned to the front end of the nuclear fuel cycle, renewing its efforts to explore uranium deposits. An exploration program had been run by the Prospecting Department at the Ministry of Geological Research and Mining since 1974, with a team of twelve geologists plus one technician and a pilot. In 1979, the AEA reached out to the IAEA, announcing a "major effort in uranium prospecting" and created a Raw Materials Division.[93] This project was envisioned on a five-year basis, and would draw on extensive foreign assistance. The uranium exploration program, led by M. A. Ghuma at the AEA, undertook sample collection and analysis.[94] The director of the AEA, Eskangy, requested that the laboratory develop the capacity to analyze yellowcake.[95]

Between 1977 and 1981, the overall progress of the nuclear program was uneven. Although there was more equipment available in the university laboratories, at the TNRC activities were kept on hold, despite having the Soviet-supplied equipment giving the option of carrying out up to thirty different types of experiments.[96] Visiting IAEA experts noted that the planned expansion had turned into an extended "transitional period" in which not much was happening. Eskangy and his staff had only started to plan research and training activities in late 1977.[97] Furthermore, "the general objectives in training and research were only vaguely defined . . . and many administrative and organizational matters on which effective implementation of the assignment depended, were not resolved."[98] The scientists "showed lack of interest in the initiatives of the [IAEA] expert to provide training aimed at improving their background in Nuclear Science."[99] The frustrated consultant instead wrote up a training manual, which could be useful in the future if the conditions at the TNRC became more amenable to support research and development activities.

One would have expected the TNRC to seek ways to adapt their existing resources to facilitate applied research tailored to meet Libya's development challenges. But the Libyan scientists were more interested in basic research and acted accordingly: "The planners of the Nuclear Research Centre were largely concerned with assembling an excellently equipped institute, and very little attention was paid to designing appropriate research programmes. As a result the type of equipment available or planned in the Centre, favours fundamental research, of the type with [only] marginal relevance to the country's requirements."[100]

Despite the IAEA's impressions, some of the inexperienced staff at the TNRC were keen to receive more training and travel abroad for fellowships. They complained privately to visiting IAEA consultants that they were prevented from doing so by regulations.[101] Still, it was unclear why they did not take advantage of opportunities to learn from visiting experts. For example, an IAEA consultant spent several months at the TNRC to advise and train the staff in radioisotope research. His lectures were halted after the Libyan staff failed to turn up. Another consultant noted that the "occasional participation [of Libyans] in these programmes is on a schedule of unpredictable randomness."[102] The Libyans were frequently absent, leaving an audience of just three or four foreign scientists and one or two Libyans in attendance at classes.[103] The AEA, which at that time had fifty or sixty employees, did not always fulfill their counterpart obligations to the IAEA when receiving such assistance.[104]

This state of affairs raised questions within the IAEA about the purpose of this expansion and about the direction of the Libyan nuclear program. It became "increasingly clear" to the IAEA consultants that "the continued existence of the Tajura Nuclear Research Center must obviously be based mainly on administrative considerations rather than any consistent plan for the effective development of its scientific capabilities within the foreseeable future."[105]

During the 1970s, Libya pursued a nuclear weapons option in two ways: as a clandestine off-shoot of a nuclear energy program and by investing in nuclear weapons programs in other states, notably Pakistan. By the early 1980s, its efforts to develop nuclear energy and carve out a weapons option at home would intensify, as Libya began to explore both the plutonium and centrifuge routes to a nuclear weapons program. But the Libyan nuclear establishment faced many hurdles: a shortage of qualified staff; a lack of necessary industrial capacities; and a leader whose main ideological project was to dismantle the state. Over the 1980s, Libya's nuclear prospects would deteriorate, adversely affected by war, international proliferation concerns, retaliatory air strikes, sanctions, and isolation.

By 1981, the Gaddafi regime anticipated the imminent arrival of nuclear power and, they believed, a weapons option. As this chapter shows, neither ambition was founded in reality. The gap between actual capabilities on the ground and the regime's ambitions increased dramatically during the 1970s. Despite assistance from the Soviet Union and the IAEA, Libya's nuclear institutions remained strangely underdeveloped. The program lacked the essential organizational capacity to plan, organize, and carry out a nuclear program in line with the regime's objectives and ambitious procurement activities. The organizational weaknesses of Libya's nuclear establishment, at both the TNRC and national levels, influenced every aspect of Libya's research and development activities, from planning to implementation. The nuclear establishment lacked a senior tier of leaders capable of organizing and running a research program and continued to suffer from a shortage of technicians and scientists. Scientists made the most of the lavish acquisition campaign carried out by the regime by developing well-equipped laboratories for basic research. Meanwhile, IAEA experts worried about the prospects of an imminent arrival of two large nuclear power reactors in a country that was clearly unprepared and ill-equipped to cope. In short, the stunted development of Libya's nuclear program during the 1970s was an overdetermined outcome.

To understand how Libyan scientists could get away with underperforming—to the point of absurdity—while the Gaddafi regime came to believe its scientists were capable of launching a nuclear energy program is impossible without considering how Gaddafi's Cultural Revolution had eroded an already weak state. Gaddafi's revolution was intended to culminate in "statelessness" in theory, but in practice it unleashed vigilante Revolutionary Committees on an already brittle state and alienated potential nuclear suppliers. Meanwhile, the Libyan nuclear program, which was modeled on Western organizations, emerged in a state that lacked the organizational resources to launch a complex technological program. It would take more than five more years before these problems became apparent to the regime, as the nuclear energy program continued to dawdle along until the mid-1980s. In the interim, the Libyan nuclear scientists launched a secret program to develop centrifuges as an alternative route to the bomb. But by the close of the 1980s this program still seemed to be going nowhere.

Nuclear Weapons Remain Elusive, 1982–1989

In 1981, Libyan nuclear scientists anticipated two Soviet nuclear power re-actors to arrive the following year. At the same time, a team of researchers began to explore centrifuges in secret, hoping to develop an alternative tech-nical route to a nuclear weapons capability. A decade later, nuclear energy remained an unfulfilled ambition while the centrifuge program failed to produce even a single operational model. After 1989 the Libyans aban-doned both tracks, disillusioned with the options of developing a nuclear weapons capability as an offshoot from an energy program or through indigenous research and development efforts, and turned to the nuclear black market.

This chapter explains how and why both the energy program and the clan-destine centrifuge project failed so completely. It also raises the question of why the Libyan regime stood idly by, and whether Muammar Gaddafi was aware of the extent to which the nuclear program was failing. Little has previously been known about the Libyan program during this decade, especially the highly secretive centrifuge program. New primary sources—including contemporary International Atomic Energy Agency (IAEA) re-ports, statements from scientists attempting to lay the foundation for nu-clear research and development, and the author's interviews with senior officials from the former Libyan regime—elucidate how the erosion of the Libyan state affected the nuclear establishment as it prepared to launch a nuclear power program. These sources show how the reactor program was stymied by the absence of planning and preparations prior to the collapse of the Soviet reactor deal in 1986. This helps to explain why the Libyan pro-gram was so vulnerable to the loss of foreign assistance, and why the decade-long research and development program focusing on centrifuges failed to launch. As Libyan scientists were increasingly left to their own devices, myriad problems due to failures of planning, management, and oversight came to the fore. It was not simply a question of investing enough, getting more foreign assistance, or making the program enough of a priority: the state lacked the organizational capability to support the planning and overseeing of a project of this size and complexity. This affected every stage from planning to implementation and oversight. There was no clear prioritization of tasks or formulation of clear and measurable objectives; neither was there a sequential approach to the acquisitions that were part of the planning for the future weapons program.

During the mid-1980s and early 1990s, the Gaddafi regime found itself increasingly isolated and vulnerable. Despite investing in a conventional arms buildup, the Libyan armed forces were also humiliated by poorly equipped Chadian forces in clashes during the 1980s. It was clear that Libya's armed forces were incapable of both defending the regime and prevailing against the forces of neighboring states. As oil revenues declined during the 1980s, the collapsing economy put new domestic pressures on the regime, and led regime factions to question the large cost of pursuing nuclear technology. The United States targeted Gaddafi's residence, as well as Libya's air force, in a series of clashes during the 1980s. The air force was in an even worse state. When the relationship between Libya and the USSR soured after 1986, the air force lost critically important support from Soviet-bloc advisers and technicians.[1] As Gaddafi began to crave a nuclear deterrent to secure his regime's political and physical survival, the nuclear program went nowhere.

Isolation and New Vulnerabilities

The 1980s were a disastrous period for Libya's foreign relations and, by extension, the nuclear program, which relied almost entirely on foreign assistance. The Gaddafi regime's foreign relations became increasingly radicalized, both in terms of policies (attempting to redraw Libya's maritime border and supporting terrorists and terrorist groups such as the Abu Nidal Organization) and methods (assassination attempts reportedly targeted expatriate Libyans, foreign ambassadors, and U.S. president Ronald Reagan).[2] This had dramatic consequences, most notably Reagan declaring regime change in Libya to be a U.S. policy objective.[3] In 1983, the Reagan administration also banned Libyans from studying nuclear science in the United States.

Relations between Libya and the United States had deteriorated badly since 1979, when the American embassy in Tripoli was closed after demonstrators burned it down. In May 1980, the United States closed its diplomatic mission in Tripoli. After the Gaddafi regime began to dispute the Libyan maritime border in the Gulf of Sirte, tensions spilled over. In September a Libyan jet fired at a U.S. reconnaissance aircraft above those waters. The following year, in August 1981, the Libyan air force fired two missiles against American aircraft, which retaliated by shooting down two Libyan jets. Two weeks later, on the twelfth anniversary of the 1969 coup, Gaddafi threatened to strike against U.S. nuclear arsenals in the Mediterranean if this happened again.[4] There was another altercation in 1983 in which no fire was exchanged.[5]

The Soviet Union was Libya's single strong ally and main supplier of nuclear technology until the Libyan economy plummeted in the mid-1980s. As detailed in the previous chapter, in 1981 the two countries had entered a broad agreement including contracts for conventional arms, technology transfers—including nuclear technology—and a promise of Soviet support if Libya were subjected to foreign aggression.[6] However, as Libya's foreign exchange reserves quickly drained during the early 1980s, the Soviets appear to have begun to question how Libya would pay for the reactors and may have considered accepting a barter arrangement.[7]

In 1986, the relationship between the Soviet Union and Libya deteriorated rapidly after Tripoli decided not to move forward with the nuclear reactor deal. The United States applied pressure on other states including Belgium, which was considering replacing the Soviets as a key supplier of technology for the Libyan nuclear energy program. Over the next few years, the Libyan program launched several initiatives to explore uranium enrichment technologies, but none of their efforts moved beyond initial studies. Libya also found it increasingly difficult to find nuclear suppliers. With or without foreign assistance, the Libyan program seemed incapable of developing an indigenous path to nuclear weapons prior to 1989.

PREPARING FOR NUCLEAR POWER

In 1981 an amendment to the Nuclear Energy Act replaced the Libyan Atomic Energy Authority (NAEA) by a new institution, the Secretariat of Atomic Energy (SAE), which was formally tasked with the highest executive role in planning, overseeing, and managing the nuclear energy program. The National Committee of Atomic Energy (NCAE), which formally oversaw the SAE, was chaired by SAE secretary Abdel-Majid Gaoud. On 7 January 1981 the Libyan General People's Congress (GPC) rubber-stamped the creation of the SAE, which had the formal status of a ministry.[8] If this gave the impression that the Libyan nuclear authorities were given more institutional powers, this was an illusion. The IAEA had advised the Libyans to create an adequate institutional framework for their nuclear energy program. The creation of the SAE and the organizational restructuring that took place in 1981 was an attempt to separate executive responsibilities inside the nuclear establishment. But creating a new set of organizations could not fix the fundamental problems facing Libyan state institutions: inadequate resources for project planning and implementation, a steady erosion of authority by Gaddafi's revolutionary agitators, and the absence of adequate monitoring mechanisms.

The SAE was led by Gaoud, a close associate of Gaddafi who would play a central role in the Libyan regime over the next several decades, and had six members.[9] Gaoud's role as SAE secretary came with the title of minister of atomic energy for peaceful uses, as well as chairman of the National Committee of Atomic Energy (NCAE). He reported directly to Gaddafi and his inner circle in the ministerial Cabinet.[10] Gaoud also played a leading role in another prestige project that was highly favored by Gaddafi, the "Great Man-Made River" intended to transport groundwater across the Libyan desert. Other members of the SAE included Under-Secretaries Fathi Nuh, Ibrahim al-Hasain and four other specialists in nuclear energy. The Under-secretaries headed the two wings of the organization; Nuh, the Executive Committee for Scientific Affairs, and al-Hasain, the Executive Committee for Financial and Administrative Affairs.[11] All six members of the SAE were university professors with no practical experience of planning or operating a nuclear power program. Figure 7.1 below provides a snapshot overview of the administrative reorganizations of the Libyan nuclear establishment during the 1970s and 1980s.

The SAE's Executive Committee for Scientific Affairs under Nuh, who also worked in the Department of Nuclear and Electronic Engineering at Al-Fateh University (as Tripoli University had been renamed in April 1976), took charge of launching and overseeing the nuclear power program. The committee was the official liaison with foreign organizations such as the IAEA and with the foreign companies assisting Libya's nuclear program.[12] A separate unit, the Committee for the Technical Review of the Nuclear Power Plant Contract, was led by former AEA director Abdel Fattah Eskangy and would study the technical aspects of the Soviet contract.[13] In 1983 the new Department for Training and Technical Cooperation led by Najib Sheibani was added to the SAE portfolio. The second wing of the SAE, the Executive Committee for Financial and Administrative Affairs, had departments focusing on legal, administrative, and financial matters, as well as foreign relations.[14]

The NCAE—which had been merged inside the now defunct NAEA—was now given a combined decision-making and advisory role with the SAE and was chaired by SAE secretary Gaoud. The NCAE was an appointed state committee, which meant that it was not part of the GPC structure. As an autonomous and essentially technocratic body, the NCAE was largely insulated from the radical actors in the Libyan regime.

Meanwhile, despite these organizational changes the nuclear program continued to face increasingly complex tasks, while struggling with inadequate institutional and human resources. Figure 7.2 gives an overview of the main tracks and organizational developments in the Libyan nuclear weapons program.

Visiting IAEA experts described the administrative and technical infrastructures of the Libyan nuclear program in late 1981 as "extremely weak."[15] The staff were all fairly recent graduates who were not only stretched thin, in the sense that they had to fulfill more functions than their job titles sug-

Libyan Nuclear Weapons Program Timeline, 1981–2003

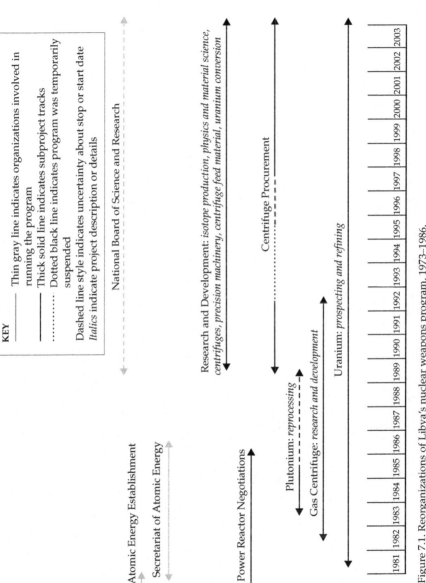

Figure 7.1. Reorganizations of Libya's nuclear weapons program, 1973–1986.

Libyan Nuclear Weapons Program Timeline, 1981–2003

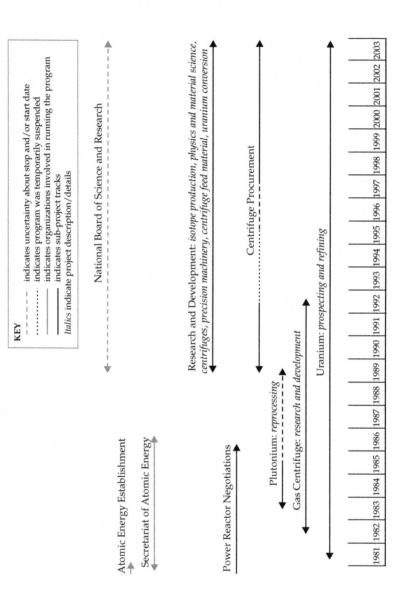

Figure 7.2. Libyan nuclear weapons program timeline, 1981–2003.

gested, but struggled to meet even the demands of their primary responsibilities.[16] For example, the SAE's Department of Power, with just five staff members, was in charge of planning and launching the nuclear power project.[17] The IAEA consultants reported to the director general that this department "must divide its present efforts between the technical proposal evaluation, nuclear power programme planning, evaluation of safety and regulatory aspects, organization and training of the future operating and maintenance team and sending away junior engineers for further training to universities, courses and industry."[18]

It was clear that the Libyans needed help. For example, as late as mid-1982 there does not appear to have been any detailed schedule at the SAE for the introduction of a nuclear energy program. The Libyan technical staff seem to have found the IAEA's advice—focus on basic capacity building and sound organizational planning rather than ambitious and abstract targets—a constructive influence. However, as contemporary U.S. intelligence assessments noted, the Libyan scientists had limited influence, and while they attempted to adopt some of this advice they lacked the human resources and institutional authority to use it to emulate the organization of nuclear programs in other states.[19]

The senior regime members had selected a site for the power reactor complex at Sirte, Gaddafi's hometown. Sirte was becoming a new home for Libya's state buildings and was intended to showcase the revolution. Placing the reactor here indicated the prestige associated with the nuclear power project. However, the SAE did not offer the IAEA any information about the specifications of the site, nor did it indicate that preparations had begun in earnest. This had a simple explanation—the SAE had not yet carried out any such assessment or started preparations. This, United States analysts suspected, reflected deeper divisions inside the SAE with regards to the need for such reactors, or, perhaps, what purpose they would actually serve.[20]

At this point, in 1981–1982, the Libyans had not started preparing institutional resources or mechanisms for tracking imported nuclear material, nor did they have safety procedures in place at nuclear facilities, despite the IAEA's advice. The notion of regulation and oversight, which the IAEA considered essential for governing a nuclear energy program, was not familiar to Libyan civil servants. Furthermore, the Libyan institutional landscape was unlike that found in other states. The Libyan regime was reluctant to set up an institutional mechanism for oversight that would be independent of the SAE, the chief agency for nuclear affairs. In Libya, oversight was carried out by individuals trusted by Gaddafi, not facilitated by institutions. After visiting the Libyan nuclear establishment in 1982, an IAEA consultant noted that the "concept of the regulatory body is not appreciated, nor have positive steps been taken to establish such a body."[21] The IAEA had encouraged the Libyan nuclear establishment to set up an independent regulatory authority for radiation protection, but the Libyans pointed out that the updated law had made the SAE the responsible agency for nuclear affairs, and were reluctant to set up an independent body for radiation protection. The IAEA consultants concluded that "it might be politically difficult and ineffectual in practice to attempt to establish a nuclear regulatory authority reporting to a different Secretariat, as would in principle be desirable to achieve full independence for the authority."[22] Nevertheless, following advice from the IAEA, SAE secretary Gaoud attempted to address these concerns by placing the NCAE (rather than the SAE) in charge of overseeing operational matters.

Although the nuclear establishment still had a "thin bench"—limited technical expertise held by a small number of individuals—it was able to launch some initiatives. At the SAE, staff members were taking steps toward creating a managerial framework for research and development activities. For example, at the Department of Radiation Protection at the SAE, a small group comprised of Nouri Ali Addaroughi, Fawzia Ali Bakkoush, and Ibrahim Abdul Rahman, prepared radiation protection guidelines. When they began, Libya had no licensing authority, nor any mechanism for control over the import, transport, or use of radioisotopes in Libya. Their recommendations, based on those of the IAEA, formed the basis of a proposed regulatory law prepared in 1981.[23] In practical terms, however, it was difficult to develop institutional capacities with such limited human resources and undefined room for maneuver. These conditions were a fragile foundation for an expansive new program.[24]

The SAE made it plain that it had ambitious plans for the future role of nuclear energy in Libya. As the Gaddafi regime continued to invest heavily to spur indigenous industrial development, energy demand rose at what IAEA officials described as "spectacular growth rates."[25] In a rare 1982 interview, SAE secretary Gaoud explained:

> Today we consume about 3,800 MW of electricity. . . . By 1995 it will be about 6,000 MW and our nuclear programme will cover about 20% of our energy needs. . . . This means we have to get about 1,200 MW, which will be distributed between four [nuclear] stations. One is in the final stages of study and negotiations right now. It is a pressurised water reactor, and it will be signed for at the beginning of 1982. It will be built by the Soviet Union and should be in operation by 1986. We are still discussing the three other power plants. The hope is that by the year 2000 we will have all four plants in operation. . . . We expect to use these power plants for a dual-use purpose— power for heavy industry and heat for desalinising brackish water.[26]

These plans were staggeringly ambitious. As IAEA experts reported in 1981, Libya sought to launch an ambitious nuclear energy program before they had managed to set up a viable research program.[27] The Libyan nuclear establishment made no secret of the urgency and ambition behind its program. In September 1981, while visiting the IAEA, M. A. Ghuma of the SAE's

Raw Materials Division characterized the nuclear program as a broad effort driven by the government, which included a five-year uranium exploration program.[28] He stressed the commitment with which his government backed the nuclear project.[29]

The regime's ambitions seem to have taken no account of the actual capabilities and resources of the Libyan nuclear establishment at that time. The shortage of qualified staff was still a critical challenge. The emergence of several new institutes at the universities and the expansion of the Tajoura Nuclear Research Center (TNRC) and the SAE, not to mention other industries, stretched Libya's trained and qualified human resources even further.[30] In 1982, of a total of four hundred staff at the TNRC, just one hundred were engineers or technicians.

To develop a nuclear power program on this limited foundation would require intensive effort and investment over a number of years. In May 1982 the Libyan government requested the IAEA "on an urgent basis" to advise them on how to prepare and plan for the launching of the nuclear power program.[31] The IAEA delegation reported its concerns to the IAEA director general in somewhat understated language, saying that the nuclear program might not "obtain the necessary national priority" to become "an island of excellence in a generally not quite satisfactory state of technological development and manpower qualifications."[32] In their internal reporting, the IAEA consultants were more blunt: this was a program facing severe challenges.

In the report following the IAEA visit in late 1982, IAEA consultants described the talks between the SAE's Department of Power and the Soviet supplier company Atomenergoexport on the nuclear reactor contract. The talks had progressed to a discussion of two 440-megawatt reactors and a water desalination unit. The contract had not been signed, and the scope of the deliverables, such as training for Libyan engineers and technical workers, was not yet decided. As a result, IAEA experts reported that "no work or training is presently being performed" by the Soviets in preparation for the delivery of these two units.[33] Apparently, the Soviets intended to complete this project as they had in the case of the TNRC, as a complete turnkey (or "superturnkey") project constructed completely by their own technicians with minimal Libyan involvement.[34]

How did the Libyan nuclear establishment attempt to cope with their inadequate basic organizational and technical resources in their efforts to plan and operate a nuclear power program? While individual staff members did their best, despite being asked to carry out tasks they were not trained for, there was a fundamental mismatch between the institutional resources and the task at hand. As a result, the Libyan nuclear establishment fell behind on all fronts. There are no indications suggesting that this was communicated to the senior regime leaders, and it does not appear that this lack of capabilities in any way affected the anticipated schedule of beginning preparations for the construction of the new power reactor site in 1982.

The Department of Power, for example, had the lead responsibility to train, operate, and initially regulate the energy program, but had only eighteen employees.[35] IAEA consultants gave advice on planning, oversight, and human resources, but they were concerned that the Libyans did not seem to make much use of their input, and struggled to operate even basic research projects. For example, the Libyan nuclear establishment, with the help of Soviet and IAEA consultants, launched research projects including "radiation and nuclear physics, nuclear and radiochemistry, shielding and radiation protection, neutron and reactor physics," but these seemed to falter at the very initial stages.[36] Meanwhile, the regime's acquisition efforts moved forward at a rapid and increasing pace. This created concern among IAEA experts, who tried to tailor their advice to target "major problem areas in a situation which would seem too full of problems."[37]

The Libyan nuclear establishment's failure to develop sufficient human resources for the planning or operation of a nuclear energy program stood in sharp contrast to the physical infrastructure they were acquiring from abroad. This was the result of several institutional shortcomings. No one drew up a plan to scale up training from basic research and development to running a nuclear energy program. In any case, the Libyan institutions were producing too few candidates, and several state institutions were competing to recruit from the small pool of graduates. When the TNRC was completed, it offered several facilities suitable for research and training, including the 10-megawatt research reactor that became operational in 1983, two accelerators, and a tokamak research device.[38] The SAE had a large room available for training activities, but this apparently saw little use.[39] The SAE planned to build a separate facility some 60 kilometers outside Tripoli, initially referred to as the Institute of Nuclear Technology, for training of up to five hundred technicians. This institute was intended to produce the necessary manpower for the nuclear energy program. It was unclear when this would be built or operational, however; according to IAEA consultants, as of late 1981 there were no plans for the proposed institute's "curricula, laboratories, or technical fields."[40] As it turned out, the institute did not materialize.

The nuclear scientists were not involved in the regime's decisions about the two Soviet reactors until they were asked to assess the technical aspects of the contract proposal in the late stage of negotiations. The SAE became belatedly involved only in 1981, just a year before the new reactors were expected to arrive, and its predecessor, the AEA, does not appear to have been consulted either. While SAE secretary Gaoud was a rising star with strong political connections, and former senior figures in the uranium exploration program had risen to senior regime positions (notably Jadallah Azzouz Ettalhi, who became minister of industry and minerals in the late 1970s), the institutions of the nuclear establishment, the SAE and the NCAE, do not appear to have been systematically consulted in high-level deliberations. As a result, the regime's assumptions about its technical options were in all likelihood inaccurate.

For example, the Gaddafi regime appears initially to have believed that the nuclear power reactors obtained from the Soviet Union could be the source of fissile material in a future weapons program.[41] This was technically possible—U.S. intelligence estimated that the two nuclear power reactors could produce enough fissile material for some thirty nuclear weapons per year—but practically it was infeasible.[42] The Soviet Union had insisted that Libya subject their nuclear facilities to IAEA safeguards and, accordingly, they were subject to monitoring and regular inspections. If Libya left the Non-Proliferation Treaty (NPT), or was caught diverting fissile material, it would risk a preemptive strike and would certainly be cut off from future assistance from the Soviet Union. This fact would have been obvious to the scientists, but apparently escaped the senior regime officials until the mid-1980s.

The two 440-megawatt Soviet reactors were meant to serve multiple purposes: they could produce nuclear energy, give Libyan scientists access to technology and training that would be essential if they later opted for a plutonium route to a nuclear weapons capability (though this would require additional infrastructure that was not subject to the NPT safeguards), and provide opportunities for scientific research. U.S. opinion was, however, that an ambitious and expanding civilian nuclear power program could create organizational pressures in favor of peaceful applications.[43] At this early stage, there appears to have been no discernible efforts in the Libyan nuclear establishment to steer the program in any particular direction: neither toward nor away from nuclear weapons.

By the mid-1980s, the Libyan regime had recognized that the power reactors could not be used directly for a weapons program as long as the country remained dependent on the Soviet Union or any other state for nuclear assistance. The senior regime leaders were believed to see the reactors as a symbol of industrial achievement, in addition to being a source of energy.[44] Thus, the nuclear energy program could both showcase an important technological achievement and develop indigenous know-how (such as plutonium reprocessing) potentially useful for a nuclear weapons program.

A Contested State: Technocrats vs. Revolutionaries

As Libya prepared to introduce nuclear power, the Cultural Revolution was intensifying. In March 1979, Gaddafi had announced the "separation of the state and the revolution," introducing a new stage in his ideological project in which nonstate actors—the Revolutionary Committees—would wield more power. As these nonstate actors became more powerful than state agencies, it was not always clear where decision-making authority was located. The power to make decisions and wield influence was increasingly a reflection of individual connections, not formal titles or organizational roles.

Gaddafi, the self-proclaimed "Leader of the Revolution," distanced himself from the official institutions of the state. By early 1981, the Revolutionary Command Council had been reduced from the original twelve to just five individuals: Gaddafi, Abdessalam Jalloud, Khaled Humeidi, Mustafa Kharroubi, and Abu Bakr Yunis Jabr. The GPC, overseen by a secretariat and twenty-three officials, met about once a year to rubber-stamp the senior regime members' decisions and appointments. Gaddafi ruled behind the scenes, based on advice from his informal "Kitchen Cabinet"—who proposed various policies for his approval—rather than formal reporting by the ministries.[45] An ambitious new generation of leaders emerged from the Revolutionary Committees who would come to play key roles in the senior tier of the regime and, in the case of Matuq M. Matuq, the nuclear program.

These changes, and the general radicalization of Libyan policies during the 1980s, caused tension in the senior tiers of the regime. Several high-profile officials in key government positions defected. By May 1981, Gaddafi had lost his first prime minister, a former head of intelligence, a former foreign minister and ambassador to the United Nations, a former minister of economy and planning, the former oil minister, and several senior ambassadors.[46] One of these defectors was Libya's ambassador to India, Mohammed Magaryef, a former auditor general who had targeted regime corruption (he would return to Libyan politics after the Arab Spring). His departure in particular resulted in a further weakening of the oversight capacities of the state. Through this string of defections, the regime lost some of its key technocratic elites and senior figures who were capable of some measure of oversight. Over the next years, tensions would continue between the radical wing of the regime and the wing advocating economic regeneration. The nuclear question would surface repeatedly as one of the divisive issues debated by these factions, particularly in the early 1990s as the "revolutionaries" favored pursuing nuclear weapons while the other group, comprising several longtime associates of Gaddafi, was critical of the rising costs associated with the program.

Institutions, such as those making up the nuclear establishment, had very little direct influence on decision making at the senior tiers of the regime. However, a small number of individual technocrats would play a significant role in managing the flagship technical projects of that era, such as the nuclear program, heavy-industry projects, and the Great Man-Made River project.[47] Some of the more prominent technocrats originally came from the nuclear program, such as Gaoud, or the oil sector, such as Shukri Ghanem, an economist who would later serve as prime minister. Ettalhi also held several key posts. He was director of the General Department of Geological

Research and Mining in 1970 and later became minister of industry and minerals, as noted above. He served as prime minister twice (1979–1984, 1986–1987) and as secretary for strategic industries in 1990.[48] He also played a leading role in the Great Man-Made River project and was a key adviser to the team participating in negotiations that would lead to the dismantlement of Libya's weapons of mass destruction (WMD) programs in 2003. Another prominent technocrat was Omar Montasser, the nephew of Libya's first prime minister, Mohammed Montasser, who served as minister for heavy industry during the late 1970s and later as prime minister himself (1987–1990), and minister for planning in 1992.[49] However, the technocrats promoted from the nuclear program had no incentives to pinpoint the many structural challenges facing this project. Nor would it be possible to blame problems on Gaddafi's effort to dismantle state institutions. Gaddafi held individuals, more than institutions, directly accountable. This created a strong incentive to keep failing projects afloat rather than point out failures.

The radical wing of the regime got the upper hand in the early 1980s, when Gaddafi was determined to realize his vision of dismantling the state. In September 1981, Gaddafi announced a broadened set of responsibilities for the Revolutionary Committees. They took over Libya's embassies abroad, where they carried out systematic assassinations targeting the exiled Libyan opposition.[50] The consequences would be dramatic. In the spring of 1984, shots were fired from the Libyan embassy in London at a group of demonstrators, killing British police officer Yvonne Fletcher. Inside the embassy were Matuq, who would take over the nuclear program in the 1990s, and Musa Kusa, the powerful head of Libyan intelligence, who swiftly left the country using diplomatic passports. Diplomatic relations between Libya and the United Kingdom were severed as a result. The regime also continued to weaken the professional armed forces. For example, Gaddafi set up a popular army to rival the professional military. In 1977 he began arming and training civilians to serve as a popular army, ostensibly to defend against foreign intervention through guerilla warfare. In 1981, the popular army counted half a million men and women.[51]

Although Gaddafi spent more than his neighbors on armaments and the number of Libyan soldiers increased, the armed forces were undermined on several fronts. Numbering only 7,000 in 1969, the armed forces expanded to 55,000 in 1982 and totaled 86,000 by 1988.[52] Still, this was one of the smallest regular armed forces in the region.[53] A series of unpopular Libyan interventions in Chad, Uganda, and the Sahara raised concerns about the loyalty of the armed forces to the Gaddafi regime.[54] As Libya and Chad clashed over the Auzou Strip, an area of uranium deposits, between 1978 and 1987, many Libyans were drafted for military service without adequate training.

The revolutionary project also set out to recast the Libyan economy, with severe consequences for industry and society. These consequences were mainly due to disruption, but the regime failed to implement its vision of a new economic order bringing industrialization and collective agriculture. Property and wealth were seized by the regime or by Revolutionary Committee members. The state seized control over large- and small-scale economic enterprises, even shops and supermarkets, and undertook new heavy-industrial projects, including a steel plant. However, the state did not provide sufficient electricity, housing, and transport for workers assigned to remote project sites. Many employees failed to turn up for work, partly because the supporting infrastructure was missing, and many were drafted to compulsory military service and sent to fight in Chad.[55] As we will see, the resulting productivity failures also afflicted the TNRC.

To make matters worse, Libya's oil income began to decrease during the 1980s due to falling world oil prices. This led to having to make choices and setting priorities, in stark contrast to the lavish "guns and butter" policies of the late 1970s. As Ghanem recounted in 1985, the regime opted for "maximum arms and minimum food"—hardly a popular move, he conceded.[56] By 1983, the regime was forced to make more trade-offs and chose, somewhat arbitrarily, to prioritize heavy industry over light industry. By 1985 all new projects had been stopped other than the steel plant, aluminum smelter, and petrochemical projects. These projects, like the nuclear energy program, continued to rely heavily on foreign expertise, raw materials, and technology.[57]

Troubles at Tajoura, 1981–1986

At the TNRC, the consequences of years of expansion without planning were becoming apparent to visiting experts. The impressive equipment and facilities offered "extraordinary possibilities for nuclear-oriented research and represents a tremendous research potential, from the equipment viewpoint," as IAEA experts noted in late 1981.[58] But the research facilities had been acquired without a definite list of objectives or activities. As the IAEA reported, "The distressing effect . . . is now realised when a number of laboratories are completed. Equipment is installed, but is idling because of the shortage of personnel and lack of research programmes."[59] Some equipment was not in use; other items, such as accelerators, were duplicated in neighboring laboratories. The senior regime leaders appear to have remained unaware of these problems, or the general inactivity on site.

The 10-megawatt research reactor finally became operational in November 1983. Between 1981 and 1983, the TNRC had hosted around two hundred Soviet specialists who assisted with testing and initial operations of the reactor and associated facilities.[60] This was not always an easy collaboration; nor did it take place in a calm work environment. According to U.S. intelligence reports, the Soviets and Libyans clashed over "the vaguely worded Tajura contract, inadequate fresh water supplies to cool the reactor, and construction problems."[61]

The Soviets had cause for concern. The Libyan regime was hoping to move away from exclusive dependence on the Soviet nuclear establishment for the acquisition and operation of the nuclear power reactors. One alternative was to discard the initial approach, which had seen the Soviets supply a complete set of turnkey facilities, and instead pursue a set of contracts with different suppliers, including the Soviets, under the leadership of Libyan officials.[62]

Meanwhile, the Libyans pursued a large number of contracts with other states—ranging from heavy-water production (essential for building power reactors) to nuclear fuel production—to support their nuclear energy and weapons programs. While there was still a large contingent of foreign specialists at the TNRC—including scientists from Egypt, Tunisia, and Sudan—there was a growing number of Libyans in the senior echelons. For these scientists, the opportunity to carry out extensive experimental research held a stronger appeal than building nuclear weapons. At this time, the scientists focused on experimental research rather than the engineering challenges associated with nuclear weapons programs. Access to new technology, combined with the absence of monitoring mechanisms capable of assessing the relevance of their research for the purposes of building nuclear weapons, gave the scientists ample opportunities to steer their research and development activities in their preferred directions.

The Libyan nuclear weapons project is better described as a plan than a program. It was based on an understanding of scientific and technological principles but the Libyans lacked both the actual experience in operating these technologies and the necessary numbers of scientists, engineers, and technicians. Libya mobilized its purchasing power hoping to buy facilities, technologies, advice, and training from others, but the shaky domestic foundations continued to undercut their efforts. There was not even a small group of scientists and engineers with the experience of operating a research program, let alone an industrial-scale project, among those attempting to plan and assess the Soviet proposal.

The Soviet-Libyan nuclear talks unsurprisingly began to run into difficulties. The Libyans realized that the Soviets were charging very high prices. For example, the Soviets requested a $450 million initial payment for signing the contract. Between 1981 and 1983, the Soviets wanted to finalize the talks—not least to recover their expenditures arising from site survey, adaptation, and preparation—but the Libyans introduced a series of technical amendments to postpone final signing.[63]

To say that the Libyan nuclear establishment was not satisfied with the Soviet reactor proposal would be an understatement. The 1981 SAE scientific assessment had revealed serious flaws, which in turn required costly and time-consuming revisions. Specifically, the review found that the reactor design was flawed and raised concerns about safety.[64] These findings further delayed the talks, and Soviet technical advisers worked on site to fix these problems. As the Libyans began to suspect that the Soviets were overcharging them, they consulted with other states, notably Belgium, to find alternative suppliers or at least pressure the Soviets to lower their price. By mid-1983 Libya was running out of foreign exchange reserves, and faced mounting economic problems at home. When the USSR ended up offering a lower price for the power reactors—perhaps in response to a more competitive bid from Belgium in May 1984—it was far from clear that Libya could afford even the revised proposal.[65] But, as Libya had few alternative suppliers for a project on this scale, and the Soviets had invested time and money in the Libyan contract, negotiations continued until March 1986, when the Libyans finally pulled the plug.

Moreover, the bilateral relationship between the two countries was steadily declining. The Soviets considered Gaddafi unstable, but were prepared to supply military equipment and nuclear technology as long as Libya could pay in cash.[66] When Libya was attacked by the United States in 1986, after having turned down the reactor contract offered by the Soviets, Tripoli appears to have made other demands on Moscow, including a de facto security guarantee against further U.S. attacks. The Soviets would not meet these demands.

As the talks with the Soviets dragged on, Libyan efforts to train manpower for the nuclear energy program stalled. The Libyans now had a larger pool of graduates to choose from: in 1981, an estimated two to three hundred Libyans studied nuclear engineering in Europe, and possibly an even larger number in the USSR.[67] But the nuclear establishment was incapable of developing a training program for these graduates to prepare the ground for a nuclear energy program. What training they did receive took place at the TNRC and at the Physics Department of Al-Fateh University. In 1981 visiting IAEA inspectors noted: "The administrative and technical infrastructure necessary to establish a nuclear power project is extremely weak. The concept of manpower planning is not understood by the Department, nor is the magnitude of the manpower requirements for the project. None of the professional staff has had significant practical experience related to a nuclear power project."[68]

Given these shortcomings, fellowships for training abroad—through the IAEA or courses offered by companies such as the Belgian company Belgonucleaire—were a very important resource. In the early 1980s Belgonucleaire trained twenty engineering students from Al-Fateh University in "the operation of research and power reactors and the metallurgy of uranium, as well as a variety of uranium processes, ranging from mining to the fabrication of fuel for power reactors."[69] However, the limited language skills of some Libyan scientists prevented them from benefiting from such opportunities. In the early 1980s several Libyans who had been selected for IAEA fellowships had to postpone their plans because they lacked sufficient English-language skills.[70]

Seeking yet another route to nuclear assistance, Libya also reached out to other Arab states seeking to develop cooperation in the nuclear field, along the lines of the European Atomic Energy Community. In 1981 Libya, Iraq, and Syria proposed setting up an Arab nuclear energy agency. In early 1982 SAE secretary Gaoud explained, "since last March a group of Arab scientists and experts have made a study of these proposals and have drafted a good report proposing many alternatives—different nuclear research centres, their tasks and so forth."[71] But as relations soured between the three countries, the initiative faltered in its very early stages.

The regime continued to recruit foreign (mainly Arab) scientists for the TNRC and Al-Fateh University. It channeled these efforts through another institution, the Arab Development Institute (ADI; later called the National Academy of Science), which also recommended scientific proposals and projects to the Libyan Cabinet. These recommendations were formally channeled through SAE secretary Gaoud.[72] The head of the ADI, Ali Ben Lashihar, set up the Nuclear Technology Group.[73] This unit recruited nuclear scientists from Arab states to work on projects exploring applications of nuclear technology. In contrast to the terms and conditions for Libyan employees, the ADI offered foreign scientists good salaries, free housing, excellent working conditions, and well-equipped laboratories.[74] In October 1981, the institute held an international conference on nuclear technology in Tripoli.[75]

ELUSIVE NUCLEAR OPTIONS

Once the regime recognized that the anticipated Soviet reactor complex would not bring them much closer to a nuclear weapons capability, they started exploring alternative technical routes. First, they considered whether they might be able to build or acquire a suitable reactor that would not be under safeguards, and explored the basic technologies associated with the plutonium route on an experimental scale. Second, they simultaneously began to consider and explore enrichment technologies as an alternative to the plutonium route.

Frustrated with their reliance on the Soviets, the Libyans attempted, without much success, to search for other ways to develop a weapons option. Libya courted a number of states for a wide range of nuclear assistance.[76] Libya already had agreements for scientific cooperation exchanges with Argentina and Pakistan, but it sought more hands-on help.[77] For example, between 1981 and 1984 Libyans sought Romanian help with developing heavy-water nuclear reactors, as well as technical assistance for the TNRC. The Romanians were tempted by the generous financial offer from the Libyan regime, but ultimately these talks failed to produce an agreement.[78] Simultaneously, the Libyan regime tried to persuade other states to supply power reactors or heavy-water production facilities.

The Libyan nuclear establishment explored plutonium reprocessing on an experimental level during the 1980s. At the TNRC, technicians fabricated dozens of uranium oxide and uranium metal targets. These targets were irradiated in the research reactor to explore fission radioisotope products.[79] In other words, they were developing some basic skills that would prove useful for a future weapons program. Between 1983 and 1985, they also received two boxes of documentation with details of the nuclear fuel cycle, which could be of value for weapons-related research and development.[80] For example, German-origin documents provided design details of nuclear reprocessing.[81] But the SAE did not make developing a reprocessing capability a priority in their research and development activities. The Radiochemistry Department was considered low priority and had not been pushed or encouraged to explore reprocessing on a systematic or large scale.[82]

As the Tajoura operations increasingly began to include clandestine activities later in the 1980s, security concerns began to affect the governance of the center as well as cooperation with foreign advisers. Security personnel from the intelligence and army were on-site to monitor the staff working at both the TNRC and the SAE. The scientists and engineers took care not to discuss with foreign experts what they perceived to be sensitive projects. The SAE did not declare the complete design information about the TNRC to the IAEA and omitted the details concerning the hot cells in the radiochemical laboratory that were used for sensitive research on irradiation of uranium targets during the second half of the 1980s.[83]

The Libyans intensively courted Belgium seeking extensive nuclear cooperation but were once again unable to secure an agreement. In May 1984, Libya offered Belgonucleaire a contract for two 440-megawatt nuclear reactors, apparently hoping this would provide an alternative to the Soviet proposal.[84] The contract was initialed in May 1984, and was expected to be signed in June, but was canceled following U.S. pressure. The proposed cooperation with Belgonucleaire was extensive, ranging from assistance with the Soviet reactor project to proposals for a plant to convert yellowcake into uranium hexafluoride (UF6), a feed material for centrifuges or nuclear fuel. The draft protocol was interpreted by U.S. intelligence to suggest that Libya could receive assistance to facilitate the indigenous construction of nuclear reactors.[85] This was, to put it mildly, a distant prospect, given Libya's lack of "any relevant industrial base."[86] The regime may have hoped for this, having no real sense of their actual capabilities in the nuclear field, and were probably delighted at the prospect of reducing Libya's long-term dependence on the Soviet Union. At a minimum, the cooperation agreement with Belgium could have enabled Libyans to operate the TNRC without reliance on Soviet on-site technicians in the longer term. In the shorter term, it could also have given Libyan engineers greater ability to explore weapons-related technologies clandestinely.

During the early 1980s, in parallel with the talks with the Soviet Union, Libyan scientists also explored gas centrifuges and alternative enrichment technologies such as laser isotope separation. In 1983, Libya probed potential suppliers for acquiring laser equipment technology. This was intended for an isotope separation project at the TNRC but, like so many other projects, appears to have faltered in the initial stages. The challenges facing the Libyan illicit enrichment projects (i.e., centrifuges and laser enrichment) were noted by other states. A 1985 U.S. intelligence assessment concluded that "both Libyan enrichment projects are at a very rudimentary stage, and there is little likelihood that Libya will be able to develop a uranium enrichment capability in the next 10 years."[87]

The only enrichment project that became a serious effort was focused on centrifuge technology. In 1982, Libyan nuclear scientists and engineers began clandestine research and development activities focusing on gas centrifuges.[88] These experiments were intended to explore gas centrifuges on an experimental scale and then to be scaled up to produce fissile material for nuclear weapons. The project was led by a German scientist who had recently been fired from the MAN company, a subcontractor to the Dutch nuclear fuel company URENCO. He was invited to the TNRC to help with the Libyan centrifuge development program.[89] He brought with him equipment and centrifuge design drawings.[90]

Under the guidance of this foreign scientist, the Libyans attempted to develop a prototype gas centrifuge. In January 1984, the Libyans sought help with their centrifuge program from Abdul Qadeer Khan, the mastermind behind Pakistan's centrifuge program, but later turned down his offer because they lacked the necessary infrastructure to scale up a centrifuge program beyond pilot-scale studies.[91] This would require extensive imports of machines, raw materials, and equipment, which the Libyans were not prepared to undertake at this stage. Nevertheless, the gas centrifuge project continued under the lead of the foreign scientist. By late 1984, after what contemporary U.S. intelligence assessments described as "years of promises and delays," the centrifuge project had made little progress.[92] The research and development project dragged on as a small-scale and low-visibility effort but was finally discontinued in 1992 without having constructed a single operational centrifuge.[93] Despite their failure, the Libyan engineers and scientists obtained valuable experience in the design, handling, and operation of centrifuge equipment.[94]

Looking for Uranium. Tripoli also pursued several other fuel-cycle capabilities during the first half of the 1980s, including uranium exploration and fuel production. These resources could have enabled the Libyans to produce the raw material for both nuclear power and nuclear weapons. True to form, the Libyans launched a Five-Year Plan in 1981 that was largely outsourced to foreign companies with minimal oversight or tangible results.

The search for uranium deposits, which had been ongoing since the 1960s, had met with little success. Early estimates assessed that one-seventh of Libya's land area could be geologically favorable for uranium deposits.[95] The SAE's aerial surveys had discovered few deposits, but the (revised) 1981

Five-Year Plan for uranium exploration recommended that aerial surveying continue nonetheless. Ultimately, none of the surveyed areas proved suitable for large-scale extraction.[96]

The Raw Materials Division explored several uranium deposits during the 1980s with the assistance of four foreign companies: Belgatom, Belgonucleaire, and Union Mirac (all Belgian), and the Mineral Resources Prospecting Company (Brazilian). By mid-1982 the Raw Material division, initially led by M.A. Ghuma and then taken over by Khaled Hangary during this year, opted to limit the access of the IAEA experts to the north and eastern sections of the Al Kufrah Basin to avoid duplicating the foreign assistance from these countries.[97] The prospecting efforts, combined with training and advice from IAEA experts, helped develop not only the prospecting program but also the skills of the local staff. The Brazilian assistance was formalized in a working group, the Group Management Committee, set up in 1984. The Libyan geologists benefited from this cooperation, which included some advice and training.

In the mid-1980s, the Libyan nuclear establishment also started to explore uranium conversion technology. In 1984, Libya started secret laboratory-scale uranium conversion experiments using the imported natural uranium at the TNRC.[98] Libya was also attempting to purchase facilities for converting uranium on a large scale. Between 1981 and 1984, Libya negotiated with a Belgian company, reportedly Belgonucleaire, for construction of a uranium conversion complex.[99] The Belgians were prepared to assist the Libyan program with what they considered to be less proliferation-sensitive technologies. However, their reluctance to provide facilities that would help Libya edge closer to a weapons option began to create tension. Libya wanted a plant for converting yellowcake into UF6. Reportedly, these talks focused on a proposal that included three sets of facilities: first, a set of processing and analytic laboratories; second, a set of laboratories to convert yellowcake to uranium tetrafluoride (UF4) along with the option of a uranium metal laboratory; and third, buildings (but not necessarily equipment) to convert UF4 to UF6.[100] These talks quickly came under U.S. pressure.[101]

In April 1983, the Libyans attempted to give Belgonucleaire an ultimatum, claiming that future business prospects depended on whether Belgium would supply a UF6 conversion facility.[102] This could have made Libya capable of producing nuclear fuel indigenously, and would have taken it closer to a weapons option through the enrichment route. The Belgians balked and instead offered a UF4 plant that produced an intermediate uranium compound. Neither project ever materialized due to several factors including U.S. pressure, the protracted talks on the power reactors, and the fact that few uranium deposits had actually been located in Libya.[103] In 1984, Libya signed an agreement with Japan for a modular uranium conversion facility. The modules arrived in 1986 later without instructions for assembly; they remained in storage for over a decade until they were partly assembled and moved to Al Khalla, a suburb of Tripoli, in 1998 and later relocated to another storage site at Sawani, on the outskirts of the city. The Libyans carried out cold tests (i.e., allegedly not processing uranium) of some of the uranium conversion components in 2002.[104]

In addition to trying to acquire their own facilities, the Libyan nuclear establishment secretly sent some of its imported yellowcake to an undisclosed nuclear weapons state in 1985. The yellowcake was processed into "natural UF6 (39 kg), UF4 (5 kg), UO2 (6 kg) and U3O8 (6 kg)" and returned to Libya the same year.[105]

EXPLORING OTHER WEAPONS OF MASS DESTRUCTION

The Gaddafi regime also tried to acquire chemical and biological weapons. The chemical weapons program in particular became closely linked with the security challenges of the 1980s, notably Libya's war in Chad. The timelines—starting from tentative exploration during the late 1970s to attempted production in the early 1980s—were similar for all of the WMD programs. This is perhaps no coincidence, as the shift toward production of clandestine weapons capabilities coincided with Libya's increasing isolation.

The chemical and biological weapons programs faced comparable processes of technological absorption. The biological weapons program does not appear to have advanced much beyond procurement, but may have included laboratory-scale experiments at a dedicated site. In contrast, the chemical weapons program made somewhat better progress.

The Libyan regime started exploring the option of a chemical weapons program as early as 1980, but efforts intensified after the effects of such weapons were demonstrated during the Iran-Iraq War.[106] In 1984 the chemical weapons program began to create a production capacity: foreign companies, including the German firm Imhausen-Chemie, built a facility at Rabta 65 kilometers southwest of Tripoli. This facility was dual-purpose: most of it was dedicated to commercial production but a small clandestine unit inside was suitable for chemical weapons production.[107] At this stage, the Libyans imported both equipment and precursors (raw materials) for weapons production. Not all of the equipment they were able to buy was useful. For example, the automatic equipment for loading mustard agent into containers was poorly constructed and caused leaks. As a result, workers resorted to filling the storage containers manually.[108]

The chemical weapons program never moved beyond small-scale production of mustard gas and initial exploration of soman and sarin.[109] The regime decided to limit the chemical weapons program to research and development, diverting resources instead to the nuclear weapons program.[110] The program ultimately produced or acquired 25 metric tons of precursors, 3,500 aerial bombs designed for dispersing chemical weapons, and three production facilities.[111] During the war between Libya and Chad, Libyan forces reportedly released chemical weapons from airplanes, but these did not have the desired effect as the wind was blowing in the wrong direction.[112]

In 1994 the Libyan chemical weapons program prepared to set up a production plant. Rumors began circulating that the intended site was in Tarhuna, east of Tripoli, where large underground tunnels were being constructed.[113] Figure 7.3 below shows key sites associated with Libya's WMD programs, as well as key military-industrial sites in the country. By the mid-1990s, several states were concerned about the Libyan chemical weapons project. In March 1996, the U.S. Central Intelligence Agency director John Deutch described Tarhuna as "the world's largest underground chemical weapons plant."[114] In April Harold P. Smith Jr., assistant to the secretary of defense, said: "If we wanted to destroy [Tarhuna], B-61 [thermonuclear bombs] will be the nuclear weapon of choice."[115] This suggestion—that the United States might use nuclear weapons in a targeted strike—sent a strong signal to the Libyan regime.

UPHEAVAL: U.S. AIRSTRIKES AND COLLAPSING NUCLEAR TALKS, 1986

In early 1986, the Libyans canceled a scheduled IAEA visit to assist with the planning of a nuclear energy program.[116] Talks had been underway for several years, an initial agreement had been signed, and in late 1985 IAEA consultants had traveled to Sirte to review the intended reactor site.[117] After the Soviet Union finally withdrew from the nuclear power reactor agreement, however, Libya's nuclear program found itself in a deepening crisis. After the two countries had spent several years attempting to iron out an agreement, it looked like the Libyan regime was not likely to find an alternative supplier, given its increasingly precarious relationship with the international community.

In March 1986, the SAE was dissolved. It is unclear why, but the timing suggests it may have been a decision triggered by the collapsed nuclear talks with the Soviet Union, which seemed to dash Libya's hopes for nuclear energy. The nuclear establishment would continue to explore alternative paths to nuclear weapons technology, and the centrifuge program continued, despite no tangible signs of progress. The former SAE minister, Abdel-Majid Gaoud, would continue to rise in the regime and became prime minister in 1994. Colonel Ahmad Mahmoud Ali, previously in charge of the military procurement office, took charge of the nuclear weapons project.[118] His cousin, Abdel Rahim Bader, was put in charge of procurement for the missile projects.[119]

Although the Libyan regime changed the personnel charged with management and oversight of the nuclear project, activities on the ground dwindled.[120] The loss of Soviet support soon had tangible consequences at the

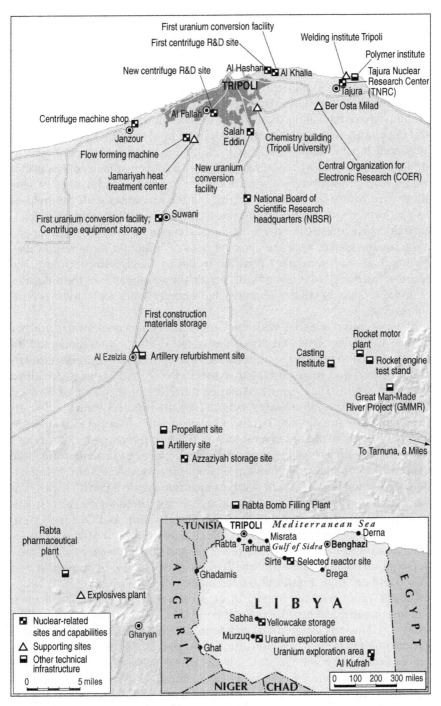

Figure 7.3. Map of nuclear and military-industrial sites, Libya.

TNRC, where the Libyans used unfiltered groundwater to cool the research reactor. This led to clogged pipes, which necessitated extensive repairs.

After 1986, the new leaders of the nuclear program had to carve out a new direction for the weapons program under difficult circumstances. Few state suppliers remained willing and able to provide what Tripoli wanted, and the nuclear black market was an increasingly appealing alternative. It was certainly more appealing than trying to scale up the clandestine research and development program, which would be held back by Libya's missing industrial capabilities. As early as 1984, the nuclear establishment considered moving toward a procurement strategy based on "major contracts that would be put together by a consultant under Libyan leadership."[121] This alternative route, developing an indigenous foundation with the help of on-site foreign experts, was more uncertain. It raised the problem of leaders' reluctance: the greater the indigenous component of a nuclear weapons program, the greater were the personal risks of failure for those responsible. Although it was sometimes possible to fail in Libya with impunity, the "Brother Leader" held senior officials personally accountable for the outcomes of projects. Blaming failures on unreliable supplier states was a more acceptable excuse.

Libya's foreign relations with the United States also deteriorated further in 1986. In January that year, concerned about WMD proliferation and Libya's sponsorship of terrorism, the United States imposed additional unilateral sanctions and froze all Libyan assets in the United States. After Libya launched six missiles against American aircraft in the Gulf of Sirte in March 1986, the United States sank a Libyan ship and struck a Soviet-supplied SA-5 missile site on the Libyan coast.[122] Two weeks later, on 5 April, a bomb exploded in a nightclub in Berlin frequented by American servicemen, killing a Turkish woman and two Americans, and injuring more than two hundred others, of whom seventy-nine were American. In retaliation, the United States launched strikes the same month against Libya's capital Tripoli and Benghazi, its second-largest city. These attacks also struck air bases, air defense, naval, and military installations, and Gaddafi's combined residence and command centre.[123] This attack was a profound shock for Gaddafi and the senior regime members and raised questions about their personal survival.[124] In the aftermath of the attack, it also became clear that they could not expect protection from the Soviet Union.

Libya's initial response to the U.S. air strikes reflected Gaddafi's shock at coming under direct attack from a superpower. His son was injured in the strikes, and he later claimed that an adopted daughter had been killed, making the point that the U.S. action affected the first family of the Libyan revolution. From this point, Gaddafi saw the prospect of U.S.-imposed regime change as a real option. In the longer term, the attack triggered a rethinking of Libyan foreign policy and also made the leadership begin to question its policy of confronting the United States.[125] The regime concluded that it "could no longer ignore the reality of American power," nor its own vulner-ability.[126] Gaddafi therefore called for deterrent capabilities: "If we had pos-sessed a deterrent—missiles that could reach New York—we would have hit it at the same moment. Consequently, we should build this force so that they and others will no longer think about an attack. . . . [If] the world has a nu-clear bomb, we should have a nuclear bomb."[127]

In addition to the U.S. attack, the regime faced a collapsing economy. The long-lasting oil boom ground to a halt in the mid-1980s, while the regime's experiments with the domestic economy, involving the banning of private enterprise, had had catastrophic consequences. This made the regime worry about its domestic prospects for survival, which seemed predicated on main-taining a high standard of living for the population. The economic down-turn triggered a rethinking of the regime's radical policies, which led to some modest attempts to reduce the radical actors and principles that had shaped Libyan domestic and foreign policy since the 1970s. The weaknesses of the state apparatus were becoming a source of growing concern for the regime. At this point, problems with mismanagement, corruption, and abuses of power by the Revolutionary Committees were becoming too apparent to ignore.[128] As a result, the regime attempted to reverse some of the more radical policies in the domestic economic sphere, but struggled to effectuate significant change given the limited resources of the state apparatus. By 1987, the Gaddafi regime also set out to improve its relations with neigh-boring countries.

Against this backdrop, the U.S. attack seems to have had a mixed impact on Libya's foreign and security policy. Tripoli's attempts to improve relations with neighboring countries stood in sharp contrast with the involvement of Libyan intelligence officers in the bombing of Pan Am Flight 103 over the Scottish town of Lockerbie in December 1988 and a French UTA flight over Niger in 1989. These apparently contradictory developments reflected a fun-damental division in the regime, which remained split between hardliners and reformists, and Gaddafi's indecision over what relationship with the in-ternational community to pursue: rapprochement with the outside world versus continued use of radical means and ends, such as support for terror-ists and terrorist acts abroad.

This tension translated as ambivalence, as Libya's political institutions de-bated pursuing WMD after the U.S. attack. For example, after the 1986 U.S. air raids, the GPC instructed the leadership to protect the regime by any and all necessary means and with any and all weapons.[129] Just two years later, however, in 1988, the GPC advocated the global destruction of WMD in a human rights declaration.[130]

In the short term, however, the idea of a nuclear deterrent to protect the Libyan regime against the consequences of its foreign adventures still car-ried a strong appeal. In June 1987, Gaddafi argued: "The Arabs must pos-sess the atom bomb to defend themselves until their numbers reach one thousand million, and until they learn to desalinate water, and until they liberate Palestine."[131] In September that year he declared: "Now that the Israelis possess the atomic weapon, the Arabs have . . . to work day and night to possess the atomic weapon in order to defend their existence."[132]

However, this securitization of Libya's nuclear proliferation project did not lead to any intensification of efforts to build or otherwise acquire nuclear weapons. Growing doubts about Libya's radical foreign policy practices and changes in its Middle East policy objectives fed the regime's ambivalence about the pursuit of nuclear weapons. The regime was also facing growing domestic discontent following failed economic reforms and revolutionary excesses. In 1987–1988, Gaddafi publically conceded that the Revolutionary Committees had "deviated, harmed, tortured" and declared that they would be brought under control. These mounting challenges led to a sharpened focus on regime security both at home and abroad, and a more critical view of the role of revolutionary ideology and actors in shaping Libyan foreign and domestic policy.

At the TNRC, the loss of Soviet technical support had significant consequences for the running of the technical equipment as well as their prospects of developing a nuclear weapons option. For example, research and development activities with possible applications in a centrifuge program—such as converting yellowcake into UF4 and uranium metal—were discontinued in the late 1980s in the absence of foreign assistance, and the Libyans struggled even to maintain the site.

While Libya's nuclear program appeared to be moving fast in the direction of nuclear energy in 1981, within five years the entire program fell apart. After the Libyan nuclear establishment was reconfigured in 1986, it soon became clear how difficult it would be to reconstitute the fledgling nuclear program without strong support from the Soviets. While this coincided with a stronger desire for nuclear weapons at the senior level of the regime, the dismantlement of the SAE and general upheaval in the state combined to undercut the development of an indigenous route. The failure of the nuclear program between 1986 and 1989 to produce nuclear energy or create a weapons option was an overdetermined outcome, as the Libyans had lost their main nuclear supplier and faced a series of crises abroad and at home.

At the core of this collapse, as this chapter has shown, was the weak Libyan state institutions. At two critical junctures during this decade, the Libyan nuclear establishment demonstrated their inability to fulfill the regime's nuclear ambitions: first, by lack of preparation for the nuclear energy program in the early 1980s; and second, by failure to devise a workable weapons option, even after Gaddafi's desire for a nuclear deterrent intensified in 1986. Despite these failures, there are few indications that the regime attempted to intervene to ensure the program moved forward. In fact, the only known action that might possibly have been such an intervention (though it is far from clear) was the dissolution of the SAE in 1986. While the regime changed the leadership and organization of the nuclear program several times, they did not attempt to micromanage, the project.

The Gaddafi regime was apparently unaware of the accumulating delays in the nuclear energy project prior to 1986, and of the ongoing failure of the centrifuge program that lasted a decade. Furthermore, because the regime rarely even consulted their scientists, they initially misunderstood the role the Soviet reactor complex could have played in a weapons program. The senior leaders of the nuclear program were promoted to other senior positions and had no incentive to point out the problems facing the program— many of which could be blamed on the supplier state, rather than attributed to the program's own shortcomings. The scientists benefited from the influx of technology and inadequate monitoring mechanisms, which left them free to focus on basic research and experiments. While the scientists explored the nuclear fuel cycle and assessed different enrichment technologies, they lacked the resources to plan or prepare for a nuclear energy program, let alone a weapons program.

As the Libyans began to explore the nuclear black market more in the mid-1980s, they appear to have believed that these clandestine suppliers could provide turnkey facilities for a weapons program, much along the lines they had expected from the failed Soviet nuclear power plant contract. As Libya began to strike deals with black-market suppliers in the 1990s, any such hopes would be proven false, at great cost.

Sanctions, Centrifuges, and Exit, 1989–2003

Between 1989 and 2003, the Libyan nuclear weapons program took a clandestine turn while the regime's ambivalence on the nuclear question deepened. The regime pursued reintegration into the global society and economy, reorganized the nuclear weapons program once more and turned to the black market. A senior regime figure, Matuq M. Matuq, took charge of the program and attempted to secretly purchase a complete turnkey centrifuge plant. But the program continued to fail, even after the scientists received thousands of centrifuge components, because the Libyan nuclear establishment lacked the capacity to operate this technology and fix problems that emerged along the way.

At this time, the regime faced compounding pressures: a collapsing economy; an Islamist uprising; and international isolation. Crippling economic sanctions and domestic turmoil triggered a rethinking of Libya's relationship with the outside world. The regime concluded that it would be in Libya's interest to abandon the pursuit of nuclear weapons if a favorable "exit strategy" could be found.[1] In other words, they did not abandon the program but pursued it as a secondary objective. While Matuq tried to revitalize the nuclear weapons track, a small group of senior officials reached out to the United States hoping to normalize relations and have sanctions lifted. Muammar Gaddafi authorized this group to offer up the nuclear weapons program as a bargaining chip to try to improve Libya's standing with the United States and the international community. They ultimately failed, as Libya faced more pressure and sanctions from 1992, and the nuclear weapons program continued.

In the late 1990s, senior regime officials returned to this debate, arguing that Libya had to choose between guns and butter, or, more specifically, between nuclear weapons and reintegration in the global economy. The regime opted to combine these two tracks, but intensified their efforts to improve their international standing. In 1999, the Libyan regime held secret talks with the United States and the United Kingdom. These resulted in the announcement, on 19 December 2003, that Libya would give up its nuclear, chemical, and biological weapons programs. The programs were dismantled and U.S. inspectors took centrifuges and the nuclear weapon designs back with them to the United States. The Libyan leadership disclosed few details about their past efforts over the following years.

Few details about Libya's nuclear program have emerged since, with one exception: the Libyan government reluctantly admitted that their turn to the nuclear black market did not begin in mid-1995, as they had first suggested, but dated back several years earlier. This chapter presents new evidence, drawing from interviews with senior Libyan regime officials and Libyan declarations about their nuclear weapons program, that shows the Libyan turn toward the black nuclear market began as early as 1989, and, for the first time, places this in the context of regime debates about grand strategy and nuclear deterrence. As we will see, the future of this program was intensely contested at the senior levels of the regime, while Gaddafi remained noncommittal. This chapter also shows that the program continued to suffer from basic problems of control and oversight, giving new insights into the organization of the nuclear weapons program that emerged on the ground. While scholars tend to dismiss the Libyan program as a nonstarter, or conclude that the Libyans downgraded their program out of a desire to rejoin the global economy, this chapter shows that the scientists on the ground laid sound plans and set sensible priorities. However, they lacked the necessary institutional resources and, as a result, suffered from underdeveloped human resources. Ultimately their efforts were stymied by the regime's mounting security concerns.

These sources show how and why the Libyan regime's attempt to bring the program back on track toward developing a weapons option failed: even after the program was reconfigured, giving the regime more direct control, Libyan scientists failed to make tangible progress toward the declared goal of giving Libya a nuclear weapons option. For example, they used funding that was intended for the weapons program for basic maintenance; even after the weapons program was revitalized in mid-1995 they focused on understanding basic processes, rather than installing centrifuges and assessing the weapons design they had acquired from their clandestine suppliers. In other words, even with Matuq at the helm the Libyan regime failed to effectively oversee and control the nuclear program. As a result, the program continued to drift.

Searching for a Nuclear Exit, 1989–1992

The regime's response to the crises of the second half of the 1980s led to a broad policy shift, with important consequences for the nuclear program.

While scholars often equate the Libyan regime, or state, with Gaddafi, we will see that regime factions and institutions played an important role in this process. Specifically, regime officials revived long-standing debates about building the revolution at home by focusing on economic development versus pursuing revolution abroad by supporting radical foreign actors. As part of these discussions, senior regime officials began to question the usefulness of a nuclear deterrent. They also launched competing initiatives, one in the form of a diplomatic overture to the West and one led by Matuq M. Matuq and the head of the intelligence services, Musa Kusa, which searched for new ways to buy nuclear technology and know-how. In 1989, Libya reconnected with the black market network led by Abdul Qadeer Khan, the Pakistani metallurgist.

The apparent discrepancy between investing in a nuclear program while seeking to open negotiations with the West, in which this program would be put on the negotiating table, was not unusual in the Gaddafi regime. Gaddafi had issued contradictory statements about weapons of mass destruction (WMD) throughout the 1970s and 1980s, and in 1996 he would sign the Treaty of Pelindaba declaring Africa a nuclear-weapons-free zone, all while actively seeking to acquire nuclear weapons. By encouraging separate and apparently contradictory policy tracks, Gaddafi could permit both options to develop further, delaying his final decision while balancing the different regime factions. Gaddafi wanted his trusted officials to develop each track until he was prepared to choose between them.

In a series of interviews carried out by the author in 2005 and 2006, some of the participants described these discussions and their consequences. These included former Libyan ambassador Mohamed Zwai to London, who was one of the three key figures in the team that began the negotiation attempts with the West in 1990–1992 and who later completed an agreement in late 2003; Seif al-Islam Gaddafi, Muammar Gaddafi's son, who also played a central role in the talks between 2001 and 2003; a former prominent Revolutionary Committee figure with close personal ties to Muammar Gaddafi; and a former speaker of the Libyan General People's Congress (GPC). Other conversations and interviews were carried out with Libyan diplomats and academics associated with the rapprochement efforts during the 1990s, some of which could be attributed while others were strictly not for attribution.

These interviews reveal that internal debate and bargaining featured in the senior leadership's decision making in the nuclear arena, as elsewhere. Zwai, for instance, noted that the costs and benefits of pursuing nuclear weapons had been debated within the Revolutionary Command Council (RCC), the GPC, and other regime institutions "since the beginning."[2] While the formal organs of the regime, such as the GPC, mainly served to rubber-stamp decisions (e.g., the establishing of the Secretariat of Atomic Energy in the early 1980s), they also served as a sounding board for debates and provided a measure of legitimacy for key decisions. Debates among senior officials, in the RCC or ministerial Cabinet, were an opportunity to promote policy preferences and launch competing initiatives.

In their discussions on the nuclear question, different regime actors expressed particular interest with regard to the nuclear program. Zwai and Gaddafi's son Seif-al-Islam each separately told the author that the military wanted to invest in conventional and nonconventional, including nuclear, weapons.[3] The latter noted that the senior figures in the regime considered the nuclear weapons program "an old dream."[4] In addition, a scholar noted that Libyan officials involved in procurement for the nuclear program during the 1990s had personal stakes, perhaps even economic incentives, to continue the program as long as their attempts to repair their relationship with the United States remained unsuccessful.[5] Nonetheless, Zwai noted, Gaddafi became convinced that the regime had to pay more attention to development at home.[6]

In the late 1980s and early 1990s, senior Libyan officials debated the strategic value of nuclear weapons and whether they were worth the costs of pursuing them. This discussion focused on the regime's analysis of clashes between nuclear and nonnuclear states, such as the Falklands War and Israel's invasion of Beirut in 1982, where nuclear weapons were not seen as having played a useful role.[7] Libyan officials perceived nuclear weapons as a passive deterrent unable to yield positive results. According to one senior official, nuclear weapons were deemed insufficient for states with weak conventional military capabilities.[8] In other words, given the imminent challenges associated with the growing U.S. pressure on Libya, conventional capabilities seemed more appropriate than the long-term option of a nuclear weapons capability. Having noted that nuclear weapons did not offer Libya the kind of security capabilities they desired, critics of the nuclear weapons option argued that Libya's security needs did not necessitate a nuclear deterrent.[9]

After this informal review, several senior officials called for the dismantlement of the program, arguing that Libya should instead spend more money on health care, education, and development.[10] This was a tense period in the regime. After the United Nations (UN) Security Council sanctions were imposed in late March 1992, the Libyan regime found itself in a critically vulnerable situation.[11] At home, the regime's support from key domestic bases began to crumble; opposition movements challenged the regime's control over parts of Libya's territory. In 1995, the Gaddafi regime faced a significant rebellion: a militant Islamist uprising in the eastern part of the country would remain undefeated until 1998. The military's inability to defeat the Islamists for three years on Libya's own territory, while other violent Islamist groups were posing a significant threat to the regimes in Egypt and Algeria, gave the regime great cause for concern. In short, the Gaddafi regime's most immediate challenges were domestic. Abdessalam Jalloud, who was widely considered the second-most prominent figure in the Libyan regime, became a vocal critic of the leadership during this period and was placed under house arrest in the spring of 1995. Gaddafi concluded that the country's international situation had to be improved in order to "enable Libya to regenerate itself and its economy."[12] This necessitated changes in Libya's foreign policy practices and her international standing, particularly with regard to the United States. The dormant nuclear program was seen as a potential bargaining chip, if talks could be opened.

In this environment, the growing influence of more moderate regime elements also led to questions about the future of the nuclear weapons program. In 1990, three senior Libyan officials—the senior diplomats Abdellati Obeidi and Mohamed Zwai, and Musa Kusa—began to reach out to U.S. and European states to signal Libya's desire to improve relations and its willingness, if necessary, to abandon the pursuit of nuclear weapons. This policy reversal, and the efforts of this group (who would later negotiate the talks leading to the 2003 agreement), have received little attention in the academic literature. However, together they suggest that the nuclear weapons program was controversial within the regime and had, at best, ambivalent support from Gaddafi. They also demonstrate that senior regime figures, with strong personal ties to Gaddafi, played a significant and proactive role in debates about the nuclear program.

Obeidi, Zwai, and Kusa were instructed by Gaddafi to reach out to the United States and European governments in the hope of improving bilateral relations and having economic sanctions lifted. Their high standing with Gaddafi gave each of them some room for independent initiative and maneuver. This group also sought advice and support from other senior regime officials, notably Jadallah Azzouz Ettalhi, who had been associated with the management of the nuclear program during the 1970s, was later appointed Libyan representative to the UN, and served as minister of strategic industries in the early 1990s; Libyan academics educated in the West were also consulted. This group attempted to reach out to U.S. officials during 1992 and 1993. Later in the 1990s, they also attempted to approach France. According to Zwai, Gaddafi was prepared to discuss the nuclear program as part of a broader negotiation framework and intended to work closely with this team if they were able to open talks with the United States.[13]

In 1990–1992, the Libyans were cautiously optimistic about their prospects of improving relations with the West. According to Zwai, they had found relations with the United States particularly difficult during the Reagan administration (1981–1989), but were hopeful that the new Bush administration would be more open to contacts with the regime. The Libyan team reached out to lower-level officials in the Bush administration. In 1992, the Libyans attempted to signal that their leader was prepared to develop a new relationship with the United States.[14] Their timing was catastrophic: faced with an increasingly hostile international environment, their overture failed.

On 13 November 1991, the United States and Britain indicted two Libyan officials, Abdelbaset al-Megrahi and Lamin Khalifah Fhimah, charging them with the murder of 270 passengers on board Pan Am Flight 103, which exploded over Lockerbie in Scotland. On 21 January 1992, the UN Security Council demanded that Libya respond to the findings of the investigation. Ettalhi, the Libyan representative at the Security Council meeting, protested that the indictments were simply "cover for military and economic aggression on a small country."[15] After Libya refused to extradite the two suspects, the Security Council imposed sanctions on air travel and banned imports of weapons and equipment on 31 March.[16] The sanctions were expanded in December that year: Libyan foreign assets were frozen and a ban on importing equipment for the oil industry was added to the existing set of restrictions. Over the next years, Tripoli watched neighboring states benefit from oil sales, while the country's economy suffered from a plummeting gross domestic product and inflation, which reached 50 percent by 1994.[17]

The imposition of sanctions undermined the efforts of moderate elements in the regime to open up to the West and to carry out reforms at home. In the short term, these developments strengthened the case for those in the regime who opposed such opening up and reform. They also fed Gaddafi's concerns, shared by several in the regime, that the United States would attempt to overthrow him.[18] Both developments strengthened the case of those in the regime who argued for the development of a nuclear weapons option. However, the added constraints on trade and imports made procurement more difficult, which created an obstacle to Matuq's efforts to import centrifuges from the nuclear black market.

Secondhand Centrifuges

In 1989, the regime started to pursue complete centrifuges, spare parts, and supporting infrastructure from the Khan network. A new body, the National Board for Scientific Research (NBSR), took charge of the nuclear weapons project. An umbrella organization, it oversaw several technical research institutes in addition to the nuclear program. The head of the NBSR was Matuq, who had risen to prominence through the ranks of the Revolutionary Committees during the 1980s; he would later become deputy prime minister in the early 2000s. Matuq had a reputation as a competent project manager, but he lacked expertise in the nuclear field. His role was to oversee the program and ensure that it ran efficiently and achieved the objective of creating a nuclear weapons capability. Matuq took this task seriously, even referring to the nuclear weapons program as his "baby" in meetings with U.S. officials in Tripoli in January 2004.[19]

The nuclear weapons program that emerged under Matuq's leadership in the 1990s was different from the earlier incarnations. From the very beginning, the program had relied heavily on foreign assistance and turn-key procurement, but under Matuq, the program cut back on its previous attempts to carry out indigenous research and development and sought instead to purchase ready-made technology. Matuq outsourced the two key technological bottlenecks—developing centrifuge cascades and acquiring suitable feed material—to the Khan network. This program would be based on a set of super-turnkey contracts from the nuclear black market, reducing the demands on the Libyans in several key areas such as planning, organization, and training. This approach was tailored to suit Libya's limited human and industrial resources. The project was also designed to minimize detectability and vulnerability, as the centrifuges and other components were designed to be mobile and could be moved between different sites. It required only a small local workforce.[20] It was also designed to be adaptable to changing opportunities and constraints, given Libya's turbulent international environment.

The Libyan regime's security concerns shaped their preferences for how the nuclear weapons program ought to be carried out. This is perhaps the only area where the regime attempted to intervene directly in the management of the program by laying ground rules for site dispersal. They duly noted how, in 1981, Israel had been able to destroy a safeguarded reactor in Iraq without drawing punishment from the international community. Concerns about similar attacks informed decisions made at the senior regime level to reduce vulnerability, for example by developing secret sites and by making sensitive units of the nuclear program mobile in the 1990s. The nuclear scientists were instructed to adopt technologies that could be moved between different sites, such as centrifuges. As a result, the technologies that they purchased were often disassembled or even kept in the shipping crates for moving between different storage sites. These security measures added to the difficulties of planning, operation, and coordination. The Libyan nuclear weapons program was designed to be modular, and while the decision to leave purchased equipment such as the uranium enrichment facility in storage was consistent with this policy, it also made it more difficult for the Libyan scientists to make these items operational.

This program was not subject to formal reviews or audits. Matuq was ultimately responsible for implementation and for reviewing its performance. A small group of six senior technicians educated in the United States worked with Matuq as advisers guiding and overseeing these efforts. One such individual was Mohamed Ennami, who had close ties with Matuq and later served as his scientific adviser in the GPC.[21] Another prominent figure was an individual referred to as Karim, who had played a leading role in the gas centrifuge program of the 1980s and the nuclear weapons program that emerged during the mid-1990s.

Matuq's first challenge was to revitalize the languishing centrifuge track. The research and development program focusing on gas centrifuges that had been started in 1982 was failing and was discontinued in 1992. The Libyans were left with the black market as their only viable track. Having reestablished contact with the Khan network in 1989, the Libyans placed an initial order for P-1 centrifuges in early 1991. Shortly after, they received some centrifuge components and designs from Khan.[22] This centrifuge model had been retired from the Pakistani program, and Khan sold it on at a handsome profit. A newer design, the P-2 centrifuge, was introduced to the Pakistani program from the mid-1980s.[23] The new sanctions imposed in March 1992 affected air cargo and travel, and made it very difficult to import equipment on a large scale. The Khan network prepared the items, but it was difficult to send centrifuges to Libya during the embargo. After the Libyans refused payment, the Khan network sold Libya's original order of centrifuges to Iran in 1993.[24]

The Libyan authorities were dissatisfied and were not persuaded that what Khan had delivered was what they had paid for. As a result, they opted out of this initial agreement.[25] This initial deal left the Libyans disillusioned with the nuclear black market. In an interview with the author, a senior Libyan academic explained that acquiring technology via the black market was cumbersome, both in the case of the nuclear program and items imported for the oil industry, because the 1993 round of UN sanctions also prohibited sales of petroleum technology.[26] For the small Libyan state, evading the UN sanctions was a difficult logistical and organizational challenge. Still, it was their only feasible option.

BUYING A CENTRIFUGE PLANT

In July 1995, the Libyan leadership placed a larger order with the Khan network. Libyan officials initially described this as a strategic decision to relaunch the centrifuge track, but in 2007–2008 admitted that the July 1995 decision simply marked the scaling up of the outsourcing efforts that dated back to 1989. During the 1990s Libya would pursue the building blocks for a nuclear weapons program through the Khan network, which could sell equipment, designs, and training. In public, Gaddafi appeared defiant: in January 1996, he called for Arab states "to try by any means" to get nuclear weapons.[27]

The Khan network was not the only source from which the Libyans attempted to clandestinely import nuclear technology. In the spring of 1995, Libyan intelligence officers approached Libyan physicists based abroad about setting up a "Libyan Science Center" as a cover for clandestine technology transfers.[28] Kusa authorized this proposal in May 1995, but the center does not appear to have materialized. The proposal stipulated that scientists would be monitored by members of the Revolutionary Committees who reported directly to Kusa. There were no formal oversight mechanisms in this project either, and the informal mechanisms consisted of individuals and groups who lacked an understanding of the technical challenges associated with operating centrifuges.

In the summer of 1997, a Libyan delegation led by Matuq and Karim met with Khan and his deputy Bukhary Seyed Tahir in Istanbul. This was the first of a series of meetings between Libyan officials and representatives of the Khan network; later meetings were held in other cities across the Middle East, including Casablanca. In 1997, the Libyans received twenty preassembled P-1 centrifuges and ordered two hundred unassembled centrifuges of this model.[29]

After Matuq caught on to the fact that what he had ordered was in fact an outdated model, he ordered a gas centrifuge plant using the newer P-2 centrifuge model for a price around $100–$200 million.[30] Specifically, he first placed an order for five thousand P-2 centrifuges, which was later expanded to ten thousand. The target date for completion of the centrifuge plant was June 2003.[31] This plant could, in theory, produce enough highly enriched uranium for several—estimates range between four and ten—nuclear weapons per year.[32]

The Khan network's offer seemed like a complete package: blueprints including a Chinese nuclear weapons design, design information, feed material (including 1.7 metric tons of uranium hexafluoride [UF6]), a turnkey centrifuge plant, and including installation and training.[33] The package also included design information and documentation from the Pakistani enrichment program including test results, calculations, and experiences. The equipment would be supplied by members of the Khan network. Its suppliers—some of whom were unaware of the destination of the equipment they sold to network members—were based in a number of countries apart from Pakistan, including the United Arab Emirates, Switzerland, South Africa, Spain, Turkey, Italy, France, the United Kingdom, Taiwan, and Japan.[34] In practice, however, the network did not deliver a complete turnkey facility, leaving the Libyans with the challenge of installing and operationalizing the centrifuge plant themselves.

The Khan network shipped designs, technology, and partly enriched uranium (UF6) in a Pakistani airplane in 2001.[35] The UF6 feed material was intended for testing the centrifuges, but the amount provided by the network—1.7 tons of approximately 1 percent enriched uranium—would have sufficed for a small nuclear weapon if it was further enriched.[36] In addition, Libya imported two smaller cylinders of UF6 in September 2000.[37]

Apart from the oversight of Matuq, the nuclear weapons program does not appear to have been subject to other technical reviews or audits. But it was clear that this was not a cost-effective project. Members of the Khan network referred to the Libyan contract as a "cash cow" and were apparently not concerned about the accumulation of rising costs or delays.[38] The Libyans grudgingly accepted these, but felt that they were being taken advantage of.[39] In an interview with the author, a senior Libyan academic described the equipment purchased by the Khan network during the 1990s as "old" and "invalid," very expensive, and apparently not well suited for a nuclear weapons program.[40]

INSTALLING CENTRIFUGES AND ORGANIZING
A WEAPONS PROGRAM

The Khan network contract provided the Libyans with the critical technological components (centrifuges), designs (including a weapons design), user manuals (from the Pakistani program), and feed material (UF6 and yellowcake) for large-scale uranium enrichment. But getting this plant up and running would require intensive efforts by the Libyan nuclear establishment. The senior engineer Mohamed Ennami would have had enough experience to recognize the scope of this challenge. According to a nuclear expert who visited all sites associated with the Libyan weapons program after the December 2003 announcement, Libyans were focusing their efforts on the mechanics and engineering of centrifuges.[41]

As noted above, the Khan network provided designs and documentation, but the assembly would be left to Libyans with, at best, marginal relevant experience.[42] Some of the items supplied were incomplete or not prepared for installation. For example, ring magnet components for the centrifuges were shipped without having been magnetized and placed in holders.[43] The Libyans had no other option than to make the most of what they had under the circumstances, but this is one example of how delays were accumulating as the nuclear weapons program prepared to enrich uranium on an industrial scale.

But to produce nuclear weapons, the Libyans also had to revive their dormant projects focusing on uranium refinement and processing in order to produce feed material for the centrifuge plant and launch new projects dedicated to weaponization. While the Khan package could in theory produce a nuclear weapon, producing an entire arsenal or becoming self-sufficient in the longer term required developing a broad range of engineering resources at the Tajoura Nuclear Research Center (TNRC). Facing these challenges with extremely limited human resources, the Libyans opted to focus on one challenge at a time. At a UN conference in 2006, Ennami, who worked closely with Matuq and the centrifuge project, provided a brief overview of the Libyan nuclear weapons program during the mid-1990s.[44] The main focus of the program at this time, Ennami explained, was to enrich uranium. Other tasks, such as weaponization, were set aside for the time being. In late 2001 or early 2002, Libya received designs and documents on nuclear weapons fabrication from the Khan network. The Libyans later declared that they did not attempt to explore this information, or even assess it, because they lacked the necessary expertise and manpower.[45]

The nuclear weapons program at the TNRC was nominally organized around six sets of activities.[46] First, research carried out in the Tajoura laboratories explored isotope production, separation and enrichment; chemical conversion of uranium; and irradiation of samples to study their properties. These activities were geared toward creating basic know-how concerning the nuclear fuel cycle, especially the front end: transforming natural uranium to suitable feed material for centrifuges. This line of research drew on skills and resources acquired in the 1980s. As described in the previous chapter, Libyan scientists had carried out uranium conversion experiments between 1983 and 1989 at the TNRC, converting yellowcake into uranium tetrafluoride (UF4) and uranium metal. Foreign scientists from a nuclear weapons state—presumably the Soviet Union—supported this research between 1983 and 1986. The Libyans used 35–40 kilograms of yellowcake for these experiments. This line of research was revived in 1994, but ultimately no UF6 was produced. The production of nuclear fuel was not the main priority of the program at that time.[47]

The second cluster of activities focused on physics and material sciences, including nuclear structure, spectroscopy, activation analysis, and radiation protection. These activities, geared toward developing basic skills and understanding processes, helped develop useful insights but were not directly related to the challenges of setting up centrifuge cascades.

The third set of activities focused on constructing and testing a uranium conversion facility to transform natural uranium concentrate (yellowcake) to feed material for the centrifuges (UF6). This line of research and development built upon earlier efforts to develop the capacity to convert yellowcake, which the Libyans had imported from several countries in large quantities since the late 1970s, to UF4 and further, they hoped, to UF6. In 1984, Libya ordered a modular uranium conversion facility from an unspecified Asian country (possibly Japan). These modules, built to Libyan specifications, arrived in 1986 without instructions for assembly or operation. They remained in storage until 1998, when they were assembled south of Tripoli at the Al Hashan Uranium Conversion Facility.[48] While Libya had ordered a conversion facility to produce UF6, what they received was a facility able to process up to 30 metric tons per year of uranium concentrate to intermediate stages: uranium oxide or UF4. Libyan scientists also requested that the government purchase equipment to produce 15–30 metric tons of UF6 annually—presumably to complement the uranium conversion facility—but no such equipment was purchased.[49] Libyan technicians carried out cold tests of the Uranium Conversion Facility modules in early 2002, before the leaders of the program moved these modules to Salah Eddin and Sawani, due to security concerns.[50] As the map of Libyan nuclear sites and other technical infrastructure shows, these sites were both south of Tripoli but at a considerable distance from each other.

The fourth cluster of activities focused on acquiring centrifuges and supporting equipment: "complete centrifugal machines, parts, auxiliary system such as feeding units, vacuum pumps, control and measurement instrumentation, balancing machines etc."[51] Libya later declared to the International Atomic Energy Agency (IAEA) that scientists received training from the Khan network in several foreign locations on "power systems, mass spectrometers, welding, gas handling, quality control, computerized machining techniques and heat treatment of materials."[52] But no practical training was given to the Libyans in how to operate or assemble centrifuges. For example, one of the attendees of a training session in northern Spain left disappointed that he had not learned how to make centrifuge components.[53]

Despite their limited training and experience, the Libyans were able to set up the simpler P-1 centrifuge models in small cascades. By October 2000, they had set up and successfully run a single P-1 centrifuge model provided by the Khan network.[54] Later that year, they began to install three P-1 centrifuge cascades at Al-Hashan. One cascade of nine centrifuges was completed; the second cascade was partly assembled, with ten of nineteen centrifuges completed; and the third cascade of sixty-four centrifuges was prepared for installation. This work was interrupted in April 2002 when the centrifuges were disassembled and placed in storage at another site in Tripoli, Al-Fallah, due to security concerns.[55]

The fifth cluster of activities focused on setting up a precision machinery workshop at Janzour, west of Tripoli. Called Project Machine Shop 1001, it would produce spare parts for centrifuges. This was intended to ensure self-sufficiency after the stocks from the Khan network were used as well as to produce tools for the program. Ennami noted that the Libyans hoped that this workshop would produce complete new centrifuges. As part of this effort, Libya purchased specialized materials for producing centrifuge components from the Khan network, including maraging steel and high-strength aluminum alloys, as these could not be produced indigenously.[56] The Khan network also provided training for Libyan technicians, reportedly on at least three occasions, so they could learn how to operate these machines.[57]

The sixth cluster of activities focused on purchasing, including feed materials for centrifuges and other chemicals for uranium conversion and high-grade manufacturing materials for equipment and centrifuges. This makes it clear that the Libyans were trying to develop the capability to produce such materials, not just to import them. As noted in previous chapters, the Libyans had encountered difficulties in the basic industrial processes involved in refining raw materials such as iron. The challenges of producing these components were of a much higher order, requiring sophisticated and specialized equipment.

The decision to delay working on weaponization and to focus on uranium conversion was arguably a necessary adaptation to the constraints of the Libyan program. Facing a host of challenges, and with such limited manpower, it was necessary to adopt an incremental approach. Matuq told the IAEA in

2004 that the program's first priority had been to set up a pilot enrichment plant to develop necessary experience, and that they had not yet started to establish a large-scale enrichment capacity.[58] Developing suitable feed material for the centrifuges was an important, but not urgent, challenge.

Ennami similarly indicated that the managers of the nuclear weapons program took an incremental approach to solving problems. As specific problems were solved, he noted, "new tasks are set, future is becoming more and more clear, and even expected date of completion was discussed."[59] Overall, Ennami concluded, the program had been "progressing reasonably well." Libyan officials who were not directly involved with the management of the program were less optimistic. According to a Libyan academic who was involved in the negotiations leading to the dismantlement of the nuclear weapons program, the program's progress was very slow.[60] Echoing these observations, several other Libyans described the nuclear program as not much more than a plan, with little actual implementation or activity on the ground.

After the dismantlement of the program in late 2003, senior Libyan diplomats and officials apparently held different views of how far the nuclear program had been from a weapons capability. Some senior figures appear to have believed that Libya was just a few years away from acquiring nuclear weapons. In 2006, Matuq told a U.S. journalist that the program could have produced weapons fairly soon, stating that the Libyan target was 2006–2008, with the option of "accelerating" the program to produce a weapon by 2007.[61] In 2005, Seif al-Islam Gaddafi estimated that, as of late 2003, a nuclear weapons option was within five years.[62] These assessments were unrealistic to say the least, given the difficulties facing the Libyan nuclear establishment. But Libyan regime officials may still have believed that a nuclear weapons option was coming within reach. Other Libyans had a more realistic impression, at least with the benefit of hindsight. In 2006, a senior Libyan diplomat who was involved in the attempts to start negotiations with the West, but lacked a bird's-eye view of the details of the nuclear weapons program, simply dismissed the nuclear project as not much of a program at all.[63]

When foreign technical experts were granted access to the Libyan nuclear program, it became apparent that a weapons option was further away than the senior Libyans believed. Mohamed el-Baradei, the IAEA director general, visited Libya on 29 December 2003, after the decision to dismantle the program. He described the project as several years away from acquiring a nuclear weapon, at the very least. Although the nuclear establishment was already receiving equipment and was expected to launch an operational centrifuge plant producing weapons quantities of fissile material within five years, which was an optimistic estimate, no one had started preparing or planning activities beyond getting the centrifuge facility up and running.[64]

OVERSIGHT AND MANAGEMENT

The management of the nuclear weapons program that emerged in the early and mid-1990s differed from the 1970s and 1980s in two important respects: there was more direct involvement by regime officials, and the development of infrastructure and technology was outsourced to a multinational profit-driven supplier network. Through these measures, the regime attempted to take direct charge over the program and reduce the influence of the scientific community that seem uninterested in pursuing regime goals. The combination of weak institutions and outsourcing proved problematic, however, because the regime's information about the progress of the program was heavily influenced by the assessments of the suppliers of the technology and the Libyan officials involved in making these contracts, especially Matuq.

The nuclear weapons program was highly compartmentalized. Few individuals outside Gaddafi's closest circle had detailed information about the program. In an interview with the author, Seif al-Islam Gaddafi said that only five individuals in the regime knew the full scope of the program's activities.[65] At the TNRC, the nuclear establishment compartmentalized the centrifuge program—which was a separate project with sites scattered around Tripoli and surrounding areas—separating it from other departments. The purpose of the activities in both the chemical and nuclear programs—weapons—was hidden even from many of the employees in each program.[66] This made effective peer review difficult, if not impossible.

In the nuclear establishment, as elsewhere in the Libyan state, the level of personal influence did not always match official titles. Senior figures in the nuclear establishment such as Ennami enjoyed personal connections with senior regime officials such as Matuq, which were more important than formal roles. Accountability and decision making continued to be based on personal relationships not institutional lines of authority. A deputy could wield more power than his nominal superior if he had better links with Gaddafi and his closest circle. This was also reflected in the flow of information in state institutions: staff would report to the minister rather than to the ministry.

While senior regime officials lacked both the technical and institutional capacity to monitor or question technical choices, they were able to follow the money trail involved in the large contracts with foreign suppliers. All procurement in the realm of security and defense tended to involve large contracts under Gaddafi's personal purview. After he shut down the Ministry of Defense following an attempted coup in 1970, there was little oversight or lateral coordination between the various security forces and the branches of the military. Instead, Gaddafi set up an informal committee to monitor contracts and distribute financial benefits to senior officials. The large amounts of money involved in the nuclear contracts gave significant incentives to the senior tier of the intelligence services, confidantes of Gaddafi, to keep a close watch over the weapons program. Two or three senior officials appear to have profited personally from the nuclear agreements, which apparently caused some tension after the program was dismantled.[67]

Tensions also emerged between the different institutional elements of the atomized Libyan military-industrial complex. Under the NBSR's aegis, several technical institutes were created between 1994 and 1998. Some of these—the Casting Institute, Welding Institute, Advanced Center of Technology, and the Higher Technical Center for Training and Production—had more relevant equipment than did the universities. The machine shop for centrifuge production was colocated with the sites. Still, the Libyan government insisted that none of these institutes were linked with the nuclear program.[68] For example, the Libyan authorities told the IAEA that no institutional interaction took place between the NBSR and the Central Organization for Electronic Research, the organization responsible for the missile program.[69] The universities appear to have had only a tangential relationship with the nuclear program at this stage; they possessed very little relevant laboratory equipment. If this is accurate, it suggests the scale of the coordination problems in the Libyan regime at a time when the nuclear weapons program was, in their eyes, approaching the operational stage.

As the building blocks for a weapons program began arriving in Tripoli in 2001–2003, the Libyan regime faced a series of challenges. Would the nuclear establishment be capable of setting up an operational nuclear weapons program? And was the regime prepared to take the risk of setting up a large-scale operational nuclear weapons program as the international community prepared for war with Iraq over its alleged WMD programs?

Negotiations, 1999–2003

While Libyan scientists and technicians were installing centrifuges, senior regime officials tried to trade the program in exchange for relief from international economic sanctions. Secret negotiations began in 1999 between Libya, Britain, and the United States to facilitate a trial of the two Libyan suspects in the Lockerbie bombing. In the fall of 2001 the talks then turned to the issue of Libya's nonconventional weapons programs.

By the late 1990s, the Libyan regime sensed that many states, particularly in Africa, were increasingly reluctant to uphold the international sanctions against Libya. This, they believed, offered a new opportunity to reach out to the West.[70] The Libyan negotiating team approached Britain seeking to reach a settlement over the 1984 shooting of police offer Yvonne Fletcher and to resolve the Lockerbie issue. In a Geneva meeting with U.S. representatives in May 1999, the Libyans offered to dismantle their WMD programs. According to a senior member of Libya's team, Gaddafi had authorized them to discuss the WMD issue at this first meeting.[71] The Libyan team made it plain that they were prepared to address all issues standing in the way of improved relations: they were ready to cooperate in the U.S. campaign against al-Qaeda; they were prepared to play a very different role in the Middle East and Africa; they were willing to support U.S.-sponsored peace talks in the Middle East and to contribute to conflict resolution in Africa.[72] In July 1999, diplomatic relations were restored between Britain and Libya; this allowed closer dialogue between those two countries, but it remained difficult for Libya to engage the Americans.

The Libyan troika from the early 1990s, comprised of senior regime figures Obeidi, Zwai, and Kusa, was supported by other senior officials, including Ettalhi, who could provide input on technical and other relevant issues. In the late 1990s, Libyan academics with doctoral degrees from the United States and the West also became involved. These academics added a "unique element" to the Libyan team, according to a senior member.[73] Furthermore, he argued, the fact that the team worked together over an extended time period, both prior to and during the negotiations between 1999 and 2003, enabled the members to iron out any disagreements on the Libyan side and craft responses to their British and American counterparts.[74] But they had to work hard, without a guarantee of success: while Gaddafi supported their efforts in principle, he had not made a binding commitment. As the talks advanced, the Libyan team had to balance their efforts to strike a deal with the United States and the United Kingdom against the risk that Gaddafi could pull back from their proposed agreement.

While Libya offered to abandon its WMD programs as early as May 1999, the Americans and the British had demanded a sequential approach, insisting first on a trial of the Lockerbie suspects in a third country (the Netherlands) before addressing the WMD issue. They did make it clear to the Libyans that the WMD programs stood in the way of improved relations, and that this issue would have to be addressed after the Lockerbie trial was completed. Furthermore, the U.S. representatives insisted that Libya cooperate with U.S. efforts against Islamist terrorism and must pay reparations to the families of the Lockerbie victims. According to Martin S. Indyk, former U.S. ambassador to Israel and leader of the U.S. delegation in subsequent talks with the Libyan team, a key U.S. goal was to ensure that the sanctions remained in force. Therefore, they agreed to proceed with secret talks on the condition that Libya would cease lobbying to have the sanctions lifted.[75] At that point, ambassador Indyk noted, the United States did not consider Libya's chemical weapons program "an imminent threat" and believed that its nuclear program "barely existed."[76]

The Libyan team—Obeidi, Zwai, and Kusa—were successful in persuading Gaddafi to extradite the two Lockerbie suspects for trial in The Hague. After the trial ended in January 2001 with the conviction of one suspect (al-Megrahi) and the acquittal of the other (Fhimah), the Libyan team wanted to return to the negotiating table. With Libya and the United Kingdom having resumed diplomatic relations, Zwai—a close associate of Gaddafi—was appointed Libya's ambassador to the United Kingdom; he moved to London in the fall of 2001. He later recalled that he was instructed to engage right away in focused disarmament talks. However, after the 9/11 terrorist attacks the talks were postponed.[77]

Resolving the Lockerbie bombing issues built confidence among the three parties, showing that they could solve difficult issues through diplomacy. From Libya's perspective, the situation was beginning to improve. The UN Security Council sanctions, in force since 1992, were lifted in October 2003. During the vote in the Security Council, the United States and France abstained; the United States explained its abstention by referring to Bush administration concerns about Libya's WMD programs.[78]

On 15 October 2001, the Libyan team met British and U.S. representatives, including the American ambassador in London, Central Intelligence Agency (CIA) and Secret Intelligence Service (MI6) officers, and the Italian deputy foreign minister.[79] The main Libyan objective was to have the bilateral U.S. sanctions lifted and to improve its relations with the United States. These sanctions stood in the way of modernizing Libya's petroleum complex and opening up its economy to the global marketplace. The United States made it clear that halting the Libyan WMD programs (nuclear, chemical, and biological) and reducing the range of Libya's SCUD-B missiles to below 300 kilometers—so that they could not reach Israel—were preconditions for moving forward on these other issues. But first, Libya was enlisted to help with the U.S. War on Terror by sharing intelligence information.

In the fall of 2002, Libyan and British officials sought to develop a new dialogue focusing specifically on WMD questions. The British had attempted to reach out to the Libyans two or three times to talk about the WMD issue, according to a senior Libyan diplomat involved in these conversations.[80] At a Camp David meeting in September 2002, Prime Minister Tony Blair persuaded President George W. Bush that they should explore whether Gaddafi would trade his WMD programs in return for relief from sanctions. In October, Blair wrote to Gaddafi, who replied tentatively that his people would be in touch.[81]

After continuing for nine months in 2003, the trilateral talks finally turned to the WMD issue. The Libyan team came to include the heads of military and foreign intelligence, the heads of the nuclear and chemical weapons programs, and Seif al-Islam Gaddafi as a self-described "trouble-shooter."[82] They worked closely with Muammar Gaddafi but faced difficulties in securing his support at critical points during the negotiations.[83]

In making their case to their leader, the Libyan negotiating team cited the changing costs and risks of pursuing nuclear weapons in the post-9/11 world. According to one of the three senior members of the team, they had concluded that pursuing nuclear weapons would be to "shoot themselves in the foot" from a security perspective.[84] After the initial meeting with the British in the fall of 2001, the Libyan delegation had become convinced that pursuing WMD carried greater risks than potential benefits: pursuing them would simply worsen struggles with the United States, now the world's only superpower. According to Seif al-Islam Gaddafi, the Libyan regime concluded that it risked a U.S. invasion or preemptive strikes after 9/11.[85] Furthermore, the leadership believed that it was necessary to channel funds toward education, health, and the economy rather than further spending on the WMD programs.[86]

In Seif al-Islam Gaddafi's recollection, it took several meetings over the course of two months in 2003 to persuade the leader to move forward with the unilateral dismantlement of the WMD programs. There were domestic hurdles to be overcome: the military had to be convinced that the negotiations were not aimed at disarming Libya but focused only on WMD.[87] The Libyan team was concerned about how to present such an agreement to the Libyan population. Seif-al-Islam later noted that such an agreement had to be presented as a "win-win" deal, and not seem to be the result of external force or pressure.[88] Furthermore, Gaddafi's son noted, as talks intensified in early 2003 the Libyan leader feared that it could be a trap, and that there was a hidden agenda at play aiming for the overthrow of his regime.

One point of tension throughout the negotiations, and even after they were completed, was Libya's demand for security guarantees and conventional military equipment as compensation for abandoning its pursuit of a nuclear deterrent. Gaddafi apparently wanted a promise that Libya would not be subject to attacks by the United States or the United Kingdom using nuclear or chemical weapons—nor presumably by their allies, including Israel. In addition, Libya wanted a security guarantee from the United States and Britain; access to advanced conventional arms; and help to expand its civilian nuclear program. In a television interview in December 2004, Gaddafi expressed his desire for a security guarantee: "The international community should ban the use of nuclear or chemical weapons against that country which has dismantled its own program on its own initiative. It must provide it with defensive weapons in order to protect itself against any danger."[89]

In early March 2003, before the U.S.-led invasion of Iraq, Libyan representatives Seif al-Islam Gaddafi and Kusa made the offer to their British counterparts that Libya would abandon its WMD programs.[90] In mid-October, fifteen U.S. inspectors led by Stephen Kappes of the CIA secretly traveled to Libya to examine the WMD facilities as well as other relevant infrastructure, including laboratories and conventional military factories.[91] Although their Libyan interlocutors had been instructed not to disclose the full scope of their programs, the inspectors found that the nuclear program was larger than they had anticipated and that Libya had more chemical weapons than expected.[92]

Also in October 2003, inspectors at the port of Taranto, Italy, found centrifuge equipment sourced by the Khan network aboard the cargo ship *BBC China* in transit from North Korea to Libya. The incident has often been described as influential on the talks: the argument is that it forced Gaddafi to commit to the deal by blowing Libya's cover.[93] Although U.S. State Department statements were initially cautious, putting this event in the context of ongoing talks in late 2003, subsequent statements by Undersecretary of State for Arms Control and International Security John Bolton and by Secretary of State Condoleezza Rice claimed that it was a key turning point.[94] British officials, however, emphasized the role of the negotiation process rather than the *BBC China* discovery. In December 2003, for example, British foreign secretary Jack Straw described the Libyan decision to give up its WMD as the product of "painstaking diplomacy . . . going back for six or seven years where we sought to re-establish a diplomatic relationship."[95]

Libyan regime figures have privately stressed that the interdiction had little effect on their willingness to abandon the WMD programs. In the years following the *BBC China* incident, persistent rumors even suggested that Libyan intelligence sources actually facilitated the interdiction, by tipping off the Americans and the British. Whether or not this is true, there is little reason to believe that the *BBC China* incident was pivotal in the Libyan decision. Incidentally, as the IAEA later noted, the inspectors overlooked one P-2 centrifuge container, which arrived in Libya in March 2004.[96]

The Libyans perceived that the Americans especially wanted to claim the dismantlement of Libya's nuclear program as a victory because of the U.S. failure to find the WMD it expected in Iraq.[97] A senior member of the negotiating team described Libya's decision to dismantle its nuclear program as a "gift to Bush and Blair."[98] Seif al-Islam Gaddafi commented that the Libyan leadership wanted to postpone the announcement, however, because they did not want it to appear as if U.S. moves against Iraq had frightened them into making the decision.[99]

While the British and the Americans had been aware of the Khan network for several years, their assessments of the Libyan program changed in the course of negotiations, and especially after the October 2003 visits. In the late 1990s, the U.S. intelligence community had indications of an enrichment program in Libya but had not gone public with this information.[100] In 2001 a Pentagon report stated that "Libya . . . made little progress" on its nuclear program because the program lacked "well-developed plans, expertise, consistent financial support, and adequate foreign suppliers."[101]

After the October visits, the parties began to iron out an agreement. As the talks were extremely sensitive, few outside the negotiating teams were aware of what was going on, even at the highest levels of the three governments. To avoid leaks or anyone spoiling the progress of the talks, the teams did not inform the IAEA about the existence of a nuclear weapons program in Libya or about the October 2003 technical visits inspecting sites associated with the program. On 16 December 2003, senior officials met at the Travellers Club in London to discuss a draft statement prepared by Kusa. The senior members of the Libyan delegation—Kusa, Obeidi, and Zwai—met British officials David Landsman and William Ehrman from the Foreign Office, two senior MI6 officials, and Robert G. Joseph of the U.S. National Security Council.[102] During a six-hour meeting, they pressed the Libyans to make more explicit what they were giving up and what they were agreeing to.[103] The Libyans wanted an explicit quid pro quo—that the United States would agree to lift sanctions in exchange for Libya's dismantlement—but the United States refused an explicit linkage.[104] The Libyan delegation also wanted to include a statement in the agreement about Libya's desire for a WMD-free zone in the Middle East—this was intended to put pressure on Israel—but the United States representatives resisted taking this route.[105] They reached an agreement but Gaddafi was still hesitant; he finally committed to the deal on 17 December after Blair telephoned him personally. Gaddafi refused, however, to make a public announcement; he left that to his Foreign Ministry. Up to the day of the announcement, U.S. officials were not certain that the deal was on.[106]

On 19 December 2003, a Libyan Foreign Ministry official announced that Libya would abandon its pursuit of internationally proscribed weapons, stating that Libya "believes that the arms race will neither serve its security nor the region's security and [that it] contradicts [Libya's] great concern for a world that enjoys peace and security."[107] The British government waited until a translation of the statement was available to be sure that it was consistent with what they had agreed; only then did Blair and Bush publicly commend Gaddafi's decision.

Between January and April 2004, Libya's nuclear weapons program was dismantled by U.S. and British inspectors, under the formal auspices of the IAEA, which had been kept out of the secret trilateral negotiations prior to December 2003. This was not an easy collaboration because the sensitive items, such as the weapons design, were seized by the United States despite the protests of the IAEA delegation. Libyan officials declared that their decision should serve as a model for other countries; that message was echoed by statements from British and American officials. Gaddafi made several statements explaining why Libya gave up the pursuit of WMD. In an interview with an Italian journalist on 17 December 2004, for example, he explained that Libya had neither the need nor the capacity to acquire nuclear weapons: "Libya [had] risked becoming involved in producing weapons at an inappropriate level. This [was] because such weapons need a solid base, great technological expertise, and vectors. Moreover, in which field could such weapons be used, in which theater of combat? Indeed, I believe that this question faces all countries producing nuclear weapons. . . . So the best decision, the most courageous decision, was to dismantle it."[108]

By late 2004, however, the Libyan government became frustrated with what they felt was a failure by the United States and the United Kingdom to deliver their part of the bargain, as Libya had not received the security assurances or weapons systems it expected, and the process of lifting the U.S. sanctions was dragging on. Libyan officials soon stopped referring to their negotiated dismantlement of their WMD programs as a model for other states. During the 2011 Arab Spring, the support from NATO forces for the insurgent forces confirmed Gaddafi's worst fears: that abandoning the nuclear weapons program left him vulnerable to being overthrown by a popular uprising backed by the West.

As this chapter has shown, the Libyan nuclear weapons program continued to underperform even after the regime revived it *and* made enormous investments. This seems baffling, as the nuclear black market appeared to solve Libya's main bottleneck: enriching uranium on a large scale. The Libyans could buy a turnkey centrifuge plant from the Khan network, complete with manuals and (some) training. There was a well-qualified senior tier of leaders in the nuclear weapons program, and Libyan scientists were making sound, incremental plans for the weapons program. Libyan engineers and technical workers appeared to be quite capable of assembling centrifuges. In other words, ineptitude was not the problem. Nonetheless, the program seemed to go nowhere.

The absence of technological determinism is a striking feature of the Libyan nuclear program: even the arrival of a complete set of imported building blocks for a nuclear program failed to trigger any real momentum. This was a recurring pattern observed since the late 1970s: after suppliers provided new nuclear technology, an initial flurry of activity was quickly followed by inertia. Here, again, the institutional weakness and small size of the Libyan nuclear establishment are critical factors. More specifically, Matuq's failure to transform the nuclear weapons program into a more effective and goal-oriented project demonstrated that money, centrifuges, and a strategic decision by Gaddafi were not enough given the structural problems their scientists faced on the ground.

Libya lacked institutionalized governance mechanisms to collect information on how the program was proceeding and to intervene where necessary to see that regime decisions were implemented. Even with Matuq at the helm, scientists continued to explore basic processes while they faced compounding problems tackling the diverse challenges associated with an operational weapons program. The lavish funding for the program, combined with an absence of technical reviews or oversight mechanisms, enabled the program to drift while the senior leadership was led to believe a nuclear weapons capability was on the horizon.

As this chapter has demonstrated, the failure of Libya's program was an overdetermined outcome. At the same time, the analysis has revealed that state capacity was an important intervening variable contributing to this result.

Given the unimpressive advances of this program, we can ask whether the nuclear weapons program was predominantly intended as a bargaining chip. Was the program ever intended to become operational? As this chapter has shown, there were different opinions on this question among senior Libyan officials. Those with more information about the program, including some who had a personal stake in the project, suggested that a nuclear weapons capability was perhaps only five years away when the program was dismantled in late 2003. Others scoffed at this notion, arguing that the program was not much more than a plan. Ultimately, the truth lies somewhere in between: the Libyans had a sound plan—thousands of centrifuges were on their way to Tripoli—but lacked the organizational resources to implement a large-scale operational weapons program. As they moved closer to an operational program, these weaknesses became increasingly obvious.

Some observers have ascribed the weaknesses of the Libyan program to the parallel pursuit of rapprochement with the United States between 2001 and 2003. While it may be tempting to assume that these deliberations and tensions were reflected in the nuclear program, this is not how the Libyan regime worked. To assume that there was such a link would be to seriously overestimate the coordination within the Libyan state.

Conclusion

In this book I have tried to accomplish three tasks. First, I have sought to explain why Iraq and Libya failed to acquire nuclear weapons and to provide a richer account of both programs than is available elsewhere. In so doing, I have argued that several facts and their implications have previously been misunderstood. Second, I have explored how state capacity worked as an intervening variable shaping the performance and governance of nuclear weapons programs in two weak states with personalist regimes. Third, my findings challenge long-standing assumptions about personalist regimes, notably the notion that they are inevitably prone to nepotism and micromanagement. Drawing on ample primary sources, many previously unexplored by scholars, I have attempted to revisit basic assumptions and long-held beliefs about each case.

My argument focused primarily on the effects of weak state capacity on nuclear weapons programs in personalist regimes. In my analysis I have tried to highlight state capacity and distinguish this from other domestic-level variables such as control mechanisms, plain ineptitude, and varying leader interest and commitment. I have used a narrow definition of state capacity, conceptualizing it as the professionalism and independence of the state apparatus, because this concept can easily become vague or unwieldy. I have sought to demonstrate how state capacity affects nuclear weapons programs from nose to tail, including planning, operationalization, oversight, and auditing. In so doing, I have treated state capacity as an intervening variable that conditions the effect of other factors, such as foreign assistance and leader interest in nuclear weapons. I have *not* argued that state capacity can explain regime decisions about pursuing or abandoning nuclear weapons programs, nor have I suggested that state capacity is the only variable that matters in shaping the performance and outcomes of these programs.

In my analysis of Iraq and Libya, I have observed how two personalist leaders attempted to address the problems associated with weak state capacity through their choice of management strategies, that is, whether they opted for centralized control, or even micromanagement, or for devolving much of the decision making to the scientific leaders of the program. Management strategy is a choice that I can't predict, but I show that there is choice variation rather than constant micromanagement in the two cases studied in this book. Whether or not leaders want to intervene directly in the management of the nuclear weapons program reflects the intensity of their desire to get the bomb, among other things. But the efficacy and impact of their interventions are shaped by state capacity via information processing and auditing mechanisms, as well as by the institutional resources at their disposal (e.g., to launch alternative research tracks or projects).

These findings matter for historians and political scientists, but also for decision makers. While fewer states today pursue nuclear weapons than before, those that do tend to be authoritarian states that cannot mobilize human and industrial resources on the scale that earlier proliferators like the Soviet Union and China were able to. As we move toward a world with more nuclear-capable authoritarian states, understanding how these states might seek to develop a weapons option—and the particular constraints they are likely to face in this process—is a pressing matter. If the arguments and analysis developed in this book are correct, we will need more refined tools capable of differentiating between authoritarian regimes with varying state capacity to understand and assess these developments.

In the following, I revisit the main findings and their implications for theory and policy, summarized in four lessons. While it falls beyond the scope of this book to apply the argument to other states, I include a mini-case study of Syria's nuclear program to see how the argument fares when applied to another personalist regime in the Middle East. Then, I assess alternative explanations for the outcomes of Iraq and Libya's nuclear programs. Finally, I conclude with some final remarks about the broader implications of the findings presented in this book.

The Findings and Their Relevance

This book has portrayed Iraq's and Libya's nuclear programs from an inside-out perspective, drawing on the contemporary perspectives of scientists and technical experts and primary sources that open up these establishments to an unprecedented degree. Where relevant, I have included perspectives from regime officials and the states' leaders on these programs and their purpose. I have argued that many of our key assumptions about how science "worked" in these regimes were misguided. Seen from this vantage point, the political leadership appears more distant from the weapons programs and, oftentimes, disinterested. Saddam and Gaddafi certainly appear to have been less omnipresent and omniscient than how they wanted to come across. This was a trade-off whose consequences were recognized, in part, because these leaders and regimes were ultimately more concerned with coup-proofing against internal threats than acquiring a nuclear deterrent.

Personalist leaders don't always get what they want—particularly if they want nuclear weapons. While leaders such as Saddam and Gaddafi try to nurture a public image as all-seeing and all-powerful, they are constrained by the mismatch between the information they have to process and the number of decisions they need to make. These challenges multiply when such leaders weaken their states to increase their own personal power. All leaders struggle to penetrate the technical details of nuclear technology, but these leaders arguable struggle more because they weaken the state's institutional resources to monitor and audit highly specialized activities such as nuclear programs. This paradox is perhaps particularly evident in the case of nuclear technology, which is difficult to understand and audit for leaders and regime elites who lack technical expertise. As this book has shown, personalist leaders may suspect or even realize that their officials are not delivering what they want. But they have limited options for addressing these problems, given the incentives facing their regime officials and the limitations of their own information-processing and auditing mechanisms in formal state institutions.

Nor should we assume that just because personalist leaders seem to want nuclear weapons, or say that they do, that they want them badly. Nuclear weapons were never Saddam's or Gaddafi's primary concern. Other crises and challenges constantly vied for their attention and, unlike Stalin, they were never convinced that nuclear weapons were their "number one problem." Their attention and commitment to these programs were inconsistent for extended periods of time. Here, the inside-out perspective applied in the case study analysis reveals a gap between the public and private rhetoric of these leaders and their actions. Furthermore, both leaders ultimately cared more about threats to their domestic survival—either in the form of domestic opposition or the longer-term risks associated with domestic discontent during economic downturns—than they did about acquiring a nuclear deterrent.

Some personalist leaders are less likely than others to get nuclear weapons. This book has attempted to demonstrate variation in the performance of Iraq's and Libya's nuclear weapons programs. I have argued that state capacity is an important part of the explanation for why Iraq got much closer to a nuclear weapons capability than Libya ever did, despite having less access to sensitive assistance and less time on their hands. The implication of this argument for other cases is that we should not expect that nuclear weapons programs in personalist regimes are likely to be the same in terms of performance based on regime type alone. This argument suggests that variation in state capacity affects the performance of nuclear weapons programs. We should not expect uniform outcomes among personalist regimes with different levels of state capacity. Nor should policymakers assume that all personalist regimes will fail in their efforts to pursue nuclear weapons: Iraq came close. Other leaders may not stumble as they approach the nuclear weapons threshold as Saddam did.

The domestic constraints facing nuclear scientists in personalist regimes do not readily reveal themselves. The cases of Iraq and Libya could be of use for analysts seeking to disentangle these constraints and their interactive effects. If the findings are correct, then coup-proofing strategies may offer important clues to how state capacity is affected by personalist leaders attempting to gain and strengthen their hold on power. State capacity is not static, even in weak states, and different coup-proofing strategies have distinct consequences. As the case of Libya suggests, erosion of formal institutions have particularly damaging, and long-lasting, consequences for state capacity.

The findings of this book also suggest that some of the observed behavior interpreted as incompetence was caused by other factors. In the analysis of Iraq's and Libya's programs, I have found several examples—including duplication of orders for laboratory equipment; failure to prepare for the introduction of nuclear energy; inadequate education and training of scientists; or simply the absence of specific targets or objectives to guide a research program—where what looked like incompetence from the outside actually reflected weak state capacity. This is not meant to suggest there was no incompetence at play in these nuclear programs. The inertia observed by visiting consultants in Libya is a different problem, but it is arguably related to the failure to plan and facilitate research.

Personalist leaders in weak states prefer not to micromanage nuclear programs. A counterintuitive finding is that neither Saddam nor Gaddafi micromanaged their nuclear weapons programs. These leaders were inconsistent in terms of their attention to their nuclear weapons programs and largely let scientists—and later other regime officials—set up and manage these programs. While I do not try to predict when a personalist leader will opt for more or less controlling management strategies, I do show that there is choice variation in the two cases studied in this book. As noted in the foregoing chapters, even scientists were surprised by how distant the leaders were.

These leaders preferred to not get too deeply involved with the detailed management of their nuclear programs. This was costly and, furthermore, both leaders preferred to delay intervening until late in the process, unless they faced a crisis. This was evident on two occasions. First, both leaders intervened—after internal bickering in the Iraqi case and after years of failure in the Libyan one—by placing a regime stalwart rather than a scientist in charge of the program. Second, both leaders set new ground rules for their programs when they began to fear military attacks: Saddam did so after the 1981 attack by Israel and Gaddafi in 2002 after increasing concerns in the Libyan regime that the program could come under fire. In these instances, rules set down by the senior political leadership led to suboptimal technical choices. In Iraq's case this was to avoid detection and a repeat strike; in Libya's this led to inertia (e.g., the disassembled Libyan nuclear facilities). However, these interventions stand in sharp contrast to the general avoidance of interference by both Saddam and Gaddafi during these programs.

Personalist leaders are more constrained than we tend to realize. Fourth, and finally, a finding with broader implications is that these leaders were more constrained than we have realized, or political scientists tend to assume. I have argued that Saddam and Gaddafi were constrained in two ways in their pursuit of nuclear weapons: first, by the weak capacity of their states; and second, by their concerns about domestic survival weighed against their desire for a nuclear deterrent to ward off foreign attack. In the case of Libya, regime elites had a direct impact on Gaddafi's decisions at key moments in the nuclear weapons program. I discuss the implications of these findings for theory below, including the long-standing debate on how authoritarian leaders make decisions about investing in military capabilities or domestic development to benefit their citizens.

Implications for Theory

This book has argued that the literature is mistaken about several important aspects of the Iraqi and Libyan programs: how they were governed; what triggered key decisions; and the outcomes of each program. Because the case universe of nuclear proliferation is very small, these findings have significant implications for theory and analysis. In this section, I highlight some of these implications and suggest how my argument might fare if applied to other cases.

Broadly, the findings shed new light on the internal politics and decision making of personalist regimes. For example, the cases of Iraq and Libya speak to long-standing debates about how leaders make choices about spending on guns or butter. A rich body of literature explores how leaders weigh different domestic-level interests in making these decisions, how different factors in their environment affect these deliberations, and whether authoritarian leaders are less constrained in making these decisions than democratic leaders who have to consider the interests of the electorate. In a study of how oil income affected different authoritarian leaders with revisionist preferences, Jeff Colgan finds that "petro-states" engage more often in armed conflict with their neighbors.[1] Both Iraq and Libya spent many petrodollars on military capabilities under Saddam's and Gaddafi's leadership. As Colgan shows, oil enabled Gaddafi to spend at least 25 percent of total revenues on arms in some years.[2] More broadly, scholars often assume that personalist leaders such as Saddam and Gaddafi are unconstrained in making decisions about spending on guns or butter, as well as conflicts and war, because they are not constrained by domestic state institutions and care less about the interests and well-being of the population.[3] Personalist leaders are less constrained than other leaders, due to the absence of strong institutional checks and balances and ample petrodollars. But, as this analysis has demonstrated, even these leaders face constraints. For example, debates about guns or butter were a recurring feature of the Libyan regime. Furthermore, these debates were consequential: the two wings of the regime—one in favor of nuclear weapons and the other lobbying for economic development at home—influenced Gaddafi's perspectives and decisions. Indeed, balancing these wings was part of Gaddafi's efforts to avoid either faction becoming too influential, thereby threatening his own relative power. Saddam also had to weigh his choices about the nuclear program against the balancing of regime factions, as was clear in his temperate public reaction to the 1981 attack on the Osirak reactor, which led hardliners to further oppose his policies at a time of widespread dissatisfaction with the Iran-Iraq War.[4]

An implication of this observation for policymakers and analysts is that personalist leaders are influenced by regime elites in their decisions about nuclear weapons, particularly if they face an economic environment where they can no longer pursue both guns and butter simultaneously. Furthermore, if personalist leaders face widespread domestic dissatisfaction due to adverse economic conditions their calculations may change. In Gaddafi's case, mounting domestic dissatisfaction contributed to his shift away from guns—including nuclear weapons—to butter. In Saddam's case, even at a time of economic hardship at home during the Iran-Iraq War, spending on the nuclear weapons program continued to soar. Understanding the mechanisms bringing about these outcomes is an important subject for further analysis.

The findings also highlight the trade-offs these leaders and regimes made between coup-proofing and the performance of their states in different issue areas. A counterintuitive finding is that even in Saddam's regime, senior officials realized that they were unable to keep track of the performance of projects in the cottage industries that emerged in the military-industrial complex. These observations speak to emerging debates about the varied performance of personalist regimes in different issue areas. They also tell us something important about implementation of decisions in these regimes, an issue area that has received less attention than why personalist leaders make particular decisions about acquiring nuclear weapons.[5]

These trade-offs can evolve over time. Saddam and Gaddafi sought to secure their hold on power initially by purges and then by weakening the standing and influence of alternative power centers—or just getting rid of them. Over time, they became more focused on balancing different state elites and regime factions. In Saddam's case, his tendency to selectively pay close attention to certain issue areas (notably the performance of the military) during the 1980s stood in contrast to his more detached style of leadership in later years, when he had fewer monitoring mechanisms in place and was difficult to get hold of even for senior regime officials.

Two central findings—that neither Saddam nor Gaddafi micromanaged the nuclear weapons programs and that their nuclear programs were not as rife with nepotism as has been widely assumed—challenge the conventional wisdom about these leaders and regimes. They also raise questions for further study. For example, the findings invite further analysis of how analysts and political scientists can interpret the behavior of nuclear scientists as indicators of intentions and decisions at the senior level of the regime. As we have seen, personalist regimes in weak states don't always know or understand what their nuclear scientists are up to. The two leaders studied in this book knew they were being misinformed and occasionally tried to impose additional control mechanisms, with mixed results. This holds significant implications for how scholars interpret observed behavior in weak states, in coding decisions as well as qualitative analyses.

More broadly, the findings challenge the enduring assumption that regime type is a reliable indicator for whether states are likely to pursue and acquire nuclear weapons. This takes many guises, from the Cold War arms races where the centralization of the Soviet state was interpreted as an obstacle to innovation, to theories arguing that neopatrimonial regimes are structurally determined to want nuclear weapons while at the same time arguing that such states are too incompetent to acquire them. The findings in this book suggest that state capacity is an important intervening variable shaping the governance and performance of these programs in authoritarian regimes.

The case universe of states pursuing nuclear weapons is small; the number of weak states run by personalist regimes is smaller. Iraq and Libya faced particular obstacles that many other states have not faced, or faced to a much lesser degree. For example, neither Pakistan nor India were subject to the restrictions of the Non-Proliferation Treaty; neither experienced a targeted strike on their nuclear establishment (even though India apparently considered striking against Pakistani nuclear sites during the 1980s); and both benefited from foreign technology and assistance. North Korea is in many ways a strong state, even if this is dominated by leaders who attempt to redefine the state in their own image. The same can be said about Iran. But other states in the Middle East that have been suspected of harboring a nuclear weapons ambition—including Algeria, Syria, and Egypt—fit the description of relatively weak states with personalist regimes. While there are several studies of the case of Egypt's past nuclear program that demonstrate how state capacity and the regime's concern about empowering new technical elites obstructed the emergence of its program, less is known about Syria and Algeria.[6] In the following, I briefly explore Syria's past program using new sources highlighting the contemporary perspectives of International Atomic Energy Agency (IAEA) consultants, including a formerly senior Iraqi nuclear scientist, to probe the explanatory power of the state capacity argument in another case.

SYRIA

Syria is a weak state governed by a personalist regime that has been suspected of seeking a nuclear weapons option. The program appears to have been dismantled or interrupted after a suspected reactor site—allegedly provided by North Korea—was destroyed by a 2007 Israeli air strike. Very little is known about the Syrian nuclear program, and even less is known about the domestic-level drivers of this program. Previously unexplored IAEA sources reveal that there are numerous similarities between the problems observed in Iraq and Libya and those that faced the Syrian nuclear program.

In Syria, foreign assistance—including technical assistance from the IAEA—offered an opportunity to launch an ambitious exploratory nuclear program despite lacking the human resources and organizational and technical infrastructure to support this effort. In February 1968, the Syrian government requested assistance from the IAEA with surveying options for possible nuclear research and development, including the drafting of a plan for the development of atomic energy.[7] In this request, the Syrian government cited its intention to launch a "preliminary" program that would be based on twenty scientists trained in relevant fields. A university scientist was, the IAEA noted, interested in acquiring a research reactor, despite the fact that there were no trained staff available and the infrastructure was not equipped to support such a reactor.[8] In other words, the Syrian program lacked the necessary support (from the political and institutional levels) and resources (technical and human) to succeed. Given these problems, IAEA experts were reluctant to provide additional support.

In Syria, the main domestic obstacles to a nuclear energy program at this time included a weak state as well as general underdevelopment. In 1969, Ghazi Derwish, a visiting IAEA consultant who was at that time director of the Tuwaitha Nuclear Research Center, summarized these challenges as follows: "staff shortage, large student population, limited funds and poor supply of equipment and laboratory facilities, are the main factors, besides poor pay, contributing to the meagreness of research done in these colleges. . . ."[9] In addition, he noted, there was no defined government policy on the issue of nuclear energy.

Despite these modest circumstances, the Syrian scientists believed that the IAEA would help them acquire a nuclear reactor and requested quotes from suppliers. The IAEA area officer for the Middle East and Europe wrote to Derwish before he traveled to his mission in Syria: "You can very well imagine this is absolutely out of the question that the Agency could enter into any expenditure of this sort. Personally I think that the best advice you could give them is to forget about such a project for several years. We understand that there is practically no trained personnel available and that the general infrastructure is not adequate to support a research reactor."[10]

After completing his assignment, Derwish noted in his final report that Syria had a "very ambitious development programme with very limited and in some cases poor scientific and technical structures to support it, with the resultant dependence on foreign or international technical aid."[11] There was no national agency at that time responsible for, or capable of, drawing up plans or overseeing implementation of a nuclear program. The Syrian Atomic Energy Committee and the Supreme Council of Sciences lacked the decision-making power and resources to carry out such tasks. Nor was there a government policy on the question of nuclear energy.[12] Despite the presence of qualified nuclear experts, the IAEA consultant concluded, the country lacked the necessary human resources and technical and organizational structures to support "scientific research and work covering wide areas in the field of atomic energy and its peaceful applications."[13] A reactor, he noted, was not something that the country could afford under present conditions.[14]

Syria continued to seek IAEA assistance with programs focusing on agriculture, health, and hydrology. In these areas, the IAEA consultants reported persistent absorption capacity problems, ranging from the absence of local counterparts and adequate working facilities (one consultant had to work from a lavatory) to a lack of interest on the part of senior authorities overseeing the nuclear program. In light of these obstacles, an IAEA consultant based in Syria in 1973 on a one-year assistance mission wrote: "I do not seem to have accomplished much at all."[15] He described the Radioisotopes in Medicine Project as "farcical."[16] The leader of this project, based in the Syrian Center for Nuclear Medicine, requested equipment worth some $78,000 without accompanying experts or training, even though the center lacked trained experts and technicians capable of handling this equipment. But, the IAEA consultant noted, "this is clearly not on."[17] Three years later another IAEA official noted their reluctance to support the isotope laboratory project in Syria: "I do not believe it is worthwhile supporting such an isotope laboratory project without genuine prospect of success, and success could only come if the trained scientists are really competent." This internal assessment came in the wake of another visiting expert's report, citing extensive problems with "the organization of hydrological research in Syria, and the ineffective performance of the Syrian Atomic Energy Commission. The root of the problem probably lies in the almost complete lack of competent scientists and a structure within which they can work effectively."[18] In other words, by the mid-1970s it was apparent that weak institutional resources were at the core of the Syrian program's troubles.

During the 1980s the Syrians, like the Libyans, tried to secure a nuclear research reactor from the Soviet Union but ultimately failed due to domestic economic difficulties. The Syrians then turned to other suppliers, reportedly including the Abdul Qadeer Khan network, over the next few years; they finally secured a research reactor from China in the 1990s. The Syrians continued to seek support from the IAEA and received assistance with the front end of the nuclear fuel cycle. But they also continued to fail to develop the infrastructure and human resources necessary to operate an indigenous nuclear energy program. However, the limited evidence that has surfaced in the wake of the 2007 Israeli strike on a suspected clandestine reactor site suggests that Syria may have benefited from more secret sensitive assistance than the outside world had realized. In 2011, the IAEA concluded that the building destroyed in the strike was similar to a North Korean reactor.[19] This suggests that Syria, like Libya, appears to have made unexpected strides in their nuclear program boosted by sensitive foreign assistance, but also indicates that the Syrian program depended on foreign expertise in light of their own shortcomings. This underscores the importance of assessing how domestic constraints, such as state capacity, work in weak states with access to extensive foreign assistance.

Implications for Policy

For policymakers, understanding how personalist leaders make decisions about nuclear weapons, and how capable their states are of implementing those decisions, is useful for risk assessments as well as crafting nonproliferation policies. Much of the recent political science literature on personalist regimes tends to emphasize two aspects: that these leaders are essentially unconstrained by state elites and domestic audiences; and that these states' scientific establishments are often inept. The findings of this book qualify these judgments, with significant implications for decision makers who need to know how personalist regimes tick.

The first insight is that personalist leaders are not as unconstrained as they might seem. Saddam and Gaddafi were influenced by their closest circle at key moments of their nuclear weapons programs. Both leaders had to manage and balance regime factions. Senior officials played a key role in negotiations with foreign suppliers and developed vested interests, which reportedly led to personal financial gain in Libya, in the continuation of the nuclear weapons programs. Both leaders maintained ambiguous positions, enabling regime factions to deliberate and promote different policies, including, in the case of Libya, on the question of nuclear weapons. Furthermore, the findings qualify the common assumption that personalist regimes are populated with yes-men who only pass on good news. The two nuclear programs appear to have been less nepotistic than many have assumed. Saddam ensured that recruitment of scientists to the nuclear program was (mostly) meritocratic. Senior managers did not voluntarily report bad news to Saddam but individuals and institutions did not hesitate to report bad news if the blame could be attributed to rival individuals or institutions. Colleagues reported on each other. Competing institutions, including units of the military-industrial complex, badmouthed other projects, such as the nuclear weapons program, to deflect potential blame when collaborative projects did not go according to plan.

A second insight is that the performance of nuclear weapons programs in personalist regimes is affected by state capacity, which varies from state to state. This suggests that the assumption that nuclear weapons programs in all personalist regimes are likely to fail, or to be inefficient, may be misleading. In this analysis of Iraq and Libya, I have argued that what might appear to be incompetence was in some cases the product of inadequate institutional resources. We cannot simply assume that scientists and engineers in personalist regimes are less capable than scientists elsewhere. However, they do face distinct obstacles, particularly if they work in states with weak institutional resources.

A third insight is that these leaders' interest in, and oversight of, their nuclear programs may have been significantly less than scholars have realized. Contrary to the conventional wisdom, the nuclear weapons programs in both states were largely delegated to scientists with little oversight and interference from the state leaders. As it turned out, this had very different consequences for each regime. Saddam's oversight was at the crux of the 2003 casus belli, when Iraq's incomplete declarations were taken as evidence that Iraq was not in compliance with United Nations resolutions. Gaddafi, in contrast, apparently got the benefit of the doubt and secretly kept stocks of undeclared chemical weapons even after the nuclear weapons program was dismantled under international supervision.

ALTERNATIVE EXPLANATIONS

In this section, I revisit alternative explanations for the performance of the Iraqi and Libyan nuclear weapons programs: access to foreign assistance; disruptive micromanagement; and economic underdevelopment.

First, I am not disputing that access to foreign technology and advice had important effects on either program. Changing access to foreign help and technology clearly had a significant impact on the performance and outcomes of both nuclear weapons programs. In my analysis, I do not conceptualize access to civilian and sensitive nuclear technology as a rival hypothesis because I treat state capacity as an intervening variable that shapes the impact of other factors, including foreign assistance.

There was significant variation in terms of how much Iraq and Libya benefited from foreign assistance, which suggests that state capacity is a significant factor affecting absorption capacity in personalist regimes. Also, this helps to explain the disproportionate impact of being cut off from technology and assistance on Libya as opposed to Iraq. An interesting finding from these two cases is the weak impact of civilian nuclear assistance on either state's efforts to edge closer to nuclear weapons.[20] In Iraq, scientists who wanted nuclear weapons lobbied to take the program in this direction before it shifted toward an energy program in 1973. After the Iraqis accessed civilian and sensitive technology during the 1970s, this did not have the effect of triggering a weapons program or attempts to move the program in this direction until after the 1981 Osirak attack.

Second, micromanagement by Saddam and Gaddafi is an alternative explanation for—or perhaps more accurately the conventional wisdom on—the performance of each program. The evidence examined in this book suggests that these leaders delegated the management of their programs without being able to monitor what their leaders were doing, and only intervened to take more control when they realized that their initial strategy had backfired. This is not to suggest there was no micromanagement or that interventions did not demotivate the scientists. For example, Jafar Dhiya Jafar was at times ordered to pursue additional technical routes by the Iraqi Atomic Energy Commission, which further stretched scant resources. But overall, these leaders were constrained rather than enabled by their weak state institutions in terms of how they could feasibly govern their nuclear scientists. This tradeoff—between the performance of these states and their leaders' hold on power—and its consequences were evident in both states. Saddam and his regime officials were aware of some of the consequences of this tradeoff, and circumstantial evidence suggests this was also the case in Libya. The mechanics of this tradeoff is an important and fertile area for further research.

Third, an alternative explanation for the stunted performance and outcomes of these nuclear weapons programs could be that they were based in developing states with limited resources. While other developing states have developed nuclear weapons without the aid of petrodollars, such as North Korea, India, and Pakistan, they too struggled. It is important to revisit the relationship between development and state capacity and the possible interactive effects. Under Saddam's rule, the Iraqi state made significant progress in education, arguably at all levels. Creating a more modern and thus powerful Iraq was at the core of the regime's self-image. In the case of Libya, poverty combined with the ravages of colonialism followed by war is clearly an important part of the explanation for why the Libyan state lacked basic resources during the early years of independence. But the uneven growth of both states after petrodollars started flowing in suggests that underdevelopment in itself is an insufficient explanation. Neither program lacked money but both were held back by weak institutional resources and capabilities. Weak management facilitated additional disruptions, such as power struggles between different factions and the expulsion of scarce expertise by the Baathists inside the nuclear establishment during the early 1970s. In the case of Libya, there were many lost opportunities to educate and train more scientists and technicians. The thin bench of scientists and technical workers was in no small part the result of the regime's reluctance to invest more in higher education, a hotbed of regime opposition.

The findings of this book challenge the conventional wisdom about why Iraq and Libya failed to acquire nuclear weapons and portray these regimes and leaders in a different light. For this reason, the findings are likely to be controversial. But this is an opportune moment to revisit our assumptions about personalist regimes, particularly in the Middle East. In the wake of wars and revolutions following the Arab Spring, mercurial regimes are collapsing or have been overthrown, while others appear to emerge in countries such as Egypt. As new sources open up these states and regimes to scrutiny, what we learn might lead us to revisit our assumptions about how they worked, in the nuclear realm and elsewhere. For example, we may develop a better understanding of the trade-offs personalist leaders make between their hold on power and state capacity on one hand, and how their calculations about guns and butter evolve in times of crisis. More broadly, these findings encourage scholars to explore the role of state capacity in different kinds of authoritarian regimes. The fates of Iraq and Libya show that the long-term costs of getting this wrong can be catastrophic. What we have learned from these cases can be of value for assessing proliferation risks in different authoritarian states in years to come. Assumptions about the intentions and capabilities of leaders such as Saddam and Gaddafi informed crucial decisions about going to war, as well as whether and how to engage these regimes through diplomacy. Realizing that personalist leaders face complex constraints inside their own states is a useful insight for leaders facing nuclear proliferators in the future. As the cases of Iraq and Libya show, the stakes are high.

Notes

Abbreviations

Arab World Documentation Unit	Arab World Documentation Unit, University of Exeter, United Kingdom
CAFCD	Iraqi National Monitoring Directorate, *Currently Accurate, Full and Complete Declaration,* National Monitoring Directorate, Baghdad, Republic of Iraq, December 4, 2002
CIA	Central Intelligence Agency
CNSAS	Romanian National Council for the Study of the Securitate Archives, Bucharest
Compendium	United Nations Monitoring, Verification and Inspection Commission, *Compendium of Iraq's Proscribed Weapons Programmes in the Chemical, Biological and Missile Areas* (New York: United Nations, 2007)
CRRC Archives	Saddam Hussein Regime Collection, The Conflict Records Research Center, National Defense University, Washington DC
CRS	Congressional Research Service
Ekéus Papers	Ambassador Rolf Ekéus Papers, private collection, Stockholm
GPC	General People's Congress, Libya
IAEA	International Atomic Energy Agency
IAEA Archives	International Atomic Energy Agency Technical Assistance Archives, Vienna
IAEC	Iraqi Atomic Energy Commission
National Archives	National Archives, Kew, Surrey, United Kingdom
National Security Archive	National Security Archive, George Washington University Washington, DC

Nuti Papers	Leopoldo Nuti Papers, Roma Tre University, Rome
Rabinowitz Papers	Or Rabinowitz Papers, Hebrew University of Jerusalem, International Relations Department
Richelson Papers	Jeffrey Richelson Papers
SAE	Secretariat of Atomic Energy, Libya
UN	United Nations
UNDP	United Nations Development Program
UNESCO	United Nations Educational, Scientific and Cultural Organization
UNSCOM	United Nations Special Commission

Introduction

1. Jafar Dhiya Jafar, unpublished manuscript (no title), Version 1, May 13, 2004, 6.

2. Etel Solingen, *Nuclear Logics: Contrasting Paths in East Asia and the Middle East* (Princeton: Princeton University Press, 2009).

3. See Jeff D. Colgan, *Petro-Aggression: When Oil Causes War* (Cambridge: Cambridge University Press, 2013); Bruce Bueno de Mesquita and Alastair Smith, "Domestic Explanations of International Relations," *Annual Review of Political Science* 15 (2012): 161–181.

4. Christopher Way and Jessica L. P. Weeks, "Making It Personal: Regime Type and Nuclear Proliferation," *American Journal of Political Science* 58, no. 3 (2013): 705–719.

5. See Jacques E. C. Hymans, *Achieving Nuclear Ambitions: Scientists, Politicians, and Proliferation* (Cambridge: Cambridge University Press, 2012).

6. Joseph Sassoon, *Saddam Hussein's Ba'th Party: Inside an Authoritarian Regime* (Cambridge: Cambridge University Press, 2011), 78.

7. Caitlin Talmadge, *The Dictator's Army: Battlefield Effectiveness in Authoritarian Regimes* (Ithaca: Cornell University Press, 2015); Caitlin Talmadge, "The Puzzle of Personalist Performance: Iraqi Battlefield Effectiveness in the Iran-Iraq War," *Security Studies* 22, no. 2 (2013): 180–221.

8. Williamson Murray and Kevin Woods, *The Iran-Iraq War: A Military and Strategic History* (Cambridge: Cambridge University Press, 2014).

9. See Marius Deeb and Mary Jane Deeb, *Libya since the Revolution: Aspects of Social and Political Development* (New York: Praeger, 1982); Ruth First, *Libya: The Elusive Revolution* (Harmondsworth, UK: Penguin African Library, 1974); Dirk Vandewalle, *Libya since Independence: Oil and State-Building* (Ithaca: Cornell University Press, 1998); John Wright, *Libya* (London: Ernest Benn, 1969).

10. Vandewalle, *Libya since Independence*, xv.

11. Alexander H. Montgomery, "Stop Helping Me: When Nuclear Assistance Impedes Nuclear Programs," in *The Nuclear Renaissance and International Security*, ed. Adam Stulberg and Matt Fuhrmann (Stanford: Stanford University Press, 2013), 177–202.

12. R. Scott Kemp, "The Nonproliferation Emperor Has No Clothes: The Gas Centrifuge, Supply-Side Controls, and the Future of Nuclear Proliferation," *International Security* 38, no. 4 (2014): 39–78.

13. Sonia Ben Ouagrham-Gormley, *Barriers to Bioweapons: The Challenges of Expertise and Organization for Weapons Development* (Ithaca: Cornell University Press, 2014).

14. See, for example, Dan Slater, "Iron Cage in an Iron Fist: Authoritarian Institutions and the Personalization of Power in Malaysia," *Comparative Politics* 36, no. 1 (2003): 81–101; James C. Scott, *Seeing Like a State: How Certain Schemes to Improve the Human Condition Have Failed* (New Haven: Yale University Press, 1998).

15. Joel S. Migdal, *Strong Societies and Weak States: State-Society Relations and State Capabilities in the Third World* (Princeton: Princeton University Press, 1988).

16. Steven Levitsky and María Victoria Murillo, "Variation in Institutional Strength," *Annual Review of Political Science* 12 (2009): 115–133.

17. See ibid., 121.

18. Here I draw on Francis Fukuyama, "What Is Governance?," *Governance* 26, no. 3 (2013): 347–368.

19. Peter B. Evans, Dietrich Rueschemeyer, and Theda Skocpol, *Bringing the State Back In* (Cambridge: Cambridge University Press, 1985).

20. Levitsky and Murillo, "Variation in Institutional Strength," 117.

21. Ibid., 118.

22. Output measures such as successful reforms or distribution of rents are better seen as dependent variables rather than indicators of state capacity. See Fukuyama, "What Is Governance?"

23. Mathew McCubbins, Roger G. Noll, and Barry R. Weingast, "Administrative Procedures as Instruments of Political Control," *Journal of Law, Economics, & Organization* 3 (Fall 1987): 243–277.

24. See, for example, Matthew Evangelista, *Innovation and the Arms Race: How the United States and the Soviet Union Develop New Military Technologies* (Ithaca: Cornell University Press, 1988); Hymans, *Achieving Nuclear Ambitions*.

25. David Holloway, *Stalin and the Bomb: The Soviet Union and Atomic Energy, 1939–1956* (New Haven: Yale University Press, 1994), 204.

26. "Saddam Meeting with Ba'ath Party Members to Discuss the Results of the UN Inspectors' Mission to Look for WMD," 1995, Record No.: SH-SHTP-A-001-295, 6–7, CRRC Archives.

27. For more details see Charles Duelfer, *Comprehensive Report of the Special Advisor to the DCI on Iraq's WMD* (Washington, DC: U.S. Government Printing Office, 2004), vol. 1: *Regime Strategic Intent.*

28. See, for example, Kent D. Peterson, "Mechanisms of Administrative Control over Managers in Educational Organizations," *Administrative Science Quarterly* 29, no. 4 (1984): 573–597.

29. I explore this in more detail in an article revisiting the controversies over the 1981 Israeli attack on an Iraqi nuclear reactor. Målfrid Braut-Hegghammer, "Revisiting Osirak: Preventive Attacks and Nuclear Proliferation Risks," *International Security* 36, no. 1 (2011): 101–132.

30. These interviews were conducted in English, except one interview with an official from the Libyan General People's Congress who brought an interpreter to the interview.

31. These aspects have been explored in more detail elsewhere. See, for example, Kevin M. Woods, David D. Palkki, and Mark Stout, *The Saddam Tapes: The Inner Workings of a Tyrant's Regime, 1978–2001* (Cambridge: Cambridge University Press, 2011); Murray and Woods, *Iran-Iraq War.*

32. See, for example, Solingen, *Nuclear Logics.*

1. Iraq Explores the Atom, 1956–1973

1. See Målfrid Braut-Hegghammer, "Revisiting Osirak: Preventive Attacks and Nuclear Proliferation Risks," *International Security* 36, no. 1 (2011): 101–132.

2. Hanna Batatu, *The Old Social Classes and the Revolutionary Movements of Iraq: A Study of Iraq's Old Landed and Commercial Classes and of Its Communists, Ba'thists, and Free Officers* (Princeton: Princeton University Press, 1978), 25–26, citing the memorandum from Abd-ur-Razzaq al-Hasani, *Tarikh-ul-Wizarat-il-Iraqiyyah* [History of the Iraqi Cabinets] (Sidon, 1953), 3:283–293.

3. Batatu, *Old Social Classes,* 5.

4. Ibid., 31.

5. Ibid., 33.

6. Ibid., 34.

7. Albert Hourani, *A History of the Arab Peoples* (London: Faber and Faber, 1991), 389.

8. Jaime Balcazar Aranibar to U. L. Goswami, "Iraq—Follow-Up Mission," 6 February 1962 (TA/IRQ-1), 2, IAEA Archives.

9. Batatu, *Old Social Classes,* 34.

10. See Joseph Sassoon, *Economic Policy in Iraq, 1932–1950* (New York: Frank Cass, 1987).

11. Alfred Bonné, *The Economic Development of the Middle East: An Outline of Planned Reconstruction after the War* (London: Kegan Paul, Trench, Trubner, 1945), 38.

12. IAEA, "Iraq Briefing Material for Preliminary Assistance Mission," Vienna, September 1959, TTI/STI/21 (TA/IRQ-1), 6, IAEA Archives.

13. *Compendium,* chap. 2, 32.

14. IAEA, "Iraq Briefing Material," 6.

15. For details see Mark S. Bell, "Beyond Emboldenment: How Acquiring Nuclear Weapons Can Change Foreign Policy," *International Security* 40, no. 1 (Summer 2015): 107.

16. Behcet Kemal Yesilbursa, *The Baghdad Pact: Anglo-American Defence Policies in the Middle East, 1950–59* (London: Routledge, 2004), 160.

17. Arne Holmberg, ed., "John Cockcroft: Banquet Speech, Les Prix Nobel en 1951," Stockholm, 1952, accessed from http://www.nobelprize.org/nobel_prizes/physics/laureates/1951/cockcroft-speech.html.

18. Jafar Dhiya Jafar, unpublished manuscript (no title), May 13, 2004, Version 1, 3.

19. John Cockcroft, "The Baghdad Pact Nuclear Training Centre," *Nature* 179, no. 4567 (1957): 936.

20. Ibid.

21. Jafar, unpublished manuscript, 2.

22. Cockcroft, "Baghdad Pact."

23. UK Foreign Office Foreign Relations Department, Baghdad Pact estimates for 1957–1958: Foreign Office minute of 17 January 1957, Baghdad Pact Economic Assistance Committee, Ref. FO 371/127840/4, Economic Committee of Baghdad Pact, National Archives.

24. Foreign Office Foreign Relation Department, "Foreign Office Supplementary Estimates 1956–57" and "Estimates 1957–58," "Technical Assistance under the Baghdad Pact," draft revised as of 11 January 1957, Baghdad Pact Economic Assistance Committee, Reference FO 371/127840, from The National Archives (hereafter Foreign Office supplementary estimates).

25. Foreign Office Foreign Relation Department, *Baghdad Despatch* no. 19, 17 January 1957, Baghdad Pact Economic Assistance Committee, Reference FO 371/127840, from the National Archives.

26. "News of Science," *Science* 127 (1958): 803–807.

27. "Foreign Office Supplementary Estimates 1956–57" and "Estimates 1957–58," *Technical Assistance under the Baghdad Pact,* revised as of January 11, 1957 (FO 371/127840), National Archives.

28. Jafar, unpublished manuscript, 4.

29. Cockcroft, "Baghdad Pact."

30. Ibid.

31. IAEA, "Iraq Briefing Material."

32. Cockcroft, "Baghdad Pact."

33. Jafar, unpublished manuscript, 2.

34. Eugene Rogan, *The Arabs: A History* (New York: Basic Books, 2011), 316.

35. Charles Tripp, *A History of Iraq* (Cambridge: Cambridge University Press, 2007), 153.

36. Batatu, *Old Social Classes,* 473–474.

37. Ibid., 289.

38. Tripp, *A History of Iraq,* 158.

39. IAEA, "Request from the Government of Iraq (Expert)," 15 February 1967, Job Description (TA/IRQ/2/03), IAEA Archives.

40. U.S. Directorate of Intelligence, *The Iraqi Nuclear Program: Progress despite Setbacks,* June 1983, 1, National Security Archive. Available at http://nsarchive.gwu.edu/NSAEBB/NSAEBB82/iraq19.pdf.

41. I. H. Usmani, the first architect of the Pakistani nuclear program, was vice-chairman of the board during this period.

42. IAEA, "Iraq Briefing Material," 11.

43. Aranibar to Goswami, 6 February 1962, 5.

44. Ibid., 4–5.

45. U Hla Maung, *Evaluation Report on the 1961 Expanded Programme of Technical Assistance in Iraq*, Confidential IAEA Report, 5 November 1961,(TA/IRQ/1), IAEA Archives.

46. Ibid., 6–7.

47. Ibid.

48. Ibid., 8.

49. Aranibar to Goswami, 6 February 1962, 4–5.

50. This hospital was originally built and staffed by American health scientists from Loma Linda University, California. After the 1958 coup, the U.S. assistance was discontinued.

51. IAEA, "Medical Isotope Applications in Iraq," *Bulletin* 42 (April 1962): 26–27.

52. "Aranibar to Goswami, 6 February 1962; Ralph Adams to Melvin Jenkins, Director, Department of Radiology, Loma Linda University School of Medicine, California, "Site Visits to Radiation Therapy and Nuclear Medicine Installations in Baghdad, Iraq, October, 1971," 17 November 1971, IAEA Archives.

53. Ibid.

54. See Pieter Buringh, *Soils and Soil Conditions in Iraq* (Baghdad: Ministry of Agriculture, 1960).

55. Aranibar to Goswami, 6 February 1962, 2.

56. Ibid., 3.

57. In 1962 the coordination committee was slimmed down to twenty-one members: Ihsan Sulaiman, director general of the Auditing Department, Council of Ministers; Colonel Duraid al-Damalouji, assistant director of Military Training, Ministry of Defense; Abdul Razzak al-Jalili, director general of Cultural Relations Ministry of Education; Abdullah Nakishbani, assistant director general of the Ministry of Finance; Nadhim Sarsam, inspector general of agriculture, Ministry of Agriculture; Sabih al-Wahbi, director general of international relations, Ministry of Health; Fuad Abdullah, president of the Grain Board, Ministry of Commerce; Brigadier Mohamed Ali al-Baghdadi, director of technical and engineering affairs at Abu Ghraib, Ministry of Guidance; Salah Izzat Tahsin, secretary-general of the IAEC, Ministry of Industry; Mohamed Ali Saib, Ministry of Communications; Badi Sharif, codification officer, Ministry of Justice; Jamal Ahmed, director general of the Legal Department, Ministry of Interior; Rahim al-Musleh, Ministry of Social Affairs; Yousef al-Ubaidi, director general of the Planning Board; Qabtan al-Madfa'I, director of planning, Ministry of Municipalities; Abdulla Shakir al-Sayyad, Ministry of Oil; Abbas al-Sarraf, secretary-general of Baghdad University; Mahdi al-Hassani, Ministry of Works and Housing; Abdul Mahdi Hassan, director general of industrial planning, Ministry of Industry; Abdul Majid al-Qaisi, Ministry of Agrarian Reform; Usamah Kadry, chairman of the committee, Ministry of Foreign Affairs; and Suha al-Turaikhi, Technical Assistance Department, Ministry of Foreign Affairs. Maung, *Evaluation Report*, 2–3.

58. Ibid.

59. IAEA, "Iraq Briefing Material," 10.

60. Aranibar to Goswami, 6 February 1962, 5.

61. Jafar, unpublished manuscript, 5.

62. Aranibar to Goswami, 6 February 1962, 1.

63. Ibid.

64. Tripp, *History of Iraq*, 169.

65. Ibid., 171–172.

66. Aranibar to Goswami, 6 February 1962, 4–5.

67. Ibid., 4.

68. A. M. Demidov, "Field Report No. 1, 13 September–6 October 1969" (TA/IRQ/1/02), 1, IAEA Archives.

69. Ibid.

70. Ibid.

71. Ihsan al-Rawi, a pharmacist, was the secretary-general of the IAEC during the construction of the center at Tuwaitha. Jafar, unpublished manuscript, 2–4.

72. Ibid., 5.

73. Ibid.

74. Dhafir Selbi, Zuhair al-Chalabi, and Imad Khadduri, *Unrevealed Milestones in Iraq's National Nuclear Program: 1981–1991* (CreateSpace Independent Publishing Platform, 2011), 18.

75. Jafar, unpublished manuscript, 6.

76. A. M. Demidov, "Final Report, 13 September, 1969–13 January, 1970" (TA/IRQ/1/02), 2, IAEA Archives.

77. Gilbert W. Smith, "Field Report No. 2, 5 January 1969" 4, IAEA Archives.

78. Josef Kajfosz, "Field Report No. 3, 29 May–15 October 1969," 10 November 1969 , 1, IAEA Archives.

79. Demidov, "Field Report No. 1." The isotopes (silicon-30, sulphur-34, selenium-74, 76, 77, 80, and 82) were on loan for a period of four to six months.

80. Tripp, *History of Iraq*, 190–191.

81. Ibid., 190.

82. *Compendium*, chap. 2, 32–38.

83. Ministry of Education, *Development of Education in Iraq during 1976/77 and 1977/78* A report presented to the XXXVII session of the International Conference on Education, Palais Wilson, Geneva, 5–14 July 1979 (Baghdad: University of Baghdad Press, 1979), 11.

84. UNESCO, *Situation Analysis of Education in Iraq* (Paris: UNESCO, 2003), 48. Available at http://unesdoc.unesco.org/images/0013/001308/130838e.pdf.

85. Ministry of Education, *Development of Education*, 28.

86. *Compendium*, chap. 2, 38.

87. Ministry of Education, *Development of Education*, 29.

88. *Compendium*, chap. 2, 38.

89. Ibid., chap. 7, 1053.

90. Tripp, *History of Iraq*, 188–189.

91. Jafar, unpublished manuscript, 7.

92. Similar institutional arrangements were made in the chemical and biological weapons programs emerging in Iraq at this time. See *Compendium*, chap. 2, 33.

93. Kajfosz, "Field Report No. 3," 2.

94. Jafar, unpublished manuscript, 7.

95. Ibid., 12.

96. Ibid., 48.

97. Smith, "Field Report No. 2," 4.

98. Ibid., 4; Demidov, "Final Report," 2.

99. Smith, "Field Report No. 2," 3.

100. Jafar, unpublished manuscript, 6.

101. Kajfosz, "Field Report No. 3," 3.

102. Ibid., 3–4.

103. Ibid.

104. Demidov, "Final Report," 3.

105. Jafar, unpublished manuscript, 9.

106. Demidov, "Final Report," 3.

107. Jafar, unpublished manuscript, 10.

108. Ibid., 16.

109. Ibid., 12.

110. Hussein Shahristani, author interview, Oslo, November 2011.

111. Jafar, unpublished manuscript, 13.

112. Shahristani interview.

113. Charles Duelfer, *Comprehensive Report of the Special Advisor to the DCI on Iraq's WMD* (Washington, DC: U.S. Government Printing Office, 2004), vol. 1: *Regime Strategic Intent*, 19.

114. "President Saddam Hussein Presiding over a Meeting with the Iraqi Revolutionary Command Council to Discuss the 'Arab Stan crisis," undated, Record No.: SH-SHTP-A-001-400, CRRC Archives.

2. Ambiguity and Ambition, 1973–1981

1. Anoushiravan Ehteshami, "Oil, Arms Procurement and Security in the Persian Gulf," *Asian Affairs* 34, no. 3 (2003): 261; Jahangir Amuzegar, *Managing the Oil Wealth: OPEC's Windfalls and Pitfalls* (London: I.B. Tauris, 1999), 216; *Compendium,* chap. 2, 32; Ahmed Hashim, "Saddam Husayn and Civil-Military Relations in Iraq: The Quest for Legitimacy and Power," *Middle East Journal* 57, no. 1 (2003): 25.

2. Hashim, "Saddam Husayn," 26; Andrew Parasiliti and Sinan Antoon, "Friends in Need, Foes to Heed: The Iraqi Military in Politics," *Middle East Policy* 7, no. 4 (2000): 135.

3. Cited in Simon Henderson, *Instant Empire: Saddam Hussein's Ambition for Iraq* (San Francisco: Mercury House, 1991), 124.

4. *Compendium,* chap. 2, 32–33.

5. Ibid., chap. 5, 768.

6. Jafar Dhiya Jafar, unpublished manuscript (no title), Version 1, May 13, 2004, 15.

7. Moyasser al-Mallah, Secretary-General of the IAEC, to A. E. Cairo, IAEA, Vienna, 12 September 1973 (TA/IRQ/3), IAEA Archives.

8. M. Mutru, Head of Europe and Middle East Section, Division of Technical Assistance, IAEA, to S. M. Mahmood, Director of the International Relations Division, IAEC, 1 November 1979, IAEA Archives.

9. Jafar, unpublished manuscript, 15.

10. Omar Adeel, Resident UN Representative in Baghdad, to U. L. Goswami, Department of Technical Assistance and Safeguards, 7 August 1973 (TA/IRQ/3/02), 1, IAEA Archives.

11. Imad Khadduri, *Iraq's Nuclear Mirage: Memoirs and Delusions* (Toronto: Springhead, 2003), 54.

12. UK Cabinet Office, Middle East Nuclear, Secret, 15 September 1980, Israel: Nuclear Energy Matters, File: MEN 166/408/1, Rabinowitz Papers.

13. Charles Duelfer, *Comprehensive Report of the Special Advisor to the DCI on Iraq's WMD* (Washington, DC: U.S. Government Printing Office, 2004), vol. 1: *Regime Strategic Intent,* 30.

14. U.S. Embassy Paris Cable 15305 to Department of State, "Interview with Shah," 24 June 1974, unclassified, National Security Archive. Available at http://nsarchive.gwu.edu/nukevault/ebb268/doc01a.pdf.

15. Khalil Ibrahim al-'Azawi, "The Third Study: Objectives and Strategic Specifics of Nuclear Armament in the Period Succeeding the Shah," 6 February 1994, Record No.: SH-GMID-D-000-342, CRRC Archives.

16. Jafar Dhiya Jafar, author interview, Rome, 4–5 May 2005.

17. Charles Tripp, *A History of Iraq* (Cambridge: Cambridge University Press, 2007), 206.

18. Ibid., 207.

19. Jafar, unpublished manuscript, 16.

20. Mutru to Mahmood, 1 November 1979.

21. IAEC to A. E. Cairo, Department of Technical Assistance, IAEA, from the, 20 November 1973 (SC/512-IRQ), IAEA Archives.

22. Jafar, unpublished manuscript, 18.

23. "Iraq, Assistance Required, Research Reactor Upgrading," GOV/COM.8/64/Add.1 (GOV/1922/Add.1), Request from the Government of Iraq, 15 February 1967 (TA/IRQ/2/03), IAEA Archives.

24. Jed C. Snyder, "The Road to Osiraq: Baghdad's Quest for the Bomb," *Middle East Journal* (1983): 568–569.

25. Leonard S. Spector, *Nuclear Proliferation Today: The Spread of Nuclear Weapons* (New York: Vintage Books, 1984), 167.

26. Jafar, unpublished manuscript, 17.

27. Duelfer, *Comprehensive Report,* 1:30.

28. Jafar, unpublished manuscript, 17.

29. Spector, *Nuclear Proliferation Today,* 167.

30. See Målfrid Braut-Hegghammer, "Revisiting Osirak: Preventive Attacks and Nuclear Proliferation Risks," *International Security* 36, no. 1 (2011): 111–112. For one scenario see Richard

Wilson, "A Visit to the Bombed Nuclear Reactor at Tuwaitha, Iraq," *Nature* 302 (31 March 1983): 376.

31. Hans Gruemm, "Safeguards Verification: Its Credibility and the Diversion Hypothesis," *IAEA Bulletin* 25, no. 4 (1983): 27.

32. "Estimation of Feasible Unreported Plutonium Production in Thermal Research Reactors in the Potential Nuclear Weapon States," Los Alamos National Laboratory, January 1997 (LA-13209-MS). Available at http://www.fas.org/sgp/othergov/doe/lanl/lib-www/la-pubs/00412501.pdf.

33. Ibid.

34. CRS, *How Long Would It Take for Iraq to Obtain a Nuclear Explosive after Its Research Reactor Began Operation?*, CRS Report for Congress, House Committee on Foreign Affairs, Hearings: Israeli Attack on Iraqi Nuclear Facility, 97th Cong., 1st sess., 25 June 1981.

35. Mahdi Obeidi and Kurt Pitzer, *The Bomb in My Garden: The Secrets of Saddam's Nuclear Mastermind* (Hoboken, NJ: John Wiley & Sons, 2004), 48.

36. Ibid.; Jafar, unpublished manuscript.

37. Khadduri, *Iraq's Nuclear Mirage*, 73; Dhafir Selbi, Zuhair Al-Chalabi, and Imad Khadduri, *Unrevealed Milestones in Iraq's National Nuclear Program: 1981–1991* (CreateSpace Independent Publishing Platform, 2011), 25.

38. Khadduri, *Iraq's Nuclear Mirage*, 75–76.

39. Ibid., 64–65.

40. Jafar, unpublished manuscript, 16–19.

41. Giulio Andreotti, President of the Council of Ministers, to General Saddam Hussein, Vice-Chairman of the Revolutionary Command Council, Baghdad, 31 December 1976, Nuti Papers.

42. *CAFCD*, extended summary, 3.

43. Italian Ministry of Foreign Affairs, Letter to the Minister, 077, Stamped by the General Secretariat on 28 September 1976, Rome, 24 September 1976., Nuti Papers.

44. Minister Plenipotentiary Umberto La Rocca, Diplomatic Adviser to the Prime Minister, Italian Ministry of Foreign Affairs, Directorate General for Economic Affairs 077/ 17771, Rome, 14 October 1976, Nuti Papers.

45. Italian Ministry of Foreign Affairs 077/ Office VII, Classified, Letter, Subject: Italy-Iraq Nuclear Cooperation—Safeguards Agreements, Rome, 14 July 1979, Nuti Papers.

46. Ministerial Telegram, Italdipl Bagdad, date 10 July 1979, Extremely Urgent, "Subject: Italy-Iraq Nuclear Cooperation," Nuti Papers.

47. Italian Ministry of Foreign Affairs, Secret: Urgent, N.060/18135, Rome, 20 October 1977, Giulio Andreotti to Carlo Donat-Cattin (Ministry of Industry) and in copy Arnaldo Forlani (Minister of Foreign Affairs), Rome, 26 October 1977, Nuti Papers.

48. U.S. Directorate of Intelligence, *The Iraqi Nuclear Program: Progress despite Setbacks*, June 1983, 12, National Security Archive. Available at http://nsarchive.gwu.edu/NSAEBB/NSAEBB82/iraq19.pdf.

49. Ibid.

50. IAEA, *Fourth Consolidated Report of the Director General of the International Atomic Energy Agency under Paragraph 16 of Security Council Resolution 1051 (1996)*, S/1997/779, 8 October 1997, appendix, 25. Available at https://www.iaea.org/OurWork/SV/Invo/reports/s_1997_779.pdf.

51. Ibid., 26.

52. Selbi et al., *Unrevealed Milestones*, 24.

53. Jafar, unpublished manuscript, 25.

54. Ibid.

55. *CAFCD*, part 2a, chap. 4.1.1, Electromagnetic Isotope Separation (EMIS), 4.1.1, strategy 1.

56. See also Braut-Hegghammer, "Revisiting Osirak," 107.

57. Selbi et al., *Unrevealed Milestones*, 19.

58. Ibid., 20.

59. Gunther H. Haase, "Field Report No. 1, 31 January–28 February 1979," 1 March 1979, 3, IAEA Archives.

60. Ibid.

61. Selbi et al., *Unrevealed Milestones*, 22.

62. Ibid., 23.

63. Haase, "Field Report No. 1," 1.

64. Ibid., 3.

65. Khadduri, *Iraq's Nuclear Mirage,* 67–68.

66. Ibid.

67. *CAFCD,* extended summary, 5.

68. Jafar, unpublished manuscript, 35.

69. Obeidi and Pitzer, *Bomb in My Garden,* 50.

70. For details see Uri Bar-Joseph, Michael Handel, and Amos Perlmutter, *Two Minutes over Baghdad* (London: Routledge, 2003).

71. Saddam and His Advisers Discussing Iraq's Decision to Go to War with Iran," 16 September 1980, Record No.: SH-SHTP-A-000-835, CRRC Archives (hereafter SH-SHTP-A-000-835).

72. "Transcript of a Speech Given by Saddam Hussein on 'The Role of the Iraqi Armed Forces in the Arab-Zionist Conflict' at Al Bakr University," Document Date: 3 June 1978, Record No.: SH-PDWN-D-000-341, 28, CRRC Archives (hereafter SH-PDWN-D-000-341).

73. Tripp, *A History of Iraq,* 211–212.

74. Ibid., 228.

75. Hussein, *Iraqi Policies in Perspective,* 9.

76. Ibid.

77. Duelfer, *Comprehensive Report,* 1:28.

78. Saddam stated: "The Arab atom will finish them off, but the Israeli atom will not finish the Arabs. But when the atom does not have a match on the other side, it would end the battle." SH-PDWN-D-000-341.

79. Meeting between Saddam Hussein and Nijirfan al-Barzani regarding the Situation in Iraq and Possibility of U.S. Attack, 14 March 2002, Record No.: SH-SPPC-D-000-304, 10, CRRC Archives.

80. "Transcript of a Meeting between Saddam Hussein and His Commanding Officers at the Armed Forces General Command," 22 November 1980, Record No.: SH-SHTP-D-000-856, 45, CRRC Archives.

81. "Revolutionary Command Council Meeting," 27 March 1979, Record No.: SH-SHTP-A-000-553, 10, CRRC Archives.

82. Meeting between Saddam Hussein and His Senior Advisers Following the Israeli Attack on Osirak, undated, Record No.: SH-SHTP-A-001-480, CRRC Archives.

83. Saddam Hussein, *Iraqi Policies in Perspective,* 13–15.

84. Hal Brands and David Palkki, "Saddam, Israel, and the Bomb: Nuclear Alarmism Justified?," *International Security* 36, no. 1 (2011): 133–166.

85. Meeting between Saddam Hussein and His Commanders regarding the Iran-Iraq War, undated (after 23 September 1980), Record No.: SH-SHTP-D-000-846, 39, CRRC Archives (hereafter SHTP-D-000-846).

86. Hussein Shahristani, author interview, Oslo, November 2011.

87. Ibid.; Jafar interview; Imad Khadduri, interview by author, Toronto, Canada, March 31, 2005.

88. Claudia Wright, "Iraq—New Power in the Middle East," *Foreign Affairs* 58 (Winter 1979–1980): 267.

89. Ibid., 268.

90. Jafar, unpublished manuscript, 23.

91. Khadduri, *Iraq's Nuclear Mirage,* 78.

92. Jafar, unpublished manuscript, 29.

93. Despite some claims to the contrary; see Etel Solingen, *Nuclear Logics: Contrasting Paths in East Asia and the Middle East* (Princeton: Princeton University Press, 2009), 157.

94. Ibid.; Jafar Dhiya Jafar, Numan Saadaldin al-Niaimi, and Lars Sigurd Sunnanå, *Oppdraget: Innsidehistorien om Saddams atomvåpen* [The mission: The inside story of Saddam's nuclear weapons] (Oslo: Spartacus, 2005).

95. Jafar, unpublished manuscript, 33.

96. Ibid., 38.

97. Shahristani interview.
98. Ibid.
99. Ibid.
100. SH-SHTP-A-000-835.
101. Discussion between Saddam Hussein and Iraqi High-Ranking Officers regarding the Iraqi Society Situation, undated, Record No.: SH-SHTP-A-001-323, CRRC Archives.
102. Meeting between Saddam Hussein and His Commanding Officers at the Armed Forces General Command regarding Preparing Forces for Battle, Estimated Document Date: November 1980Record No.: SH-SHTP-D-000-847, 7, CRRC Archives (hereafter SH-SHTP-D-000-847).
103. SH-SHTP-D-000-846, 39.
104. Khadduri, *Iraq's Nuclear Mirage*, 72.
105. Ibid., 71.
106. SH-SHTP-D-000-847, 25.
107. Ibid.
108. "Saddam and Senior Iraqi Officials Discussing the Conflict with Iran, Iraqi Targets and Plans, a Recent Attack on the Osirak Reactor, and Various Foreign Countries," Document Date: 1 October 1980, Record No.: SH-MISC-D-000-827, 11, CRRC Archives.
109. Ibid.
110. Selbi et al., *Unrevealed Milestones*, 26.
111. Ibid.
112. U.S. Deputy Director for National Foreign Assessment, "Request for Review of Draft Paper on the Security Dimension of Nonproliferation," 9 April 1981, 9, National Security Archive. Also available at https://www.documentcloud.org/documents/347018-doc-5-4-9-81-state-dept-draft-paper.html.

3. Saddam's Nuclear Weapons Program, 1981–1987

1. See, for example, Jeremy Tamsett, "The Israeli Bombing of Osiraq Reconsidered: Successful Counterproliferation?" *Nonproliferation Review* 11, no. 3 (2004): 70–85, 114–142; Dan Reiter, "Preventive Attacks against Nuclear Programs and the 'Success' at Osiraq," *Nonproliferation Review* 12, no. 2 (2005): 355–371; Richard K. Betts, "The Osirak Fallacy," *National Interest* 83 (2006): 22–25.
2. Iraqi Atomic Energy Commission, "Preface," in Iraqi Nuclear Programme, 1956–1991 (Baghdad: Al-Adib, 1992), vii.
3. U.S. Interagency Intelligence Assessment, "Implications of Israeli Attack on Iraq," 1 July 1981, 8, National Security Archive (hereafter "Implications of Israeli Attack on Iraq").
4. Dhafir Selbi, Zuhair Al-Chalabi, and Imad Khadduri, *Unrevealed Milestones in Iraq's National Nuclear Program: 1981–1991* (CreateSpace Independent Publishing Platform, 2011), 27.
5. "Factfile: How Osirak Was Bombed," *BBC News,* http://news.bbc.co.uk/2/hi/middle_east/5020778.stm.
6. Selbi et al., *Unrevealed Milestones*, 28.
7. *President Saddam Hussein's Speech on National Day (1981), Thirteenth Anniversary of the 17–30 July 1968 Revolution,* trans. Naji Al-Hadithi (Baghdad: Dar Al-Ma'mun, 1981), 17.
8. Sa'adoun Hammadi , *The Israeli Aggression against the Peaceful Nuclear Installations in Iraq: Statement Made by Dr. Sa'adoun Hammadi, Minister for Foreign Affairs of Iraq, before the Security Council, 12 June 1981* (Baghdad: Ministry of Foreign Affairs, 1981), 4.
9. Ibid.
10. Ibid., 12.
11. "Implications of Israeli Attack on Iraq," 4.
12. Ibid., 4–8.
13. Ibid., 8.
14. Hans Gruemm, Deputy, "Safeguards and Tamuz: Setting the Record Straight," *International Atomic Energy Agency Bulletin* 23, no. 4 (1981): 10–14.

15. IAEA, "Text of the Statement Made by the Director General to the Security Council," GC (XXV)/INF/196/Rev.1, , 4, Annex, 3. Available at https://www.iaea.org/About/Policy/GC /GC25/GC25InfDocuments/English/gc25inf-196-rev1_en.pdf. See also Sigvard Eklund, "Peaceful Nuclear Development Must Continue," *International Atomic Energy Agency Bulletin* 23, no. 3 (1981): 3.

16. Eklund, "Peaceful Nuclear Development," 3.

17. UN Security Council Resolution 487 (1981), adopted on 19 June 1981.

18. Ibid., 1.

19. "Implications of Israeli Attack on Iraq," 2.

20. Selbi et al., *Unrevealed Milestones*, 29.

21. Ibid.

22. Jafar Dhiya Jafar, unpublished manuscript (no title), Version 1, May 13, 2004, 38.

23. Jafar Dhiya Jafar, author interview, Rome, 4–5 May 2005.

24. *President Saddam Hussein Interviewed on Zionist Raid on Iraqi Reactor,* trans. Naji Al-Hadithi (Baghdad: Dar Al-Ma'mun for Translation and Publishing, 1981), 10–11. This is the Iraqi transcript of Barbara Walters's interview with Saddam Hussein on 28 June 1981 for the ABC network.

25. *President Hussein's Press Conference on Iraq's Internal, Arab and International Policies (July 19, 1981)* (Baghdad: Dar Al-Ma'mun for Translation and Publishing, 1981), 14.

26. *President Saddam Hussein Addresses Cabinet of Conflict with Iran,* trans. Namir A. Mudhaffer (Baghdad: Dar Al-Ma'mun for Translation and Publishing, 1981), 17.

27. "Saddam Meeting with His Cabinet to Discuss the 1982 Budget," undated (c. 1982), Record Number: SH-SHTP-A-000-635, 21, CRRC Archives.

28. Jafar, unpublished manuscript, 39.

29. Ibid., 35.

30. Ibid., 36.

31. Ibid.

32. Charles Tripp, *A History of Iraq* (Cambridge: Cambridge University Press, 2007), 226.

33. *Compendium,* chap. 2, 34.

34. Ibid., 35.

35. Ibid., 139.

36. Ibid., 140.

37. Ibid.

38. Ibid., 151.

39. Ibid., 153.

40. UNSCOM, "Note for the File: Meeting at Military Industrial Commission," 1 July 1995, Ekéus Papers.

41. Jafar, unpublished manuscript, 49.

42. Steven Heydemann, *War, Institutions, and Social Change in the Middle East* (London: University of California Press, 2000), 273.

43. Charles Duelfer, "Addendums to the Comprehensive Report of the Special Advisor to the DCI on Iraq's WMD," March 2005, 39. Available at https://www.cia.gov/library/reports /general-reports-1/iraq_wmd_2004/addenda.pdf.

44. UNSCOM, "Note for the File: Rolf Ekéus Meeting with Tariq Aziz, Deputy Prime Minister of Iraq," 5 August 1995, 8–12, Ekéus Papers.

45. *CAFCD,* part 1, chap. 3, 2–3.

46. Jafar, unpublished manuscript, 39.

47. *CAFCD,* part 1, chap. 1, 9.

48. Selbi et al., *Unrevealed Milestones,* 38.

49. Ibid.

50. Ibid., 18–19.

51. *CAFCD,* part 1, chap. 1, 10–11.

52. Robert E. Kelley, "The Iraqi and South African Nuclear Weapon Programs: The Importance of Management," *Security Dialogue* 27, no. 1 (1996): 27–38.

53. Jafar, unpublished manuscript, 43–44.

54. Ibid.

55. Ibid., 4; *CAFCD,* part 1, chap. 2, 1.
56. *CAFCD,* part 1, chap. 2, 1.
57. Jafar, unpublished manuscript, 49.
58. Iraqi nuclear scientist, author interview, Doha, 17 November 2006.
59. Ibid.
60. For more on this collaboration see Jafar, unpublished manuscript, 54–57.
61. *CAFCD,* extended summary, 6.
62. Ibid., 25.
63. Jafar, unpublished manuscript, 66.
64. Ibid., 124.
65. *CAFCD,* part 1, chap. 2, 1.
66. *Compendium,* chap. 7, 1044–1045.
67. *CAFCD,* part 1, chap. 3, 12.
68. Ibid., chap. 1, 8.
69. Ibid., part 2a, chap. 1, 1.
70. Ibid., part 1, chap. 1, 10–11.
71. Ibid.
72. Iraqi nuclear scientist interview.
73. *CAFCD,* part 1, chaps. 1, 2, 15.
74. Selbi et al., *Unrevealed Milestones,* 59.
75. *CAFCD,* extended summary, 9.
76. Jafar, unpublished manuscript, 41.
77. *CAFCD,* part 1.1, 9.
78. Mahdi Obeidi and Kurt Pitzer, *The Bomb in My Garden: The Secrets of Saddam's Nuclear Mastermind* (Hoboken, NJ: John Wiley & Sons, 2004), 54.
79. Jafar, unpublished manuscript, 67.
80. Ibid., 45.
81. *CAFCD,* part 2a, chap. 4, 4.1.1, 1.
82. Ibid., part 5, chap. 11, 11.
83. *Compendium,* chap. 7, 1047.
84. *CAFCD,* part 5, chap. 11, Achievements, 1–2.
85. Ibid.
86. Jafar, unpublished manuscript, 68.
87. *CAFCD,* part 5, chap. 11, Achievements, 3–4.
88. Ibid.
89. Jafar, unpublished manuscript, 64.
90. Ibid.
91. Ibid., 63–64.
92. *CAFCD,* part 1, chap. 1, 1.2.1, 8.
93. Ibid., part 5, chap. 11, Achievements, 5.
94. *Compendium,* chap. 7, Interlinks between Iraq's Weapons Programmes, 1049.
95. Ibid., 1051.
96. *CAFCD,* part 5, chap. 11, Achievements,14–15.
97. Jafar, unpublished manuscript, 20.
98. *CAFCD,* part 5, chap. 11, Achievements, 14–15.
99. Ibid., 16.
100. Ibid.
101. Selbi et al., *Unrevealed Milestones,* 41–44.
102. Ibid.
103. Ibid.
104. *Compendium,* chap. 5, Biological Weapons Programme, 152.
105. Selbi et al., *Unrevealed Milestones,* 45–46.
106. Jafar, unpublished manuscript, 56.
107. Selbi et al., *Unrevealed Milestones,* 26.
108. Kelley, "Iraqi and South African Nuclear Weapons Programs."

109. Selbi et al., 58–59.

110. Ibid., 59–60.

111. Ibid.

112. Iraqi nuclear scientist interview.

113. Selbi et al., *Unrevealed Milestones*, 48.

114. Ibid., 51.

115. Ibid., 49.

116. Ibid.

117. Jafar, unpublished manuscript, 50.

118. Ibid., 51.

119. Ibid.

120. Selbi et al., *Unrevealed Milestones*, 80.

121. Duelfer, "Addendums," 40.

122. Simon Henderson, *Instant Empire: Saddam Hussein's Ambition for Iraq* (San Francisco: Mercury House, 1991), 88–89.

123. Jafar, unpublished manuscript, 52.

124. "Note for the File: Meeting between General Hussein Kamal, Ambassador Rolf Ekéus, Prof. Maurizio Zifferero, Nikita Smidovich, Amman 22 August 1995, UNSCOM/IAEA Sensitive." Available at http://www.informationclearinghouse.info/pdf/unscom950822.pdf.

125. *CAFCD*, part 3a, chap. 5, Device Development., 2.

126. Ibid.

127. Ibid.; Jafar, unpublished manuscript, 52–53.

128. Jafar, unpublished manuscript, 77.

4. Crises and a Crash Program, 1988–1991

1. Dhafir Selbi, Zuhair Al-Chalabi, and Imad Khadduri, *Unrevealed Milestones in Iraq's National Nuclear Program: 1981–1991* (CreateSpace Independent Publishing Platform, 2011), 83–84.

2. Ibid.

3. Jafar Dhiya Jafar, unpublished manuscript (no title), May 13, 2004, 15, 57.

4. "Correspondence from the Presidential Cabinet regarding Designation of a New Administration for the Iraqi Atomic Energy Department," 1 April 1988, Record No.: SH-PDWN-D-000-419, CRRC Archives.

5. For example, he had taken charge of a large new undertaking called Petrochemical Project 2 and selected a group of experts from the oil ministry to join this separate effort. Simon Henderson, *Instant Empire: Saddam Hussein's Ambition for Iraq* (San Francisco: Mercury House, 1991), 49–50.

6. Mahdi Obeidi and Kurt Pitzer, *The Bomb in My Garden: The Secrets of Saddam's Nuclear Mastermind* (Hoboken, NJ: John Wiley & Sons, 2004), 158.

7. Selbi et al., *Unrevealed Milestones*, 70–71.

8. Ibid.

9. Obeidi and Pitzer, *Bomb in My Garden*.

10. *CAFCD*, part 1, chap. 3, 3.1, 1.

11. Ibid., 10.

12. Ibid., part 2b, chap. 4.4, 72–73.

13. Ibid., part 1, chap. 1, 23–38.

14. Ibid.

15. Ibid., extended summary, 33–34.

16. Ibid.

17. Ibid., 32.

18. See Obeidi and Pitzer, *Bomb in My Garden*, 92.

19. *CAFCD*, part 2b, chap. 4.4, 4.

20. Ibid., 4–6. See also Obeidi and Pitzer, *Bomb in My Garden*.

21. *CAFCD*, part 2b, chap. 4.4, 6–7.

22. Ibid., extended summary, 33–34.
23. David Albright and Mark Hibbs, "Supplier-Spotting," *Bulletin of the Atomic Scientists* (January–February 1993): 8.
24. Ibid.
25. See, for example, Jeff Gerth, "Atom Bomb Parts Seized in Britain En Route to Iraq," *New York Times*, 29 March 1990; "Iraq's Silent Allies in Its Quest for the Bomb," *Businessweek*, 13 January 1991.
26. Elaine Sciolino, "Iraq's Nuclear Program Shows the Holes in U.S. Intelligence," *New York Times*, 20 October 1991.
27. Obeidi and Pitzer, *Bomb in My Garden*, 120.
28. *CAFCD*, extended summary, 35.
29. Ibid., part 2b, chap. 4.4, 4–6.
30. Ibid.
31. Ibid., part 1, chap. 1, 12–15.
32. Ibid, part 5, chap. 11, 22.
33. Ibid, 17.
34. *CAFCD*, part 5, chap. 11, 23.
35. Jafar, unpublished manuscript, 64; Selbi et al., *Unrevealed Milestones*, 122.
36. *CAFCD*, part 2a, chap. 4.1, 4–5.
37. Ibid., part 5, chap. 11, 6–8.
38. Ibid.
39. Ibid., 20–23.
40. Ibid., part 3a, chap. 5.1, 1.
41. Ibid., part 1, chap. 1, 1.2.3, 27.
42. Jafar, unpublished manuscript, 78.
43. *CAFCD*, part 3a, chap. 5, 3–6.
44. *CAFCD*, part 5, chap. 11, 11.3 Nuclear Device Development, 49.
45. *CAFCD*, part 3a), chap. 5, 5.2.4, 6. S/1997/779, Attachment 1, 56.
46. S/1997/779, Attachment 1, 56.
47. *CAFCD*, part 3a), chap. 5, 5.2.4, 6.
48. Ibid.
49. Ibid., part 3a, chap. 5.7, 28.
50. Ibid., 17.
51. Ibid.
52. *CAFCD*, part 3a, chap. 5.2. 3.
53. Jafar, unpublished manuscript, 79.
54. Selbi et al., *Unrevealed Milestones*, 98.
55. *CAFCD*, part 3a, chap. 5.2, 17–18.
56. Ibid., part 3a, chap. 5.2 5.
57. Selbi et al., *Unrevealed Milestones*, 97.
58. *CAFCD*, part 3a, chap. 5.3, 36–37.
59. Ibid., 38.
60. Ibid., part 3a, chap. 5.2, 26.
61. Jafar, unpublished manuscript, 78–80.
62. Ibid., 82.
63. "Meeting between Saddam and Senior Iraqi Officials Discussing the Execution of British Journalist Farzad Bazoft, Modifications to Iraq's Constitution, and an Israeli Attack on Iraq's Nuclear Reactor", undated (after 1981 Israeli strike on Osirak reactor), Record No.: SH-SHTP-A-000-910, CRRC Archives, 5. Available at http://crrc.dodlive.mil/files/2013/01/SH-SHTP-A-000-910_English.pdf.
64. "The Impact of a 20-Kiloton Nuclear Bomb on the City of Baghdad," Deputy Director of the Nuclear Energy Organization, Presidency of the Republic Secretariat, General Security Directorate Number: (IL) 51723, 29 December 1990, Top Secret and Confidential, CRRC Archives; Handwritten note, 19 November 1990, Ministry of Interior, Supreme Control Command, nr. 88,

top secret and confidential, meeting minutes, Office of the Presidency, 18:00 hours on 17 November 1990, SH-idgs-d-001-4311.pdf, CRRC archives.

65. *CAFCD*, extended summary, 25–26.

66. "Minutes of Meeting the President of Iraq: Saddam Hussein with the President of Yemen: Ali 'Abdallah Salih," 8 April 1990, Record No.: SH-MISC-D-000-652, CRRC Archives.

67. Ali al-Dabagh interview with Tariq Aziz, Parts 1 and 2 [this interview took place in summer 2010 but was given to Al-Arabiya News Channel by Al-Dabagh in spring 2013], translated by Mohammed Baban. Available at http://crrc.dodlive.mil/2013/07/23/crrc-releases -translation-of-interview-with-tariq-aziz/.

68. Al-Dabagh interview with Aziz.

69. Jafar, unpublished manuscript, 86.

70. Joseph Sassoon, *Saddam Hussein's Ba'th Party: Inside an Authoritarian Regime* (Cambridge: Cambridge University Press, 2011), 145.

71. *CAFCD*, extended summary, 45–46, citing 18 August as the date of the order.

72. Ibid.

73. Jafar, unpublished manuscript, 86–7.

74. Jafar Dhiya Jafar, author interview, Rome, 4–5 May 2005.

75. *CAFCD*, part 5, chap. 5.11, 1.

76. See UN Security Council Report, Appendix, S/1997/779, 17–18, and Attachment 1, 1.3: "The Intended Diversion of Research Reactor Fuel", 48; Charles Duelfer, *Comprehensive Report of the Special Advisor to the DCI on Iraq's WMD* (Washington, DC: U.S. Government Printing Office, 2004), vol. 1: *Regime Strategic Intent*, appendix, 3.

77. Jafar, unpublished manuscript, 87.

78. Ibid.

79. *CAFCD*, part 3b, chap. 5.11, 1.

80. Ibid., extended summary, 47.

81. Ibid., 18.

82. Ibid., 21.

83. Ibid., 19.

84. Ibid., 50.

85. Ibid., 48.

86. Ibid., 56.

87. Ibid., 64.

88. Ibid., 45.

89. "Correspondence between the Military Industrialization Commission and the Petro Chemical Group regarding Letter from A.Q. Khan Offering Assistance to the Iraqi Government in Developing a Uranium Enrichment Program," Estimated Document Date: October 1990, Record No.: SH-MICN-D-000-741, CRRC Archives (hereafter SH-MICN-D-000-741).

90. Dhafir Selbi, author interview, Amman, 2005.

91. SH-MICN-D-000-741.

92. Jafar, unpublished manuscript, 88.

93. *CAFCD*, part 3b, chap. 5.11, 29.

94. IAEA, *Fourth Consolidated Report of the Director General of the International Atomic Energy Agency under Paragraph 16 of Security Council Resolution 1051 (1996)*, S/1997/779, 8 October 1997, 21. Accessed from https://www.iaea.org/OurWork/SV/Invo/reports/s_1997_779.pdf.

95. Ibid, Attachment 1, 48.

96. Jafar, unpublished manuscript, 69.

97. David Albright, Frans Berkhout and William Walker, *Plutonium and Highly Enriched Uranium 1996: World Inventories, Capabilities and Policies* (Oxford: Oxford University Press, 1997), 337. Accessed from http://books.sipri.org/files/books/SIPRI97AlBeWa/SIPRI97AlBe Wa.pdf

98. Jafar Dhiya Jafar, Numan Saadaldin al-Niaimi, and Lars Sigurd Sunnanå, *Oppdraget: Innsidehistorien om Saddams atomvåpen* [The mission: The inside story of Saddam's nuclear weapons] (Oslo: Spartacus, 2005), 98–99.

99. Hussam Mohammad Ameen al-Yassin, Director of the National Monitoring, to Director of the Private Security Forces, August 1995, Record No.: SH-INMD-D-000-657, 1, CRRC Archives.

100. Obeidi and Pitzer, *Bomb in My Garden*, 134.

101. Jafar, author interview, Dubai, United Arab Emirates, November 12, 2006.

102. "Meeting at the Ministry of Defence with the Minister of State for the Armed Forces Mr. Hamilton—October 22, 1992," Ekéus Papers.

103. Ibid.

104. "Note for the File: Meeting with Joxe [French Minister for Defense], November 17, 1992, Compiled at 12:25 hours, October 21, 1992," Ekéus Papers.

105. Jacques E. C. Hymans, *Achieving Nuclear Ambitions: Scientists, Politicians, and Proliferation* (Cambridge: Cambridge University Press, 2012), 115.

5. Searching for Uranium in Libya, 1951-1973

1. Jacques E. C. Hymans, *Achieving Nuclear Ambitions: Scientists, Politicians, and Proliferation* (Cambridge: Cambridge University Press, 2012), 242.

2. See Marius Deeb and Mary Jane Deeb, *Libya since the Revolution: Aspects of Social and Political Development* (New York: Praeger, 1982), 112.

3. See Benjamin Higgins and Jacques Royer, "Economic Development with Unlimited Supplies of Capital: The Libyan Case," *Libyan Economic and Business Review* 3, no. 2: 1–28.

4. Ruth First, *Libya: The Elusive Revolution* (Harmondsworth, UK: Penguin African Library, 1974), 142.

5. John Wright, *Libya* (London: Ernest Benn, 1969), 199.

6. Higgins and Royer, "Economic Development," 3.

7. Wright, *Libya*, 224.

8. Ibid., 222.

9. Youssef Mohammad Sawani, "Post-Qadhafi Libya: Interactive Dynamics and the Political Future," *Contemporary Arab Affairs* 5, no. 1 (2012): 1–26.

10. Wright, *Libya*, 260–261.

11. First, *Libya*, 89.

12. Ibid.

13. Wright, *Libya*, 260.

14. Ibid., 223.

15. First, *Libya*, 80.

16. Ibid., 79–80; Wright, *Libya*, 264.

17. Wright, *Libya*, 241.

18. First, *Libya*, 102.

19. Ibid.

20. Benjamin Higgins, *Economic Development: Problems, Principles, and Policies* (New York: Constable, 1959), 26.

21. Wright, *Libya*, 183.

22. Adrian Pelt, *Libyan Independence and the United Nations: A Case of Planned Decolonization* (New Haven: Yale University Press, 1970), 671.

23. Deeb and Deeb, *Libya since the Revolution*, 26.

24. Wright, *Libya*, 243.

25. Mohammed Faraj Dghaim, "Al Jami'a Al Libiya fi Eidi'a Al Khamseen: Safha Mushriqa fi tarikh Libia," *Al Jamei Magazine*, no. 10 (2005), Al-Fateh University.

26. Deeb and Deeb, *Libya since the Revolution*, 31.

27. Ibid., 40.

28. Wright, *Libya*, 260.

29. Higgins and Royer, "Economic Development," 3.

30. Ibid., 3–4.

31. Ibid., 6.

32. Waniss Otman and Erling Karlberg, *The Libyan Economy: Economic Diversification and International Repositioning* (New York: Springer, 2007), 322.

33. Pelt, *Libyan Independence*, 693.

34. Higgins and Royer, "Economic Development," 4; Wright, *Libya*, 261.

35. Wright, *Libya*, 261.

36. "Daily Brief," *Central Intelligence Bulletin*, 22 June 1960, 1.

37. U.S. Senate, *United States Security Agreements and Commitments Abroad, Hearings before the Subcommittee on United States Security Agreements and Commitments Abroad of the Committee on Foreign Relations, Ninety-first Congress, first [and second] session[s]* (Washington, DC: U.S. Government Printing Office, 1969–1970), 2000–2001.

38. Ibid.

39. Ragaei El Mallakh, "The Economics of Rapid Growth: Libya," *Middle East Journal* (1969): 308.

40. Ibid.

41. Higgins and Royer, "Economic Development," 8.

42. First, *Libya*, 81.

43. Wright, *Libya*, 272.

44. Ibid., 271.

45. This number excludes quarries. Deeb and Deeb, *Libya since the Revolution*, 111–112.

46. J. Cameron to Ol. Lloyd, "Technical Assistance Mission to Libya, 4–11 December 1970," 15 December 1970 (C2-LIB-3.002), 4, IAEA Archives.

47. Ibid.

48. A. Shaari, Deputy Director General for Industrial Research Department, Ministry of Industry, Kingdom of Libya, to the IAEA, 16 June 1969, IAEA Archives.

49. Ahmed El-Atrash, Assistant Under-Secretary of State, Kingdom of Libya, to Resident Representative of the UNDP, 19 August 1969 (LIB/3/002), IAEA Archives.

50. Wright, *Libya*, 274.

51. Ibid.

52. Wright, *Libya*, 278; First, *Libya*, 82–83.

53. Wright, *Libya*, 278.

54. Ibid., 279.

55. Wright, *Libya*, 274.

56. First, *Libya*, 95.

57. Ibid., citing "Arms and the Super Salesman," *Sunday Times*, 2 June 1968.

58. First, *Libya*, 94.

59. Ibid.

60. Ibid., 107.

61. Ibid., 106.

62. Ibid., 119.

63. Ibid., 112.

64. Ibid., 113.

65. Umar Ibrāhaim Fatòhalai, Monte Palmer, and Richard Chackerian, *Political Development and Bureaucracy in Libya* (Lexington, MA: Lexington Books, 1977), 75.

66. First, *Libya*, 120.

67. Ibid., 121.

68. Dirk Vandewalle, *Libya since Independence: Oil and State Building* (Ithaca: Cornell University Press, 1998), 185.

69. Cited in First, *Libya*, 162, note 41.

70. First, *Libya*, 123.

71. See oral histories from former political prisoners on the "42 Years of Oppression: Personal Accounts of human rights abuses during the Gaddafi era in Libya" website: http://en.libya42.org/.

72. Fatòhalai et al., *Political Development*, 95–96.

73. First, *Libya*, 132.

74. Fatòhalai et al., *Political Development*, 96.

75. Mohamed M. Ennami, Scientific Adviser to the Secretary of the General People's Committee for Manpower, Training and Employment, "The Libyan Case" (paper presented at the 18th UN Conference on Disarmament Issues in Yokohama, 21–23 August 2006, Yokohama, Japan).

76. First, *Libya*, 154; Lisa Anderson, "Libya and American Foreign Policy," *Middle East Journal* 36, no. 4 (1982): 526.

77. Wyn Q. Bowen, *Libya and Nuclear Proliferation: Stepping Back from the Brink* (London: International Institute for Strategic Studies/Routledge, 2006), 15.

78. First, *Libya*, 204–211.

79. Libya had to rely on external sources for military equipment as it had not developed production capabilities of its own. Pierre Shammas, ed., "Libya Survey—Part 2—Arms Consumption Is Rising: Chad Drama Is Imminent," *Strategic Balance in the Middle East* 15, no. 4 (11 April 1988): 29.

80. "Middle East Arms Race, Libya: Qadhafi Games Endanger Military Power Base," *Strategic Balance in the Middle East*, Arab Press Service Organization, Beirut, January 1981, 7.

81. Memorandum of Conversation between Mansor Kikhia, Libyan Permanent Representative to the UN, and Secretary of State Henry Kissinger, 2 December 1976, American Embassy Residence, Mexico City, 2. National Security Archive.

82. Fatòhalai et al., *Political Development*, 159.

83. Ennami, "Libyan Case," n.p.

84. Senior official of the Libyan GPC, author interview, Tripoli, 16 June 2005.

85. Former Revolutionary Committee member, author interview, Tripoli, 15 June 2005.

86. "Libya: Al-Qadhafi Addresses General People's Congress," Tripoli, Great Jamahiriyah TV (in Arabic), 2 March 2004, from FBIS.

87. J. A. K. Quartey, "Report to the Government of Libya: Atomic Energy Planning," Technical Assistance Report No. 846, 14 May 1973, limited distribution, 1, IAEA Archives.

88. James Cameron, "Nuclear Raw Materials Prospection Programme: Report to the Government of Libya, 4–11 December 1970," 18 December 1970, limited distribution (LIB/3/002), IAEA Archives.

89. Quartey, "Report to the Government of Libya," 18.

90. Ibid., 17.

91. Ibid., 18.

92. "Attachment 1 to Travel Report: Background Information on Libya, Report on Nuclear Power Manpower Development, Mission to the Socialist People's Libyan Arab Jamahiriya, 15 to 24 June 1982, December 3 1982, Report to Director General" (TA-LIB-0/005), 1, IAEA Archives.

93. J. Dolnicar and S. B. Hammond, "IAEA, Nuclear Programming: Report to the Secretariat for Atomic Energy of the Socialist People's Libyan Arab Jamahiriya" (draft), November 1981(LIB/0/004), 9, IAEA Archives.

94. "Attachment 1 to Travel Report," 1.

95. On the Egyptian program and decision see Maria Rost Rublee, "Egypt's Nuclear Weapons Program: Lessons Learned," *Nonproliferation Review* 13, no. 3 (November 2006): 555–567.

96. See Bowen, *Libya and Nuclear Proliferation*.

97. Zainab Abbas, ed., *The Battle of Destiny: Speeches and Interviews by Colonel Muammar Gadhafi* (London: Kalahari Publications, 1976), 55.

98. References to Libyan requests for nuclear assistance can be found in the following: Evan S. Medeiros, *Reluctant Restraint: The Evolution of China's Nonproliferation Policies and Practices, 1980–2004* (Singapore: NUS Press, 2009), 35; Gordon Corera, *Shopping for Bombs: Nuclear Proliferation, Global Insecurity, and the Rise and Fall of the AQ Khan Network* (Oxford: Oxford University Press, 2006), 12; Stephen M. Meyer, *The Dynamics of Nuclear Proliferation* (Chicago: University of Chicago Press, 1986), 7; Etel Solingen, *Nuclear Logics: Contrasting Paths in East Asia and the Middle East* (Princeton: Princeton University Press, 2009), 212; Gawdat Bahgat, *Proliferation of Nuclear Weapons in the Middle East* (Gainesville: University Press of Florida, 2007), 129; Joseph Cirincione, Jon B. Wolfsthal, and Miriam Rajkumar, *Deadly Arsenals, Tracking Weapons of Mass Destruction* (Washington, DC: Carnegie Endowment for International Peace, 2002), 307; Kenneth Timmerman, *Weapons of Mass Destruction: The Cases of Iran, Syria, and Libya* (Los Angeles: Simon Wiesenthal Center, 1992), 88. See also "Writer Reports Libya A-Bomb Bid," *Washington Post*, 16 April 1979.

99. Bowen, *Libya and Nuclear Proliferation*, 28.

100. Ibid.

101. CIA, Intelligence Memorandum 279, "Qadhafi's Nuclear Weapon Aims," May 1975 (approved for release 4 February 2002), 2, Richelson Papers.

102. Quartey, "Report to the Government of Libya," 21.

103. S. Habib Ahmed, Resident Representative of the UNDP, to O. E. S. Lloyd, Area Officer for Africa, Division of Technical Assistance, IAEA, "Prospecting for Radioactive Materials in Libya," 29 April 1970 (LIB/3/002), IAEA Archives.

104. IAEA request from the Government of Libya, Job Description, New Materials Prospection, 25 November 1969 (LIB/3/002), IAEA Archives.

105. Mohamed Mughrabi, Deputy Director General, Office of Technical Cooperation, Libyan Arab Ministry of Planning, to Resident Representative of the UNDP, 26 April 1970 (TA/3/002), IAEA Archives.

106. First, *Libya*, 153–156. The budget allocations in the new regime's second development plan (1972–1975) set aside more money for industrial and mineral projects (15 percent) than any other budget element (agriculture was a close second).

107. Quartey, "Report to the Government of Libya."

108. Source lists figures in pounds, but Libya changed the name of their currency from pounds to dinars after the 1969 revolution. The value of both currencies was equivalent. First, *Libya*, 157.

109. Ibid., 170.

110. Ibid., 171.

111. Ibid., 160.

112. Ibid., 169.

113. Shukri Ghanem, "Changing Planning Policies in Libya," in *Planning and Development in Modern Libya*, ed. Mukhtar M. Buru, Shukri Mohammed Ghanem, and Keith S. McLachlan (London: Lynne Rienner, 1985), 225. Projects were planned for Jifarah Plain, Jabal Al Akhdar, Fezzan, Al Kufrah, and Sarir Salul Elkhudor.

114. The state set up about one hundred factories between 1970 and 1980 (ibid.).

115. Quartey, "Report to the Government of Libya," 20.

116. Ibid., 1–2.

117. J. Cameron to O. Lloyd, 15 December 1970, 1.

118. Quartey, "Report to the Government of Libya," 15.

119. Ibid., 2.

120. Ibid.

121. Ibid.

122. Ibid., 3.

123. Ibid.

124. Deeb and Deeb, *Libya since the Revolution*, 40.

125. Quartey, "Report to the Government of Libya," 6.

126. Cameron, "Nuclear Raw Materials," 2. Ettalhi became secretary-general of the GPC (equivalent to prime minister) in the mid-1980s.

127. Ibid., 4.

128. Quartey, "Report to the Government of Libya," 23.

129. Ibid., 9.

130. Ibid., 7.

131. Ibid., 8.

132. Ibid., 6.

133. Ibid., 9.

134. Ibid., 20.

135. Ibid., 20. Most sources, including official Libyan statements, instead date the beginning of Libya's nuclear energy program to 1973. See, for example, Ali Gashut, Atomic Energy Establishment, Libyan Arab Jamahiriya, "Ministerial Presentation: Libya," in *Nuclear Energy in the 21st Century: Addressing Energy Needs and Environmental Challenges: Proceedings of an International Ministerial Conference, Beijing, 20–22 April 2009* (IAEA: Vienna, 2009).

136. Quartey, "Report to the Government of Libya," 20.

137. Ibid., 21.
138. Ibrahim Adly, Resident Representative of the UNDP, to O. E. S. Lloyd, Area Officer for Africa, Division for Technical Assistance, IAEA, "Establishment of the Board of Directors of the Atomic Energy Authority in the LAR," 22 December 1973 (TA/LIB-2), IAEA Archives.
139. IAEA, "Legal Aspects of Nuclear Regulation and Establishment of the Nuclear Regulatory Body, Report to the Government of the Socialist People's Libyan Arab Jamahiriya," Technical Cooperation Report No. 1946, August 1982 (LIB/0/005), IAEA Archives.
140. Quartey, "Report to the Government of Libya," 17.
141. Ghanem, "Changing Planning Policies in Libya," 225.
142. Ibid.
143. Ibid.
144. Ibid., 226.
145. Ibid.

6. Cultural Revolution and Nuclear Power, 1973–1981

1. Lindsey Hilsum, *Sandstorm: Libya in the Time of Revolution* (London: Penguin, 2012), 55.
2. John Wright, *A History of Libya* (London: C. Hurst, 2012), 207.
3. Ruth First, *Libya: The Elusive Revolution* (Harmondsworth, UK: Penguin African Library, 1974), 137; Dirk J. Vandewalle, ed., *Qadhafi's Libya, 1969–1994* (London: St. Martin's Press, 1995), 182.
4. Vandewalle, *Qadhafi's Libya*, 182.
5. Ibid., 102, 182.
6. First, *Libya*, 138–140.
7. J. A. K. Quartey, "Report to the Government of Libya: Atomic Energy Planning," Technical Assistance Report No. 846, 14 May 1973, limited distribution, 2–3, IAEA Archives.–
8. Faculty of Science, University of Libya, "Request for Technical Assistance from IAEA" (TA/LIB/4/002), 3–4, IAEA Archives.
9. Quartey, "Report to the Government of Libya," 6; J. Dolnicar to A. Abu Bakr, "1974 Regular Programme of Technical Assistance—Libya," 6 July 1973, IAEA Archives.
10. J. Dolnicar and S. B. Hammond, "IAEA, Nuclear Programming: Report to the Secretariat for Atomic Energy of the Socialist People's Libyan Arab Jamahiriya" (draft), November 1981, (TA/LIB/0/004), 20–21, IAEA Archives.
11. Yusuf Elmehrik, Dean of the Faculty of Science, University of Libya, to U. Goswami, (TA/LIB/4/002), 12 June 1973, IAEA Archives.
12. Quartey, "Report to the Government of Libya," 5.
13. Faculty of Science, "Request for Technical Assistance from IAEA," 4.
14. Quartey, "Report to the Government of Libya," 6.
15. Ibid., 9.
16. CIA, Intelligence Memorandum 279, "Qadhafi's Nuclear Weapon Aims," May 1975 (approved for release 4 February 2002), Richelson Papers.
17. A. M. J. Spits, IAEA Expert, Tripoli, to J. Dolnicar, Division of Technical Assistance, 12 November 1976 (TA/LIB/4/02), IAEA Archives.
18. Faculty of Science, University of Libya, "Request for Technical Assistance from IAEA: Nuclear Measurements Project," attached to Elmehrik to Goswami, 12 June 1973, 3. This request was supported by letter from Mohamed al-Mabruk al-Bahi of the Libyan Arab Republic Ministry of Foreign Affairs (with a carbon copy to the Ministry of Planning, Tripoli), 29 March 1973 (TR/505), IAEA Archives.
19. Faculty of Science, "Request for Technical Assistance from IAEA: Nuclear Measurements Project," 1.
20. Ibid.
21. For example, the Libyans requested assistance with electronics and the installation and operation of the analytic equipment (Libyan Government to M. Kenyeres and A. Abu Bakr, 4 July 1973, IAEA Archives).

22. Dolnicar to Bakr, 6 July 1973.

23. Dolnicar and Hammond, "IAEA, Nuclear Programming," 22.

24. J. Dolnicar, IAEA, to A. Ben Hameida, Vice Dean, Faculty of Science, University of Tripoli, 8 May 1974 (TA/LIB/4/02), IAEA Archives.

25. Milovan Vidmar, IAEA Expert, to A. Abu Bakr, 27 December 1975 (TA/LIB/9/02), 1, IAEA Archives.

26. A. J. M. Spits, "Libya: Final Report," 12 July 1976–11 April 1977 (TA/LIB/4/02), IAEA Archives.

27. O. E. S. Lloyd, Area Officer for Africa, Division of Technical Assistance, IAEA, to Ibrahim Adly, Resident Representative of the UNDP, Libya, 10 May 1973 (TA/LIB-2), IAEA Archives.

28. A. J. M. Spits, "Libya: Field Report No. 1," 13 July–6 August 1976) (TA/LIB/4/02), 2, IAEA Archives.

29. In late 1977, an IAEA consultant offered to develop some guidelines for selection of candidates for fellowships. Robert W. Thiele, "Radioisotopes Centre (LIB/0/03) Report to the Government of Libya," 20 January 1977–20 March 1978 (TA/LIB/0/003), 4, IAEA Archives.

30. J. Dolnicar, Physics Section, to A. J. M. Spits, IAEA Expert, Tripoli, 2 November 1976 (TA/LIB/4/02), IAEA Archives.

31. See "Libya: Tajura Nuclear Reactor Senior Scientist on Its Construction, Capabilities," *Al-Majallah* (London), 1 February 2004, 26–29, FBIS; Wyn Q. Bowen, *Libya and Nuclear Proliferation: Stepping Back from the Brink* (London: International Institute for Strategic Studies/Routledge, 2006), chap. 2.

32. "Libya."

33. Vidmar to Bakr, 27 December 1975, 1.

34. CIA, "Qadhafi's Nuclear Weapon Aims," 2.

35. Memorandum of Conversation between Mansor Kikhia, Libyan Permanent Representative to the UN, and Secretary of State Henry Kissinger, 2 December 1976, American Embassy Residence, Mexico City, 2, National Security Archive.

36. Wright, *Libya*, 209.

37. A. M. J. Spits, "Libya: Field Report No. 2," 7 August–12 November 1976, 1, IAEA Archives.

38. J. Dolnicar, Physics Section, IAEA, to A. M. J. Spits, IAEA Expert, Tripoli, 23 November 1976 (TA/LIB/4/02), IAEA Archives.

39. "Rumors of Libyan Atomic Bomb Quest Raise Fears," *Washington Post*, 30 July 1979. The Libyan nuclear chronology is available at http://www.nti.org/media/pdfs/libya_nuclear.pdf?_=1316466791.

40. See Målfrid Braut-Hegghammer, "Libya's Nuclear Turnaround: Perspectives from Tripoli," *Middle East Journal* 62, no. 1 (2008): 55–72.

41. CIA, "Qadhafi's Nuclear Weapon Aims," 1.

42. Author's interview with a senior Libyan GPC official, Tripoli 2005, cited in Braut-Hegghammer, "Libya's Nuclear Turnaround," 8.

43. CIA, "Qadhafi's Nuclear Weapon Aims," 1.

44. Ibid.

45. IAEA, "Implementation of the NPT Safeguards Agreement in the Libyan Arab Jamahiriya," Report by Director General to the Board of Governors, GOV/2008/39, 12 September 2008, annex, 2.

46. U.S. Directorate of Intelligence, *The Libyan Nuclear Program: A Technical Perspective, An Intelligence Assessment*, February 1985 (approved for release 22 November 2011), 8, National Security Archive.

47. Leonard Spector, *Nuclear Proliferation Today: The Spread of Nuclear Weapons* (New York: Vintage, 1984), 151; Bowen, *Libya and Nuclear Proliferation*, 28.

48. A. J. M. Spits, IAEA Expert, Tripoli, to J. Dolnicar, Division of Technical Assistance, IAEA, 1 August 1976, IAEA Archives.

49. CIA, "Qadhafi's Nuclear Weapons Aims," 3.

50. Kenneth Timmerman, *Weapons of Mass Destruction: The Cases of Iran, Syria, and Libya* (Los Angeles: Simon Wiesenthal Center, 1992), 89.

51. U.S. Directorate of Intelligence, *Libyan Nuclear Program*, 13.

52. Feroz Khan, *Eating Grass: The Making of the Pakistani Bomb* (Palo Alto, CA: Stanford University Press, 2012), 111.

53. Ibid.

54. Bowen, *Libya and Nuclear Proliferation*, 31.

55. Robert W. Thiele, "Final Report, Project: LIB/0/03—Establishment of Radioisotope Laboratory," 20 January 1977–20 March 1978 (TA/LIB/0/003), 1, IAEA Archives.

56. Spits, "Field Report No. 1," 1.

57. Ibid., 2

58. Ibid.

59. Spits to Dolnicar, 1 August 1976.

60. J. Dolnicar, Division of Technical Assistance, IAEA, to B. Radischat, Division of Technical Assistance, 31 August 1976 (LIB/4/03) IAEA Archives.

61. A. M. J. Spits, IAEA Expert, Tripoli, to J. Dolnicar, Division of Technical Assistance, IAEA, 2; Frank Barnaby, *The Invisible Bomb: The Nuclear Race in the Middle East* (London: I.B. Tauris, 1993), 98; "Soviet Union Denies It Plans Bases in Libya," *New York Times*, 28 May 1975; "Libya Said to Buy Soviet A-Power Plant," *Washington Post*, 12 December 1977; "Nuclear Power Agreements," *Washington Post*, 4 October 1978.

62. Roland Timarbaev, "On Libya, Antimissile Defense, As Well As Other Autobiographical Events," *Security Index* 14, no. 1 (1983): 113.

63. Ibid.

64. Bowen, *Libya and Nuclear Proliferation*, 29.

65. U.S. Directorate of Intelligence, *Libyan Nuclear Program*, 1–2.

66. Ibid., 13.

67. Dolnicar and Hammond, "IAEA, Nuclear Programming," 9.

68. U.S. Directorate of Intelligence, *Libyan Nuclear Program*, 14.

69. U.S. Deputy Director for National Foreign Assessment, "Request for Review of Draft Paper on the Security Dimension of Nonproliferation, Libya: The Proliferation Threat," 9 April 1981, 1. National Security Archive.

70. Spits to Dolnicar, 12 November 1976, 2.

71. Timarbaev, "On Libya," 113.

72. Joseph V. R. Micallef, "A Nuclear Bomb for Libya?," *Bulletin of the Atomic Scientists* (August–September 1981): 14.

73. Dolnicar and Hammond, "IAEA, Nuclear Programming," 9.

74. Vidmar to Bakr, 27 December 1975, 1; Spits, "Field Report No. 1," 1.

75. The government had made plans in the 1980s for an agro-industrial project comprising two hundred wells expected to produce 200 million gallons of water per day. F. M. Swailem, M. S. Hamza, and A. I. M. Aly, "Isotope Composition of Groundwater in Kufra, Libya," *Water Resources Development* 1, no. 4 (1983): 333.

76. "Libya."

77. "1977 Plan: Establishment of a Neutron Activation Analysis Laboratory," Radioisotopes Centre, 24 May 1975, TA Report No. 1345, 9–10, IAEA Archives.

78. Ibid., 6.

79. Dolnicar and Hammond, "IAEA, Nuclear Programming," 9.

80. Robert W. Thiele, "Libya: Field Report No. 1," 23 January–28 February 1977 (TA/LIB/0/003), 1, IAEA Archives.

81. A. M. J. Spits IAEA Expert, Tripoli, to J. Dolnicar, Division of Technical Assistance, IAEA, 29 November 1976 (TA/LIB/4/02), IAEA Archives.

82. Thiele, "Field Report No. 1," 2.

83. Thiele, "Field Report No, 1," 3–5.

84. Pierre Shammas, ed., "Libya Survey—Part 2—Arms Consumption Is Rising: Chad Drama Is Imminent," *Strategic Balance in the Middle East* 15, no. 4 (11 April 1988): 35.

85. Memorandum of Conversation between Mansor Kikhia, Libyan Permanent Representative to the UN, and Secretary of State Henry Kissinger, 2 December 1976, American Embassy Residence, Mexico City, 2, National Security Archive.

86. Spits, "Field Report No. 2," 2.

87. Dolnicar and Hammond, "IAEA, Nuclear Programming," 21.
88. "Libya."
89. Ibid.
90. Thiele, "Field Report No. 1"; Robert W. Thiele, "Field Report No. 2," 1 March–31 May 1977 (TA/LIB/0/003), 1, IAEA Archives; Robert W. Thiele, "Field Report No. 3," 1 June–30 September 1977 (TA/LIB/0/003), IAEA Archives.
91. Thiele, "Radioisotopes Centre," 5.
92. Ibid., 1–7
93. P. Barretto, "Uranium Exploration Programme in Libya," Interoffice Memorandum, 9 May 1979 (LIB/03), 1, IAEA Archives.
94. Thiele, "Radioisotopes Centre."
95. Ibid., 4.
96. Ibid., 1.
97. A. M. Eskangy, General Director, Atomic Energy Authority, to A. Abu Bakr, Division of Technical Assistance, IAEA, received 18 November 1977 (TA LIB/03/03), IAEA Archives.
98. Thiele, "Radioisotopes Centre," 1.
99. Ibid.
100. Dolnicar and Hammond, "IAEA, Nuclear Programming," 19.
101. Thiele, "Final Report."
102. Thiele, "Field Report No. 2," 1.
103. Thiele, "Final Report," 3.
104. A. Abu Bakr, Area Officer for Africa, Division of Technical Assistance, to Robert W. Thiele, 13 June 1977, IAEA Archives.
105. Thiele, "Field Report No. 2," 1.

7. Nuclear Weapons Remain Elusive, 1982–1989

1. Pierre Shammas, ed., "Middle East Arms Race, Libya: Qadhafi Games Endanger Military Power Base," *Strategic Balance in the Middle East*, Published by the Arab Press Service Organization, January 1981, Beirut, Lebanon, 7.
2. CRS, *Issue Brief for Congress: Libya*, 24 February 2003, Foreign Affairs, Defense, and Trade Division, 6, available at http://fpc.state.gov/documents/organization/18216.pdf.
3. Robert Litwak, *Rogue States and US Foreign Policy: Containment after the Cold War* (Washington, DC: Woodrow Wilson Center Press, 2000), 173.
4. Leonard S. Spector, *Nuclear Proliferation Today* (New York: Vintage, 1984), 156.
5. CRS, *Issue Brief for Congress*, 6.
6. Wyn Q. Bowen, *Libya and Nuclear Proliferation: Stepping Back from the Brink*, (London: International Institute for Strategic Studies/Routledge, 2006), 15.
7. U.S. Directorate of Intelligence, *The Libyan Nuclear Program: A Technical Perspective*, Intelligence Assessment, February 1985 (approved for release 22 November 2011), 14, National Security Archive.
8. The new SAE was established through an amendment to the 1973 Nuclear Energy Act.
9. "Nuclear Energy Aide and Foreign Adviser Appointed in Tripoli," *New York Times*, 8 January 1981.
10. U.S. Directorate of Intelligence, *Libyan Nuclear Program*, 17–18.
11. Ibid.
12. The Executive Committee for Scientific Affairs initially consisted of five subdepartments: the Department of Power led by M. Bara Fathi with initially five staff; the Department of Fuel Cycle headed Elborai Mahmed with eight staff members; the Department of Radiation Protection led by Nouri Ali Addarougi with three staff members; the Department of Exploration and Mines (also known as the Raw Materials Division), led by M. A. Ghuma with thirteen staff; and the Department of the Nuclear Research Centre led by Ibrahim al-Hasain, who was

also a member of the SAE (and director of the Executive Committee for Financial and Administrative Affairs). J. Dolnicar and S. B. Hammond, "IAEA, Nuclear Programming: Report to the Secretariat for Atomic Energy of the Socialist People's Libyan Arab Jamahiriya" (draft), November 1981 (TA/LIB/0/004), 7, IAEA Archives.

13. U.S. Directorate of Intelligence, *Libyan Nuclear Program*, 17.

14. IAEA Interoffice Memorandum from J. Dolnicar and S. B. Hammond to Director General, "Travel Report: Programming Mission to Libya, 1–8 November 1981," 9 November 1981 2, IAEA Archives (hereafter "Travel Report: Programming Mission").

15. Ibid., 5.

16. Ibid., 2.

17. Ibid., 5.

18. IAEA Interoffice Memorandum to the Director General from R. Schmidt, "Report on Nuclear Power Manpower Development," 3 December 1982 (C2-LIB-0.005), 1, IAEA Archives.

19. U.S. Directorate of Intelligence, *Libyan Nuclear Program*, 2.

20. U.S. Directorate of Intelligence, *Libyan Nuclear Program*, 14.

21. IAEA, "Travel Report: Programming Mission," 5.

22. IAEA Interoffice Memorandum from L. W. Herron and A. Vuorinen to the Director General, "Travel Report—Mission to Libya, 25 April–2 May 1982," 25 May 1982, 1, IAEA Archives.

23. "Travel Report: Programming Mission," 3.

24. Ibid., 5.

25. "Report on Nuclear Power Manpower Development Mission to the Socialist People's Libyan Arab Jamahiriya, 15 to 24 June 1982," Attachment 1 to "Travel Report: Programming Mission" (TA/LIB/0/005), 1, IAEA Archives.

26. Claudia Wright, "Libya's Nuclear Programme," *Middle East*, February 1982, 47.

27. "Travel Report: Programming Mission," 5.

28. IAEA Interoffice Memorandum from M. Tauchid to A. Abu Bakr, "T.A. Programme in Uranium Exploration in Libya," 30 September 1981 (LIB/3/003-004), IAEA Archives.

29. Ibid.

30. "Report on Nuclear Power Manpower", 2.

31. IAEA, "Nuclear Power Manpower Planning," 2.

32. "Report on Nuclear Power Manpower," 2.

33. IAEA, "Nuclear Power Manpower Planning," 7.

34. Ibid., 8.

35. Ibid., 11.

36. Mohamed M. Ennami, Scientific Adviser to the Secretary of the General People's Committee for Manpower, Training, and Employment, "The Libyan Case" (paper presented at the 18th UN Conference on Disarmament Issues in Yokohama, 21–23 August 2006, Yokohama, Japan).

37. IAEA Interoffice Memorandum from H. J. Laue to J. A. K. Quartey, "Comments on the Travel Report 'Programming Mission to Libya by Messrs. Dolnicar and Hammond,'" 14 January 1982 (TA/LIB/0/005), 1, IAEA Archives.

38. A tokamak is a research device that can be used for studying nuclear fusion. Dolnicar and Hammond, "IAEA Nuclear Programming," 17.

39. Ibid., 16.

40. Ibid.

41. U.S. Directorate of Intelligence, *Libyan Nuclear Program*, 1–2.

42. Ibid., 13.

43. Ibid.

44. Ibid.

45. "Nuclear Energy Aide."

46. "Qaddafi Opposition Is Getting Stronger," *New York Times*, 27 May 1981.

47. "Libya: Members of the Libyan Cabinet," The Free Library, http://www.thefreelibrary.com/LIBYA+-+Members+of+the+Libyan+Cabinet.-a055288463.

48. Ibid.

49. Ibid.

50. Dirk Vandewalle, *A History of Modern Libya* (Cambridge: Cambridge University Press, 2012), 123–124.

51. John Wright, *A History of Libya* (London: C. Hurst, 2012), 236.

52. Hanspeter Mattes, "Challenges to Security Sector Governance in the Middle East: The Libyan Case" (paper presented at a workshop on "Challenges of Security Sector Governance in the Middle East," 12–13 July 2004, Geneva).

53. "Libya Survey—Part 1—A Military Structure Set for Big Geo-Political Games," *Strategic Balance in the Middle East* 15, no. 3 (21 March 1988).

54. Pierre Shammas, ed., *Strategic Balance in the Middle East, January 1981: Middle East Arms Race* (Beirut: Arab Press Service Organization, 1981).

55. Shukri Ghanem, "Changing Planning Policies in Libya," in *Planning and Development in Modern Libya*, ed. M. M. Bury, S. M. Ghanem, and K. S. McLachlan (London: Lynne Reiner, 1985), 226–227.

56. Ibid., 228.

57. Ibid., 229.

58. "Travel Report: Programming Mission," 4.

59. Ibid.

60. U.S. Directorate of Intelligence, *Libyan Nuclear Program*, 14.

61. Ibid., 2.

62. Ann MacLachlan and Mike Knapik, "Belgium and Libya Will Sign an Agreement on Nuclear Cooperation," *Nucleonics Week*, 24 May 1984, 6.

63. U.S. Directorate of Intelligence, *Libyan Nuclear Program*, 14.

64. Ibid.

65. Ibid.

66. Lisa Anderson, "Libya and American Foreign Policy," *Middle East Journal* 36, no. 4 (Autumn 1982): 526.

67. Joseph V. R. Micallef, "A Nuclear Bomb for Libya?," *Bulletin of the Atomic Scientists* (August–September 1981): 15.

68. "Travel Report: Programming Mission," 5.

69. U.S. Directorate of Intelligence, *Libyan Nuclear Program*, 13.

70. A. Abu Bakr to M. Tauchid, "Field Report of Mr. Kanaziewicz," 7 September 1982 (LIB/3/003), IAEA Archives.

71. Claudia Wright, "Libya's Nuclear Programme," 47.

72. U.S. Directorate of Intelligence, *Libyan Nuclear Program*, 17.

73. Mohamed Ezzat Abdelaziz, *Particle Accelerators* (Beirut: Arab Development Institute, 1980).

74. Bowen, *Libya and Nuclear Proliferation*, 27.

75. Ibid.

76. U.S. Directorate of Intelligence, *Libyan Nuclear Program*, 9–10. Among the countries Libya approached were West Germany, Iran, Belgium, Romania, Finland, Yugoslavia, Britain, Pakistan, China, Italy, Argentina, Canada, Switzerland, and India.

77. "Nuclear Energy Aide."

78. Case File "OLGA," D13891/Vol. 43, 1985, CNSAS. I am grateful to Eliza Gheorghe for sharing this source.

79. Ibid., 6.

80. IAEA, "Implementation of the NPT Safeguards Agreement in the Libyan Arab Jamahiriya," Report by the Director General to the Board of Governors, GOV/2008/39, 12 September 2008, accessed from http://www.globalsecurity.org/wmd/library/report/2008/libya_iaea _gov-2008-39_080912.htm.

81. Peter Crail, "Libya Adds New Pieces to Its Nuclear History," *Arms Control Today*, 6 October 2008.

82. IAEA, "Implementation" (GOV/2008/39).

83. Ibid.

84. "Belgium in Dilemma over Libyan N-Power Offer," *Financial Times*, 19 May 1984.

85. U.S. Directorate of Intelligence, *Libyan Nuclear Program*, 15.

86. Ibid.

87. Ibid., 11.

88. Bowen, *Libya and Nuclear Proliferation*, 35.

89. David Albright, *Peddling Peril: How the Secret Nuclear Trade Arms America's Enemies* (New York: Free Press, 2010), 116.

90. IAEA, "Implementation of the NPT Safeguards Agreement of the Socialist People's Libyan Arab Jamahiriya," Report by the Director General to the Board of Governors, GOV/2004/12, 20 February 2004, 5.

91. IAEA, "Implementation" (GOV/2008/39), annex, 3.

92. U.S. Directorate of Intelligence, *Libyan Nuclear Program*, 8.

93. Bowen, *Libya and Nuclear Proliferation*, 35; IAEA, "Implementation" (GOV/2004/12), 5.

94. IAEA, "Implementation" (GOV/2004/12), 4.

95. M. Petrovic, "Nuclear Radiometric Surveying: Report to the Government of the Libyan Arab Jamahiriya LIB/3/003," abstract (LIB/3/003), IAEA Archives.

96. Bowen, *Libya and Nuclear Proliferation*, 29.

97. Jerzy Kanasiewics, "Interim Report: Project LIB/3/003, 23.05-22.11.82," Tripoli, 20 August 1982 (LIB/3/003), IAEA archives.

98. IAEA, "Implementation" (GOV/2004/12), 4.

99. IAEA, "Implementation" (GOV/2008/39), 4. See IAEA, "Implementation of the NPT Safeguards Agreement of the Socialist People's Libyan Arab Jamahiriya," Report by the Director General to the Board of Governors, GOV/2004/33, 28 May 2004, Restricted distribution, annex 1, paragraph 27; Bowen, *Libya and Nuclear Proliferation*, chap. 2, p. 35.

100. IAEA, "Implementation of the NPT Safeguards Agreement of the Socialist People's Libyan Arab Jamahiriya," Report by the Director General to the Board of Governors, GOV/2004/59, 30 August 2004, 4.

101. Bowen, *Libya and Nuclear Proliferation*, 35.

102. U.S. Directorate of Intelligence, *Libyan Nuclear Program*, 8.

103. MacLachlan and Knapik, "Belgium and Libya," 6.

104. IAEA, "Implementation" (GOV/2004/12), 4.

105. Ibid., 3.

106. Andrew Terrill, "Libya and the Quest for Chemical Weapons," *Conflict Quarterly* 14, no. 1 (1994): 49.

107. Jonathan Tucker, "The Rollback of Libya's Chemical Weapons Program," *Nonproliferation Review* 16, no. 3 (November 2009): 372.

108. Ibid.

109. Ibid., 373.

110. Ibid., 376.

111. Patrick Wintour, "Britain Sends Officials to Libya to Help Destroy Chemical Weapons," *Guardian*, 14 November 2011.

112. Michael R. Gordon, "U.S. Thinks Libya May Plan to Make Chemical Weapons," *New York Times*, 24 December, 1987.

113. Tucker, "Rollback," 373.

114. Ibid.

115. Art Pine, "Only A-Bomb Could Destroy Libya Plant, Scientist Says: Pentagon: Expert Declares Ordinary Weapons Incapable of Carrying Out U.S. Threat to Hit Suspected Chemical Arms Facility," *LA Times*, 24 April 1996; "U.S. Said to Have No Non-Nuclear Way to Destroy Suspect Libyan Plant," Associated Press, 23 April 1996.

116. Bowen, *Libya and Nuclear Proliferation*, 33.

117. Libya reported to the IAEA that the talks were canceled in 1985. IAEA, "Implementation" (GOV/2008/39), 4.

118. Pierre Shammas, ed., "Libya Survey—Part 2—Arms Consumption Is Rising: Chad Drama Is Imminent," *Strategic Balance in the Middle East* 15, no. 4 (11 April 1988): 35.

119. Ibid.

120. Ennami, "Libyan Case."

121. Bowen, *Libya and Nuclear Proliferation*, 33.

122. Eleanor Clift and James Gerstenzang, "U.S. Warplanes Destroy Libya Missile Site, Sink Patrol Craft: Strike after Attack by Kadafi Forces; No American Losses," *Los Angeles Times,* 25 March 1986.
123. Litwak, *Rogue States,* 176.
124. Målfrid Braut-Hegghammer, "Libya's Nuclear Turnaround: Perspectives from Tripoli," *Middle East Journal* 62, no. 1 (2008): 55–72.
125. Ibid.; senior official in the Libyan GPC, author interview, Tripoli, 16 June 2005.
126. George Joffé, "Libya: Who Blinked, and Why," *Current History* 103, no. 673 (May 2004), 221–225.
127. Leonard S. Spector, *Nuclear Ambitions: The Spread of Nuclear Weapons, 1989–1990* (Boulder, CO: Westview Press, 1990), 183.
128. Dirk Vandewalle, *Libya since Independence: Oil and State Building* (Ithaca: Cornell University Press, 1998), 140.
129. Ibid.; Senior official in the Libyan GPC interview.
130. *La Grande Charte Verte des Droits de L'Homme de l'ere Jamahiriyenne,* Le Congrés Général du Peuple de la Grande Jamahiriya Arabe Libyenne Populaire et Socialiste, 12 June 1988, 14.
131. Frank Barnaby, *The Invisible Bomb: The Nuclear Race in the Middle East* (London: I.B. Tauris, 1993), 150.
132. "Arabs Need Atomic Weapons to Counter Israel, Khadafy Says," *Toronto Star,* 2 September 1987.

8. Sanctions, Centrifuges, and Exit, 1989–2003

1. Libyan journalist, author interview, Tripoli, 26 January 2006.
2. Ambassador Mohamed Zwai, author interview, London, 2 May 2006.
3. Ibid.; Seif al-Islam Gaddafi, author interview, Tripoli, 18 June 2005.
4. Seif al-Islam Gadhafi interview.
5. Libyan academic 1, author interview, Tripoli, 24 January 2006.
6. Zwai interview.
7. Senior official in the Libyan GPC, author interview, Tripoli, 16 June 2005.
8. Ibid.
9. Målfrid Braut-Hegghammer, "Libya's Nuclear Turnaround: Perspectives from Tripoli," *Middle East Journal* 62, no. 1 (2008): 55.
10. Senior official in the Libyan GPC, author interview, Foreign Ministry, Tripoli, 28 January 2006 (via interpreter).
11. "Defence in Peacetime—Part 2C—Libya," *Strategic Balance in the Middle East* 31, no. 2 (5 February 1996), in Arab World Documentation Unit.
12. Alison Pargeter, "Libya: Reforming the Impossible?," *Review of African Political Economy* 33, no. 108 (2006): 221.
13. Zwai interview.
14. Ron Suskind, "The Tyrant Who Came in from the Cold," *Washington Monthly,* October 2006. Available at http://www.washingtonmonthly.com/features/2006/0610.suskind.html.
15. Trevor Rowe, "U.N. Presses Libya on Bombing," *Washington Post,* 22 January 1992, A01.
16. UN Security Council Resolution 748 (31 March 1992). Adopted by the Security Council at its 3,063rd meeting on 31 March 1992.
17. Pargeter, "Libya," 220.
18. Former central Revolutionary Committee figure, author interview, Tripoli, 15 June 2005.
19. William Tobey, "Analysis: A Message from Tripoli: How Libya Gave Up Its WMD, Part 3: What Do You Do with a Plastic Shopping Bag Full of Nuclear Weapon Designs?," *Bulletin of Atomic Scientists,* 5 December 2014, http://thebulletin.org/message-tripoli-part-3-how-libya-gave-its-wmd7843.
20. Ambassador Donald Mahley, author interview, Washington, DC, 6 March 2007.

21. "ISN/CTR Visit: Libya Moves Forward on Scientist Engagement Programs," cable sent by U.S. Embassy, Tripoli, 3 November 2009, WikiLeaks, http://wikileaks.org/cable/2009/11/09TRIPOLI886.html.

22. David Albright, *Peddling Peril: How the Secret Nuclear Trade Arms America's Enemies* (New York: Free Press, 2010), 117.

23. David Albright, *Libya: A Major Sale at Last,* Institute for Science and International Security Special Report, 1 December 2010. Available at http://isis-online.org/uploads/isis-reports/documents/Libya_and_the_Khan_Network_1Dec2010.pdf.

24. Ibid., 5.

25. Peter Crail, "Libya Adds New Pieces to Its Nuclear History," *Arms Control Today,* 6 October 2008.

26. Libyan academic 1, author interview, Tripoli, 24 January 2006.

27. "Defence in Peacetime."

28. "(S/NF) Kudos for biographic reporting on Libyan Nuclear officials (C-ME9-01366)," 17 July 2009, WikiLeaks, https://wikileaks.org/plusd/cables/09STATE74778_a.html; "Bazelya's Possible Involvement in Technology Transfer Secret and Personal," Covering Top Secret Delicate Source UK Eyes A The Security Service G9A/S Our Ref: PF690551/G9/0, 1 December 1995, Wikileaks, https://cryptome.wikileaks.org/mi5-lis-uk.htm.

29. Albright, *Peddling Peril,* 122.

30. Ibid.

31. Plea and Sentence Agreement of G. Wisser in *State vs. Geiges, Wisser, and Krisch Engineering,* available at http://isis-online.org/uploads/conferences/documents/Southaf_Relevant_Facts.pdf (hereafter Plea and Sentence Agreement).

32. Raymond Bonner and Craig S. Smith, "Pakistani Said to Have Given Libya Uranium," *New York Times,* 21 February 2004; Albright, *Peddling Peril,* 124; Gordon Corera, *Shopping for Bombs: Nuclear Proliferation, Global Insecurity, and the Rise and Fall of the AQ Khan Network* (Oxford: Oxford University Press, 2006), 109.

33. Henry D. Sokolski, ed., *Pakistan's Nuclear Future: Worries Beyond War* (Carlisle, PA: Army War College, Strategic Studies Institute, 2008) 26, available at http://www.dtic.mil/dtic/tr/fulltext/u2/a475702.pdf.

34. Ibid., 15.

35. Bonner and Smith, "Pakistani."

36. Ibid.

37. IAEA, "Implementation of the NPT Safeguards Agreement of the Socialist People's Libyan Arab Jamahiriya," Report by the Director General to the Board of Governors, GOV/2004/12, 20 February 2004, Annex 1, 3, accessed from https://fas.org/nuke/guide/libya/iaea0504.pdf.

38. Albright, *Libya,* 19.

39. Libyan academic 1, author interview, Tripoli, January 24, 2006.

40. Ibid.

41. Yojana Sharma, "Libya: Nuclear Research 'Not Up to Scratch,'" *University World News* 169, 1 May 2011.

42. Plea and Sentence Agreement.

43. Albright, *Libya,* 33.

44. Mohamed M. Ennami, Scientific Adviser to the Secretary of the General People's Committee for Manpower, Training and Employment, "The Libyan Case" (paper presented at the 18th UN Conference on Disarmament Issues in Yokohama, 21–23 August 2006, Yokohama, Japan). The Libyan regime provided a very sparse account of their nuclear weapons program to the IAEA. The most detailed overview was a four-page summary of the program's activities submitted on 29 December 2003, with very little supporting information. That account is not publicly available.

45. IAEA, "Implementation of the NPT Safeguards Agreement of the Socialist People's Libyan Arab Jamahiriya," Report by the Director General to the Board of Governors, GOV/2004/12, 20 February 2004, IAEA, 6, accessed from http://www.securitycouncilreport.org/atf/cf/%7B65BFCF9B-6D27-4E9C-8CD3-CF6E4FF96FF9%7D/Disarm%20GOV200412.pdf.

46. Ennami, "Libyan Case."

47. IAEA, "Implementation of the NPT Safeguards Agreement of the Socialist People's Libyan Arab Jamahiriya," Report by the Director General to the Board of Governors, GOV/2004/33, 28 May 2004, annex 1, 3–4.

48. Ibid., 4.

49. Ibid., 5.

50. Ibid., 4.

51. Ennami, "Libyan Case."

52. IAEA, "Implementation" (GOV/2004/33), annex 1, 6.

53. Albright, *Libya*, 40; "Técnicos libios fueron instruidos en España sobre maquinaria de posible uso nuclear," *El Pais*, 24 February 2004.

54. IAEA, "Implementation" (GOV/2004/12), 5.

55. Ibid.

56. Ibid., 6.

57. Bonner and Smith, "Pakistani."

58. IAEA, "Implementation" (GOV/2004/12), 2.

59. Ennami, "Libyan Case."

60. Libyan academic, author interview, Tripoli, 24 January 2006.

61. Judith Miller, "How Gadhafi Lost His Groove: The Complex Surrender of Libya's WMD," *Wall Street Journal*, 16 May 2006.

62. Seif al-Islam Gadhafi interview.

63. Libyan ambassador involved in trilateral negotiations, author interview, Tripoli, 18 January 2006.

64. Andrea Koppel, "ElBaradei: Libya nuclear program dismantled," *CNN.com*, 29 December 2003, http://edition.cnn.com/2003/WORLD/africa/12/29/libya.nuclear/.

65. Seif al-Islam Gadhafi interview; Libyan journalist, author interview, Tripoli, 2005.

66. Miller, "How Gadhafi Lost His Groove"; Zwai interview.

67. Mahley interview.

68. IAEA, "Implementation" (GOV/2004/33), annex 1, 7.

69. Ibid.

70. Zwai interview.

71. Ibid.

72. Ibid.

73. Ibid.

74. Libyan academic 1, author interview, Tripoli, 24 January 2006.

75. Martin S. Indyk, "The Iraq War Did Not Force Gadaffi's Hand," *Financial Times*, 9 March 2004.

76. Ibid.

77. Zwai interview.

78. Paul Kerr, "U.S. Refuses to Lift Sanctions against Libya," *Arms Control Today*, 1 October 2003, available at http://www.armscontrol.org/act/2003_10/Libya.

79. Peter Beaumont, Kamal Ahmed, and Martin Bright, "The Meeting That Brought Libya in from the Cold," *Observer*, 21 December 2003.

80. Zwai interview.

81. Miller, "How Gadhafi Lost His Groove."

82. Seif al-Islam Gadhafi interview.

83. Zwai interview.

84. Ibid.

85. Seif al-Islam Gadhafi interview.

86. Zwai interview.

87. Seif al-Islam Gadhafi interview.

88. Ibid.

89. "Libyan Leader Laments No 'Concrete' Reward for Giving up WMD," *RAI Tre* [in Italian], 17 December 2004, FBIS.

90. Sharon A. Squassoni and Andrew Feickert, *Disarming Libya: Weapons of Mass Destruction*, CRS Report for Congress, Congressional Research Service, Library of Congress, 22 April 2004, 3; Miller, "How Gadhafi Lost His Groove."

91. Miller, "How Gadhafi Lost His Groove."
92. Squassoni and Feickert, *Disarming Libya,* 3.
93. See also Miller, "How Gadhafi Lost His Groove."
94. Paul Kerr, "Libya Vows to Dismantle WMD Program," *Arms Control Today,* 1 January 2004, available at http://www.armscontrol.org/act/2004_01-02/Libya.
95. Ibid.
96. IAEA "Implementation" (GOV/2004/33), annex 1, 6.
97. Seif al-Islam Gadhafi interview.
98. Zwai interview.
99. Seif al-Islam Gadhafi interview.
100. Kerr, "Libya Vows to Dismantle WMD Program."
101. Ibid.
102. Beaumont et al., "Meeting That Brought Libya In from the Cold"; William Tobey, "Analysis: A Message from Tripoli: How Libya Gave Up Its WMD, Part 2: Qaddafi Agrees 'So That the Color Green Will Be All Over the World,'" *Bulletin of Atomic Scientists,* 3 December 2014, http://thebulletin.org/message-tripoli-part-2-how-libya-gave-its-wmd7839.
103. Tobey, "Message from Tripoli, Part 2."
104. Judith Miller, "Gadhafi's Leap of Faith," *Wall Street Journal,* 17 May 2006.
105. Tobey, "Message from Tripoli, Part 2."
106. William Tobey, "Analysis: A Message from Tripoli: How Libya Gave Up Its WMD, Part 1: The Path to Interdiction," *Bulletin of Atomic Scientists,* 3 December 2014, http://thebulletin.org/message-tripoli-how-libya-gave-its-wmd7834.
107. "On This Day: 19 December: 2003: Libya Gives Up Chemical Weapons," *BBC News,* http://news.bbc.co.uk/onthisday/hi/dates/stories/december/19/newsid_4002000/4002441.stm.
108. "Libyan Leader Laments."

Conclusion

1. Jeff D. Colgan, *Petro-Aggression: When Oil Causes War* (Cambridge: Cambridge University Press, 2013).
2. Ibid., 149.
3. Bruce Bueno de Mesquita and Alastair Smith, "Domestic Explanations of International Relations," *Annual Review of Political Science* 15 (2012): 161–181.
4. U.S. Interagency Intelligence Assessment, "Implications of Israeli Attack on Iraq," 1 July 1981, 8, National Security Archive.
5. See Jacques E. C. Hymans, *Achieving Nuclear Ambitions: Scientists, Politicians, and Proliferation* (Cambridge: Cambridge University Press, 2012).
6. See, for example, Rublee, "Egypt's Nuclear Weapons Program" *The nonproliferation review* 13, no. 3 (2006), 555–567.
7. Request from the Government of the Syrian Arab Republic for an Atomic Energy Planning Expert, 26 February 1968, IAEA Archives.
8. A. E. Cairo, Area Officer for the Middle East and Europe, Division of Technical Assistance, to Ghazi Derwish, 7 August 1968 (TA/SYR/0/002), IAEA Archives.
9. Ghazi Derwish, "Syrian Arab Republic: Plans for Nuclear Research with Special Reference to Radioisotope Applications," IAEA Report, 1969 (TA/SYR/0/002), 6, IAEA Archives.
10. Cairo to Derwish.
11. Derwish, "Plans for Nuclear Research," 6.
12. Ibid., 7.
13. Ibid.
14. Ibid., 31.
15. Peter Watson to R. A. Northwick, Safeguards Section, IAEA, Syrian Arab Republic, 4 May 1973 (TA/SYR/6/02), IAEA Archives.

16. Ibid.

17. Ibid.

18. Interoffice Memorandum from C. B. Taylor, Division of Research and Laboratories, to M. Mutru, Technical Assistance, "Evaluation of Final Report by Mr. Kuoppamaki on His Visit to Syria," 2 November 1976 (SYR/8/02), IAEA Archives.

19. See IAEA, "Implementation of the NPT Safeguards Agreement in the Syrian Arab Republic," Report by the Director General to the Board of Governors, GOV/2011/30, 24 May 2011, IAEA Archives. See also "Syria: Nuclear," NTI.org, http://www.nti.org/country-profiles/syria/nuclear/.

20. See Matthew Fuhrmann, *Atomic Assistance: How "Atoms for Peace" Programs Cause Nuclear Insecurity* (Ithaca: Cornell University Press, 2012).

Index

Note: Italic page numbers refer to illustrations.

CPSIA information can be obtained at www.ICGtesting.com
Printed in the USA
BVOW08*0615270716

456999BV00001B/2/P

9 781501 702785